The Top 100 American Situation Comedies

D1131894

The Top 100 American Situation Comedies

An Objective Ranking

MITCHELL E. SHAPIRO *and*
TOM JICHA

McFarland & Company, Inc., Publishers
Jefferson, North Carolina

OTHER WORKS BY MITCHELL E. SHAPIRO
AND FROM MCFARLAND

Cable Television Prime Time Programming, 1990–2010 (2012)

Television Network Prime Time Programming, 1985–2007 (2009)

Radio Network Prime Time Programming, 1926–1967 (2002; softcover 2008)

Television Network Weekend Programming, 1950–1990 (1992)

Television Network Daytime and Late-Night Programming, 1959–1989 (1990; softcover 2013)

Television Network Prime-Time Programming, 1948–1988 (1989)

LIBRARY OF CONGRESS CATALOGUING-IN-PUBLICATION DATA [new form]

Names: Shapiro, Mitchell E., 1953– | Jicha, Tom, 1945–
Title: The top 100 American situation comedies : an objective ranking / Mitchell E. Shapiro and Tom Jicha.
Other titles: Top one hundred American situation comedies
Description: Jefferson, North Carolina : McFarland & Company, Inc., Publishers, 2016. | Includes index.
Identifiers: LCCN 2015037329| ISBN 9781476664040 (softcover : acid free paper) | ISBN 9781476623405 (ebook)
Subjects: LCSH: Situation comedies (Television programs)—United States—Plots, themes, etc.
Classification: LCC PN1992.8.C66 S45 2016 | DDC 791.45/617—dc23
LC record available at http://lccn.loc.gov/2015037329

BRITISH LIBRARY CATALOGUING DATA ARE AVAILABLE

Front cover image © 2015 RUSSELLTATEdotCOM/iStock

Printed in the United States of America

McFarland & Company, Inc., Publishers
 Box 611, Jefferson, North Carolina 28640
 www.mcfarlandpub.com

Table of Contents

Introduction   1

1. *All in the Family*   5
2. *Cheers*   7
3. *Frasier*   10
4. *M*A*S*H*   12
5. *The Mary Tyler Moore Show*   15
6. *Friends*   18
7. *Everybody Loves Raymond*   20
8. *I Love Lucy*   23
9. *The Cosby Show*   25
10. *Seinfeld*   27
11. *Modern Family*   30
12. *Murphy Brown*   32
13. *The Golden Girls*   34
14. *The Danny Thomas Show*   36
15. *The Dick Van Dyke Show*   38
16. *30 Rock*   40
17. *Will & Grace*   43
18. *The Andy Griffith Show*   45
19. *Taxi*   47
20. *Roseanne*   49
21. *Barney Miller*   52
22. *Mad About You*   54
23. *The Big Bang Theory*   56
24. *The Phil Silvers Show*   59
25. *Family Ties*   61
26. *Bewitched*   63
27. *Two and a Half Men*   65
28. *Happy Days*   68
29. *Home Improvement*   71
30. *Sex and the City*   73
31. *Get Smart*   75
32. *The Beverly Hillbillies*   77
33. *Father Knows Best*   79
34. *The Larry Sanders Show*   82
35. *The Lucy Show*   84
36. *Night Court*   86
37. *The Office*   89
38. *Three's Company*   92
39. *The Wonder Years*   94
40. *The Jeffersons*   96
41. *Sanford and Son*   99
42. *Maude*   101
43. *Laverne & Shirley*   103
44. *Curb Your Enthusiasm*   105
45. *Newhart*   108
46. *Kate & Allie*   111
47. *Malcolm in the Middle*   113
48. *Coach*   115
49. *Entourage*   118
50. *Alice*   120
51. *Hogan's Heroes*   123
52. *3rd Rock from the Sun*   125
53. *One Day at a Time*   128
54. *Rhoda*   131
55. *The George Burns & Gracie Allen Show*   133

56. *Soap* 136
57. *Family Affair* 139
58. *Designing Women* 141
59. *The Bob Cummings Show (Love That Bob)* 144
60. *The Odd Couple* 146
61. *Room 222* 149
62. *December Bride* 151
63. *Hazel* 153
64. *Who's the Boss?* 155
65. *My Three Sons* 158
66. *The Real McCoys* 160
67. *A Different World* 163
68. *The Life of Riley* 165
69. *Our Miss Brooks* 167
70. *Mama* 170
71. *Evening Shade* 172
72. *Here's Lucy* 174
73. *Empty Nest* 176
74. *Petticoat Junction* 178
75. *Gomer Pyle, U.S.M.C.* 181
76. *Veep* 183
77. *Nurse Jackie* 186
78. *Dream On* 188
79. *Benson* 190

80. *Full House* 193
81. *Weeds* 195
82. *Growing Pains* 198
83. *Arrested Development* 200
84. *Ellen (These Friends of Mine)* 203
85. *The Donna Reed Show* 205
86. *The Adventures of Ozzie & Harriet* 207
87. *How I Met Your Mother* 210
88. *The Bob Newhart Show* 212
89. *Diff'rent Strokes* 215
90. *Scrubs* 217
91. *Green Acres* 220
92. *The Facts of Life* 222
93. *The Wizards of Waverly Place* 225
94. *iCarly* 227
95. *Wings* 230
96. *Married ... with Children* 232
97. *Perfect Strangers* 234
98. *The King of Queens* 237
99. *McHale's Navy* 239
100. *Family Matters* 242

Appendices
A. *Ranked List of All Qualifying Situation Comedies* 245
B. *Top 25 Situation Comedies by Decade* 254
C. *Top Situation Comedies by Network* 259
D. *Top 25 Situation Comedies That Aired for One Season or Less* 263

Index 265

Introduction

One of the oldest arguments is what is the "best" of all time? All subjects are fair game. This book attempts to provide an answer to one such subject— the best American television situation comedy of all time. In fact, it provides a ranked list of the 100 best.

There have been a number of books and articles written addressing this subject. All have something very important in common—they all provide subjective lists, i.e., lists based on the opinions of their authors. While these attempts at determining the "best of all time" are interesting, they are still only the opinions of their creators. It is difficult to make true or meaningful comparisons, let alone rankings, when subjective criteria are applied. Such criteria will vary, sometimes significantly, from one list to another. There will even be variations in how and what criteria are applied to programs within the same list.

This book presents an attempt to come to an objective answer to the question of what are the best American situation comedies of all time. The authors are both experts from differing backgrounds that have been studying or following the world of television content—one has been a scholar and educator who has been researching television programming from both empirical and historical perspectives for the past 40 years and has published six reference books on the topic; the other has been one of the nation's leading television journalists and critics for more than 30 years. Both authors also share a lifelong passion and love for television.

Seeking an objective solution, the authors developed a mathematical formula that would rank television programs—in this case, situation comedies. There are four components to this formula—ratings, longevity, peer acceptance and spawning other programs. These components were treated as equally important. While each component was treated as mutually exclusive, the authors recognize that there is a connection between each and every one of these components (however, this connection will exist for all programs in a similar manner). For example, the higher the rating a series achieves is a major factor in deciding whether or not a network will bring that series back for another season (hence, affecting its longevity). A series that achieves high ratings for a number of seasons might lead the network to spin off a new series from the original, and so on.

Each of the four components of our formula is discussed below: ***Ratings:*** This component consisted of a program's season-long ranking in the A.C. Nielsen television household ratings (a rating is a percentage of the number of total television households watching a specific program at a specific time). Each television season (usually September through May) will produce a ranking, based on these Nielsen ratings, of all programs that aired during that season. For example, if in a specific television season there were 145 different series that aired the rankings will be from 1 (the highest-rated program) through 145 (the lowest-rated program).

The reason we chose to use these rankings instead of the actual ratings was because the ratings for series that aired in the pre-cable era (prior to 1981) were significantly higher than series in the post-cable era because there was much less competition for the viewing audience.

When *I Love Lucy* aired there were only three options for most viewers, whereas when *The Big Bang Theory* aired viewers had more than 100 viewing options. The more options available, the lower the rating will be for any program. Using the rankings was more even—for example, a program that had the 4th highest ratings in the 1957–58 television season was treated the same as a program that had the 4th highest ratings for the 2002–03 television season.

Longevity: This component was simply how long the series lasted during its original run (the period when new episodes were being produced). The number of television seasons during which a program aired was counted.

Peer Acceptance: This component was comprised of results of voting by the National Academy of Television Arts and Sciences—the Emmy Awards. Only the "major" Emmy categories were included—Best Series, Best Acting (Lead, Supporting and Guest), Best Writing and Best Directing. Points were awarded for both winning and being nominated for an Emmy. Winning the award counted five times more than simply being nominated. The points for winning or being nominated for the series categories counted twice as much as points awarded for the acting categories which, in turn, counted twice as much as points awarded for the writing and directing categories.

Spawning Other Programs: This component credited series responsible for producing spin-off series. For example, *Maude* was a spin-off from the series *All in the Family* so *All in the Family* was credited with spawning another series. *Good Times* was a spin-off from *Maude* so *Maude* was credited with spawning another series. Because *All in the Family* was responsible for *Maude*, it was also credited with spawning *Good Times*. It should be pointed out that the series that it spawned did not have to also be a situation comedy (e.g., *The Mary Tyler Moore Show* spawned *Lou Grant*, a drama series).

While every American television live-action situation comedy series that aired on television was initially examined, not all of them merited consideration for the "best." In order for a series to be considered it had to meet at least one of four different criteria—it had to air for at least three seasons; or it had to rank among the top 30 series in at least one television season; or it had to receive at least one nomination for any of the major Emmy Award categories previously mentioned; or it had to have spawned at least one other series. The result was that 377 different American television live-action situation comedies met at least one of the aforementioned criteria and were thus evaluated by our formula.

Because we were striving for an objective result, we made every attempt to keep our personal feelings about certain series out of the process. There were series that both of us felt were not great, but because they lasted for many seasons or had high rankings (or both) they made the list. Also, one series, *The Honeymooners*, which was a personal favorite of both of us, did not make the Top 100—this was due primarily to the fact that it ran for only one season. A testament to its worth is that it still ranked 122.

In order to write about each of the Top 100 situation comedies, we obtained and viewed episodes of each of the series in the list—all of the episodes for many of them. We did this to refresh our memories about certain programs and also to make sure that our factual information was correct. After our viewings, we discussed what we would say about each series. Drawing on both of our lifetimes of expertise and knowledge, each of us added information that we had obtained through the years.

Several sources were used in compiling air date information and cast listings for each series. These sources include *TV Guide* and the following reference works: *Television Network Prime Time Programming, 1948–1988*, *Television Network Prime Time Programming, 1985–2007*, *Cable Television Prime Time Programming, 1990–2010*, all by Mitchell E. Shapiro, and *The Complete Directory to Prime Time Network TV Shows: 1946–2007* by Tim

Brooks and Earle Marsh. Emmy award information was obtained from the official web site of the Academy of Television Arts & Sciences.

There will still be arguments. Such is human nature. However, we hope you enjoy reading about the 100 best American situation comedies. We believe you will agree with us but it is inevitable that there will still be disagreements.

1. *All in the Family*

Broadcast History:

Tuesday	9:30–10:00	January 1971–July 1971	CBS
Saturday	8:00–8:30	September 1971–September 1975	CBS
Monday	9:00–9:30	September 1975–September 1976	CBS
Wednesday	9:00–9:30	September 1976–October 1976	CBS
Saturday	9:00–9:30	November 1976–September 1977	CBS
Sunday	9:00–9:30	October 1977–October 1978	CBS
Sunday	8:00–8:30	October 1978–September 1979	CBS

#1 rated series in 1971–72	#1 rated series in 1975–76
#1 rated series in 1972–73	#12 rated series in 1976–77
#1 rated series in 1973–74	#4 rated series in 1977–78
#1 rated series in 1974–75	#9 rated series in 1978–79

20 Major Emmy Awards (51 nominations):
5 Emmy Awards for Best Series (9 nominations)
4 Emmy Awards for Best Actor (8 nominations)
3 Emmy Awards for Best Actress (8 nominations)
2 Emmy Awards for Best Supporting Actor (5 nominations)
1 Emmy Award for Best Supporting Actress (5 nominations)
3 Emmy Awards for Best Writing (10 nominations)
2 Emmy Awards for Best Direction (6 nominations)

Cast: Carroll O'Connor; Jean Stapleton; Sally Struthers (1971–78); Rob Reiner (1971–78); Mike Evans (1971–75); Isabel Sanford (1971–75); Mel Stewart (1971–73); Sherman Hemsley (1973–75); Betty Garrett (1973–75); Vincent Gardenia (1973–74); Billy Halop (1972–77); Brendon Dillon (1972–73); Bob Hastings (1973–77); Burt Mustin (1973–76); Allan Melvin (1973–79); Ruth McDevitt (1973–75); James Cromwell (1974); Liz Torres (1976–77); Danielle Brisebois (1978–79); Jason Wingreen (1977–79); Danny Dayton (1977–79); Bill Quinn (1978–79).

There is no more surefire conversation or argument starter than "Who's No. 1?" The topic can be college football, Leno or Letterman, the Beatles or Stones. But there is a noteworthy exception: TV's all-time number 1 situation comedy. The answer has to be *All in the Family*.

Television changed forever on January 12, 1971, with the debut of Nor-

5

man Lear's ground-breaking series. Viewers had never been introduced to a character like Archie Bunker, whose ethnic slurs and Neanderthal social viewpoints might have been commonplace in the blue collar, white male dominated taverns of the Queens (New York) neighborhood where the series was set. However, it was shocking to viewers accustomed to traditional saccharine comedies such as *The Brady Bunch*, *The Partridge Family* and *My Three Sons*. Archie spared no group. African-Americans were "spades," "coons" and "jungle bunnies." Latinos were "spics." Italians (or Eye-talians, as Archie pronounced it) were "guineas." Jews were "kikes." Michael, his son-in-law of Polish heritage, was a "dumb Polack."

The imprudence of discussing politics and religion in open company is legend. Both were fair game to Archie and company. He went with the Biblical version of creation, including a bizarrely unique take on the Garden of Eden. Adam and Eve were running around naked, in Archie World. Then Eve got Adam to take a bite of the apple. Immediately they heard a command from above. "Get your clothes on and get out of here."

In the charged era of Watergate, Archie was a fan and defender of Richard Nixon. "How do they get away with this?" roiled water cooler conversations and op-ed opinion pages. The answer could be partially traced to an off-the-record, snarky observation once made by a network executive. "TV would have given Hitler his own show if he produced ratings." *All in the Family* generated huge ratings. Not immediately. It took several months for word of mouth to bring the midseason arrival to the attention of the masses. However, by the summer of 1971, Norman Lear's ground-breaking comedy had soared to the top of the Nielsens, where it stayed for five seasons. The Television Academy took note as *All in the Family* was named best new series of the 1970–71 season as well as outstanding comedy series, the first of four times it was cited as best in class. Even after *All in the Family* was bumped from Nielsen's top rung by ABC's nostalgia siblings *Happy Days* and *Laverne and Shirley*, it remained one of the top 10 series in the Nielsen ratings through the end of the decade when it was rechristened *Archie Bunker's Place* in recognition of changes that had taken place in the story-telling and casting.

A less cynical reason *All in the Family* was able to "get away with it" was the realization that Lear, an ardent liberal, wasn't celebrating prejudice but was holding it up to a mirror for disapproval. Carroll O'Connor's iconic character was an isolated strawman, whose ignorance was illuminated and cold-cocked weekly. His wife Edith, sympathetically portrayed by Jean Stapleton, might have been "the dingbat" to Archie but she was prejudice-free and irresistibly likeable. With a disapproving glance or exasperated "Oh, Archie," she made it clear she couldn't believe the toxic waste coming out of the mouth of the man she loved. Rob Reiner's career student Michael, a color blind, left wing, anti-war activist unfailingly out-thought and out-reasoned Archie. Miraculously, the relatively brief time Michael had been with Archie's overly-emotional only child Gloria (Sally Struthers) outweighed her formative years under the influence of her father.

It was a pitch perfect ensemble, as each of the core four went on to win multiple Emmys. Michael's next door African-American running mate, Lionel Jefferson (Mike Evans), delighted Archie while subtly mocking him by repeatedly vowing, in black dialect remote from his normal speech pattern, to become an "e-lectrical engineer." Lionel became the vehicle to introduce additional tormentors for Archie. Lionel's Uncle Henry (Mel Stewart) challenged Archie on matters of race but he gave way in season three to Lionel's dad, George, as outspokenly bigoted from the black perspective as Archie was from his point of view. Sensing additional ratings gold Sherman Hemsley's George was spun off in 1975 into his own series as the patriarch of *The Jeffersons*. *The Jeffersons* was not the first spinoff of *All in the Family*. Archie's ultra-liberal cousin Maude (Bea Arthur), who reveled in humiliating Archie, transitioned into her own show in 1972.

All in the Family was as prodigious in siring a couple of generations of offspring as it was in producing ratings and Emmys. Struthers eventually went out on her own in the aptly titled *Gloria*. *The Jeffersons* became the parents of *Checking In*. Maude gave birth to *Good Times*. No series has ever been responsible for more second and third generation series. This doesn't include *Archie Bunker's Place*, which was more a continuation than a new entity. *All in the Family* continued to challenge the status quo by delving into previously unexplored subject matter such as Edith being raped in her own home and when Stapleton felt she had strip-mined every facet of her character, Edith was killed off, a traumatic event for fans of such a beloved character. Ratings, awards, an enduring impact on the culture; by any standard, there is no argument what is the number one situation comedy of all time.

2. *Cheers*

Broadcast History:

Thursday	9:00–9:30	September 1982–December 1982	NBC
Thursday	9:30–10:00	January 1983–December 1983	NBC
Thursday	9:00–9:30	December 1983–August 1993	NBC

#12 rated series in 1984–85
#5 rated series in 1985–86
#3 rated series in 1986–87
#3 rated series in 1987–88
#4 rated series in 1988–89

#3 rated series in 1989–90
#1 rated series in 1990–91
#4 rated series in 1991–92
#8 rated series in 1992–93

20 Major Emmy Awards (95 nominations):
4 Emmy Awards for Best Series (11 nominations)
2 Emmy Awards for Best Actor (11 nominations)
2 Emmy Awards for Best Actress (9 nominations)
1 Emmy Award for Best Supporting Actor (19 nominations)
6 Emmy Awards for Best Supporting Actress (13 nominations)
1 Emmy Award for Guest Actor/Actress (8 nominations)
2 Emmy Awards for Best Writing (13 nominations)
2 Emmy Awards for Best Direction (11 nominations)

Cast: Ted Danson; Shelley Long (1982–87); Rhea Perlman; Nicholas Colasanto (1982–85); George Wendt; John Ratzenberger; Kelsey Grammer (1984–93); Woody Harrelson (1985–93); Kirstie Alley (1987–93); Bebe Neuwirth (1986–93); Tom Skerritt (1987–88); Jay Thomas (1987–89); Roger Rees (1989–91); Jackie Swanson (1989–93); Paul Wilson (1991–93); Philip Perlman (1991–93).

It took a couple of seasons for most of America to become familiar with the names of the barflies in the Boston pub that became renowned as the place where everybody knows your name. *Cheers* was an immediate critical darling and NBC in-house favorite when it premiered in the fall of 1982. In those days, the late NBC Entertainment President Brandon Tartifkoff liked to joke that he thought his low-rated network's full name was "Perennially Third Place NBC." (At that time, for all intents and purposes, there were only three networks.) NBC's Nielsen woes worked against any new series being sampled as they had no strong programs to serve as lead-ins to new series. The season after *Cheers* made its debut, Tartikoff infamously struck out with all eight new series on its fall schedule. (Forays into foolishness such as *Manimal, Boone, We Got It Made, Jennifer Slept Here* and talking chimpanzee *Mr. Smith* probably would have failed under the best of circumstances.)

However, *Cheers* was a trailblazer of NBC's transformation into "The Quality Network," as it came to be known for more than a decade starting in the mid-'80s. So its low ratings be damned, Tartikoff and his boss, NBC Chairman Grant Tinker, made *Cheers* the lowest rated comedy series ever picked up for a second season, then did it again for season three. Everything changed in 1984. *The Cosby Show* became one of the hottest newcomers in years, energizing Thursday's lineup, which quickly came to be christened "Must See TV." Tens of millions of viewers brought to NBC at the start of the night by *The Cosby Show* fed into *Family Ties* at 8:30, *Cheers* at 9:00, *Night Court* at 9:30 and *Hill Street Blues* at 10:00.

Cheers which had languished so deep into the Nielsen rankings that it didn't make the cut in many newspaper ratings reports, jumped into the Top 15 in its first *Cosby*-fueled season, then the top 5 through the rest of the decade until it peaked at number 1 in 1990–91—a rarity for a show so deep into its run.

Although the workplace humor concept broke no new ground, the writing was brilliant, the characters rich and well fleshed out and the superlative cast, none of whom brought glitzy credentials to the project, eventually racked up more than a dozen individual Emmys to accompany the series' four Emmys, as TV's outstanding comedy. Before last call in the spring of 1993, *Cheers* had racked up 28 Emmys. Ted Danson, as the series pivot man, bar owner Sam Malone, a washed-up former pitcher for the Red Sox, was nominated nine times as best lead actor in a comedy but he didn't capture his first of two Emmys until 1990. Danson had a long resume of TV credits when he was cast but most were for one-shot guest roles. Indeed, he was in two pilots in 1982, the leading man in *Cheers* and a villainous guest role as an elevator rapist in the CBS series *Good Witch of Laurel Canyon/Tucker's Witch*. Legend has it that the more prominent William Devane was ticketed for the role of Sam Malone until he turned in an off-the-wall audition, including playing Sam bare-footed behind the bar.

Each of Danson's leading ladies, Shelley Long as Diane Chambers and Kirstie Alley (twice) as Rebecca Howe, also were honored with lead actress trophies by the Television Academy. Alley was the beneficiary of Long's decision to leave the series after six seasons to pursue a career in film. Despite her early exit, Sam and Diane became a catch phrase for love-hate romances. However, it was Rhea Perlman as caustic waitress Carla Tortelli, who became the series' Emmy over-achiever with four golden statues. Long wasn't the first regular to check out. Nicholas Colasanto, who played slow-witted but beloved Coach, had to exit after the third season with a heart ailment, which took his life the following February. Newcomer Woody Harrelson was hired as *Cheers* new bartender and it became a career-making role, which earned him an Emmy, too.

Ironically, one of the regulars who didn't win an Emmy for *Cheers* was Kelsey Grammer, as twittish psychologist Frasier Crane. The character was created for the third season as a love interest for Diane, who wound up jilting Frasier at the altar because of her lingering feelings for Sam. Adding to the irony, Bebe Neuwirth, who played Frasier's rebound romance, cold fish Lilith, was honored with a pair of Emmys for *Cheers*. The twice nominated Grammer more than made up for the *Cheers* snub, winning four Emmys for spinoff *Frasier*, which also ran 11 seasons.

---

3. *Frasier*

Broadcast History:

Thursday	9:30–10:00	September 1993–September 1994	NBC
Tuesday	9:00–9:30	September 1994–September 1998	NBC
Thursday	9:00–9:30	September 1998–July 2000	NBC
Tuesday	9:00–9:30	July 2000–May 2004	NBC

#7 rated series in 1993–94	#6 rated series in 1999–2000
#15 rated series in 1994–95	#17 rated series in 2000–01
#11 rated series in 1995–96	#14 rated series in 2001–02
#16 rated series in 1996–97	#26 rated series in 2002–03
#10 rated series in 1997–98	#30 rated series in 2003–04
#3 rated series in 1998–99	

26 Major Emmy Awards (68 nominations):
5 Emmy Award for Best Series (8 nominations)
4 Emmy Awards for Best Actor (10 nominations)
4 Emmy Awards for Best Supporting Actor (13 nominations)
No Emmy Award for Best Supporting Actress (1 nomination)
5 Emmy Awards for Best Guest Actor/Actress (23 nominations)
4 Emmy Awards for Best Writing (9 nominations)
4 Emmy Awards for Best Directing (4 nominations)

Cast: Kelsey Grammer; David Hyde Pierce; John Mahoney; Jane Leeves; Peri Gilpin; Dan Butler; Edward Hibbert (1994–2004); Patrick Kerr (1994–2004); Tom McGowan (1998–2004); Saul Rubinek (1999–2000); Jane Adams (1999–2000); Millicent Martin (2000–03); Wendie Malick (2003–04).

A guy walks into a bar. Twenty years later he is the most enduring comedic character in the history of television. No one could have predicted that Frasier Crane, a pompous psychiatrist introduced on *Cheers* as a fringe character designed to be jilted by Shelley Long's Diane Chambers, would not only outlive *Cheers* but would match its longevity and become the pivotal figure of the most successful spinoff ever, winner of a record five straight best comedy laurels. In the process, the iconic twit created by Kelsey Grammer equaled the record 20 seasons of *Gunsmoke*'s Matt Dillon. However, James Arness, who played Mr. Dillon, could not match Grammer's distinction of being the only actor ever nominated for an Emmy for playing the same character on three series—*Cheers*, *Frasier* and a guest appearance on *Wings*. (All three sitcoms were from the creative team of Peter Casey, David Lee and David Angell. The latter came to a tragic end as one of the passengers on the American Airline flight that became the first to crash into the World Trade Center on September 11, 2001.)

Frasier departed from the *Cheers* formula. Unlike its ancestor, which essentially played out on only one set, the bar, Frasier had workplace and home life components. Frasier's role as host of a popular Seattle radio advice program made him a local celebrity and became a vehicle for voice cameos by a constellation of stars calling into the show. "Name That Voice" became a fun guessing game for viewers. But the series' heart and soul was the complex relationships in Frasier's personal life at his fashionable high rise apartment. As extraordinary as Grammer was, he was not a one-man band. Grammer was complemented by a cast seemingly designed by divine inspiration. As on *Cheers*, each of the key supporting players was a virtual unknown with limited primarily guest credits—some of them on *Cheers*.

David Hyde Pierce, who coincidentally bore an uncanny resemblance to Grammer, was a revelation as Fraser's equally snooty, social climbing brother Niles. Pierce matched Grammer's haul of four Emmys but went a step further, ringing up the Hall of Fame distinction of being nominated each of the 11 seasons *Frasier* was on NBC. (The previous record was eight.) The creation of Niles required creative contortions inasmuch as Frasier had told the Cheers gang that he was an only child. (Playing with series history wasn't groundbreaking. Harry Morgan played a loony general on *M*A*S*H* before becoming a regular as kindly Col. Potter.)

A similar situation pertained to Frasier's father, Martin, portrayed by John Mahoney. In another *Cheers* barroom conversation, Frasier mentioned his father was a research scientist who had died. On *Frasier*, Martin was a former Seattle police officer, forced into retirement when he was shot in the hip while on duty by a fleeing felon. Challenged on this, Frasier explained that he had been involved in a "you're dead to me" feud with Martin when he said his father had passed away. Martin's recovery from his wounds necessitated a full-time, live-in therapist, Daphne Moon, played by British actress Jane Leeves.

Although Niles was married to shrewish but never seen Maris (mirroring the never seen Vera, spouse of *Cheers'* Norm) he carried on like a teenager in love around the vivacious Daphne. This infatuation was achingly obvious to everyone but her. It wasn't until seven years into the series that Niles let his feelings be known to her. By then Daphne was engaged. But, like *Cheers'* Diane, Daphne left her fiancé at the altar to run away with Niles and eventually marry him, an arguably jumping the shark turn of events. Mahoney and Leeves were each Emmy nominated for their roles. If there were an Emmy for animal performances, Martin's pet Eddie, a Jack Russell terrier played by Moose, would have been a cinch for a supporting player nod.

Frasier's assistant and call screener at the radio station, unabashedly randy Roz Doyle (Peri Gilpin), became a surrogate member of the Crane clan, a presence in both parts of Frasier's life. The common ground was a coffee shop near the radio station, which became a regular meeting place. Roz was open to overtures from virtually any potential suitor with one notable exception, the obnoxiously aggressive sports talk host Bulldog Briscoe (Dan Butler), who couldn't accept that any woman, let alone the promiscuous Roz, could resist him. Meanwhile a sexual tension driven by personal affection evolved between Frasier and Roz, which they finally gave into, but only once.

Although locating Frasier on the West Coast was a conscious decision to establish narrative distance between the series, most of the *Cheers* regulars eventually made guest appearances. Woody Harrelson, Shelley Long and Bebe Neuwirth, as Frasier's estranged wife Lilith, the mother of their son, each were honored with Emmy nominations for guest roles on *Frasier*. The award-winning writing extended beyond the two series' familiar characters. Laura Linney, Anthony LaPaglia, Derek Jacobi and Jean Smart (twice) won Emmys for guest roles. By the time the final credits rolled, Frasier had rung up a record 37 Emmys, to vault over previous leader *The Mary Tyler Moore Show*.

---

4. *M*A*S*H*

Broadcast History:

Sunday	8:00–8:30	September 1972–September 1973	CBS
Saturday	8:30–9:00	September 1973–September 1974	CBS
Tuesday	8:30–9:00	September 1974–September 1975	CBS
Friday	8:30–9:00	September 1975–November 1975	CBS
Tuesday	9:00–9:30	December 1975–January 1978	CBS
Monday	9:00–9:30	January 1978–September 1983	CBS

#4 rated series in 1973–74	#7 rated series in 1978–79
#5 rated series in 1974–75	#4 rated series in 1979–80
#14 rated series in 1975–76	#4 rated series in 1980–81
#4 rated series in 1976–77	#9 rated series in 1981–82
#8 rated series in 1977–78	#3 rated series in 1982–83

13 Major Emmy Awards (93 nominations):
1 Emmy Award for Best Series (11 nominations)

3 Emmy Awards for Best Actor (12 nominations)
2 Emmy Awards for Best Supporting Actor (22 nominations)
2 Emmy Awards for Best Supporting Actress (10 nominations)
1 Emmy Award for Best Writing (12 nominations)
4 Emmy Awards for Best Direction (26 nominations)

Cast: Alan Alda; Wayne Rogers (1972–75); Loretta Swit; Larry Linville (1972–77); Gary Burghoff (1972–79); McLean Stevenson (1972–75); William Christopher; Jamie Farr (1973–83); Harry Morgan (1975–83); Mike Farrell (1975–83); David Ogden Stiers (1977–83); Karen Philipp (1972); Timothy Brown (1972); Patrick Adiarte (1972); John Orchard (1972–73); Linda Meiklejohn (1972–73); Herb Voland (1972–73); Odessa Cleveland (1972–74); Marcia Strassman (1972–73); Kelly Jean Peters (1973); Lynette Mettey (1973); Bobbie Mitchell (1973–77); Robert Simon (1973–74); Kellye Nakahara (1974–83); Patricia Stevens (1974–78); Judy Farrell (1976–83); Jeff Maxwell (1976–83); Enid Kent (1977–79); Johnny Haymer (1977–79); Jan Jordan (1977–83); Gwen Farrell (1979–83); Connie Izay (1979–81); Jennifer Davis (1979–80); Shari Sabo (1980–83); G.W. Bailey (1981–83); Roy Goldman (1981–83); Rosalind Chao (1983).

M*A*S*H will forever have a place in TV history. Its 251st and final episode on February 28, 1983, became Nielsen's highest rated entertainment program of all time, a distinction it still holds. It is inconceivable that in the multi-channel universe the 2½ hour special's 60.2 rating (percent of all homes in America with TV) will ever be surpassed. Pretty good for a series in danger of early cancellation after its boot camp season. In season two, CBS moved it from Sunday into the Saturday slot behind the white hot *All in the Family* and it remained in the Nielsen Top 10 for almost all of the rest of its run.

Generals are said to fight the last war in the current war. M*A*S*H—the initials stood for Mobile Army Surgical Hospital—took a similar approach. The adaptation of a hit film premiered in the fall of 1972 as the Vietnam War and virulent protests at home against it raged. The dark comedy was set in the Korean War but it was clear the series and some of the smartest dialog ever heard on television was a commentary on the conflict in Southeast Asia.

M*A*S*H, a winner of 14 Emmys, might have been one of the most uneven comedies ever, a factor that added to its strength. Some episodes were laugh out loud hilarious, others somber and poignant. A few were shot in black and white to enhance authenticity. The producers pushed to be liberated from a laugh track but CBS, at the time still a stalwart advocate of canned laughter, stood firm. The network relented slightly, agreeing to allow scenes in the operating room to go laugh track free. Once the series became established as a bona fide hit, CBS allowed a handful of episodes with especially dark tones to go laugh track free throughout.

The characterizations also fluctuated over time. Picking up from the movie, surgeons Hawkeye Pierce (Alan Alda) and Trapper John McIntyre (Wayne Rogers) were hard partying playboys with a booze-producing still and often a couple of nubile nurses in their tent, which more resembled a frat house. Their healing duties were treated as inconvenient interruptions to their revelry, although when called upon they were extraordinarily gifted healers. Col. Henry Blake was a like-minded soul but his duties as commanding officer necessitated a more sober approach. Like Hawkeye, Trapper and almost everyone else in the unit had been drafted and was not happy about it. Maj. Frank Burns (Larry Linville) and Maj. Margaret "Hot Lips" Houlihan (Loretta Swit) were the banes of the base. In an otherwise laissez faire milieu, they were sticklers for Army regulations—with one exception. They were carrying on a torrid romance despite the fact that Frank had a wife and children back home.

A parade of cast departures brought about more than character changes. MacLean Stevenson, who played Col. Blake, miscalculated his value as an actor and importance to M*A*S*H and left for his own series on NBC after the third season. Apparently miffed at Stevenson's disloyalty, the show had Henry perish in a plane crash on his way home—a move that so unsettled the audience that the producers vowed to never repeat it. Stevenson, a relative unknown before M*A*S*H, came to be mocked as a symbol for actors who make horrid career choices. Col. Blake's exit from the series epitomized his future TV endeavors. All his shows crashed and burned.

M*A*S*H hired veteran Harry Morgan to play the new commanding officer, Col. Sherman Potter. A dedicated career military man, Col. Potter preferred to do things by the book but he tempered his leadership with compassion and common sense. (Morgan had previously played a guest role as a different character, a loony general.) Where Col. Blake was at heart as much a cut-up as Hawkeye and Trapper, Col. Potter was more a father figure to the men and women under him. This was especially true with his efficient but naive clerk Radar O'Reilly (Gary Burghoff), who had a knack for anticipating Col. Potter's requests.

A few months after Stevenson departed, Wayne Rogers, who played Trapper, decided he wasn't being fairly compensated and also left the show. Trapper was allowed by the writers to go home in one piece. The casting of Mike Farrell as Hawkeye's new tent mate, B.J. Hunnicut, resulted in the most drastic change in tone. The drinking all but disappeared and Hawkeye no longer had a running mate for skirt chasing. B.J. was a devoted father, who spoke rapturously about his beloved spouse Peg. Despite being an almost perfect husband, B.J. gave in to temptation and did stray with one of the nurses—

an act he regretted. Hawkeye still had an eye for the ladies but his pursuit of amorous conquests declined precipitously.

Even though the series was mired in the 1950s, the woman's movement was gaining traction in the real world. Without fanfare, Hawkeye and the others abruptly refrained from calling Maj. Houlihan "Hot Lips." The storylines veered in another direction again when Larry Linville, who played Maj. Burns, left the series in 1977. The plot catalyst was Maj. Houlihan falling in love with another officer and getting married. A broken hearted Frank went AWOL. He was replaced by Maj. Charles Winchester Emerson (David Ogden Stiers), a prim, proper and pompous Bostonian, who became the constant foil for pranks by Hawkeye and B.J. The final significant cast departure came when Gary Burghoff, who had played Radar in the movie and the TV series, left in 1979. Radar's clerk duties were inherited by the suddenly responsible Cpl. Klinger (Jamie Farr), who had spent his entire hitch up to this point at the 4077th cross dressing in the hopes of being granted an early psychological discharge.

Farr, Morgan and William Christopher, who played Father Mulcahy, enlisted in a spinoff, *Aftermash*, which was as insipid as its parent was brilliant. It lasted only just over one season, less than half as long as the Korean conflict, which *M*A*S*H* mined for 11 years of superlative television.

---

5. *The Mary Tyler Moore Show*

Broadcast History:

Saturday	9:30–10:00	September 1970–December 1971	CBS
Saturday	8:30–9:00	December 1971–September 1972	CBS
Saturday	9:00–9:30	September 1972–October 1976	CBS
Saturday	8:00–8:30	November 1976–September 1977	CBS

#22 rated series in 1970–71   #9 rated series in 1973–74
#10 rated series in 1971–72   #11 rated series in 1974–75
#7 rated series in 1972–73   #19 rated series in 1975–76

27 Major Emmy Awards (61 nominations):
3 Emmy Awards for Best Series (8 nominations)
4 Emmy Awards for Best Actress (8 nominations)
5 Emmy Awards for Best Supporting Actor (12 nominations)
7 Emmy Awards for Best Supporting Actress (15 nominations)
6 Emmy Awards for Best Writing (10 nominations)
2 Emmy Awards for Best Direction (8 nominations)

Cast: Mary Tyler Moore; Edward Asner; Ted Knight; Gavin MacLeod; Valerie Harper (1970–74); Cloris Leachman (1970–75); Lisa Gerritsen (1970–75); John Amos (1970–73); Georgia Engel (1973–77); Betty White (1973–77); Joyce Bulifant (1971–77); Priscilla Morrill (1973–74); Robbie Rist (1976–77).

Mary Tyler Moore was loved by America for her charming turn as Laura Petrie in *The Dick Van Dyke Show*. She elevated herself to iconic status with her follow up as Mary Richards in the eponymous situation comedy. Her impact and popularity was such that a statue of her was erected in downtown Minneapolis, a singular honor for a situation comedy character. *The Mary Tyler Moore Show* was more than a star vehicle. It pointed a mirror to the aspirations and obstacles of American women, particularly single women, in the fourth quarter of the 20th century. Emmy-nominated all seven seasons it was on the air and a three-time winner as television's outstanding comedy, it is on most short lists of the finest situation comedies of all time.

While fulfilling its primary mission to entertain and elicit laughs, the series offered low key social commentary on issues such as equal pay for equal work, a woman having sex outside marriage, pharmaceutical addiction, divorce and homosexuality. These were untouchable topics in mostly saccharine television comedy when the show premiered in 1970. The setting, the newsroom of low-rated WJM-TV, serving Minnesota's Twin Cities, provided an ideal forum to shine a light on society's mores and failings. It was a time when manual typewriters were still in vogue, drunks were still cute and gay meant a person was unusually happy. Unlike the in-your-face heavy-handedness of *All in the Family*, which arrived four months later, *The Mary Tyler Moore Show* made its points while maintaining a happy face. This was true even of the death of a colleague that was beloved by many of the staff members at WJM. The episode on the death of Chuckles the Clown was so simultaneously poignant and hilarious that it has been mentioned on several lists of the finest of all time.

Mary Richards is television's gold standard for portraying a self-reliant woman, who could be content in a career with a satisfying personal life sans husband. She dated but the relationships never led to marriage. Moore was Emmy nominated eight times as top comedic actress and won four statues (one in 1974 for Actress of the Year, a subsequently abandoned category). Mary was a naïve 30-year-old coming off a breakup of a long-term relationship when she walked into WJM looking for a job as a secretary. By the time she got there, the position had been filled. However, there was an opening for an assistant producer of the six o'clock news show. It was a subtle commentary on television news that she would be offered such a role with absolutely no experience. What's more, the assistant producer's position paid $10 less than the secretarial job.

The news executive who hired Mary, Lou Grant (Ed Asner), was a gruff, sarcastic, hard-drinking taskmaster, whose bluster was camouflage for a good heart. He managed to keep this well under wraps most of the time. Mr. Grant—the only way Mary ever addressed him—became a mentor and father figure for Mary. He was just Lou to everyone else. When the series ended, Lou Grant was spun off into a new show, a rare instance of a comedy spawning a drama.

Every village needs an idiot. Pompous, self-important anchor Ted Baxter filled this role to perfection. For a man in his position, the silver-maned, nattily attired face of the station was egregiously prone to malapropos—vegetarians were veterinarians—and mispronunciations, including simple words like Chicago. The character endures as the model for vacuous television news people. News writer Murray Slaughter (Gavin MacLeod), Lou's first lieutenant, was vicious in relentlessly zinging Ted, who wasn't sharp enough to realize he was being mocked. When Ted was asked to front a broadcasting school, which turned out to be a scam, he wondered aloud what the founder needed him for. "Fertilizer," Murray retorted without missing a beat.

Mary had another extended family at the Victorian home in which she rented an apartment. Her landlord, Phyllis Lindstrom (Cloris Leachman), was controlling and meddlesome but she and Mary formed a bond. Phyllis was married to the never seen Lars, whose death after the fifth season was the catalyst for Phyllis moving to San Francisco, the locale for another spinoff (*Phyllis*). Rhoda Morgenstern (Valerie Harper) was a neighbor of Mary. They got off to a bad start when Phyllis rented to Mary the apartment Rhoda thought she was going to get. Rhoda got over this and became Mary's closest non-workplace friend. Rhoda, who could be as pushy as Phyllis but had a better sense of humor, was constantly on the hunt for a boyfriend but always for naught. After season four, she also was spun off into her own series (*Rhoda*) with her character moving to New York where she felt the pickings for a boyfriend would be greater.

Sue Ann Nevins (Betty White) and Georgette Franklin (Georgia Engel) joined the series in progress. Sue Ann was the host of WJM's "Happy Home-maker" program. She spent every moment not working on the show pursuing male companionship with Lou, her number one prey. Georgette wasn't the brightest bulb in the chandelier, evidenced by the fact that she shared Ted's assessment that he was the greatest. He proposed to her on the air then got buyer's remorse. But they eventually married and adopted one child before having another biologically.

Every member of the supporting cast, each of whom won at least one Emmy, returned for the widely praised finale. An exceedingly long group hug segued into Mary, who had worked her way up to news producer, shutting off the newsroom lights for the final time.

---

6. *Friends*

Broadcast History:

Thursday	8:30–9:00	September 1994–February 1995	NBC
Thursday	9:30–10:00	February 1995–August 1995	NBC
Thursday	8:00–8:30	August 1995–July 2004	NBC

#8 rated series in 1994–95	#5 rated series in 1999–2000
#3 rated series in 1995–96	#5 rated series in 2000–01
#4 rated series in 1996–97	#1 rated series in 2001–02
#4 rated series in 1997–98	#2 rated series in 2002–03
#2 rated series in 1998–99	#4 rated series in 2003–04

5 Major Emmy Awards (37 nominations):
1 Emmy Award for Best Series (6 nominations)
1 Emmy Award for Best Actress (3 nominations)
No Emmy Awards for Best Actor (4 nominations)
No Emmy Awards for Best Supporting Actor (1 nomination)
1 Emmy Award for Best Supporting Actress (8 nominations)
1 Emmy Award for Best Guest Actor/Actress (9 nominations)
No Emmy Awards for Best Writing (2 nominations)
1 Emmy Award for Best Direction (4 nominations)

Cast: Courteney Cox; Jennifer Aniston; David Schwimmer; Matthew Perry; Matt LeBlanc; Lisa Kudrow; Elliott Gould (1994–2003); Christina Pickles (1994–2003); Jane Sibbett (1994–2001); Jessica Hecht (1994–2000); Tom Selleck (1996–97); Helen Baxendale (1998–99); James Michael Tyler (1995–2004); Paul Rudd (2002–04); Aisha Tyler (2003); Cali & Noelle Sheldon (2003–04).

Friends was the most-favored-son new series of the 1994–95 season. Months before it debuted on NBC its development process was the subject of a series of articles in *The New York Times*. When *The Times* affords this kind of publicity to a series, other entertainment vehicles follow. Thus *Friends* had an uncommon public awareness for a new series. The other side of this coin is this becomes a challenge to live up to the extraordinary expectations. *Friends* managed to do this from beginning to end. The series was a Nielsen top 10 hit with viewers in each of its 10 seasons. Its finale in 2004 garnered more than 52 million viewers, the fourth biggest tune-in for a series ender (behind *M*A*S*H, Cheers* and *Seinfeld*). When NBC's long dominance of Thursday night went into eclipse, programming boss Jeff Zucker ordered super-sized 40-minute episodes to buck up the network's standing.

Friends was also a smash with its peers. It earned 62 Emmy nominations, including 37 major nominations—six as television's outstanding comedy. It won its only series Emmy for season 8. Five of the six regulars were Emmy nominated (Matt LeBlanc was the odd one out). Jennifer Aniston was named best lead actress in 2002. Lisa Kudrow took home the supporting actress statue in 1997. The popularity of the series enabled it to attract big name guests, some of whom, such as Brad Pitt (then Aniston's boyfriend) and Susan Sarandon, rarely showed up in episodic television. Bruce Willis won a guest performer Emmy.

One of the series most noteworthy achievements was keeping the entire regular cast intact from beginning to end. Screen-time equality was a significant factor. Episode titles were fairly self-descriptive: "The One Where Monica Gets a Roommate," "The One After Joey and Rachel Kiss," "The One with Phoebe's Ex-Partner," "The One with Ross's Thing" and "The One with Chandler's Work Laugh." However, no matter whose name might have been in the title, each of the six got almost the exact screen time as the others. What's more, none came to the series with a bigger name than any of the others. The best known was probably Courteney Cox, whose claim to fame was being plucked out of the audience by Bruce Springsteen in his "Dancing in the Dark" video. With no reason for jealousy, the cast remained extremely tight. They negotiated as a group, eventually raising their salaries to $1 million per episode apiece. They entered the Emmys in the same category; as supporting actors through the first seven seasons, lead actors after that. Even after the series left the air, they remained close friends (no pun intended), according to each of them.

Friends had a strong pedigree behind the scenes. It's creators, Marta Kauffman and David Crane, had been responsible for what then was the most successful HBO comedy ever, *Dream On*. Also it was airing on NBC, still on an extraordinary roll ignited by *The Cosby Show* and reinvigorated by *Seinfeld*. The concept was simple, six young single people ubiquitous in each other's lives. Most of the plots took place in the lower Manhattan apartments of Monica Geller (Courteney Cox) and Rachel Green (Aniston) or their across-the-hall neighbors Chandler Bing (Matthew Perry) and Joey Tribiani (LeBlanc).

Monica, a chef with obsessive compulsive disorder, was the controlling mother of the group. Her long-time friend Rachel moved into her place as a runaway bride on what was to be her wedding day. She eventually became a fashion buyer. However, with the expectation that she would become a pampered spouse, she was desperate for a place to crash while she planned the rest of her life. Monica's brother Ross (David Schwimmer), a paleontologist at the Museum of Natural History, was a regular presence, as was Phoebe Buffay (Kudrow), an eccentric street musician. Their hangout was a nearby coffee house, Central Perk, where a white-haired server named Gunther (James Michael Tyler) became a semi-regular.

Chandler, a corporate numbers cruncher, and Joey, a soap opera actor yearning for bigger stages, were opposites in most ways. Joey's all-purpose greeting, "How you doin'?" became his trademark. Their apartment was part arcade, part zoo. A foosball table dominated the living room and Joey made pets of non-domesticated animals, such as a duck. Schwimmer, whose big credit was as a fringe player during the first season of *NYPD Blue*—David Caruso's character mockingly tagged him "4B," his apartment number— played Ross, whose first marriage collapsed when his wife, Carol, the mother of their son Ben, revealed she was a lesbian.

Before the series wrapped, Ross also would have a brief marriage to an English woman named Emily. But the real love of his life was Rachel, for whom he pined whenever he wasn't involved with someone else. Together, they conceived a daughter, although there was some question whether Joey, with whom Rachel also had a fling, was the father. In the end, Ross and Rachel became husband and wife. Before the final credits, Chandler and Monica, who had a long father figure relationship with Dr. Richard Burke played by Tom Selleck, also married and Phoebe wed a guy named Mike Hannigan (Paul Rudd), with whom she had an on-again, off-again relationship over the final two seasons. Only Joey was left single, a fortuitous choice since he became the only *Friends* character to be spun off into his own series. Lightning didn't strike twice. *Joey* was an artistic and ratings disaster, canceled after two seasons.

7. *Everybody Loves Raymond*

Broadcast History:

Friday	8:30–9:00	September 1996–February 1997	CBS
Monday	8:30–9:00	March 1997–August 1998	CBS
Monday	9:00–9:30	September 1998–June 2005	CBS
Monday	8:30–9:00	July 2005–September 2005	CBS

#30 rated series in 1997–98
#11 rated series in 1998–99
#12 rated series in 1999–2000
#5 rated series in 2000–01

#4 rated series in 2001–02
#7 rated series in 2002–03
#9 rated series in 2003–04
#9 rated series in 2004–05

12 Major Emmy Awards (54 nominations):
2 Emmy Awards for Best Series (7 nominations)
1 Emmy Award for Best Actor (6 nominations)
2 Emmy Awards for Best Actress (7 nominations)
3 Emmy Awards for Best Supporting Actor (12 nominations)
3 Emmy Award for Best Supporting Actress (6 nominations)
No Emmy Awards for Best Guest Actor/Actress (7 nominations)
1 Emmy Award for Best Writing (6 nominations)
No Emmy Awards for Best Directing (3 nominations)

Cast: Ray Romano; Patricia Heaton; Brad Garrett; Doris Roberts; Peter Boyle; Madylin Sweeten; Sawyer Sweeten; Sullivan Sweeten; Andy Kindler; Kevin James (1996–98); Monica Horan (1997–2005); Joe Manfrellotti (1997–2005); Fred Willard (2003–05); Georgia Engel (2003–05); Chris Elliott (2003–05).

Everybody Loves Raymond was another in a procession of sitcoms—*Welcome Back, Kotter, Seinfeld, Home Improvement, Roseanne,* among others—adapted from the standup comedy of its star, in this case Ray Romano, an infectiously likeable Everyman. It wasn't a heavy lift. Romano's stage show was steeped in incidents from his domestic experiences in Long Island. His big break came as a result of an appearance on *Late Night with David Letterman.* The host was so impressed that he signed Romano to a development deal with his production company, World Wide Pants. *Everybody Loves Raymond* was a product of that deal.

Romano maintained his real first name in the series but his character, married and the father of three (a daughter and twin sons, who were heard about more than seen), was given the surname Barone. A sportswriter for the suburban daily *Newsday,* Ray was the darling of his parents, Frank (Peter Boyle) and Marie (Doris Roberts). This grated on his only sibling, king-sized older brother Robert (Brad Garrett), a policeman who still lived at home, and gave the series its title. Garrett, an accomplished standup himself, who once opened for Sinatra, was given more laugh lines than Romano, most complaining about the favoritism shown his brother (a theme used successfully decades earlier by the Smothers Brothers). His body language and exaggerated facial expressions generated almost as many laughs as the punchlines. Among his unique quirks was a habit of touching his chin before putting food into his mouth.

Ray didn't land far from the family tree after he married Debra (Patricia

Heaton). In fact, he wound up only across the street from his parents and Robert. Debra, who had been subjected to the other Barones in only small doses when she and Ray had a tiny apartment, thought it would be a good idea to have the children grow up near their grandparents in a spacious house, a decision she came to rue on a daily basis as her in-laws wound up spending more time in Ray's living room and kitchen than their own. Few episodes took place outside the Barone home. Marie made it clear that she didn't consider Debra a worthy spouse for her beloved Raymond. Not that Ray also wasn't the occasional target of her insulting comments. She just couldn't help herself. As far as meddling Marie was concerned, Debra's cooking wasn't up to the level she provided Raymond; Debra's housekeeping left a lot to be desired and her child-rearing was fault ridden. It could have been worse. Marie wasn't aware that Raymond, like many men, constantly complained about the lack of action in his bedroom. (Also like most men, his bellyaching was unjustified.)

Fortunately for Debra, her cantankerous father-in-law didn't pile on. He was just happy that someone other than him was being verbally bludgeoned by his wife. But he would get in a few sarcastic zingers of his own now and then. The vignettes that drove the series weren't ground-breaking. Most came from issues mined by family sitcoms throughout the history of television. This was art imitating life, according to executive producer Philip Rosenthal. He said each episode evolved from a brain storming session in the writers' room, which began with an inquiry whether anyone had a funny experience at home during the previous week.

It was the impeccable timing and delivery by the cast that made the episodes shine, a reality illustrated by the ensemble' Emmy hauls. The series was named television's outstanding comedy twice. Romano was cited as best lead actor in a comedy once. Heaton won a pair of lead actress Emmys. Roberts was the biggest winner with four Emmys. Garrett took home three statues. For some inexplicable reason the Television Academy failed to award a trophy to Boyle in spite of him being nominated six times.

As new scenarios for the core group became harder to improvise, the series expanded its cast. When it was decided that it was time for Robert to find a wife and leave the nest, Rosenthal didn't look far. He cast his wife, Monica Horan, to play Amy McDougall, a friend of Debra, who captured Robert's heart. Although she had limited credits, Horan fit the role well. (She and Rosenthal met while attending Long Island's Hofstra University.) Horan's entrance created an opening for a couple more comedic veterans, Georgia Engel and Fred Willard, to make periodic visits as Amy's off-the-wall parents,

Pat and Hank McDougall. They were each nominated for an Emmy for guest roles on the series.

---

8. *I Love Lucy*

Broadcast History:

Monday   9:00–9:30   October 1951–June 1957   CBS

#3 rated series in 1951–52	#1 rated series in 1954–55
#1 rated series in 1952–53	#2 rated series in 1955–56
#1 rated series in 1953–54	#1 rated series in 1956–57

5 Major Emmy Awards (24 nominations):
2 Emmy Awards for Best Series (4 nominations)
2 Emmy Awards for Best Actress (9 nominations)
No Emmy Awards for Best Supporting Actor (5 nominations)
1 Emmy Award for Best Supporting Actress (4 nominations)
No Emmy Awards for Best Writing (2 nominations)

Cast: Lucille Ball; Desi Arnaz; Vivian Vance; William Frawley; Richard Keith (1956–57); Jerry Hausner (1951–54); Elizabeth Patterson (1953–56); Doris Singleton (1953–57); Kathryn Card (1953–56); Mary Jane Croft (1957); Frank Nelson (1957).

Many would be surprised and some would argue vociferously about why *I Love Lucy* is not the all-time number one situation comedy. It was television's first super hit comedy, if not program of any genre. Legend had it that through the 20th century there was never a time when *I Love Lucy* reruns weren't on television somewhere in the world. The show established Lucille Ball as the queen of physical comedy, arguably for all time. If ratings were compiled as scrupulously as they came to be, the January 19, 1953 episode, in which Lucy gave birth to Desi Jr., might rank as the highest rated entertainment program of all time. (Of course, the number of homes with television was only a small fraction of what it has become.)

Desi Arnaz's inspired decision to shoot on film rather than use the then-in-vogue kinescope for distribution laid the foundation for rerun syndication, which became the mother's milk of the industry's bottom line. This became the catalyst for the gradual relocation of the center of the television industry from New York to the sound stages of Hollywood. Desi also is the father of the three-camera shooting technique, which is still the format used by the majority of sitcoms in the new millennium. Desi would go on to establish his own production company, named for him and his wife, Desilu, which was responsible for a slew of hits, the most noteworthy being *The Untouchables*.

Oh, yeah, it was funny as hell, too, and the humor holds up more than a half-century after *I Love Lucy* made its debut in 1951. Every *Lucy* fan has a favorite but the ones most often cited include Lucy stomping wine grapes in Italy, another in which she and her gal pal Ethel became overwhelmed by an out-of-control conveyor belt of candy bonbons, the one where Lucy gives birth to Desi Jr., and one in which Lucy got bombed while doing a commercial for a health tonic. The admonition by Desi, "Lucy, you got some 'splaining' to do," is parroted by fans who weren't born when it was uttered.

Like many comedies at the dawn of television, *I Love Lucy* was a lift from a popular radio program, *My Favorite Husband*. As the transition to the burgeoning new medium was being discussed, CBS had reservations about Desi "being believable" as Lucy's husband, even though the couple was married in real life. Some things never change. More than 35 years later, as *thirtysomething* was being cast, the same concerns were raised about real life spouses Ken Olin and Patricia Wettig. ABC didn't think they looked right for each other and cast each with a different spouse in what became the hit series.

Lucy and Desi went into their own pockets to film a pilot and prove the network wrong. The gambit was a success and *I Love Lucy* was given a slot on the 1951 fall schedule. The format wasn't a direct lift from the radio show. In the television version, Desi owned a New York nightclub, where his band performed. Lucy was a homemaker although she yearned to break into show business like her husband. Some of the funniest episodes derived from her attempts to prove to Desi's chagrin that she could do it.

Lucy and Desi lived in an apartment on the East Side of Manhattan. Their landlords, Fred and Ethel Mertz, became their best friends. Ethel, played by Vivian Vance, was Lucy's co-conspirator in many of her most zany schemes, which frustrated Fred. Vance had reservations at the casting of William Frawley as Fred. Frawley was in his mid–60s, 22 years older than Vance, when the series debuted. To compensate, Ethel was frumped up a bit to appear closer to her husband's age.

But the chemistry all around clicked immediately. *I Love Lucy* was the third highest rated series on television for its maiden season (The established *Arthur Godfrey's Talent Scouts* and the *Texaco Star Theatre*, starring Milton Berle, held the top two spots). For four of the next five seasons, *I Love Lucy* ascended to television's throne room. The exception was 1955–56 when the eventually disgraced *$64,000 Question* became all the rage with *I Love Lucy* number two.

Although *I Love Lucy* remained on the network in reruns, original production on the mothership ceased in 1957. The concept was partially mined in follow-up series *The Lucy-Desi Comedy Hour*, *The Lucy Show* and *Here's Lucy* but *I Love Lucy* endured only six seasons. This relative lack of longevity, and the fact that there were far fewer Emmy awards given during television's early years, is a primary reason why *I Love Lucy* isn't ranked above series such as *All in the Family*, *M*A*S*H*, *Cheers*, *Frasier*, *The Mary Tyler Moore Show*, *Friends* and *Everybody Loves Raymond*, which endured almost twice as long. Nevertheless, in the hearts of many, *I Love Lucy* will always be the standard against which all television comedies are measured.

9. The Cosby Show

Broadcast History:

Thursday	8:00–8:30	September 1984–June 1992	NBC
Thursday	8:30–9:00	July 1992–September 1992	NBC

#3 rated series in 1984–85	#1 rated series in 1988–89
#1 rated series in 1985–86	#2 rated series in 1989–90
#1 rated series in 1986–87	#5 rated series in 1990–91
#1 rated series in 1987–88	#18 rated series in 1991–92

5 Major Emmy Awards (22 nominations):
1 Emmy Award for Best Series (3 nominations)
No Emmy Award for Best Actress (2 nominations)
No Emmy Awards for Best Supporting Actor (1 nomination)
No Emmy Awards for Best Supporting Actress (2 nominations)
1 Emmy Award for Best Guest Actor/Actress (7 nominations)
1 Emmy Award for Best Writing (4 nominations)
2 Emmy Awards for Best Direction (3 nominations)

Cast: Bill Cosby; Phylicia Rashad; Sabrina Le Beauf; Lisa Bonet (1984–91); Malcolm-Jamal Warner; Tempestt Bledsoe; Keshia Knight Pulliam; Clarice Taylor; Earle Hyman; Peter Costa (1985–89); Geoffrey Owens (1986–92); Deon Richmond (1986–92); Carl Anthony Payne II (1986–87); Troy Winbush (1987–91); Joseph C. Phillips (1989–92); Raven-Symone (1989–92); Erika Alexander (1990–92); William Thomas, Jr. (1991–92).

Bill Cosby caused a stir among TV writers on the 1984 summer press junket. Appearing at the semi-annual event to promote new series for fall, Cosby offered an uncharacteristically boastful response to a question about why he wanted to return to episodic TV. "I'm doing it to save NBC," he said. The Peacock network had been at low ebb for years. Cosby said he felt he owed NBC for making him the first African-American actor to get equal billing with a white co-star in a drama series when he and Robert Culp headlined

I Spy. But that show was only a moderate success and previous comedy series featuring Cosby in a lead role had been failures. His main claim to fame when *The Cosby Show* premiered was as a spokesman for Jell-O. Moreover, his new sitcom was scheduled against Tom Selleck's *Magnum, P.I.*, one of television's highest rated dramas. Critics in the room smiled knowingly at each other and when the session ended, they joked among themselves that Cosby had become full of himself and delusional.

There was nothing really ground-breaking or gimmicky about *The Cosby Show* concept beyond the fact that its focus was a prosperous African-American family: Cliff Huxtable, a doctor; his wife Clair (Phylicia Rashad), a lawyer; and their five children: Theo, the only son (Malcolm-Jamal Warner); Denise, the oldest at home (Lisa Bonet); elementary schooler Vanessa (Tempestt Bledsoe); Rudy, the baby of the family (Keshia Knight Pulliam), and college student Sondra (Sabrina LeBeauf). None were especially precocious nor obnoxious, the types who sometimes break out in family comedies. Plots, especially the early ones, were lifted from Cosby's stand-up act, which centered around humorous episodes from his personal and family life. Cosby was a rarity. He worked clean, no matter the venue. This made his routines easy to adapt for broadcast television.

Cosby's boast became prophetic. *The Cosby Show* was an immediate monster hit. It finished its debut season third in the Nielsen ratings (behind white hot soaps *Dallas* and *Dynasty* but well ahead of *Magnum, P.I.*) Its next five seasons it was the top rated show on television, with full season average Nielsen ratings in the 30s (percentage of all households in America with television), a plateau that hasn't been seen since and in the multi-channel universe likely will be seen again. Its popularity was such that NBC got Major League Baseball to delay the start of Thursday night World Series games on the network so *The Cosby Show* would not have to be pre-empted.

The Cosby Show also had a broad halo effect. The comedies that followed—*Family Ties* and *Cheers*, highly regarded for their quality but low-rated pre–*Cosby*—vaulted into the Nielsen Top Five. NBC would dominate Thursday into the new millennium and the success on this night afforded promotional platforms to spread the success to other nights. The perennial third place network started a long run in the Nielsen penthouse. ABC would be reminded regularly during this era that it had first crack at *The Cosby Show* but passed.

A trait that distinguished the series, a black, upper income nuclear family, became a source of criticism from some African-Americans, who contended that the show wasn't black enough, that it didn't portray the reality of many black families. The counter argument was that the Huxtable family was a role model and inspiration. *The Cosby Show* might not have depicted life in the inner city (it was set in a fashionable Brooklyn neighborhood) but did celebrate African-American authors, artists and entertainers. Sammy Davis, Jr., Stevie Wonder (who was rewarded with an Emmy nomination) and B.B. King made guest appearances. Also episodes delved into issues such as teen pregnancy and Theo's struggle to overcome dyslexia. Late in the series run, the Huxtables welcomed Clair's cousin Pam, a 17-year-old who grew up in the ghetto. Also, it spun off the series *A Different World*, starring Bonet as a student at Hillman, a predominantly black college in the South, and encouraged NBC to schedule a couple of other black-oriented NBC sitcoms, *Amen* and *227*.

The Cosby Show not only revived NBC, it ignited a renaissance of situation comedy, a form that had been declared dead by many in the business as drama series dominated the ratings. The season before the Huxtables arrived, only one sitcom (*Kate & Allie*) ranked among Nielsen's Top 10. The season after it became a sensation, half the Top 10 were sitcoms. The year after that, the number was seven. For whatever reasons, the Television Academy voters weren't as enamored of *The Cosby Show* as the audience was (possibly due to Bill Cosby's public indifference to awards). The series was rewarded with a best comedy Emmy only once and none of the regulars got to take home an Emmy.

---

10. *Seinfeld*

Broadcast History:

Thursday	9:30–10:00	May 1990–July 1990	NBC
Wednesday	9:30–10:00	January 1991–February 1991	NBC
Thursday	9:30–10:00	April 1991–June 1991	NBC
Wednesday	9:30–10:00	June 1991–December 1991	NBC
Wednesday	9:00–9:30	December 1991–January 1993	NBC
Thursday	9:30–10:00	February 1993–August 1993	NBC
Thursday	9:00–9:30	August 1993–September 1998	NBC
Wednesday	8:30–9:00	January 1998–September 1998	NBC

#25 rated series in 1992–93	#2 rated series in 1995–96
#3 rated series in 1993–94	#2 rated series in 1996–97
#1 rated series in 1994–95	#1 rated series in 1997–98

7 Major Emmy Awards (54 nominations):
1 Emmy Award for Best Series (7 nominations)

No Emmy Awards for Best Actor (5 nominations)
3 Emmy Awards for Best Supporting Actor (12 nominations)
1 Emmy Award for Best Supporting Actress (7 nominations)
No Emmy Awards for Best Guest Actor/Actress (6 nominations)
2 Emmy Awards for Best Writing (11 nominations)
No Emmy Awards for Best Directing (6 nominations)

Cast: Jerry Seinfeld; Julia Louis-Dreyfus; Jason Alexander; Michael Richards; Liz Sheridan; Barney Martin (1991–98); Len Lesser (1991–98); Wayne Knight (1991–98); Sandy Baron (1991–97); Richard Fancy (1991–98); Bob Balaban (1992–93); Heidi Swedberg (1992–97); Peter Crombie (1992–93); Estelle Harris (1992–98); Jerry Stiller (1993–98); Danny Woodburn (1994–98); Ian Abercrombie (1994–98); Steve Hytner (1994–98); Bryan Cranston (1994–97); Richard Herd (1995–98); Patrick Warburton (1995–98); John O'Hurley (1995–98); Phil Morris (1995–98).

"The TV show about nothing" was really something. The self-styled tagline for *Seinfeld* was more marketing ploy than apt description. *Seinfeld* episodes were, of course, always about something, offshoots of humorous observational bits from Jerry Seinfeld's standup comedy act. The opening scenes presented the comedian in a club setting describing incidents that segued into an episode. In the early years these tended toward situations and conundrums identifiable to viewers: forgetting where a car is parked in a huge mall garage and an interminable wait to be seated in a restaurant. Once the series was an established hit, storylines veered brazenly toward the risqué and absurd: "The Contest" among four adults to see which one could hold out longest without masturbating; hoarding of "the sponge," birth control devices that had been removed from the market; a bride-to-be dying from licking poisoned glue on the envelopes for her wedding invitations, bought on the cheap by her fiancé.

Of all television's landmark series, *Seinfeld* started life as the most improbable. The pilot aired on July 5, 1989, with television viewing at its seasonal nadir. Even without formidable competition (cable was still in its infantile three R's era: reruns, religion and rasslin'), opening night ratings were dismal. The series wasn't even called *Seinfeld* at birth. It was *The Seinfeld Chronicles*. The Nielsen ratings were so under-achieving that when an initial four-episode trial run ended, there weren't many expectations that the show would be seen again. Indeed, it disappeared for almost a year, not resurfacing until the following May—again in a viewing dead zone a week after the official television season ended. Despite the repechage, NBC clearly did not value it as a prize property. However, word of mouth gradually built about this show with an off-kilter worldview, spurring a gradual uptick in the ratings.

Jerry Seinfeld kept his name and real-life occupation but the characters orbiting the star were fictional, albeit based on people Seinfeld and his creative partner, Larry David, were familiar with. Indeed, David, credited by many as the real genius behind the show, fashioned George Costanza (Jason Alexander) after himself. George was depicted as a self-absorbed face in the crowd ne'er-do-well, who depended upon Jerry to prop him up or bail him out of his latest misadventure. Many were the product of schemes to beat the system or scam a woman into his bed. He was the cheapskate who inadvertently was responsible for the death of his fiancée, who he tried to dump when he became convinced he had a shot at dating Marissa Tomei. George's employment history was as bleak as his love life. He even managed to screw up a dream job with the New York Yankees by cutting every conceivable corner to get out of work. David in effect talked to himself while playing Yankees owner and George's boss George Steinbrenner, although David was only seen from behind.

Jerry's across-the-hall neighbor Kramer (Michael Richards) was modeled after one of David's friends and neighbors, a colorful dreamer with a million get-rich schemes named Kenny Kramer. Richards' Kramer went for years before it was revealed that his first name was Kosmo. Kramer's trademark was to slide, stumble or crash into Jerry's place, sans invitation or knocking. Kramer's goofy gambits ranged from setting up a stage in his apartment to present his own knockoff of the iconic daytime talk show *The Merv Griffin Show*, transporting used beverage containers from New York, where there is a 5-cent deposit to other states where the deposits were a dime or more and publishing a coffee table book about coffee tables. When the mood struck him, Kramer built a hot tub in his living room.

Kramer's frequent co-conspirator was another neighbor, Newman (Wayne Knight), an unscrupulous mailman. Jerry despised Newman to such an extent that he couldn't mention his name without his voice dripping disdain.

Elaine Benes (Julia Louis-Dreyfus) was Jerry's former girlfriend and still a constant in his life. Elaine used the guys as confidantes, advisors and occasional wingmen in her efforts to bag her "Mr. Right." Among the candidates was the late John F. Kennedy, Jr. Another was an oddball named Puddy, an over-the-top sports buff, a career-making role for Patrick Warburton. John O'Hurley also ascended from bit player status as J. Peterman, Elaine's clueless boss at a catalog company.

Jerry's fortunes with women weren't appreciably better than Elaine for a shared trait. Both were extraordinarily choosy, picking apart the slightest imperfections of appearance of character or a potential mate. Jerry frittered potential mates over issues such as man hands, a rash ointment he found in a medicine cabinet, their voices or laughs. He suspected a beauty played by pre–*Desperate Housewives* Terri Hatcher of having cosmetically enhanced breasts. When she learned of his suspicion, Hatcher's character kissed him off with the line, "They're real and they're spectacular."

While *Seinfeld* didn't spawn any spinoff series, it did seem to have a magical touch for actresses that played guest spots opposite him in one or more episodes as the Seinfeld exposure led to series of their own. Among them were the aforementioned Hatcher, Courteney Cox (*Friends*), Jane Leeves (*Frasier*), Jami Gertz (*Still Standing*), Anna Gunn (*Breaking Bad*), Kristin Davis (*Sex & the City*) and Debra Messing (*Will & Grace*).

---

11. *Modern Family*

Broadcast History:

Wednesday   9:00–9:30   September 2009–present   ABC

#24 rated series in 2010–11   #18 rated series in 2012–13
#17 rated series in 2011–12   #19 rated series in 2013–14

16 Major Emmy Awards (45 nominations):
5 Emmy Awards for Best program (5 nominations)
3 Emmy Awards for Best Supporting Actor (16 nominations)
2 Emmy Awards for Best Supporting Actress (9 nominations)
No Emmy Awards for Best Guest Actor/Actress (5 nominations)
2 Emmy Awards for Best Writing (2 nominations)
4 Emmy Awards for Best Directing (8 nomination)

Cast: Ed O'Neill; Sofia Vergara; Julie Bowen; Ty Burrell; Jesse Tyler Ferguson; Eric Stonestreet; Rico Rodriguez; Nolan Gould; Sarah Hyland; Ariel Winter.

Modern Family should have been titled "Extended Family." Cumulatively three related clans cover the gamut of contemporary units: a traditional nuclear family, a blended family and a gay couple, who adopted a daughter and, when California's ban on same sex marriages was thrown out by the courts, finally wed.

Ed O'Neill as Jay Pritchett is again married with children but also grandchildren and a step son. After a May-December courtship, long divorced Jay married sassy Columbian Gloria, a career-making role for shapely Sofia Vergara. Previously married Gloria brought with her a son, Manny (Rico Rodriguez), an adolescent with a middle-aged soul. In season five, somewhat to Jay's initial dismay, Gloria became pregnant with the couple's only biological child, a son. Jay already had two adult children, Mitchell Pritchett (Jesse Tyler Ferguson) and Claire Dunphy (Julie Bowen). The latter has three kids, all of whom are considerably older than their new uncle. The sixtyish Jay is constantly mistaken for his new son's grandfather. Mitchell is in a committed long-term relationship with Cameron Tucker, a double Emmy winning role for Eric Stonestreet.

Mitchell is a job-hopping corporate and environmental lawyer while Cameron, for the most part, plays Mr. Mom. He does, however, work part-time as a teacher, drama instructor and football coach. Each of the occupations is a rich source of humor because of the unabashedly flamboyant approach he brings to the jobs. The loving couple jumps through all the frustrating hoops before finally being able to adopt a Vietnamese toddler they name Lily. In characteristic fashion, Cameron introduces Lily to the rest of the family *Lion King* style, triumphantly holding her in both hands over his head. Taking advantage of her father's obsession to be the perfect parents, Lily (Aubrey Anderson-Emmons) evolves into a manipulative smart-mouth.

Claire is primarily a stay-at-home mother, although she dabbles from time to time in rejoining the work force. One of her jobs is in Jay's home supply business, where she is resented as an under-qualified product of nepotism—which she is. Her husband, Phil Dunphy (Ty Burrell), a good natured realtor, is a throwback to the bumbling but well meaning spouse in vogue on television series decades earlier. Both roles produced supporting character Emmys, two for Bowen, one for Burrell. Haley Dunphy (Sarah Hyland), the oldest of their offspring, is a boy-crazy conniver, who quickly enrolls then drops out of college, returning back home to live. Her sister Alex (Ariel Winter) is Haley's opposite, a scholarly student indifferent to boys, partially because none have shown a lot of interest in her. However, beneath the surface is a beautiful young lady seemingly destined to blossom into a stunning heart-breaker. Their brother Luke (Nolan Gould), an awkward tweener, lives in the shadows of his two older sisters and even that of his cousin Manny. But as the only other male in the home, he gets ample attention from his father, who wants Luke to be a younger version of himself, even trying desperately to transmit to the youngster his love of amateur magic.

The Dunphy children are seen in every episode but their involvement is almost always relegated to the "B" stories, as the adults move to the fore. Each episode is almost evenly divided between the three households (a lesson wisely learned from *Friends*) with a connecting thread that weaves through the entire extended family.

The former spouses of Jay and Gloria show up infrequently, generally to create turmoil in their ex-mates' new families. Shelley Long plays the flighty DeDe Pritchett, the mother of Claire and Mitchell. Benjamin Bratt plays Javier Delgado, a free-wheeling playboy. In spite of his irresponsibility and the many times he has made promises he failed to keep, Javier is idolized by Manny, a situation that grates on Jay. The saving grace is that Gloria clearly has no use for the guy who once swept her off her feet.

Nathan Lane makes infrequent appearances as Pepper, the self appointed leader of the gay social circle in which Cameron and Mitchell used to travel. As soon as he learns Cameron and Mitchell are planning nuptials, Pepper seizes control and creates a never-to-be-forgotten series of calamities. However, as always, all is well that ends well.

---

12. *Murphy Brown*

Broadcast History:

Monday	9:00–9:30	November 1988–February 1997	CBS
Monday	8:30–9:00	April 1997–May 1997	CBS
Monday	9:30–10:00	June 1997–September 1997	CBS
Wednesday	8:30–9:00	October 1997–January 1998	CBS
Monday	9:30–10:00	April 1998–May 1998	CBS
Monday	9:30–10:00	July 1998–August 1998	CBS

#27 rated series in 1989–90	#9 rated series in 1993–94
#6 rated series in 1990–91	#16 rated series in 1994–95
#3 rated series in 1991–92	#18 rated series in 1995–96
#4 rated series in 1992–93	

15 Major Emmy Awards (43 nominations):
2 Emmy Awards for Best Series (5 nominations)
5 Emmy Awards for Best Actress (7 nominations)
No Emmy Award for Best Supporting Actor (3 nominations)
No Emmy Awards for Best Supporting Actress (5 nominations)
5 Emmy Award for Guest Actor/Actress (11 nominations)
2 Emmy Awards for Best Writing (6 nominations)
1 Emmy Award for Best Direction (6 nominations)

Cast: Candice Bergen; Charles Kimbrough; Joe Regalbuto; Faith Ford; Grant Shaud (1988–96); Pat Corley (1988–96); Robert Pastorelli (1988–94); Ritch Brinkley (1988–97); John Hostetter; Alan Oppenheimer (1988–92); Scott Bakula (1993–96); Dyllan Christopher (1994–95); Jackson Buckley (1996); Haley Joel Osment (1997–98); Garry Marshall (1994–97); Christopher Rich (1995–97); Paul Reubens (1995–97); Paula Korologos (1995); Pat Finn (1995–98); Matt Griesser (1996–97); Lily Tomlin (1996–98).

Murphy Brown was an attempt to take what worked for Mary Tyler Moore and make it work again for another popular actress, Candice Bergen. It succeeded beyond anyone's hopes, dominating the ratings in its time slot, winning a pair of Emmys as television's outstanding comedy and five Emmys for Bergen. It could have been more. After the fifth, she withdrew herself from consideration in order to give other actresses she considered worthy a shot. (Not to diminish Bergen's accomplishments but the fact that her father, ventriloquist Edgar Bergen, was a founder of the Television Academy, might have had something to do with her enduring Emmy success.)

Murphy was a star correspondent for the CBS news magazine *FYI*, a thinly camouflaged imitation of *60 Minutes*. A strident feminist, Murphy had strong opinions about everything, including the contemporary political scene in Washington, D.C., the base for her program. Murphy did nothing in moderation, including drinking. At the series outset she had just returned to work after a rehab stint at the Betty Ford Center. Thanks to her reputation as a take-no-prisoners journalist and personal popularity, her job was waiting for her. She was greeted affectionately by FYI's old hands, especially Frank Fontana (Joe Regalbuto), her confidante and closest friend even while they occasionally competed for prize "gets" and big stories. Another welcoming her back warmly was Jim Dial (Charles Kimbrough), who had more gravitas than common sense and zero sense of humor. He was the series answer to *The Mary Tyler Moore Show*'s Ted Baxter although not as cartoonish.

Things were not entirely the same. In Murphy's absence, Corky Sherwood (Faith Ford), a former Miss America, had been hired to take over some of Murphy's duties. Corky was perky, extroverted and a bit of a bubblehead; everything Murphy was not. However, she had such an endearing personality, Corky was universally embraced and kept around even with Murphy back. FYI had a new 25-year-old executive producer, Miles Silverberg (Grant Shaud), with virtually zero credentials but formidable connections at the network. His title might have given Miles the role of the boss but the staff treated him like a newbie office clerk. None were tougher on him and less respectful than Murphy. Murphy's secretary was not retained during her absence, so she had to rely on temps while seeking someone acceptable to fill the position on a permanent basis. The fact that she found something wrong with every one of them or they had a problem with her became a running punchline. Murphy wound up going through almost 100 candidates, including Paul (Pee-Wee Herman) Reubens and Bette Midler.

Another similarity to *The Mary Tyler Moore Show* was the division of plots between the FYI studio and Murphy's fashionable townhome in D.C.

Actually, it was the neighborhood and exterior that was fashionable. The interior was a never-ending work in progress. Murphy put the makeover in the hands of Eldin Bernecky (Robert Pastorelli), a free-thinking painter who turned the renovations into his life's work. A third front was a tavern near FYI headquarters run by a colorful owner/bartender named Phil (Pat Corley), who claimed to know all of Washington's secrets. The *Murphy Brown* gang suspected he might actually be as inside as he boasted.

Judgmental commentary on the political scene was a big part of the behind-the-scenes activity at FYI. When the tables were turned it turned into a national cause celebre. Murphy became pregnant after a fling with her former husband, who decided he didn't want to become a daddy. Murphy opted to raise the child, eventually named Avery for Murphy's late mother, as a single working mom. Murphy Brown's real-life counterparts, including Katie Couric, Joan Lunden and Paula Zahn, appeared as themselves at Murphy's baby shower. This evoked criticism from Vice President Dan Quayle during the 1992 election season. He contended that Murphy's lifestyle decision set a bad example for the nation's women and trivialized the role of fathers. Editorial pages, op-eds and late night comedy shows erupted into a frenzy. The mainstream media lined up behind Bergen and the show, which struck back with veiled shots at Quayle. As it always is, such controversy was a windfall for the show's ratings.

---

13. *The Golden Girls*

Broadcast History:

Saturday	9:00–9:30	September 1985–July 1991	NBC
Saturday	8:00–8:30	August 1991–September 1991	NBC
Saturday	8:30–9:00	September 1991–September 1992	NBC

#7 rated series in 1985–86	#6 rated series in 1989–90
#5 rated series in 1986–87	#10 rated series in 1990–91
#4 rated series in 1987–88	#30 rated series in 1991–92
#6 rated series in 1988–89	

8 Major Emmy Awards (46 nominations):
2 Emmy Awards for Best Series (6 nominations)
3 Emmy Awards for Best Actress (15 nominations)
1 Emmy Award for Best Supporting Actress (7 nominations)
No Emmy Award for Guest Actor/Actress (9 nominations)
1 Emmy Award for Best Writing (3 nominations)
1 Emmy Award for Best Direction (6 nominations)

Cast: Bea Arthur; Betty White; Rue McClanahan; Estelle Getty; Herb Edelman; Harold Gould.

The Golden Girls is one of television's unlikeliest mega-hits. It was close to miraculous that it was picked up by NBC at all. When *The Golden Girls* premiered in 1985, the major networks were obsessed with chasing the 18-to-49 demographic cherished by the advertising industry of Madison Avenue. This extended to the casting of series. Veteran actors were somewhat tolerable playing peripheral roles but that was it. Youth had to be served. But thanks to the raging success of *Miami Vice*, *The A-Team* and its Thursday "must see TV" situation comedies, NBC could afford to take a chance on a series about four golden-agers sharing a house in Miami. (However, the series was shot entirely on the West Coast.) The network owed the Magic City one, given its Wild West depiction on *Miami Vice*. Some dubbed *The Golden Girls* "Miami Nice."

In spite of the worldwide hype for *Miami Vice*, *The Golden Girls* earned higher ratings from the start and lasted seven seasons to *Miami Vice*'s five. Bea Arthur was the most equal of the quartet, at least at the outset, as bitter divorcee Dorothy Zbornak. Herb Edelman appeared sporadically, starting with the second episode, as Dorothy's former spouse, who left her for a much younger woman. Outspoken, opinionated and acid-tongued, Dorothy could have been a DNA match for Arthur's Maude.

Estelle Getty as Dorothy's mother Sophie became the show stealer. (In real life, Arthur was a year older than her television mother.) Sophie came to live with the other three when her retirement facility burned down. She was said to have suffered a stroke, which stripped away any inhibitions and control of her mouth. This excused the outrageously politically incorrect outbursts and insults, which became the trademark of her character. Betty White played Rose Nylund, a good-hearted widow, who was a little slow on the uptake and became easily confused. Rue McClanahan filled out the foursome as over-sexed, perennially horny Blanche Devereaux.

In the pilot, Blanche was on the verge of marrying a guy she had known for only a week. This was just one of the reasons Dorothy and Blanche were wary that she might be making a mistake getting hitched to a guy they regarded as shady. They also were worried where they were going to live with Blanche taking a husband. It became a moot point when their suspicions about the groom-to-be were borne out and the wedding was called off. The series came full circle in the finale, centered around the preparation for Dorothy's nuptials to a lover named Lucas, played by Leslie Nielsen. The other women were prepared to use this as the catalyst for each of them going their own way. In the end, however, Blanche, Rose and Sophie decided to stay together.

The ensemble was pitch perfect and stayed intact throughout the show's run. It is said to be one of two series in which this was the case, the other being *Friends*. Each of the four actresses was honored with an Emmy and their collaboration helped *The Golden Girls* win two Emmys as best comedy series.

By the time the show ended, *The Golden Girls* had slumped out of the Nielsen Top 10 for the first time. Undaunted CBS coaxed the remaining threesome to transition to a spinoff, *The Golden Palace*. The premise was Blanche sold her home and used the proceeds to buy a small hotel, which had seen better days. The idea was the women would pool their efforts to run the place. In the not-so-grand tradition of *AfterMASH*, the sequel was poorly conceived and executed and was rejected by the audience in its only season.

---

14. *The Danny Thomas Show*

Broadcast History:

Tuesday	9:00–9:30	September 1953–June 1956	ABC
Monday	8:00–8:30	October 1956–February 1957	ABC
Thursday	9:00–9:30	February 1957–July 1957	ABC
Monday	9:00–9:30	October 1957–September 1964	CBS
Monday	9:30–10:00	April 1965–September 1965	CBS

#2 rated series in 1957–58   #8 rated series in 1961–62
#5 rated series in 1958–59   #7 rated series in 1962–63
#4 rated series in 1959–60   #9 rated series in 1963–64
#12 rated series in 1960–61

5 Major Emmy Awards (20 nominations):
2 Emmy Awards for Best Series (5 nominations)
1 Emmy Award for Best Actor (4 nominations)
No Emmy Awards for Best Actress (1 nominations)
No Emmy Award for Best Supporting Actress (2 nominations)
No Emmy Awards for Best Writing (2 nominations)
2 Emmy Awards for Best Direction (6 nominations)

Cast: Danny Thomas; Jean Hagen (1953–56); Marjorie Lord (1957–65); Rusty Hamer; Sherry Jackson (1953–58); Penney Parker (1959–60); Angela Cartwright (1957–65); Louise Beavers (1953–54); Amanda Rudolph (1955–64); Horace McMahon (1953–54); Ben Lessy (1953–59); Jesse White (1953–57); Hans Conried (1956–65); Mary Wickes (1956–57); Sheldon Leonard (1957–61); Pat Harrington, Jr. (1959–60); Annette Funicello (1959); Sid Melton (1959–65); Pat Carroll (1961–64).

The Danny Thomas Show endured for 12 seasons on two networks. One simple explanation—it was good during a lot of seasons when most of television wasn't very good. When *The Danny Thomas Show* (the series was known as *Make Room for Daddy* during its first three seasons) premiered on ABC in 1953 prime time also included *Junior Press Conference, The Big Issue, Pantomime Quiz, Johns Hopkins Science Review, Colonel Humphrey Flack*, at least three boxing programs and one wrestling show. The ABC network was dark (no programming) in the hour preceding *The Danny Thomas Show*. The Dumont Network (then one of the Big Four) was dark opposite *The Danny Thomas Show*. This is not to damn with faint praise. *The Danny Thomas Show* was a delightful half-hour, which won an Emmy in its rookie season as best new series (a category subsequently discontinued) and was named overall best comedy the following season when Thomas won as best actor in a comedy. Sheldon Leonard also won a couple of directing Emmys.

In this milieu, an established entertainer/personality like Thomas shone. Interestingly, legend has it that ABC wasn't that high on Thomas, who had failed in his only other TV show, fronting a sitcom. It agreed to pick him up in order to get another program starring Ray Bolger (*Where's Raymond?*), a bigger name. *Where's Raymond?* lasted only two seasons. Thomas was another sitcom star who played a character much like himself. Danny Williams was an entertainer who was frequently out on the road. His regular absences forced his wife Margaret (Jean Hagen) into almost a single parent role to their two children, Terry (Sherry Jackson) and Rusty (Rusty Hamer), an early example of a precocious youngster spouting lines that could come only from a team of adult script writers.

Danny was loud and abrasive but beneath his gruff exterior he had a good heart. The real Danny shared these traits, which created issues on the set. Hagen abruptly left the series after the third season, reportedly fed up with Thomas' dictatorial manner. Thomas closed the door to Hagen ever returning by killing off Margaret. This led to a season of Danny Williams dating a bevy of attractive potential replacement mothers for his kids. He settled on a woman named Kathy (Marjorie Lord). When the series jumped to CBS in the fall of 1957, Kathy had already settled in as the new woman of the house. With her came a young daughter, Linda (Angela Cartwright), by a previous marriage. Linda gradually replaced Rusty as the cutie pie of the family.

Jackson followed Hagen out the door in 1958. Ostensibly her character was going away to college but a year later Terry was back, this time played by Penney Parker. One season later, Terry was gone for good, having gotten married. Among an array of recurring characters was an eccentric uncle, Tonoose, a tour de force for Hans Conreid.

Danny Williams' bombast was responsible for one of the show's enduring legacies. On one of his road trips, Danny was stopped for a minor traffic infraction in Mayberry, North Carolina. Danny became so verbally abusive and condescending to what he regarded as the bumpkin sheriff, Andy Taylor, that he wound up in the Mayberry jail. That episode, which was designed as a backdoor pilot, was such a sensation *The Andy Griffith Show* was rushed into production.

The real Danny Thomas also had a role in what would become a long running hit, *That Girl*, starring his daughter Mario. His son Tony also was a creative force for *The Golden Girls*. Five years after *The Danny Thomas Show* left the air in 1965, Thomas attempted to recreate the magic with *Make Room for Granddaddy*, again on ABC. By then, competition was a lot more formidable and the follow-up series quietly expired after its one and only season.

---

15. *The Dick Van Dyke Show*

Broadcast History:

Tuesday	8:00–8:30	October 1961–December 1961	CBS
Wednesday	9:30–10:00	January 1962–September 1964	CBS
Wednesday	9:00–9:30	September 1964–September 1965	CBS
Wednesday	9:30–10:00	September 1965–September 1966	CBS

#9 rated series in 1962–63   #7 rated series in 1964–65
#3 rated series in 1963–64   #16 rated series in 1965–66

15 Major Emmy Awards (25 nominations):
4 Emmy Awards for Best Series (4 nominations)
3 Emmy Awards for Best Actor (4 nominations)
2 Emmy Awards for Best Actress (3 nominations)
No Emmy Awards for Best Supporting Actor (1 nomination)
No Emmy Award for Best Supporting Actress (3 nominations)
4 Emmy Awards for Best Writing (6 nominations)
2 Emmy Awards for Best Directing (4 nominations)

Cast: Dick Van Dyke; Mary Tyler Moore; Rose Marie; Morey Amsterdam; Larry Mathews; Richard Deacon; Jerry Paris; Ann Morgan Guilbert; Carl Reiner.

America embraced a new unofficial royal couple in 1961, John and Jackie Kennedy. The same year, television viewers fell in love with Rob and Laura Petrie on *The Dick Van Dyke Show*. The roles became career-makers for the then little known Van Dyke and Mary Tyler Moore, whose stars continued to blaze for more than a half-century. Previously, each had a succession of bit roles in TV and movies. Van Dyke made his debut in an episode of *The Phil Silvers Show* and had small parts on the big screen in *Bye Bye Birdie* and *Mary Poppins*. Mary Tyler Moore had a less imposing resume. She made her debut in a commercial, which played on *The Adventures of Ozzie and Harriet*. Her first fairly steady work was as a voice (only her legs were seen on screen) in *Richard Diamond, Private Detective*, which went uncredited. For a *77 Sunset Strip* role, she was billed simply as "Girl." On *The Tab Hunter Show*, she was "Brunette." Together they made TV gold in black and white.

The Petries, who met while Rob was in the army and engaged to someone else and Laura was a USO entertainer, followed the family comedy paradigm of the day. Television was still in its era of innocence. Rob and Laura slept in separate beds, separated by a nightstand. They frequently displayed affection for each other but their kisses were passion-free. It was not even hinted they might have been foreplay. This didn't diminish the ardor America and peers felt for them. The Television Academy voted the series television's outstanding comedy three times and best new series once. The stars were multiple Emmy nominees and won twice apiece.

The show flourished in Nielsen's Top 10 for its first three of five seasons. Legend has it that when MTM moved on to her own eponymous series, it was decided that her character, a completely different single woman, could not be divorced because viewers might become confused and would revolt at the notion that Laura had divorced Rob.

Rob, a smart, good-natured but oafish guy given to pratfalls and other physical humor, was the bread-winner. He was rarely seen in anything less formal than a suit coat and tie, even while relaxing at home. Once in a while, when he was feeling wild and crazy, he would doff the coat for a cardigan sweater. But the tie stayed. Laura's uniform consisted of fashionable ensembles, even first thing in the morning. She was content to stay home and run the house while awaiting Rob's return from his workday.

The Petries had a pre-adolescent son, Richie (Larry Matthews), who was fed a funny line or two by the writers while otherwise remaining mostly in the background. Plots were tame, non-controversial, free of anything resembling edginess and they always dissolved into happily-ever-after resolutions: Rob brings home ducklings, which cause chaos in the house; Richie gets sick on a night when Rob and Laura were looking forward to going to a party; Rob fears he might have developed an allergy to Laura and the series of mishaps that almost kept Rob and Laura from getting to the altar. It was a time when Rob saying, "I've got to get married," elicited shocked double takes and images of a shotgun wedding (which wasn't the case).

In addition to the formula for the family situation comedy, *The Dick Van Dyke Show* also built in the workplace situation comedy, thus combining the two formulae into one series (a television first). Rob's workplace, the writers' room of "The Alan Brady Show," a comedy variety series, shared center stage with the Petries' domestic life. Rob was the head writer, modeled on series creator Carl Reiner's experiences writing for Sid Caesar's *Your Show of Shows*. Reiner played Alan Brady, who was referred to in almost every episode but Reiner did not appear in character until the fourth season.

Rob had a couple of partners in the creation of each show, Buddy Sorrell (Maury Amsterdam) and Sally Rogers (Rose Marie), both show business veterans. Buddy, who liked to flaunt his quarter-century in show business, was a sarcastic producer of a steady stream of corny jokes. Level-headed Sally was the ballast for Buddy's excesses but usually wound up serving as straight woman for his sense of humor. Sally was treated like one of the guys but was always on the lookout for a single guy. Occasionally, the threesome would break into song and dance.

Richard Deacon had a minor but steady presence as Mel Cooley, a humorless producer who, not coincidentally, was the star's brother-in-law. Buddy was merciless in putting him down. Throughout the run of the show, Rob was working on an autobiography of his experiences. In the finale, a series of reminiscences, Alan brought the story full circle by buying Rob's book with the intentions of turning it into a television show. *The Dick Van Dyke Show* set itself apart from other situation comedies of its time, as it was smart and based in reality, while most other situation comedies of the early 1960s were mindless and based in fantasy or far-fetchedness (e.g., *Mr. Ed*, *The Beverly Hillbillies*, *Bewitched*, *Gilligan's Island*, etc.).

---

16. 30 Rock

Broadcast History:

Wednesday	8:00–8:30	October 2006–November 2006	NBC
Thursday	9:30–10:00	November 2006–March 2007	NBC
Thursday	9:00–9:30	April 2007	NBC
Thursday	8:30–9:00	May 2007–November 2007	NBC
Thursday	9:30–10:00	December 2007	NBC
Thursday	8:30–9:00	April 2008–May 2008	NBC

Thursday	9:30–10:00	November 2008–August 2009	NBC
Thursday	9:30–10:00	November 2009–August 2010	NBC
Thursday	8:30–9:00	September 2010–December 2010	NBC
Thursday	10:00–10:30	January 2011–April 2011	NBC
Thursday	8:30–9:00	June 2011–July 2011	NBC
Thursday	9:30–10:00	August 2011	NBC
Thursday	8:00–8:30	January 2012–March 2012	NBC
Thursday	8:30–9:00	April 2012–June 2012	NBC
Thursday	8:00–8:30	September 2012–January 2013	NBC

11 Major Emmy Awards (73 nominations):
3 Emmy Awards for Best Series (7 nominations)
1 Emmy Award for Best Actress (7 nominations)
2 Emmy Awards for Best Actor (7 nominations)
No Emmy Awards for Best Supporting Actress (4 nominations)
No Emmy Awards for Best Supporting Actor (2 nominations)
1 Emmy Award for Best Guest Actress (11 nominations)
1 Emmy Award for Best Guest Actor (14 nominations)
3 Emmy Awards for Best Writing (13 nominations)
No Emmy Awards for Best Direction (8 nominations)

Cast: Tina Fey; Alec Baldwin; Tracy Morgan; Jane Krakowski; Lonny Ross; Scott Adsit; Judah Friedlander; Keith Powell; Jack McBrayer; Katrina Bowden; Rachel Dratch; Maulik Pancholy.

Self-esteem deficiency is a recurring issue for television. Rarely, if ever, does the medium portray itself in a positive light. When television depicts itself on screen it almost always focuses on vain performers, insensitive news people and pompous executives with a cynical view of the intelligence of the audience. *30 Rock* adhered to this paradigm, albeit in a smarter way than most of its predecessors. Tina Fey essentially played herself as Liz Lemon, the producer of *The Girlie Show* (TGS), a *Saturday Night Live–like* sketch comedy show. Fey was the head writer of *Saturday Night Live* before segueing to running her own sitcom. Writers are often advised to write what they know. Fey did that. She created a world populated by out of control talent, who turned her days on the set into nightmares and filled her evenings with dread of a phone call for comment on some anti-social antic, which was making Page Six of the *New York Post*; temperamental writers, whose egos need relentless massaging; and meddling network bosses with suggestions only they recognized as brilliant.

No one made Liz's life more miserable than unabashed narcissist Jack Donaghy (Alec Baldwin), NBC's Vice President of East Coast Television and Microwave Oven Programming. (NBC was owned at the time by General Electric, under whose bumbling stewardship the network plunged from the undisputed king of the ratings to a distant also-ran frequently out-rated by Spanish language and cable networks.) Jack's first act was to insist that "The Girlie Show" broaden its comedy and demographic reach by hiring Tracy Jordan (Tracy Morgan, another *SNL* alum), a comic known for being volatile, difficult to control and liable to say anything that came to his mind, no matter how offensive it might be. Donaghy also dictated that the name of the series be extended to "TGS with Tracy Jordan." Another of Jack's dunderheaded schemes involved inserting Jerry Seinfeld, using footage owned by the network, into every series on NBC. This brought a visit from Seinfeld with a cease and desist demand.

Like Fey, Morgan didn't have to reach far to get into character. Fey's uncanny resemblance to 2008 Republican Vice Presidential candidate Sarah Palin became an incalculable asset to *30 Rock* as well as *Saturday Night Live*, which Fey revisited during the campaign to mimic Palin. During an appearance on an NBA pre-game show, Morgan was asked to compare Fey and Palin. "Sarah Palin is good masturbation material," Morgan retorted.

Morgan wasn't alone in making the wrong kind of headlines. A nasty phone message Baldwin left for his 11-year-old daughter became public. He also caused a plane to return to the boarding area at JFK because he refused to shut off his cell phone for departure. Perhaps reaffirming that a little controversy never hurts; these incidents didn't seem to have a negative impact on the show. Then again the ratings for *30 Rock* were so sub-par that it didn't have far to fall. The series never cracked Nielsen's Top 50 rated series.

Only the extraordinary support from the Television Academy vaulted it into our all-time Top 20. *30 Rock* won three Emmys as TV's outstanding comedy series. In one season, *30 Rock* scored a record 22 Emmy nominations. Fey and Baldwin took home lead actor Emmys in 2008 and Baldwin repeated in 2009.

Donaghy's decree of top billing for Tracy Jordan made a basket case of neurotic Jenna Maroney (Jane Krakowski), who had been the nominal star of TGS. Jenna craved regular reassurance that her star still shone. The arrival of Tracy Jordan exacerbated her insecurities. She also saw TGS as merely a springboard for her career and moonlighted during the offseason in theater and film. One foray saw her return to TGS for a new season looking like she had spent the summer at fat camp—getting fat.

Previously little known Jack McBrayer became a scene stealer as Kenneth Parcell, a hayseed NBC page. Kenneth was so starstruck at being at the hub of a TV network he behaved like an indentured servant, especially to Jack Donaghy. Despite its ratings deficiencies, *30 Rock* became a magnet for celebrities not often associated with situation comedy. Oprah Winfrey made a guest appearance, as did Jon Bon Jovi. Former Vice President Al Gore appeared twice and Condoleezza Rice, Secretary of State for George W. Bush, played one of Jack Donaghy's former lovers. This support didn't extend to NBC. For its final season, 2012–13, the network commissioned only 13 episodes, the same order given to unproven rookies.

17. *Will & Grace*

Broadcast History:

Monday	9:00–9:30	September 1998–November 1998	NBC
Tuesday	9:30–10:00	December 1998–March 1999	NBC
Thursday	8:30–9:00	April 1999–May 1999	NBC
Thursday	9:30–10:00	May 1999–July 1999	NBC
Tuesday	9:30–10:00	June 1999–September 1999	NBC
Thursday	9:00–9:30	August 1999–August 2003	NBC
Thursday	8:30–9:00	August 2003–September 2003	NBC
Thursday	9:00–9:30	September 2003–January 2004	NBC
Thursday	8:30–9:00	February 2004–April 2004	NBC
Thursday	9:00–9:30	April 2004–July 2004	NBC
Thursday	8:00–8:30	July 2004–September 2004	NBC
Thursday	8:30–9:00	September 2004–December 2004	NBC
Thursday	9:30–10:00	December 2004–January 2005	NBC
Thursday	8:30–9:00	February 2005–December 2005	NBC
Thursday	8:00–8:30	January 2006–May 2006	NBC

#14 rated series in 2000–01   #11 rated series in 2002–03
#9 rated series in 2001–02   #13 rated series in 2003–04

10 Major Emmy Awards (51 nominations):
1 Emmy Award for Best Series (6 nominations)
1 Emmy Award for Best Actor (4 nominations)
1 Emmy Award for Best Actress (5 nominations)
1 Emmy Award for Best Supporting Actor (7 nominations)
3 Emmy Award for Best Supporting Actress (8 nominations)
3 Emmy Awards for Best Guest Actor/Actress (14 nominations)
No Emmy Awards for Best Writing (1 nomination)
No Emmy Awards for Best Directing (6 nominations)

Cast: Eric McCormack; Debra Messing; Sean Hayes; Megan Mullally; Shelley Morrison (1999–2006); Gary Grubbs (1998–99); Harry Connick, Jr. (2002–06).

Will Truman and Grace Adler disproved the theory that men and women can't be best friends without sex getting in the way. It helped that Will was gay. Gay characters began infiltrating prime time in the 1970s, primarily in dramas and made-for-television movies. *Will & Grace* broke new ground in the fall of 1998 as the first major network series in which homosexuality was the prevailing theme. Gay characters were not only featured, they were the central figures of the episodes. (Ellen DeGeneres had come out in her ABC sitcom in the spring of 1997. However *Ellen*, in which she initially was presented as straight, was in its fourth season when "The Puppy Episode" aired and it left the air the following year.)

Will (Eric McCormack) and Grace (Debra Messing) met as students at Columbia University in New York. Will didn't immediately divulge his sexual orientation and they briefly dated. His "celibacy" became an issue and they moved on to other people while remaining friends. This all took place before the events in the series. At the outset, Grace was set to marry against the counsel of Will, who felt her fiancé was not right for Grace. She balked at the advice but ultimately realized Will was right. She called off the wedding, leaving herself without a place to live. By this time Will, a successful attorney, had come out to her, so there were no misconceptions when he invited her to share his fashionable West Side apartment. It was supposed to be a temporary arrangement until she found a place of her own. The first place she found was across the hall but she returned to Will's, which seemed more like home.

This injected each into the other's circle of friends. Will's best pal was flamboyantly gay Jack McFarland (Sean Hayes). Grace's assistant at her interior design shop was pill-popping, booze-addled Karen Walker (Megan Mullally). Jack fancied himself an entertainer but like many in his field he worked numerous side jobs between gigs. Karen, who said she was bisexual, had married fabulously well. She worked only to give herself something to do. She and Jack became fast friends. Indeed, when Karen's maid Rosario, an illegal alien, was in danger of being deported, Jack agreed to a sham marriage to keep her in the United States. He was good like that. It was revealed that way back when he had donated his sperm to a lesbian, played by Rosie O'Donnell, wanting a child.

Grace had an active romantic life. Among those who showed up in guest roles as her lovers was *Cheers* alumnus Woody Harrelson. Meanwhile Will dated sparingly and his relationships all were chaste. This became a contentious issue with gay activist groups, who complained if the series was going to be an accurate depiction of gay life, Will's love life should be as open as Grace's. NBC relented and Will also began to date. Patrick Dempsey, who would go on to become "McDreamy" on *Grey's Anatomy*, had a guest starring arc as one of Will's more serious relationships.

A doctor, Leo Markus emerged as Grace's main man and eventually husband in season five, with Harry Connick, Jr., making about two dozen appearances in the role over the final four seasons. Despite Leo's womanizing, which ended their marriage, the two kept returning to each other and conceived a child, Lila. They split again and Grace raised their daughter with a little help from her friends. After a chance meeting, which rekindled their romance, Leo and Grace reconciled and became husband and wife for the second time in the final episode.

In keeping with the new "what's good for one is good for the other" paradigm, Will fell in love with a cop named Vince D'Angelo, played by Bobby Cannevale. This relationship also had its rough spots and the two split. Will then became involved in a rebound romance with a guy named James (Taye Diggs). However, James was not a citizen and, like Rosario, was in danger of deportation. Just as Jack did with Rosario, then-single Grace offered to marry James in a green card wedding. Before it happened, Will realized James was not such a nice guy and the wedding was called off. Will eventually resumed his romance with Vince and they, too, got married before the final curtain came down.

As all long-running series do, the circle of characters gradually expanded to include family and extended family. Debbie Reynolds made appearances as Grace's mother, an entertainer. Blythe Danner showed up as Will's mom and Sydney Pollack played his father. Lesley Ann Warren appeared in four well-spaced episodes as the mistress of Will's father. *Will & Grace* has the rare distinction of having all four of its core cast win Emmys (Mullally won two) as well as winning for best comedy series.

---

18. *The Andy Griffith Show*

Broadcast History:

Monday	9:30–10:00	October 1960–September 1964	CBS
Monday	8:30–9:00	September 1964–September 1965	CBS
Monday	9:00–9:30	September 1965–September 1968	CBS

#4 rated series in 1960–61	#4 rated series in 1964–65
#7 rated series in 1961–62	#6 rated series in 1965–66
#6 rated series in 1962–63	#3 rated series in 1966–67
#5 rated series in 1963–64	#1 rated series in 1967–68

6 Major Emmy Awards (9 nominations):
No Emmy Awards for Best Series (3 nominations)

5 Emmy Awards for Best Supporting Actor (5 nominations)
1 Emmy Award for Best Supporting Actress (1 nomination)

Cast: Andy Griffith; Ronny Howard; Don Knotts (1960–65); Elinor Donahue (1960–61); Frances Bavier; Hope Summers; Jim Nabors (1963–64); Aneta Corsaut (1964–68); George Lindsey (1965–68); Howard McNear; Hal Smith (1960–67); Jack Dodson (1966–68); Paul Hartman (1967–68); Betty Lynn (1960–65); Jack Burns (1965–66); Parley Baer (1962–63); Burt Mustin (1961–66); Ken Berry (1968).

The Andy Griffith Show was a state of mind as much as a television series. The feel-good fictional town of Mayberry, North Carolina, and its inhabitants were throwbacks to the kindest and gentlest times in America. The series evolved from a not-so-kind and gentle encounter on *The Danny Thomas Show*. Thomas in his persona as entertainer Danny Williams was returning to New York when he was stopped for blowing through a stop sign by Mayberry's Sheriff Andy Taylor, Griffith in a one-shot guest role. Danny bellowed and howled about what he perceived to be an injustice, insulting Mayberry, its people and every other small town in Middle America. Andy maintained the low-key demeanor that was the mark of his character, in the process allowing Danny to come off as a typical obnoxious New Yorker. America loved it and *The Andy Griffith Show* was commissioned.

The spinoff followed that paradigm. Mayberry was a place where people didn't feel it necessary to lock their doors and where everyone in town knew and had certain affection for everyone else, with Sheriff Taylor the role model. Crime was almost non-existent, if you didn't count an occasional moonshiner or Otis (Hal Smith), the town drunk, tying one on. On those occasions Otis would conduct a citizen's arrest of himself, check into the town jail, then check himself out in the morning when he sobered up. For convenience sake, the jail cell key was kept within reach.

Mayberry must have been on a special map provided to the world's dumbest criminals, because every now and then a serious felon would pass through, only to be outsmarted and apprehended by Andy with the assistance (or sometimes despite the hindrance) of his manic deputy Barney Fife (Don Knotts). No matter, Barney claimed all the credit as if he were Elliot Ness busting Al Capone. Barney fancied himself a one-man crime-busting dynamo. It didn't matter that the crimes he had to deal with were of the jaywalking, illegal parking variety. He brought a self important G-man intensity to the job. Andy, who didn't feel it necessary to be armed, served as a governor on his gung ho deputy, allowing him to carry a firearm but insisting that it not be loaded. As a compromise to soothe Barney's ego, Andy allowed him one bullet, but insisted that Barney keep it in his shirt pocket. Griffith allowed Knotts to be the scene-stealer, serving as a straight man to Barney's over-exuberance.

Amazingly, Griffith was not Emmy nominated for his iconic role, nor was the series, but the star's unselfishness helped Knotts win five supporting actor awards. In his personal life, Sheriff Taylor was a widower with a young son, Opie (Ron Howard). No matter what else was going on Andy always had time to be a father first, whether that entailed providing Solomon-like solutions to Opie's childhood problems or spending a day with him at the local fishing hole. The title credits were played with Andy and Opie heading to the pond, accompanied by composer Earle Hagen whistling the title tune, "The Fishing Hole."

Andy was assisted in raising Opie by Aunt Bea (Frances Bavier), a matronly woman given to become easily flustered. Bavier won the show's only other performance Emmy. Mayberry was dense with colorful figures. Slow witted Floyd Lawson (Howard McNear) ran the town barbershop where issues of the day were chewed over. Gomer Pyle (Jim Nabors) operated the local filling station before segueing into his own spinoff, *Gomer Pyle, U.S.M.C.* His cousin Goober (George Lindsay) then took over.

The Andy Griffith Show was in Nielsen's Top 10 for all eight of its seasons (the first five in black-and-white) and is one of a handful of series that left the air when it was ranked the number one show on television. When Griffith decided it was time to step away, many of the show's characters transitioned to another spinoff, *Mayberry, RFD.*

19. *Taxi*

Broadcast History:

Tuesday	9:30–10:00	September 1978–October 1980	ABC
Wednesday	9:00–9:30	November 1980–January 1981	ABC
Thursday	9:30–10:00	February 1981–June 1982	ABC
Thursday	9:30–10:00	September 1982–December 1982	NBC
Saturday	9:30–10:00	January 1983–February 1983	NBC
Wednesday	9:30–10:00	March 1983–May 1983	NBC
Wednesday	10:30–11:00	June 1983–July 1983	NBC

#9 rated series in 1978–79 #13 rated series in 1979–80

15 Major Emmy Awards (31 nominations):
3 Emmy Awards for Best Series (5 nominations)
2 Emmy Awards for Best Actor (5 nominations)

19. *Taxi*

3 Emmy Awards for Best Actress (4 nominations)
3 Emmy Awards for Best Supporting Actor (6 nominations)
2 Emmy Awards for Best Writing (8 nominations)
2 Emmy Awards for Best Direction (3 nominations)

Cast: Judd Hirsch; Jeff Conaway (1978–81); Danny DeVito; Marilu Henner; Tony Danza; Randall Carver (1978–79); Andy Kaufman; Christopher Lloyd (1979–83); Carol Kane (1981–83).

Situation comedy is rarely, if ever, plot-driven. Story lines exist merely to serve colorful, loopy, quirky characters, the more the merrier. *Taxi* had a garage full, perhaps the most ever in the 30-minute genre. Their common denominators were they all worked for the same Manhattan cab company and with one exception they all wished they were doing something else. The odd man out was Alex Rieger (Judd Hirsch). He drove a cab because it was an expedient way to make a living. A reformed gambler, Alex served as the moral compass for his colleagues; a decent, compassionate guy, who fell into the role of workplace confidante, common sense advisor and shoulder to lean on.

His opposite number was Louie DePalma (Danny DeVito), a diminutive despot, who cracked the whip from the garage's management cage, a comedic metaphor for the people being protected from a dangerous beast. Alas Louie had the freedom to leave his enclosure and inflict his evil up close and personal. Devoid of conscience and any semblance of common decency, black-hearted Louie ruled with an iron fist and reveled in taunting and tormenting the help. As undersized as he was, there was nothing beneath him. This included sneaking a peek into restrooms and dressing areas set aside for female drivers. Another reprehensible tactic was to proffer the temptations of juicier assignments in exchange for submitting to his depraved carnal desires.

The lone female character not disgusted by Louie was Zena Shuman. Life imitated art as Rhea Perlman, who played Zena, became DeVito's real-life wife. The most frequent victim of Louie's fantasies was Elaine Nardo (Marilu Henner), who didn't make sufficient money at her day job at an art gallery, her true love, to liberate herself from a second job as a cabbie. Alex did his best to protect her from Louie's tyranny and vile propositions and succeeded only to a degree. (Henner, is one of those unique individuals with the uncanny ability to remember every detail of every moment of her life— the conceit of the CBS series *Unforgettable*—and had a randy side in real life. She told Howard Stern on his radio program that she had her way with several of her cast mates.)

Tony Banta (Tony Danza) was a frustrated boxer, who took too many shots to the head in a career that never saw his hand raised in triumph.

Nevertheless, he refused to abandon his aspiration to someday become a champion. Driving a cab was something to do in the interim. Danza liked to joke that his character had the same first name so that he wouldn't miss his cues when someone called out Tony. If there is validity to the expression, "If you remember anything about the 1960s, you weren't there," Rev. Jim Ignatowski (Christopher Lloyd) is the poster boy for the decade. He did it all when it came to any mind altering substance that could be injected, ingested or inhaled. Consequently, he couldn't remember 60 seconds ago let alone the 1960s. It was a wonder he could grasp why he was behind the wheel of a cab. His honorary suffix had something to do with being ordained by a cult whose credo involved hallucinogens.

As bizarre as Rev. Jim was, he met his equal in Latka Gravas (Andy Kaufman), a mechanic from an unnamed Eastern European nation. Latka's native tongue was incomprehensible gibberish to his colleagues. Latka, who had a heart of gold, also mastered fractured English. However, in some of his multiple personalities, such as obnoxious Tony Clifton and Vic Ferrari, he had Prof. Higgins command of English. Latka found his soul mate in a feisty woman from his homeland named Simka (Carol Kane), a relationship that would have been forbidden in their native land because mountain people hated valley people and vice versa.

Bobby Wheeler (Jeff Conaway) fancied himself an actor, but parts being few and far between, he had to drive a cab to eat. Ironically, Conaway, who scored a featured role in *Grease*, left *Taxi* to pursue a big-screen career, which never materialized to the extent he hoped.

Unfortunately *Taxi* earned more critical plaudits than audience support. It won 18 Emmys, including three for best comedy series. Hirsch (twice), DeVito, Lloyd and Kane also were honored with golden statues by the Television Academy. After four low-rated seasons, ABC gave up on *Taxi*. However, NBC riding high in the ratings, made a bid to save it, picking it up and scheduling it after monster hit *Cheers*. Coincidentally, *Cheers'* Ted Danson and George Wendt had guest shots on *Taxi* prior to being cast in *Cheers*. The gilded lead-in was no help to *Taxi* and NBC threw in the towel after one season.

20. *Roseanne*

Broadcast History:

| Tuesday | 8:30–9:00 | October 1988–February 1989 | ABC |
| Tuesday | 9:00–9:30 | February 1989–September 1994 | ABC |

Wednesday	9:00–9:30	September 1994–March 1995	ABC
Wednesday	8:00–8:30	March 1995–May 1995	ABC
Wednesday	9:30–10:00	May 1995–July 1995	ABC
Tuesday	8:30–9:00	August 1995–September 1995	ABC
Tuesday	8:00–8:30	September 1995–August 1997	ABC

#2 rated series in 1988–89	#2 rated series in 1992–93
#1 rated series in 1989–90	#4 rated series in 1993–94
#3 rated series in 1990–91	#10 rated series in 1994–95
#2 rated series in 1991–92	#16 rated series in 1995–96

3 Major Emmy Awards (17 nominations):
No Emmy Awards for Best Actor (7 nominations)
1 Emmy Award for Best Actress (5 nominations)
2 Emmy Awards for Best Supporting Actress (4 nominations)
No Emmy Awards for Best Writing (1 nomination)

Cast: Roseanne Barr; John Goodman; Lecy Goranson (1988–92, 1995–96); Sarah Chalke (1993–95, 1996–97); Sara Gilbert; Sal Barone (pilot); Michael Fishman; Laurie Metcalf; Natalie West (1988–92); George Clooney (1988–89); Ron Perkins (1988–89); Evelina Fernandez (1988–89); Anne Falkner (1988–89); Ned Beatty (1989–95); Estelle Parsons (1989–97); Tom Arnold (1989–94); Glenn Quinn (1990–97); Johnny Galecki (1992–97); Martin Mull (1991–97); Bonnie Sheridan (1991–92); Sandra Bernhard (1991–97); Michael O'Keefe (1993–96).

Blue-collar families have been a staple of situation comedies since the early years of *The Life of Riley*, but *Roseanne* broke new ground in the genre. The Connors of a fictional community in Illinois were not the typical-looking television family. Roseanne and her husband Dan both had serious weight problems and neither had a magazine cover face. Their children Becky, Darlene and D.J. (a fourth, Jerry, would be born in season eight) didn't look like they came from central casting, either. Sara Gilbert played Darlene. Lacey Goranson originated the role of Becky, then turned it over to Sarah Chalke in season six when it was time for college in Goranson's real life (Goranson came back in season 8, then left again to be replaced again by Chalke). Michael Fishman took over as D.J. after the pilot.

The Connors were relatable to Middle America for reasons beyond not looking like Hollywood stars. Just getting by was a paycheck-to-paycheck struggle. Dan and Roseanne each worked outside the home, a rarity for a sitcom. Both bounced from job to job. In the beginning Dan was in construction and Roseanne worked in a plastics factory. Both would eventually wind up entrepreneurs. Dan opened a motorcycle repair shop and Roseanne was a partner in a diner. Neither was a threat to crack the Fortune 500 (or 500,000). The family dealt with many of the issues confronting families everywhere:

paying the bills, medical crises, coping with extended family, getting the kids through childhood and adolescence and just maintaining a marriage through hard times. In the process, the storylines delved into hot button social issues—drugs, race, abortion, gay rights, etc.—but it was redeemed by not coming up with a tidy, crowd-pleasing resolution within 30 minutes.

America responded. *Roseanne* was among the top five highest rated series on television for each of its first six seasons and was television's number one show in 1989–90, its second season. The Emmy voters were a different situation. As popular as the series was, it never was named television's best comedy.

Roseanne, transitioning from a career in standup comedy, was the center of the universe. Her forceful and snarky personality carried the show. She was rewarded with her only Emmy as best lead actress in a comedy in 1993. At the outset she went by her given name, Roseanne Barr. When she divorced her first husband, Bill Pentland, and married Tom Arnold, who occasionally showed up in episodes as a friend of Dan, she changed her billing to Roseanne Arnold. When Roseanne and Tom split and she married her bodyguard, she appeared as just Roseanne.

Roseanne cultivated an image as a jovial "domestic goddess"—but as the series progressed, she became as prominent on the gossip pages as the television pages. She developed a reputation as an out of control, demanding monster on the set. John Goodman, an unlikely leading man as Dan, became the more popular figure with the public. The Television Academy liked him, too, but never enough to be their favorite. He was nominated seven times as lead actor in a comedy but never had his name called to come to the stage to pick up a trophy. While Goodman wasn't romantic lead material, a then little known actor, who would go on to become a global heartthrob, had a bit role as Roseanne's boss—George Clooney. As payback after he had become a superstar, Clooney returned to the series for the finale playing himself.

Clooney wasn't the only world-class star in waiting to play a minor role on the show. Leonardo DiCaprio and Tobey Maguire also had guest roles. The series arguably overstayed its welcome as it veered away from what had made it popular in its final season. The Connors won a mega million lottery, lifting them to super rich status. Alas, in the final episode the lottery windfall, the entire series for that matter, was revealed to be a dream by Roseanne.

21. *Barney Miller*

Broadcast History:

Thursday	8:00–8:30	January 1975–January 1976	ABC
Thursday	8:30–9:00	January 1976–December 1976	ABC
Thursday	9:00–9:30	December 1976–March 1982	ABC
Friday	8:30–9:00	March 1982–April 1982	ABC
Thursday	9:00–9:30	April 1982–September 1982	ABC

#17 rated series in 1976–77   #15 rated series in 1978–79
#17 rated series in 1977–78   #20 rated series in 1979–80

3 Major Emmy Awards (30 nominations):
1 Emmy Award for Best Series (7 nominations)
No Emmy Awards for Best Actor (7 nominations)
No Emmy Awards for Best Supporting Actor (8 nominations)
No Emmy Awards for Best Guest Actor/Actress (2 nominations)
1 Emmy Award for Best Writing (4 nominations)
1 Emmy Award for Best Direction (2 nominations)

Cast: Hal Linden; Abe Vigoda (1975–77); Gregory Sierra (1975–76); Maxwell Gail; Jack Soo (1975–78); Ron Glass; Barbara Barrie (1975–76); Anne Wyndham (1975); Michael Tessier (1975); Florence Stanley (1975–77); Linda Lavin (1975–76); James Gregory; Ron Carey (1976–82); June Gable (1976–77); Steve Landesberg (1976–82); George Murdock (1978–82).

It doesn't make for compelling television but a lot of cops go their entire career without un-holstering their service revolver, let alone firing it. They don't dash down alleys, climb over fences and leap from rooftop to rooftop in pursuit of suspects. A typical workday is dominated by filling out paperwork and dealing with minor breaches of the law. *Barney Miller* was the first television series to recognize this. Perhaps this is why it has often been said that it was the favorite show of real life cops, although evidence to back this boast was strictly anecdotal. Life in Manhattan's fictional 12th Precinct, a set from which the show rarely strayed, was frequently dull but never uninteresting, even when there was a lull in the parade of inept miscreants, bargain basement street-walkers and delusional sidewalk characters, who passed through the squad room.

The ABC comedy was more about the diverse array of detectives who dealt with them. Hal Linden played the title character, a low-key leader of the detective division, who resorted to common sense and compassion more than following "the book." Barney was married but his wife Elizabeth (played after the pilot by Barbara Barrie) was a rarely seen point of reference.

The detectives under Barney were a quirky bunch, none more so than Abe Vigoda as hypochondriac senior detective Phil Fish, whose personal plumbing necessitated he spend almost as much time in the men's room as at his desk. Each day's shift meant he was one day closer to retirement. Fish's relentless bellyaching about his aches and pains proved endearing to viewers and Vigoda was spun off into his own series, *Fish*, co-starring his wife Bernice (Florence Stanley), about whom he also constantly complained. When the offspring series didn't work, *Fish* returned to the 12th Precinct.

Stanley "Wojo" Wojohowicz (Maxwell Gail), a former Marine, was the room's gung-ho but not-too-bright amiable cop, who wished police work was more like what he saw on television. He also fancied himself a lady's man, though there was scant evidence of romantic triumphs. Like most of his colleagues, he also had a strong compassionate streak.

Nick Yemana was loved by one and all for his quick wit even as the coffee he made, his self-appointed duty, was brutally critiqued. Jack Soo, who played Yemana, died at midseason in 1979. The sad occasion was acknowledged by the show with a poignant special episode featuring his colleagues breaking the fourth wall to share reminiscences and expressions of affection for him.

Det. Ron Harris (Ron Glass) made no attempt to disguise his feelings that the mundane duties of his job were beneath him, annoyances and distractions from his primary goal of becoming a published novelist. The nattily dressed social climber spent much of his on-duty hours writing "Blood on the Badge," which he hoped would liberate him from the station house and catapult him into the ranks of the beautiful people.

Arthur Dietrich (Steve Landesberg) was a know-it-all, who actually seemed to know it all. The warehouse of factoids and anecdotes at his command during any discussion or situation was astounding. Unlike some who flaunt their superior intellect, he was well liked by his co-workers. Dietrich was a late arrival. The character was introduced in the third season and became a regular the following year. Prior to taking on the role, Landesberg had appeared as a priest in season two.

Gregory Sierra worked only the first two seasons as high strung Det. Chano Amenguale, whose Puerto Rican ancestry was an asset in multi-cultural New York City. Ron Carey joined the regular ensemble in season three as obsequious patrolman Carl Levitt, who was convinced the only thing keeping him from getting out of uniform was his short stature. To compensate, he unabashedly brown-nosed Barney and any other superior officer. His determination was rewarded in the series finale when he was finally given his gold badge. Like Landesberg, Carey had been seen earlier in the show's run. In his case it was as a perp.

James Gregory recurred as world weary Inspector Frank Lugar, who yearned for the good old days (whatever they were) and did his best to not draw attention to himself or the cops over whom he had supervisory duties. The series came to an end when the 12th Precinct was declared a historic landmark, which brought about its closing, with the detectives reassigned throughout the city.

Barney Miller was loved by audiences, critics and Emmy voters. The show garnered thirty major Emmy nominations during its eight-year run, winning an Emmy for Best Comedy Series. The series was a ratings success, placing in the Nielsen top twenty for four years—from its third season through its sixth season. The series also broke ground during its day by having possibly the most diverse regular cast ever assembled to that time.

22. *Mad About You*

Broadcast History:

Wednesday	9:30–10:00	September 1992–January 1993	NBC
Saturday	9:30–10:00	February 1993–July 1993	NBC
Thursday	8:00–8:30	July 1993–August 1995	NBC
Thursday	8:30–9:00	August 1995	NBC
Sunday	8:00–8:30	September 1995–July 1996	NBC
Tuesday	8:00–8:30	August 1996–December 1998	NBC
Monday	9:00–9:30	December 1998–January 1999	NBC
Monday	8:30–9:00	February 1999–May 1999	NBC
Monday	9:00–9:30	May 1999–July 1999	NBC
Thursday	10:30–11:00	August 1999	NBC

#11 rated series in 1994–95
#23 rated series in 1996–97
#23 rated series in 1997–98

4 Major Emmy Awards (17 nominations):
No Emmy Awards for Best Series (4 nominations)
4 Emmy Awards for Best Actress (7 nominations)
No Emmy Awards for Best Actor (6 nominations)

Cast: Paul Reiser; Helen Hunt; Anne Elizabeth Ramsey; Tommy Hinkley (1992–93); Leila Kenzle (1992–98); Richard Kind (1992–93); John Pankow (1993–99); Judy Geeson (1993–99); Paxton Whitehead (1993–99); Jeff Garlin; Cynthia Harris; Louis Zorich; Robin Bartlett; Suzie Plakson (1996–99); Mo Gaffney (1997–99).

The popularity and longevity of *Mad About You* can be explained in two words: Helen Hunt. Her personal appeal propped up an otherwise slight comedy. The Television Academy recognized this. Hunt won four Emmys. Her co-star in what was essentially a two-character show, Paul Reiser, was shut out on Emmy nights. However, Reiser was shrewd enough to have a clause in his contract that he and Hunt would be paid equally throughout the show's run. As a result, he rode Hunt's coattails to a then almost unheard of $1 million weekly paycheck.

In many ways, *Mad About You* was more of a show about nothing than was *Seinfeld*. Early episodes were built around trivialities such as what to do on a Sunday when there is nothing to do; fretting over whether their sex life was growing stale; dealing with untimely intrusions by family and friends; how to handle a chance encounter with a former lover; debating the right time to have a baby and becoming frantic when conception doesn't happen as quickly as they expected. Once the show became established, story lines became more poignant and dramatic, including Paul having problems dealing with his wife enjoying more professional success and a wrenching breakup as a result of a romantic indiscretion.

Jamie (Hunt) and Paul Buchman (Reiser) were newlyweds when the romantic comedy joined the NBC schedule in 1992. They were a well matched couple, neurotic young professionals striving to make their way in their chosen careers in Manhattan; Jamie in public relations, Paul as a documentary filmmaker. Fortuitously they were supportive of each other's ambitions inasmuch as they were rife with personality quirks and insecurities. Until they had a daughter, Mabel (an acronym for Mothers Always Bring Extra Love), late in the series run, the Buchmans lavished their affection on their not very bright but very lovable dog Murray, who had a tendency to run into furniture and walls.

An ensemble of friends and family dropped into and out of the Buchmans' apartment. Fran Devanow (Leila Kenzle) was Jamie's boss who became one of her closest friends. Paul's bosom buddy was his cousin Ira (John Pankow), who worked at the sporting goods store owned by Paul's father Burt (Louis Zorich). Burt's retirement created rare tension between Paul and Ira over who should have the final say about the management of the store. Sylvia Buchman (Cynthia Harris) was cordial but cool (more the former than the latter) toward her daughter-in-law. Burt and Sylvia had another daughter, Lisa (Ann Ramsey), an emotional wreck, whose issues included an eating disorder.

Continuity was not a major concern in casting. Jamie's mother Theresa was played by three different actresses: Nancy Dussault, Penny Fuller and Carol Burnett for the final three seasons. Paul Dooley was originally Jamie's father, Gus Stemple, but Carroll O'Connor took over the part for the final three seasons. As compelling storylines involving Paul and Jamie became more challenging to concoct, peripheral players were introduced. Hank Azaria, who would later have a one-year marriage to Hunt after meeting her on the show, recurred as a dog walker named Hank, who had a heavy Scandinavian accent. Mel Brooks was introduced as Paul's uncle Phil. Cyndi Lauper showed up as Ira's estranged wife. Lisa Kudrow played a forgetful waitress, Ursula Buffay, at a restaurant frequented by the Buchmans. It was a character Kudrow would segue into Ursula's ditzy twin Phoebe on *Friends*.

The stunt casting, Jamie and Paul's breakup and the addition of a child was illustrative of how the series was running out of creative momentum. The birth of Mabel, traditionally a device intended to pump life into fading concepts, was the final nail in the show's coffin, altering the original concept into just another cutesy family comedy. By the time the plug was mercifully pulled, the audience had dropped by almost 50 percent and a series that was generally within or on the fringe of Nielsen's Top 30 became one of the lowest ranked series on a major network.

23. *The Big Bang Theory*

Broadcast History:

Monday	9:30–10:00	September 2007–February 2008	CBS
Monday	8:30–9:00	March 2008–September 2010	CBS
Thursday	8:00–8:30	September 2010–August 2014	CBS
Monday	8:00–8:30	September 2014–October 2014	CBS
Thursday	8:00–8:30	November 2014–present	CBS

#12 rated series in 2009–10   #3 rated series in 2012–13
#15 rated series in 2010–11   #2 rated series in 2013–14
#8 rated series in 2011–12

5 Major Emmy Awards (19 nominations):
No Emmy Awards for Best Program (4 nominations)
4 Emmy Awards for Best Actor (8 nominations)
No Emmy Awards for Best Supporting Actress (3 nominations)
1 Emmy Award for Best Guest Actor/Actress (4 nominations)

Cast: Johnny Galecki; Jim Parsons; Kaley Cuoco; Simon Helberg; Kunal Nayyar; Sara Gilbert (2007–10); Melissa Rauch (2009–present); Mayim Bialik (2009–present); Kevin Sussman (2008–present).

The Big Bang Theory is arguably the smartest sitcom ever. Many comedies have had smart writing and smartly drawn characters. No other show has had characters the intellectual equal of Sheldon Cooper, Leonard Hofstader, Rajeesh Koothrapalli and Howard Wolowitz. All but Howard hold Ph.D.s. Sheldon, a theoretical physicist, is the self-proclaimed most intelligent person on the planet. He finds it incredible that his neck is able to support a head filled with so much knowledge. One of his goals is to live long enough to be preserved forever as a cyber-being.

Sheldon started college at 11 years of age and earned his doctorate at 15. He's a genetic outlier. His never seen father was an uncouth, hard-drinking, womanizing Texan. His mother (Laurie Metcalf) is a good-natured religious fanatic of limited intellect but broad common sense. The apple fell a galaxy away from the tree. Sheldon is an avowed atheist, because religion can't be scientifically proven. He also rarely makes an attempt at handling alcohol. On the rare occasions he does drink, he does so badly and usually winds up spitting it out.

Jim Parsons brings the character vividly to life and, at least at the outset, was almost singularly responsible for the success of the show. As sharp as Sheldon is book-wise, he is hopelessly inept in social settings and suffers from OCD (Obsessive Compulsive Disorder). He sits on the same corner of the couch and insists on the same ethnic cuisine from the same restaurants on the same night of every week. He has no patience for those he considers his intellectual inferior. This includes Stephen Hawking. Sheldon's non-working hours are dominated by science fiction movies and television series and superhero comic books. He can't stand physical contact, which rules out intimate romantic relationships, even after he finds his match on the internet in plainish Amy Farrah Fowler (Mayim Bialik), also a Ph.D. He finally kisses her on a Valentine's Day date aboard a vintage train but through the rest of the season and the subsequent ones encores were rare and with a dearth of passion, to the dismay of his openly frustrated girlfriend.

Leonard (the lead characters' names are homage to veteran television producer Sheldon Leonard), an experimental physicist, is almost as smart (but not quite, Sheldon relentlessly reminds him) and almost as socially dorkish as his roommate. His personality was greatly influenced by a domineering mother (Christine Baranski), a published sociologist who in spite of her son's academic credentials and professional status regards him as an under-achiever. Leonard shares many of Sheldon's tastes in entertainment but yearns for a more traditional lifestyle, which beckons when Penny (Kaley Cuoco), a knockout aspiring actress/Cheesecake Factory waitress of limited intellect from Nebraska, moves across the hall.

Leonard's initial attempt to ingratiate himself to her results in Sheldon and him getting de-pantsed by one of her former hulking boyfriends. Penny is the kind of girl a geek like Leonard (Johnny Galecki) usually has no shot with. His only previous romance was with a woman who turned out to be a North Korean spy intent on picking his brain. Nevertheless, Leonard and Penny eventually become an on-again, off-again couple (which reportedly briefly mirrored real life—Cuoco and Galecki had dated on and off). During the off periods with Penny, Leonard has flings with co-worker Leslie Winkle (Sarah Gilbert), a professional nemesis of Sheldon's, and Raj's attractive sister Priya (Aaarti Mann), an international attorney.

Howard and Raj, co-workers at Cal Tech, are constant presences in the Pasadena apartment shared by Sheldon and Leonard. Howard, the only member of the group without a doctorate, holds a masters degree in engineering and works with NASA. Among his projects is an experimental toilet for the space shuttle, which winds up flushing up instead of down. He also wrecks the Mars Rover while trying to impress a date. Nevertheless, NASA sends him on a mission into space, which makes him insufferable on his return.

Howard (Simon Helberg) fancies himself a ladies man but most members of the opposite sex find him as appealing as a yeast infection. Among myriad undesirable traits, he still lived with his over-bearing, grotesquely overweight mother (Carol Ann Susi) whose shrill voice was often heard although she was never seen. The untimely death of Susi during season eight prompted the writers to also have Mrs. Wolowitz die. Howard improbably winds up courting and marrying shapely Bernadette Rostenkowski after they are fixed up by Leonard and Penny. Bernadette (Melissa Rauch) finds Howard's idiosyncrasies endearing.

Raj (Kunal Nayyar), an astrophysicist, migrated from India, where his father is a wealthy gynecologist. Raj's strongest fear was having to return to his homeland because of its "filth and overpopulation." He's allows himself to say this often but when one of his buddies does, Raj chastises him with "That's racist." Raj's social life was impeded through the first six seasons by his inability to talk to a woman unless he has had some alcohol. He seemed to meet his match when he falls for an attractive deaf mute but she turns out to be a gold-digger. Another of his romantic interests climbed out a window to escape him on their first date. This heartbreak was inexplicably instrumental in him suddenly being able to talk to women while sober. Then he never shut up.

The core group dominated the early seasons until Bernadette, then Amy Farrah Fowler (always pronounced as if it was all one name) were integrated into the cast. Stuart Bloom (Kevin Sussman) joined the regular ensemble in season six as the owner of the failing comic book store frequented by the gang. A poor soul with a beaten down puppy dog personality, he also is a loser when it comes to dating. When he gets up the courage to ask Penny for a date, she winds up blurting out Leonard's name during an amorous moment. He has no more luck when Amy Farrah Fowler goes to a movie with him to make Sheldon jealous, a scheme that improbably succeeds.

Interestingly, Galecki, Gilbert and Metcalf also worked together on the highly successful situation comedy, *Roseanne*, on which *Big Bang* co-creator Chuck Lorre was a writer.

The Big Bang Theory was enormously popular during its run—it was the highest rated situation comedy, both on the network with new episodes and in syndication with reruns. Due to this, and its growing popularity each year CBS announced at least a three-year renewal for the series during the 2013–14 television season.

24. *The Phil Silvers Show*

Broadcast History:

Tuesday	8:30–9:00	September 1955–October 1955	CBS
Tuesday	8:00–8:30	November 1955–February 1958	CBS
Friday	9:00–9:30	February 1958–September 1959	CBS

#30 rated series in 1955–56
#22 rated series in 1956–57

9 Major Emmy Awards (18 nominations):
3 Emmy Awards for Best Series (4 nominations)
2 Emmy Awards for Best Actor (5 nominations)
No Emmy Awards for Best Supporting Actor (4 nominations)
3 Emmy Awards for Best Writing (4 nominations)
1 Emmy Award for Best Directing (1 nomination)

Cast: Phil Silvers; Harvey Lembeck; Herbie Faye; Paul Ford; Maurice Gosfield; Joe E. Ross; Allan Melvin; Billy Sands; Mickey Freeman; Hope Sansberry; Jimmy Little; Elisabeth Fraser (1955–58).

Master Sgt. Ernest G. Bilko was one of television's earliest lovable rogues. He was a motor mouth con man, who ran the motor pool and all forms of gambling in the peacetime army at Fort Baxter in a fictional Kansas town.

Emmy winning Phil Silvers was one of a kind in the lead role. Not even a comedic actor as masterful as Steve Martin, who starred as *Sgt. Bilko* in a 1996 theatrical, could impart Silvers' magic to the character. The series was also one of the first of its genre to extend the traditional nuclear family concept, the norm in the 1950s, to an extended workplace family of characters.

Ernie Bilko could turn any circumstance into a betting scheme or opportunity for personal gain. He created gambling action on activities as ridiculous as pigeon racing or even what the colonel had for breakfast. When he learned an officer's wife had a twitch during her deadly boring classical music recitals, Bilko organized a base-wide pool on the number of times she would twitch during a performance. Briefly misidentified as a genius, Bilko used his time among the military's best and brightest to concoct a way to unfailingly predict the results of horse races.

Bilko's belief that he had a secret map to a treasure trove of gold in California led to the setting for the series being changed from the Midwest to the West Coast for its final season. This coincided with actual shooting shifting from New York to Hollywood. The proximity to the movie capital allowed for guest appearances by show business giants such as Lucille Ball.

The 1950s being America's last age of innocence, bad behavior by a leading character on television had to have negative consequences. Ergo most of Bilko's scams were thwarted by his commanding officer, Colonel Hall (Paul Ford), who was haunted by the thought that somewhere, somehow, Bilko was up to something. Their games of cat and mouse included Bilko devising a radar watch on the colonel and the commanding officer installing a closed circuit TV to monitor Bilko's every move. The series finale had Bilko and some of his men in a base prison cell under the constant closed circuit surveillance of the colonel, who cackled ironically, "This is a show that will never be canceled."

Bilko's golden tongue helped him charm the colonel's wife, Nell (Hope Sansberry), and turn her into a frequent ally. Bilko even had a soft spot for her husband, although it was motivated primarily by self interest. When Col. Hall became chagrined at being passed over for a long overdue promotion Bilko used all his wiles, including wangling the colonel a spot in a golf foursome with a prominent tour pro and President Eisenhower, to get the colonel to reconsider his retirement plans. Better the enemy you know than the one you might get, Bilko decided.

Bilko had a paternalistic attitude about the men who served under him. No one had better cheat any of them was his credo, because if anyone was going to do it, it was going to be him. Most of the time, however, his men served as co-conspirators. Corporal Rocco Barbella (Harvey Lembeck) and Corporal Steve Henshaw (Allan Melvin) were Bilko's primary aides-de-camp. Their loyalty to him was such that they were willing to take figurative bullets for him.

Also among Bilko's loyalists was slovenly Private Duane Doberman (Maurice Gosfield). There was nothing Doberman wouldn't do for his sergeant. When Bilko needed the army to finance a trip to Washington for a rendezvous with an old flame, he outfitted Doberman like an alien from Mars, so that he could be dispatched to a UFO investigation in the capital. Also prominent in the large ensemble was Herbie Faye as Private Sam Fender, Billy Sands as Private Dino Paparelli and Joe E. Ross as Sergeant Rupert Ritzik.

For the most part, Bilko was too busy getting into his own brand of mischief to allow romantic entanglements. An exception was a long-running flirtation with one of the base secretaries, Sergeant Joan Hogan (Elisabeth Fraser). The series was such a tour de force for Silvers that its title was revised in its first season from *You'll Never Get Rich* to *The Phil Silvers Show*. In reruns it was often known as *Sgt. Bilko* or just *Bilko*.

The series was a favorite of the Emmy voters, being nominated for best comedy each of its four seasons on the air (winning three times). Silvers also won twice as best actor. The series also won three times for best comedy writing and once for best directing.

25. *Family Ties*

Broadcast History:

Wednesday	9:30–10:00	September 1982–March 1983	NBC
Monday	8:30–9:00	March 1983–August 1983	NBC
Wednesday	9:30–10:00	August 1983–December 1983	NBC
Thursday	8:30–9:00	January 1984–August 1987	NBC
Sunday	8:00–8:30	August 1987–September 1989	NBC

#5 rated series in 1984–85	#2 rated series in 1986–87
#2 rated series in 1985–86	#17 rated series in 1987–88

4 Major Emmy Awards (14 nominations):
No Emmy Awards for Best Series (4 nominations)
3 Emmy Awards for Best Actor (4 nominations)
No Emmy Awards for Best Supporting Actress (2 nominations)
No Emmy Awards for Best Supporting Actor (1 nomination)
1 Emmy Award for Best Writing (2 nominations)
No Emmy Awards for Best Direction (1 nomination)

Cast: Meredith Baxter-Birney; Michael Gross; Michael J. Fox; Justine Bateman; Tina Yothers; Brian Bonsall (1986–89); Marc Price; Tracy Pollan (1985–86); Scott Valentine (1985–89); Courteney Cox (1987–89).

The times were changing in the early 1980s. The sex and drugs and rock 'n' roll, anti-establishment attitudes of the 1960s and 1970s had morphed into the Me Generation's "greed is good" Reagan years. The shift to conservatism was a tough adjustment for many who had grown up demonstrating in the streets for the liberal cause du jour. It was especially challenging for Steven and Elyse Keaton. The couple, played by Michael Gross and Meredith Baxter, still were socially active, once getting arrested at an anti-nukes rally. But they had given birth to a living, breathing example of society's course correction. The former hippies' first-born, Alex P. Keaton (Michael J. Fox), was a strident right-winger with a poster of Richard Nixon on his wall and reverence to the Reagan philosophy in his heart. *Family Ties* was designed to answer the questions "How could this happen?" and "Now that is has, how do we deal with it?"

Steven and Elyse were designed as sympathetic figures and Alex was charted to be the designated oddball, who would be instructed in the error of his ways. Fox, in his first major role, turned this upside down. Alex was embraced by America as the breakout character. To his credit, series creator Gary David Goldberg, who identified with Steven and Elyse, recognized what was happening in Middle America and shifted emphasis toward what amounted to The Alex P. Keaton Show. Steven, the general manager of a local PBS station, and Elyse, an architect, had two other children at the outset, early teen Mallory (Justine Bateman), a budding material girl deficient in real world sense, and her younger sister Jennifer (Tina Yothers), who, for the most part, was just there. In the third season, the Keatons had another child, Andy (Brian Bonsall). However, the younger Keaton siblings were merely supporting characters for the Alex-centric vignettes.

Fox went on to win three consecutive best actor Emmys (he was nominated a fourth time—as supporting actor) and helped the show to be nominated as best comedy four times, although it never got to bring home the series gold. Fox's cast mates earned two other Emmy nominations among them, both a supporting actress nod to Bateman. Goldberg, whose single writing Emmy was the show's only other major laurel from the Television Academy, prudently put aside his own politics to write to Alex's strengths. A classic moment came when an excited Mallory was describing her first part-time job. She told him how she was being paid for four hours but could get her duties finished in about half that. Alex asked why then she didn't do more. A confused Mallory rationalized that she wouldn't get any extra pay, an opening for Alex to retort, "Mallory, in your own simple way, you've just explained why socialism will never work." (Fox himself later became an advocate for the Democratic Party.)

Some big names walked through the Keaton living room over the series' seven-year run. Tom Hanks had a recurring role as Elyse's ne'er-do-well brother Ned Donnelly, who always seemed to on the lam from someone. Geena Davis had a three-episode arc as the Keatons' housekeeper, Karen Nicholson. Courteney Cox, then most familiar as the girl Bruce Springsteen pulled out of the audience in the "Dancing in the Dark" music video, played Alex's second serious girlfriend, Lauren Miller. Tracy Pollan, who played Alex's first long-term girlfriend, Ellen Reed, would become his real-life wife in an enduring marriage.

Family Ties was a classic example of the value of advantageous scheduling in the pre-cable era when there were essentially only three major players: ABC, CBS and NBC. For its first two seasons, it struggled on Wednesday following the fading *Facts of Life*. In the fall of 1984 NBC shifted it to Thursday following *The Cosby Show*, which became one of television's biggest hits ever. *Family Ties* rode *Cosby*'s coattails to number 5 in the Nielsen ratings that season, then became number 2 to only *Cosby* for the following two seasons.

When NBC decided to use the post–*Cosby* half-hour to launch a spinoff, *A Different World*, *Family Ties* was moved to Sunday and its audience dropped in half. After one more season it was out of the Top 30 and ended its run with a two-part episode in which Alex left the security of the nest and heads to New York to pursue his dreams.

26. *Bewitched*

Broadcast History:

Thursday	9:00–9:30	September 1964–January 1967	ABC
Thursday	8:30–9:00	January 1967–September 1971	ABC
Wednesday	8:00–8:30	September 1971–January 1972	ABC
Saturday	8:00–8:30	January 1972–July 1972	ABC

#2 rated series in 1964–65	#11 rated series in 1967–68
#7 rated series in 1965–66	#11 rated series in 1968–69
#7 rated series in 1966–67	#24 rated series in 1969–70

26. Bewitched

3 Major Emmy Awards (20 nominations):
No Emmy Awards for Best Series (3 nominations)
No Emmy Awards for Best Actress (6 nominations)
No Emmy Awards for Best Actor (1 nomination)
2 Emmy Awards for Best Supporting Actress (8 nominations)
1 Emmy Award for Best Direction (2 nominations)

Cast: Elizabeth Montgomery; Dick York (1964–69); Dick Sargent (1969–72); Agnes Moorehead; Maurice Evans; David White; Irene Vernon (1964–66); Kasey Rogers (1966–72); Diane Murphy (1966–72); Erin Murphy (1966–72); George Tobias; Alice Pearce (1964–66); Marion Lorne (1964–68); Paul Lynde (1965–72); Alice Ghostley (1969–72); Bernard Fox (1967–72).

The popular perception of the 1960s, especially among those who weren't there, was of an entire decade of explosive demonstrations and riots in the streets, civil disobedience, sex, drugs and rock 'n' roll. Actually, this didn't take hold until the back end of the 1960s, with the assassinations of Bobby Kennedy and Martin Luther King, the enduring, widely despised Vietnam War and the tumultuous 1968 presidential election season. TV always has been a few years behind the curve. The saying "TV doesn't lead society, it follows" could have been coined for this decade. In 1964, less than a year after America grieved the loss of John F. Kennedy, the Beatles were singing "I Want to Hold Your Hand" (the harder stuff came later) and the prime time network landscape was dominated by trifles such as *My Favorite Martian*, *McHale's Navy*, *My Three Sons* and *Gilligan's Island*. *The Adventures of Ozzie and Harriet* was still hanging on. *All in the Family* and the socially relevant, often angry comedies it spawned didn't appear until the early 1970s. *Bewitched* fit snugly into this mindless paradigm.

Whereas Superman could bend steel, leap over tall buildings with a single bound and fly faster than a speeding bullet, Samantha Stephens could achieve miraculous ends with a mere twitch of her nose. She might have been a witch but she was a good witch. Her means were often questionable, especially to her frustrated spouse Darrin, but her ends were always well intended. Coyishly portrayed by Elizabeth Montgomery, she was also a quite a looker. Samantha was the kind of woman most men would dream of marrying, with delightful anticipation of what she could do for him with her magical powers a sweetener to the already complete package. Who wouldn't want a knockout bride, who could produce diamonds, furs and fancy cars with a twitch of her nose? The answer was Darrin Stephens. He loved Samantha but hated that she was a witch. He begged, cajoled and sometimes demanded that she cease and desist making magic.

Darrin was not most men in another way. There was two of him. Dick York inaugurated the role of the constantly frustrated foil for his wife's antics and stayed with it until health issues forced him to step aside after five seasons. Coincidentally, an actor with the same first name, Dick Sargent, stepped in for what became a seamless transition. You got the feeling there could have been a different Darrin every week and the audience would have neither noticed nor cared as long as Montgomery's Samantha was up to her old tricks.

To make matters worse for buzz kill Darrin, he was badly outnumbered by a coven of family members and friends of Samantha, led by her mother Endora (Agnes Moorehead), who never missed an opportunity to attempt to break up her daughter's mixed marriage to a mortal. She relentlessly but unsuccessfully tempted Darrin with knockout women she conjured, including bringing to life Venus de Milo. Endora had a battalion of allies, including flamboyant Uncle Arthur (Paul Lynde), Samantha's lookalike cousin Serena (also played by Montgomery), flighty housekeeper Esmeralda (Alice Ghostley), whose witch powers batteries needed recharging, and the Witches Council, which demanded that Samantha make her marriage to a mortal disappear.

Long-time film actress Agnes Morehead was a scene stealer as the cunning Endora, a role for which she was Emmy-nominated six times as outstanding supporting actress. Montgomery was nominated five times and the series was thrice up for best comedy. In a ghoulish coincidence, the series only performing Emmys went posthumously to Marion Lorne, as Aunt Clara, and Alice Pearce as the Stephens nosy neighbor Gladys Kravitz, who suspected there were strange goings-on in the Stephens household. (No disrespect to either fine actress but death has frequently been a career move during Hollywood award season.)

The lack of love from Hollywood peers was more than compensated for by the embrace of the viewing audience. *Bewitched* soared to the number 2 most watched series during its first season, the loftiest ranking to that time for an ABC series, and remained in the Top 15 for the first five of its eight seasons. The series also produced one very short-lived, spinoff series, *Tabitha*, about the Stephens' daughter (also a witch).

27. *Two and a Half Men*

Broadcast History:

Monday	9:30–10:00	September 2003–September 2005	CBS
Monday	9:00–9:30	September 2005–July 2012	CBS

Thursday	8:30–9:00	July 2012–August 2013	CBS
Thursday	9:30–10:00	September 2013–February 2014	CBS
Thursday	9:00–9:30	March 2014–May 2014	CBS
Monday	9:30–10:00	June 2014–August 2015	CBS

#15 rated series in 2003–04   #11 rated series in 2009–10
#11 rated series in 2004–05   #17 rated series in 2010–11
#17 rated series in 2005–06   #11 rated series in 2011–12
#21 rated series in 2006–07   #11 rated series in 2012–13
#17 rated series in 2007–08   #27 rated series in 2013–14
#10 rated series in 2008–09

3 Major Emmy Awards (23 nominations):
No Emmy Awards for Best Series (3 nominations)
1 Emmy Award for Best Actor (5 nominations)
1 Emmy Award for Best Supporting Actor (6 nominations)
No Emmy Awards for Best Supporting Actress (6 nominations)
1 Emmy Award for Best Guest Actor/Actress (3 nominations)

Cast: Charlie Sheen (2003–11); Jon Cryer; Angus T. Jones (2003–13); Holland Taylor; Conchata Ferrell; Melanie Lynskey (2003–07); Marin Hinkle; April Bowlby (2005–08); Emmanuelle Vaugier (2005–12); Ryan Stiles (2006–present); Jennifer Bini Taylor (2006–10); Courtney Thorne-Smith (2010–15); Ashton Kutcher (2011–15); Amber Tamblyn (2013–15).

Some guys have all the luck. Charlie Harper (Charlie Sheen) was one of those. Handsome, charming and ridiculously wealthy from writing commercial jingles, he lived in a Malibu beachfront mansion. Gorgeous women found his hedonist lifestyle irresistible. Some guys have no luck. These would include Alan Harper (Jon Cryer), Charlie's ne'er-do-well brother. A chiropractor with a failing practice, he got put out of his house by his estranged wife Judith (Marin Hinkle) when she decided she wanted to experiment with becoming a lesbian. (Once she had Alan out of her life, she went back to men.) With no place to live, Alan got Charlie to let him crash with him. Supposedly it was a temporary arrangement. But once Alan got his foot in the door, there was no getting him out, to Charlie's chagrin.

Alan was a package deal. He had shared custody of his adolescent son Jake (Angus T. Jones), a lad of limited intellectual prowess and common sense. But he received a masters degree level education in sex and partying from witnessing his Uncle Charlie's free-wheeling, free-loving lifestyle. The frank and sexually provocative dialog and story lines pushed the envelope to new frontiers for broadcast television. CBS used the show's popularity as testimony to its acceptance by viewers and further argued it was on in the evening at a time when parents should have had control over what their children watched.

This argument lost its credibility when the series went into syndication where it was often presented by local stations during dinner hours. However, by then, *Two and a Half Men* was a part of the culture and had numerous imitators pushing the boundaries of propriety even further.

Until Alan moved in, the only constant presence in Charlie's life was his plus-size housekeeper Berta (Conchata Ferrell). Berta had a sharp tongue with which she often lashed Charlie. He tolerated her disrespect because she was one of the few people willing to put up with, and clean up after, his hard-partying ways. A presence in Charlie's life much more than he wanted was his next door neighbor Rose (Melanie Lynskey). A one-night stand ended so badly that she Super Glued Charlie's genitals to his leg, then became his stalker. The way in which Rose, who made her exits by leaping off his porch, monitored his every move, especially with other women, was creepy in a comical way.

If there was a role model to blame for Charlie's lifestyle it was his oft-married mother Evelyn (Holland Taylor), who flaunted her own sexually liberated attitudes. This was an enduring source of resentment for Charlie and Alan, who felt she neglected them growing up while pursuing lovers. She made it clear this bothered them more than it did her.

One woman, a ballet dancer named Chelsea (Jennifer Bini Taylor), got Charlie as far as the altar in a Las Vegas wedding chapel but the nuptials fell apart at the last minute. As long as they were there, Alan, who was to be the best man, decided to take advantage of the situation and marry a ditzy, buxom woman named Kandi (April Bowlby), who was one of Charlie's former lovers. The marriage flamed out as quickly as MySpace.

Charlie Harper's hard living turned out to be tame compared to Sheen's real life. He made no apologies for his fondness for alcohol, narcotics and prostitutes, several at a time. This led to a ferocious feud with *Two and a Half Men* co-creator Chuck Lorre, who said it was affecting the show. Their back and forth barbs titillated tabloid readers for months in 2011 until Lorre decided Sheen wasn't worth the aggravation he brought and fired him. The future of the series hung in the balance until Lorre and CBS opted to go on with a new leading man. Ashton Kutcher was cast for season nine as Walden Schmidt, a computer whiz billionaire. Walden was heartbroken as a result of his divorce from his beloved Bridget. Judy Greer, who recurred as Bridget, had previously played Myra, the sister of Judith's then fiancée Herb Melnick. She and Charlie had a couple of amorous days together.

Lorre made certain there was no way Charlie Harper could ever return. The plot for the season nine premiere explained that Rose had finally won

Charlie's heart. They had married and gone to France for their honeymoon. Alas, Charlie could never change. Rose caught him cheating and he wound up "falling" in front of a Paris subway train. Feeling alone in the world, Walden improbably invited the shameless Alan to continue to live in Charlie's former house. It wasn't long before Walden regretted this decision as much as Charlie had. Not even the possibility of marrying a hot woman named Lyndsey (Courtney Thorne Smith) was enough to induce Alan to move out and begin life on his own.

Angus Jones also was written out of the series after season nine in the wake of him making unflattering comments about how wrong it was for him to have been subjected to raunch as a child actor. Jake joined the army and was soon deployed to Japan. With Jake gone, Amber Tamblyn joined the cast as Jenny, the daughter Charlie never knew he had. Jenny, a lesbian, inherited her father's love for booze and alley cat morality, going through beautiful woman at a pace Charlie would have admired. By then, it was no big deal for television. With the new cast, the series ran four more years, but it was never the same.

---

28. *Happy Days*

Broadcast History:

Tuesday	8:00–8:30	January 1974–September 1983	ABC
Tuesday	8:30–9:00	September 1983–January 1984	ABC
Tuesday	8:30–9:00	April 1984–May 1984	ABC
Thursday	8:00–8:30	June 1984–July 1984	ABC

#16 rated series in 1973–74	#17 rated series in 1979–80
#11 rated series in 1975–76	#15 rated series in 1980–81
#1 rated series in 1976–77	#18 rated series in 1981–82
#2 rated series in 1977–78	#28 rated series in 1982–83
#3 rated series in 1978–79	

No Major Emmy Awards (8 nominations):
No Emmy Awards for Best Actor (3 nominations)
No Emmy Awards for Best Supporting Actor (1 nomination)
No Emmy Awards for Best Supporting Actress (2 nominations)
No Emmy Awards for Best Direction (2 nominations)

åRon Howard (1974–80); Henry Winkler; Tom Bosley; Marion Ross; Anson Williams (1974–83); Donny Most (1974–80); Erin Moran; Gavan O'Herlihy (1974); Randolph Roberts (1974–75); Neil J. Schwartz (1974–75); Beatrice Colen (1974–76); Linda Purl (1974–75; 1982–83); Misty Rowe (1974–75); Tita Bell (1974–75);

Pat Morita (1975–76; 1982–83); Al Molinaro (1976–82); Scott Baio (1977–84); Lynda Goodfriend (1977–82); Cathy Silvers (1980–83); Ted McGinley (1980–84); Billy Warlock (1982–83); Crystal Bernard (1982–83); Heather O'Rourke (1982–83).

Happy Days was widely perceived to be an homage to the similarly themed *American Graffiti*, a big screen blockbuster the year before *Happy Days* premiered on ABC in 1974. That Ron Howard, at the time best known as Andy Griffith's boy Opie, had a prominent role in both the film and television series bolstered this belief as did utilizing early rock era anthem "Rock Around the Clock" as its theme song. (It was replaced for the second season by an original theme.) However the genesis of *Happy Days* preceded *American Graffiti* as a 1972 vignette, "Love and the Television Set" (subsequently retitled "Love and the Happy Days"), on the fluffy ABC anthology series *Love American Style*. Even before that, ABC passed on a pilot, *New Family in Town*, which featured many of the *Happy Days* characters and actors, including Howard. Thus it is fair to say the success of *American Graffiti* influenced ABC to take what became *Happy Days* to series.

The light-hearted period piece set in the idyllic 1950s also was an ideal alternative to harder edged, topical comedies such as *All in the Family* and *Maude*, which had come into vogue. Howard was the pivotal character as Richie Cunningham, a clean cut teen living in Milwaukee with his father Howard (Tom Bosley), who ran a hardware store, stay-at-home mom Marion (Marion Ross) and kid sister Joanie (Erin Moran). Richie's college age brother Chuck was an occasional presence in seasons one and two. However, a way to effectively use this character was never devised. So, he was first sent away to school then written out of the show as if he had never existed. In one of the final episodes, Howard referred to his "two" children. Chuck was such a non-factor he was played by different actors, Gavan O'Herlihy and Randolph Roberts, without viewers paying much notice.

One of the most fortuitous accidents in television history occurred when what was designed to be a minor character, Arthur Fonzarelli (Henry Winkler), was introduced. "The Fonz," a high school dropout whose trademark look was a leather motorcycle jacket, was crafted as a counterweight to Richie and his clean cut pals Potsie (Anson Williams) and Ralph Malph (Donny Most). They all hung out at Arnold's Drive In—a malt and burger joint similar to the ground zero of *American Graffiti*. Fonzie was too cool for school. Any girl was his with a snap of his fingers. A karate-like chop of his hand fired up Arnold's jukebox. There was nothing he couldn't fix with the same thump. His thumbs up gesture and "Ayyyyy" expression of approval became parts of the culture. So did the negative expression "Sit on it."

At the end of the series run, the Smithsonian Institution requested Fonzie's leather jacket for permanent display. Producers took note. The secondary character was promoted to equal billing with Richie, at the expense of Potsie, Ralph and the others. When Ron Howard left the show in season eight, Winkler's name was elevated to the head of the credits.

Happy Days' ratings soared with the popularity of The Fonz. By its third season, it was the number one show in the Nielsen ratings. The writers also cleaned up the Fonz's act, transforming the rebel into a role model for the other characters. He went to night school and earned his high school diploma, surprising Richie and the gang by graduating with them. He was welcomed to live above the Cunninghams' garage, allowing him to be an even more constant presence in their lives. Eventually, he became a businessman, with his own garage and part ownership of Arnold's. After a brief relationship with a single mom, played by Linda Purl (who had a previous appearance as one of Richie's dates), Fonzie adopted a young boy on his own.

As *Happy Days* matured and the originals started to leave the show, emphasis shifted to Joanie and her romance with Fonzie's cousin Chachi (Scott Baio). The young lovers were spun off into their own short-lived series, *Joanie Loves Chachi.* When it failed, they returned to the mothership. Other series offspring enjoyed more success, most notably *Laverne & Shirley* and *Mork & Mindy.* The title characters of *Laverne & Shirley* were a couple of not especially sharp girls who were insinuated into *Happy Days* as double dates for Richie and Fonzie. In 1976–77, *Happy Days* and *Laverne & Shirley* were the top two series on the Nielsen charts.

The following season, they reversed that order. *Happy Days* also introduced the world to Robin Williams, who appeared as an outer space alien named Mork from the planet Ork. He came to earth to study humans and chose Richie as his prime subject. Overwhelmingly positive response led Williams to be spun off into his own series, which enjoyed a meteoric rise toward the top of the ratings. In 1978–79, *Laverne & Shirley, Happy Days* and *Mork & Mindy* were three of television's four highest rated series. (*Three's Company* split them.) A fourth spinoff, *Blansky's Beauties,* starring Pat Morita, who showed up occasionally on *Happy Days* as the eponymous Arnold, was rejected even quicker than *Joanie Loves Chachi.*

Another seeming misstep became part of *Happy Days* legacy. In season five, the writers designed an episode with a preposterous plot, which had Fonzie water ski jumping over a pool of sharks. "Jumping the shark" became a euphemism (as well as the title of a book) for series that had become so creatively bankrupt that the writers had to resort to outlandish storylines. Winkler liked to point out that no matter what the detractors might have said, *Happy Days* went on for six years after "jumping the shark."

---

29. *Home Improvement*

Broadcast History:

Tuesday	8:30–9:00	September 1991–August 1992	ABC
Wednesday	9:00–9:30	August 1992–September 1994	ABC
Tuesday	9:00–9:30	September 1994–July 1998	ABC
Tuesday	8:00–8:30	July 1998–May 1999	ABC
Friday	8:00–8:30	July 1999–September 1999	ABC

#5 rated series in 1991–92	#7 rated series in 1995–96
#3 rated series in 1992–93	#9 rated series in 1996–97
#2 rated series in 1993–94	#10 rated series in 1997–98
#3 rated series in 1994–95	#10 rated series in 1998–99

No Major Emmy Awards (7 nominations):
No Emmy Awards for Best Series (2 nominations)
No Emmy Awards for Best Actor (1 nomination)
No Emmy Awards for Best Actress (4 nominations)

Cast: Tim Allen; Patricia Richardson; Zachery Ty Bryan; Jonathan Taylor Thomas (1991–98); Taran Noah Smith; Earl Hindman; Richard Karn; Pamela Anderson (1991–93); Debbe Dunning (1993–99).

Fueled by the extraordinary success of *The Cosby Show*, sitcoms adapted from the acts of standup comedians came into vogue during the 1990s (*Roseanne, Seinfeld, Everybody Loves Raymond*, etc.). *Home Improvement* was another in this line and became one of the major successes of the genre. Tim Allen's nightclub act was steeped in the comedian's uber-macho alter ego. This became the basis for his television character, Tim Taylor. The host of a local do-it-yourself cable television show in Detroit, *Tool Time*, Tim's philosophy was there was no job around the house that couldn't be accomplished by turning up the power of the machines involved.

Allen's personal popularity powered *Home Improvement* to an eight-year run near the top of the Nielsen ratings. It was greatly aided at launch by a cushy hammock between *Full House* and *Roseanne*. However, it quickly became a viewer favorite in its own right. In its third season, it was the second highest rated series in prime time. Tim's mania for power usually wound up making any small problem a bigger one. He was the first responder to any fix-it job around the Taylor household. This unfailingly resulted in a need for a second responder, someone who knew what he was doing and could handle the original problem as well as any new ones created by Tim's bungling.

Not only was he somewhat inept, Tim was also accident-prone. When he got his hands on a power tool, his patient wife Jill (Patricia Richardson) and their children, Brad (Zachary Ty Bryan), Randy (Jonathan Taylor Thomas) and Mark (Taran Noah Smith) ran for cover and tried to hide anything they valued. The youngsters ranged from ages 8 to 10 when *Home Improvement* debuted in 1991. Brad, athletic and a big man on campus, had a knack for doing the wrong thing. Nothing major but enough to be called to the attention of his parents. Andy was more cerebral and had a smart mouth, which often got him into hot water. Mark, the baby of the family, generally played third fiddle in the shadow of his older brothers. As he got older he began to rebel, including dabbling in the dark world of Goth.

As the series progressed, the kids antics and issues matured with them. The younger characters became more integral to the show's generally soft plots and their popularity soared among their contemporaries in the real world. Thomas left the series after season seven, ostensibly to concentrate on his studies. He did graduate with honors from a toney Los Angeles area prep school and went on to Harvard. However, he also found time to play in a couple of "B" movies, *Speedway Junkie* and *Walking Across Egypt.* The fact that he did this after exiting the series might have been a source of ill will because he was not asked back to participate in the three-part series finale, although his character was shown in flashbacks. If there were problems, they must have eventually been smoothed over, since Thomas was invited to appear in guest roles in Allen's next ABC series, *Last Man Standing.*

Tim's co-star on *Tool Time,* the mild-mannered Al Borland (Richard Karn), served as a governor for Tim's tendency to take things over the top. Tim was such a klutz that viewers assumed it was all a part of the act, to lighten the show. Thankfully, Al was always there to smooth over the rough edges left by Tim. A then little known actress named Pamela Anderson occasionally appeared during the first two seasons as Lisa the Tool Girl, the eye candy on *Tool Time.* Anderson left for another series, *Baywatch,* which turned her into an international sensation. Debbe Dunning replaced her for the show's final six seasons.

The core cast was completed by Tim's philosophical next-door-neighbor Wilson (Earl Hindman), which turned out to be both his first and last names. Wilson and Tim had man-to-man chats over the fence separating their properties in every episode, although it was more like mentor, Wilson, and student. They shared thoughts about the vagaries of life and family. The height of the fence allowed Wilson to be seen only from the bridge of his nose upward, a gimmick that became a trademark of the series. The fence didn't come down until the final episode.

Although *Home Improvement* was immensely popular with audiences (during its entire eight year run it was never out of the Nielsen top ten), critics and Emmy voters weren't as enthralled with the show.

---

30. *Sex and the City*

Cable History:

Sunday	9:00–9:30	June 1998–August 1998	HBO
Sunday	9:00–9:30	June 1999–October 1999	HBO
Sunday	9:30–10:00	June 2000–October 2000	HBO
Sunday	9:00–9:30	June 2001–August 2001	HBO
Sunday	9:00–9:30	January 2002–February 2002	HBO
Sunday	9:00–9:30	July 2002–September 2002	HBO
Sunday	9:00–9:30	June 2003–September 2003	HBO
Sunday	9:00–9:30	January 2004–February 2004	HBO

4 Major Emmy Awards (32 nominations):
1 Emmy Award for Best Series (5 nominations)
1 Emmy Award for Best Actress (6 nominations)
1 Emmy Award for Best Supporting Actress (9 nominations)
No Emmy Awards for Best Guest Actress (1 nomination)
No Emmy Awards for Best Writing (7 nominations)
1 Emmy Award for Best Direction (4 nominations)

Cast: Sarah Jessica Parker; Kim Cattrall, Kristin Davis; Cynthia Nixon; Chris Noth; Willie Garson; Ben Weber (1998–99); David Eigenberg (1999–2004); Bridget Moynahan (1999–2000); John Corbett (2000–02, 2004); Kyle MacLachlan (2000–02); Lynn Cohen (2000–04); Mario Cantone (2000–04); Frances Sternhagen (2000–02); James Remar (2001–04); Candice Bergen (2001–04); Sonia Braga (2001); Evan Handler (2002–04); Ron Livingston (2002–04); Sean Palmer (2002–04); Jason Lewis (2003–04); Blair Underwood (2003–04); Mikhail Baryshnikov (2004).

Sex and the City became the biggest comedy hit in the history of cable, as well as its first series Emmy winner, by appealing to both genders for different reasons. Females loved the depiction of four attractive, independent-minded career women having the time of their lives in New York City while aggressively pursuing men and seeking to climb the social and professional ladders. Males were drawn to the T&A worked into every episode. (No sense not taking advantage of being on HBO.)

The series was based on a book and columns written by New York journalist Candace Bushnell. However the crafting of the four bawdy gal pals, arguably among the most well rounded female characters ever crafted for television, was the product of a gay man, producer/writer Darren Star, whose credits also include *Melrose Place* and *Beverly Hills 90210*. It could be said that these four man-hungry women essentially served as surrogates for the fantasies of gay males. As the series progressed several gay male characters were insinuated regularly into the plots.

Sarah Jessica Parker starred as Bushnell's alter ego, Carrie Bradshaw, a populist sex and relationships specialist for a New York newspaper. Each of the episodes was kicked off by Carrie, serving as narrator, commenting about some facet of being young, single and on the prowl in Manhattan. The other boroughs might as well have floated away into the ocean.

Carrie's circle of BFFs included sexually adventuresome publicist Samantha Jones (Kim Cattrall), who was open to any sexual escapade, with the gender of her partner(s) not a consideration. Cattrall, who came to fame as the sexual screamer teacher in the motion picture *Porky's*, was wildly uninhibited personally and gleefully appeared nude in the majority of episodes. Kristin Davis played Charlotte York, an art specialist, who was Samantha's sexual opposite. Charlotte, the seemingly wholesome girl-next-door type, loved action between the sheets as much as the other three but was reluctant to ape their free love attitude. Her goal, which she occasionally fell short of achieving, was to save herself for her Prince Charming. Frequent buzz killer Miranda Hobbes (Cynthia Nixon) was a sour lawyer, who trusted no one outside her immediate circle, especially men.

All the women, including Carrie, played the field, dating some guys for extended periods, others for one-night stands. However, Carrie's heart belonged to the ultra suave, extremely wealthy Big, a tour de force for Chris Noth. Although male physical endowment was recurring conversational fodder for Carrie and her pals, it was not suggested that this is how Noth's character earned his name. Carrie knew him and referred to him as nothing else. It was not revealed until the end of the series that his birth name was John Preston.

Big seemed as taken with Carrie as she was with him, but he was commitment phobic, at least when it came to Carrie. This might have been a result of his failed marriage. However, during one of the lulls in their relationship, Big married again, a woman named Natasha, played by Bridget Moynahan, who in real life is the first wife of superstar quarterback Tom Brady. Her screen marriage to Big didn't last, either. When things were going well between

Carrie and Big, who finally committed to her in Paris in the series finale, hopeless romantics swooned.

Sex and the City won four major Emmy awards during its run. The success and popularity of the series ultimately led to the production of two motion picture versions (with full cast intact).

---

31. *Get Smart*

Broadcast History:

Saturday	8:30–9:00	September 1965–September 1968	NBC
Saturday	8:00–8:30	September 1968–September 1969	NBC
Friday	7:30–8:00	September 1969–September 1970	CBS

#12 rated series in 1965–66
#22 rated series in 1966–67

7 Major Emmy Awards (14 nominations):
2 Emmy Awards for Best Series (4 nominations)
3 Emmy Awards for Best Actor (4 nominations)
No Emmy Awards for Best Actress (2 nominations)
1 Emmy Award for Best Writing (2 nominations)
1 Emmy Award for Best Direction (2 nominations)

Cast: Don Adams; Barbara Feldon; Edward Platt; Dave Ketchum (1966–67); Stacy Keach, Sr. (1966–67); Bernie Kopell (1966–69); King Moody (1966–69); Dick Gautier (1966–69); Victor French (1965–70); Robert Karvelas (1967–70); Jane Dulo (1968–69).

James Bond films were all the rage in the 1960s. As always, television producers and networks took notice. Knockoff dramas such as *The Man from U.N.C.L.E.* began to appear on the small screen. Even pop music jumped on the bandwagon with Johnny Rivers' "Secret Agent Man." Two of the most creative comedic minds ever, Buck Henry and Mel Brooks, opted to zig when everyone else was zagging. They created *Get Smart* as a satiric takeoff on the genre. Just as James Bond had his 007 designation, Maxwell Smart (Don Adams) was Agent 86. In spite of unconventional, often foolish methods, he was amazingly efficient.

James Bond might have had his ejector seat super sports car and other gadgets. Maxwell Smart had ridiculous gimmickry such as a shoe phone (decades before compact cell phones). He also had phones built into various articles of clothing and accessories—ties, belts, eyeglasses, etc. Occasionally several would ring at the same time, usually at inopportune times. Bond had Goldfinger. Max had an art theft villain dubbed Bronzefinger.

The series launched a lexicon of Max's pet expressions, which worked their way into the pop vernacular. When he could see an absurdly implausible tale he was trying to sell wasn't being well received, he tried to shift gears with "Would you believe...?" A misfire would be followed by "Missed by that much." If one of his gambits failed to achieve the desired result with unfortunate consequences, he would apologize with "Sorry about that."

The 007 series had its Bond girls. Agent 86 had 99, played by husky voiced beauty Barbara Feldon. Business-like 99 essentially served as a straight woman and occasionally a damsel in distress for Maxwell. Other than when operating under an alias, 99 never went by anything other than her numerical designation. Her real name was never revealed. She had her spy toys, too, among which was a phone built into her fingernails.

Max and 99 worked for a United States counter-intelligence agency dubbed CONTROL, whose Cold War nemesis was KAOS, an anti–American operation founded in Romania—but incorporated in Delaware for tax purposes. The seeming acronyms were typical *Get Smart* inanity. They stood for nothing. KAOS was headed by a duo named Siegfried (Bernie Koppel) and Starker (King Moody), whose goal was world domination. They had their own gadgetry, including a robot with super human powers (but not super human intelligence) named Hymie (Dick Gautier). Eventually, Max was able to turn Hymie, bringing him over to the side of CONTROL.

Another of Max's unlikely allies was Agent Armstrong, an ape surgically transformed to look like a human. Agents 86 and 99 reported to "The Chief" (Edward Platt), the cranky head of CONTROL, who was often frustrated by Max's missteps and close calls but kept him around because of his uncanny ability to transform a screw-up into a mission accomplished. Max saved The Chief's life when Hymie was programmed to assassinate him.

Maxwell and 99 eventually became romantically involved and married at the end of the fourth season. With other candidates disappearing as soon as they were asked, Max turned to Hymie to serve as his best man. The honeymoon didn't go as planned. Max and 99 wound up marooned on an uncharted island, deserted except for Siegfried and Starker. The following season, after *Get Smart* had migrated from its birthplace on NBC to CBS for its final season, 99 gave birth to twins.

The Bond movies weren't alone in being paid homage. With *I Spy* a big winner, *Get Smart* did a takeoff that had Max touring the globe with a black table tennis pro. An episode on Siegfried trying to destroy the world's potato crops was inspired by *Snoopy and the Red Baron*. Max and 99 once went undercover as Connie and Floyd, *Get Smart*'s answer to *Bonnie and Clyde*. Max was a man of many disguises: a servant, a flamenco dancer and a motorcycle gang member, to name just a few.

Memories of *Get Smart* were so warm and enduring that several attempts were made to bring back the concept. Adams and Feldon took a shot at remaking the magic in a 1988 made-for-TV movie and seven years later in a short-lived series revival on the Fox network. Steve Carell and Anne Hathaway tried on the big screen in 2008. But with the Cold War long over and without Henry and Brooks, it just wasn't the same.

32. *The Beverly Hillbillies*

Broadcast History:

Wednesday	9:00–9:30	September 1962–September 1964	CBS
Wednesday	8:30–9:00	September 1964–September 1968	CBS
Wednesday	9:00–9:30	September 1968–September 1969	CBS
Wednesday	8:30–9:00	September 1969–September 1970	CBS
Tuesday	7:30–8:00	September 1970–September 1971	CBS

#1 rated series in 1962–63	#7 rated series in 1966–67
#1 rated series in 1963–64	#12 rated series in 1967–68
#12 rated series in 1964–65	#10 rated series in 1968–69
#7 rated series in 1965–66	#18 rated series in 1969–70

No Major Emmy Awards (7 nominations):
No Emmy Awards for Best Series (1 nomination)
No Emmy Awards for Best Actress (2 nominations)
No Emmy Award for Best Supporting Actress (1 nomination)
No Emmy Awards for Best Writing (1 nomination)
No Emmy Awards for Best Direction (2 nominations)

Cast: Buddy Ebsen; Irene Ryan; Donna Douglas; Max Baer, Jr.; Raymond Bailey; Nancy Kulp; Bea Benaderet (1962–63); Harriet MacGibbon (1962–69); Frank Wilcox (1962–66); Lisa Seagram (1965–66); Phil Gordon (1962–63); Arthur Gould Porter (1962–65); Sirry Steffan (1962–63); Louis Nye (1962); Sharon Tate (1963–65); Milton Frome (1964–67); Ray Kellogg (1964–66); Roy Roberts (1964–67); Larry Pennell (1965–69); Percy Helton (1968–71); Elvia Allman (1969–71); George "Shug" Fisher (1969–71); Judy Jordan (1969–70); Danielle Mardi (1969–71); Judy McConnell (1969); Mady Maguire (1969–71); Bettina Brenna (1969–71); Phil Silvers (1969–71); Kathleen Freeman (1969–71); Diana Bartlett (1970–71); Roger Torrey (1970–71).

The Beverly Hillbillies was a show for its time. In 1962 a gallon of gas cost less than what a pack of chewing gum does a half-century later. So, as unthinkable as it might be in the 21st century, America found it easy to embrace a family of oil barons. It helped that the Clampett clan was living an American dream, ascending from dirt poor Appalachia to filthy rich in one of the nation's most glamorous addresses. It was all thanks to a fortuitous accident. The show's theme song told the story about Jed Clampett discovering oil on his land while out hunting. The Clampetts become instant millionaires and move into a Beverly Hills mansion.

The Clampetts became the ultimate fish out of water. You could take them out of the hills but you couldn't take the hills out of them. Soft spoken Jed (Buddy Ebsen) was as rich in down home common sense as he was in petro dollars. Vexed over something, he'd sit out front of his opulent mansion and go to whittling to clear his head, just as he did on the porch back home. Jed wasn't very sophisticated but he was no one's fool. Scammers, who took him for an easy mark, inevitably wound up regretting it.

Jed, a widower, was the nominal head of the clan, although his mother-in-law Granny (Irene Ryan), as feisty a woman as has ever emerged from the hills, might have mounted a minority challenge. Granny hated her new "high fallutin" environment. Her incessant gripes included an inability to get the "fixin's for possum stew," one of her pet recipes. Grocers looked at her like she belonged in an institution and Rodeo Drive might have a wild west name but there was no forest to hunt her own ingredients. Neighbors turned apoplectic every time she fired up her moonshine still or cooked another vat of foul-smelling lye soap. She couldn't catch a fish in the "cement pond" out back and she learned to her dismay, it was against the law to practice her own brand of backwoods medicine, even if it was often more effective than the traditional kind.

Another bee in Granny's bonnet was what she saw as the dearth of young men to court her nubile and naive tomboy granddaughter Ellie Mae (Donna Douglas). A blond knockout in tight clothes, Elly Mae would take any guy's breath away. However, the prospect of facing a shotgun-toting Granny if he stepped out of line might have been a factor in a scarcity of suitors. This is not to say Elly May needed reinforcements. She was gentle and loving with all manner of critters, even raccoons and skunks, but also was capable of man-handling any guy until he cried "uncle." Eventually, Jed used some of his windfall to buy a movie studio, which the Clampetts used as a fishing hole for potential mates, with monikers like Dash Riprock (this was the era of Rock Hudson, Tab Hunter, et al.).

Every village (and sitcom) needs an idiot and cousin Jethro Bodine (Max Baer, Jr.) filled the bill on *The Beverly Hillbillies*—this despite the fact that

Jethro was the Clampetts' academic over-achiever. He made it all the way to sixth grade back home, where grading must have been done on a generous curve. Jethro, totally unaware that he was dumb as a rock quarry, vacillated between aspiring to be a brain surgeon or a double-naught spy (remember, this was the decade America fell in love with James Bond 007). He took to the Clampetts' new lifestyle with a gullible zest and became a willing target for every gold-digging hottie in Hollywood.

It wasn't only knockouts that were hot for Jethro. Miss (plain) Jane Hathaway (Nancy Kulp), girl Friday for the Clampetts' banker Millburn Drysdale (Raymond Bailey), yearned for Jethro but not for the money. She was warm for his hulking form. It was her boss who was all about the money. Mr. Drysdale went into cardiac arrest every time Jed suggested he might take his money and go home or use it for some other purpose that entailed withdrawing it from Mr. Drysdale's bank. His wife Harriet (Harriet MacGibbon) didn't share his affection for the Clampetts. She detested having them as next-door neighbors and would have been happier than a sow in slop if the Clampetts took their money and went home, no matter what it meant to her husband's fiscal and physical health.

The Beverly Hillbillies was sitcom gold for CBS, topping the ratings for its first two seasons and never finishing out of Nielsen's Top 20 for the first eight years of its nine-year run. It also triggered almost a decade of similarly themed hit sitcoms, including *Petticoat Junction* and *Green Acres*. The Television Academy wasn't as enamored of the unsophisticated humor as the public. *The Beverly Hillbillies* was honored with only seven Emmy nominations over its long run and was totally shut out on Awards Night. It is believed that this show, more than any other, led then FCC Chairman Newton Minnow to proclaim television as a "vast wasteland."

33. *Father Knows Best*

Broadcast History:

Sunday	10:00–10:30	October 1954–March 1955	CBS
Wednesday	8:30–9:00	August 1955–September 1958	NBC
Monday	8:30–9:00	September 1958–September 1960	CBS

#17 rated series in 1957–58
#14 rated series in 1958–59
#6 rated series in 1959–60

5 Major Emmy Awards (18 nominations):
No Emmy Awards for Best Series (4 nominations)
3 Emmy Awards for Best Actress (3 nominations)
2 Emmy Awards for Best Actor (4 nominations)
No Emmy Awards for Best Supporting Actor (1 nomination)
No Emmy Awards for Best Supporting Actress (1 nomination)
No Emmy Awards for Best Writing (4 nominations)
No Emmy Awards for Best Direction (1 nomination)

Cast: Robert Young; Jane Wyatt; Elinor Donahue; Billy Gray; Lauren Chapin; Sarah Selby; Yvonne Lime (1954–57); Paul Wallace (1954–59); Jimmy Bates (1954–59); Robert Foulk (1955–59); Vivi Jannis (1955–59); Roger Smith (1957–58); Robert Chapman (1957–58); Sue George (1957–58); Roberta Shore (1958–59).

Father Knows Best followed what was a familiar path to television in the early days of the medium. Like *The Lone Ranger, Amos and Andy, Dragnet* and *The Adventures of Ozzie and Harriet*, which it most resembled in tone, *Father Knows Best* was adapted from a successful radio series. Although the core characters remained the same, Robert Young was the only cast member to make the transition from the radio program, which ran from 1949 to 1954, to the television series, which debuted on the CBS television network in the fall of 1954.

Young, a popular big screen actor in the 1930s and 1940s, played to his charisma deficient nice guy type as Jim Anderson, a soft spoken insurance spokesman, who was patriarch of a stereotypical Midwestern family in the fictional town of Springfield. On radio, Jim was a bit of a bumbler. He quickly transitioned to a wise Father of the Year, adept at Solomon-like decisions, on the tube. Young stayed with the series through the 1960 season when he decided he had done all he could with the character and wanted to explore other options. His personal appeal didn't travel well initially. His first post–*Father Knows Best* series, *Window on Main Street*, was canceled after one season. It wasn't until 1969 that Young would find the role that defined his career even more than Jim Anderson, *Marcus Welby, M.D.*

Jane Wyatt, who enjoyed a moderately successful early career on Broadway and film, took over the role of Jim's spouse Margaret upon the transition to television. Margaret was a homemaker who willingly ceded Jim's primacy in the home. Even when he encouraged her to take courses at Springfield Junior College to become more independent, she demurred. "I don't want to be independent. I want to be dependent upon you." Jim and Margaret donned the television uniforms of the day. He was rarely seen out of a sports coat, dress shirt and tie. Margaret's ensemble of choice was a prim dress, often accentuated by pearls. This was true even when they were relaxing around the house. They slept in twin beds and displays of affection were confined to passionless pecks.

Nevertheless, the Andersons managed to conceive three children. Betty (Elinor Donahue), their first born, was 17 when the series premiered. She was her mother's daughter in almost every way, including her wardrobe choices and pre-feminist conformity to societal norms. Bud (Billy Gray), the Anderson's middle child, was three years younger. He was a hot rod enthusiast but embraced none of the rebellious attitudes and behavior associated with souped-up cars. Shy around the opposite sex at the outset, he matured into a romantic, who became smitten with almost every woman in his orbit, including a college professor, a football coach's daughter and his tutor. Kathy (Lauren Chapin), the baby of the family, was five years younger than Bud. "Kitten" to her family, she was a happy-go-lucky cutie pie, whose role was to blurt out precious one-liners beyond her age. Her evolution from tomboy to pretty young woman, which she resisted, provided fertile terrain for story lines.

Most of the episodes were simplistic mini-morality plays devoid of controversy or edge. Problems that would a couple of decades later become staples of situation comedy—pre-marital sex, alcohol and drug use—were not a part of the Andersons' world. College students at mixers were clean cut, conservatively dressed and drank soft drinks through straws. Troubling issues, tame as they were, were thrashed out around the Anderson dinner table.

Betty was disappointed when she was assigned to tutor an oafish member of the high school football team. But once she got to know him, she realized he was a great guy and a prize catch. A new teacher at school, who replaced one of the most popular members of the faculty, became a target for pranks by Bud's classmates. Bud knew the newbie was a standup guy because of an act of kindness on his behalf but went along with the in-crowd. However, when things got out of hand, Bud displayed judgment and leadership in getting his pals to ease up and give the teacher a fair chance. Margaret led by example. Inheriting a piece of property adjoining a home owned by a cranky senior citizen, who resented her mere presence, she kept working to find common ground until she got through to him in time for a heart-tugging curtain scene.

The series had an unusual history in that it ran on all three major networks. Its first season was on CBS, where it struggled to find an audience and was canceled. NBC picked it up and turned it into a viewer favorite. Three years later, it returned to CBS for its final first-run season, which broke into Nielsen's top 10. CBS tried to sustain the magic, scheduling reruns for two years. After CBS gave up on this strategy, then-fledgling ABC picked it up for another season of prime time repeats. Fans got to revisit the Andersons in a couple of TV movie reunions in 1977. *Father Knows Best* was nominated for four best series Emmys, winning none. However, Young and Wyatt picked up multiple Emmys for Best Actor (twice) and Best Actress (three times).

34. *The Larry Sanders Show*

Cable History:

Saturday	10:30–11:00	August 1992–November 1992	HBO
Wednesday	10:00–10:30	June 1993–September 1993	HBO
Wednesday	10:30–11:00	October 1993–January 1996	HBO
Wednesday	10:00–10:30	November 1996–February 1997	HBO
Wednesday	10:30–11:00	March 1997–May 1997	HBO
Sunday	10:00–10:30	March 1998–May 1998	HBO

3 Major Emmy Awards (48 nominations):
No Emmy Awards for Best Series (6 nominations)
No Emmy Awards for Best Actor (5 nominations)
1 Emmy Award for Best Supporting Actor (10 nominations)
No Emmy Awards for Best Supporting Actress (2 nominations)
No Emmy Awards for Best Guest Actor/Actress (6 nominations)
1 Emmy Award for Best Writing (13 nominations)
1 Emmy Award for Best Direction (6 nominations)

Cast: Garry Shandling; Rip Torn; Jeffrey Tambor; Penny Johnson; Janeane Garafalo (1992–96); Jeremy Piven (1992–93); Wallace Langham; Linda Doucett (1992–95); Megan Gallagher (1992); Deborah May; Bob Odenkirk; Kathryn Harrold (1993–94); Scott Thompson (1995–98); Mary Lynn Rajskub (1996–98).

Garry Shandling followed the counsel given to every writer in creating *The Larry Sanders Show*. He wrote what he knew. He knew the in's and out's of late night network television as well as anyone who wasn't a permanent host of one of the shows. Shandling was a regular guest on *The Tonight Show* and, for a time after Joan Rivers alienated Johnny Carson by venturing into her own show on Fox, Shandling was *Tonight's* permanent guest host. However, he wasn't considered a serious candidate to replace Carson, a job that went to fellow standup comedian Jay Leno. Shandling, in effect, created his own late night program, starring himself, for HBO.

Larry Sanders was a show within a show with Shandling's alter ego in the title role. Episodes were split between the backstage antics and politicking on film and snippets of the fictional late night program on tape. Little attempt was made to camouflage the fact that *The Larry Sanders Show* was a thinly veiled takeoff on *The Tonight Show,* although the liberties of premium cable allowed language on the faux show that was out of bounds on the broadcast late night shows into the 21st century.

The sets were almost identical and Larry's sidekick, Hank Kingsley (Jeffrey Tambor), had a pet phrase, "Hey now," modeled after *Tonight Show* sidekick Ed McMahon's "Hi yo." Hank, who did the show's warm-up, was full of himself and felt he could do as good or better job as host as his boss. His runaway ego and ambition led him to regularly chase get-rich schemes and put out feelers for television and film roles or his own show.

HBO had enjoyed moderate success with original comedy series such as *First and Ten* and *Dream On* but *The Larry Sanders Show* became its biggest original comedy—the first cable show nominated for an Emmy as outstanding comedy series. Its fifth season set a record for most Emmy nominations with 16. It brought HBO its first major series Emmys, for writing and directing. Shandling and his co-stars, Tambor and Rip Torn, were nominated almost every year but had the misfortune of being up against the *Frasier* juggernaut. Consequently, only Torn took home a performing Emmy as outstanding supporting actor for his portrayal of *Larry Sanders* producer Artie (his surname was not revealed).

Previously, *The Larry Sanders Show* had captured five Cable ACE Awards, which were created because the Television Academy dragged its feet in allowing cable to compete for Emmys. The awards recognition and strong subscriber satisfaction encouraged HBO to go forward with other comedies that would capture Emmys, most notably *Sex and the City.* It also enabled *The Larry Sanders Show* to attract a roster of A-list guests playing themselves, the equal of the late night gabfests on the broadcast networks. Dana Carvey, Carol Burnett, Ellen DeGeneres, David Duchovny and Rosie O'Donnell won Emmy nominations for guest roles. The ultimate recognition might have been Leno and David Letterman appearing as guests.

Although his late night program was a success by most standards, Larry Sanders was haunted by the insecurities commonplace in show business. Network executives exacerbated this by constantly meddling in the program, suggesting guests and demanding he take steps to attract younger demographics, all realities in the real world of television. Larry interpreted these incursions as votes of no confidence and feared each guest suggested by the network was an attempt to find a replacement for him. This was especially true of Jon Stewart's frequent appearances. (The faux suits might have been right given Stewart's subsequent popularity in a late night format for Comedy Central.)

Torn's Artie was a show-stealer. Ferociously protective of Larry and the show, he was, on the surface, a prim and proper gentleman. Out of public earshot, he spewed cascades of expletives that would take the paint off a wall. He also had a secret harem.

The series would occasionally veer away from the studio, its primary set, to delve into Larry's tormented private life. He was unable to maintain a relationship with either of his wives (Kathryn Harrold and Megan Gallagher) or a parade of knockouts and celebrities, some of whom he met backstage and others he hit upon while they were on the show. For a brief time, Larry was engaged to Roseanne.

The series also proved a grand showcase for actors who would go on to long and prosperous careers: Janeane Garofolo, who was Emmy nominated as talent booker Paula; Mary Lynn Rajskub as booking assistant Marylou; Jeremy Piven as head writer Jerry; Wallace Langham, who succeeded Piven's character; Penny Johnson as Larry's assistant Beverly; Sarah Silverman as a writer; and Bob Odenkirk as Larry's agent Stevie.

The series ended when Larry finally became fed up with network interference. One of the guests on the series finale was Jerry Seinfeld, two weeks after ending his own landmark series. The widespread opinion was *The Larry Sanders* finale was superior.

---

35. *The Lucy Show*

Broadcast History:

Monday	8:30–9:00	October 1962–June 1964	CBS
Monday	9:00–9:30	September 1964–July 1965	CBS
Monday	8:30–9:00	September 1965–June 1967	CBS
Monday	8:30–9:00	September 1967–August 1968	CBS

#4 rated series in 1962–63	#3 rated series in 1965–66
#6 rated series in 1963–64	#4 rated series in 1966–67
#8 rated series in 1964–65	#2 rated series in 1967–68

2 Major Emmy Awards (9 nominations):
No Emmy Awards for Best Series (1 nomination)
2 Emmy Awards for Best Actress (4 nominations)
No Emmy Awards for Best Supporting Actor (2 nominations)
No Emmy Awards for Best Writing (1 nomination)
No Emmy Awards for Best Direction (1 nomination)

Cast: Lucille Ball; Vivian Vance (1962–65); Charles Lane (1962–63); Gale Gordon (1963–68); Dick Martin (1962–64); Candy Moore (1962–65); Jimmy Garrett (1962–

66); Ralph Hart (1962–65); Ann Sothern (1965–66); Roy Roberts (1965–68); Mary Jane Croft (1965–68).

America never stopped loving Lucy even if Desi did. The divorce of Lucille Ball and Desi Arnaz, which led to the end of *I Love Lucy*, television's first super hit, became the catalyst for *The Lucy Show*. The premise adhered to the paradigm that worked so spectacularly, only without Desi. Lucy played a new character, Lucy Carmichael, but was up to her usual antics, including the signature "Waaah!" cry when her foolhardy schemes went awry. The thinking was America wasn't ready for Lucy as a divorcee so she was cast as a widow left with a substantial trust fund by her late husband.

Plots had Lucy up to all her familiar tricks. Many involved pratfall humor and preposterous scenarios, such as being locked in a bank vault and a space capsule, glued to her basement wall and getting mistakenly inducted into the Marines as Lou C. Carmichael. She volunteered to referee a football game and predictably fouled things up gloriously, inasmuch as she knew nothing about the sport. The writers weren't bashful about going back to the tried and true. In other episodes, Lucy wound up in vignettes that had her attempting to play softball, golf and ski, skills at which she was hilariously inept.

Desi might have been gone but Lucy hired *I Love Lucy* sidekick Vivian Vance to play her roommate, Vivian Bagley, who was divorced. (William Frawley from *I Love Lucy* made a cameo appearance in season six.) The two women shared a home with their children: Lucy's son Jerry (Jimmy Garrett) and daughter Chris (Candy Moore) and Viv's son Sherman (Ralph Hart). Lucy also reunited with another long-time pal, Gale Gordon, who had a history with her going back to radio in the 1930s.

Initially Lucy's trust fund was managed by a banker named Mr. Barnsdahl (Charles Lane) but he was replaced after the first season by Gordon, as cantankerous banker Theodore Mooney. The series underwent even more significant revisions after its third season. The location was changed from a fictional town in upstate New York to Los Angeles. Vance asked to be relieved of her regular status and made only occasional appearances over the final three seasons. The children also were written out of the show as Gordon's role was stepped up. With Vance mostly out of the picture, Ann Sothern, was brought in to play an occasional new running mate, pretentious Countess Framboise, who was really a commoner named Rose Harrison. However, the chemistry wasn't the same as it was with Vance and Sothern made contractual demands Lucy chose not to meet, so her appearances were limited to season four and a few in season five.

The Tinseltown location allowed big names from the movie and television business to show up in ridiculous scenarios driven by Lucy's penchant to become starstruck around A-list talent of the era. Trying to help Mr. Mooney land a major depositor for his bank, Lucy turned hick to recruit Tennessee Ernie Ford, playing an unsophisticated but fabulously rich hillbilly music sensation, in an episode capped by a country hoedown. Again returning to what worked, another episode featured Lucy trying to get the notoriously tight Jack Benny to put his money in Mooney's bank. Asked to deliver contracts to John Wayne, with explicit instructions not to bother The Duke, Lucy, of course did exactly the opposite, creating havoc on a movie set.

Milton Berle made several guest appearances. In one, Lucy became convinced Uncle Miltie was cheating on his wife (he wasn't) and tried to stage an intervention. Carol Burnett guested in a two-parter as a flight attendant trainee, who winds up working a flight with the clueless Lucy. Among many other stars that agreed to guest shots on the series were Dean Martin, Ethel Merman, Mickey Rooney, Robert Goulet and Art Linkletter. Lucy opted for another change of pace after the sixth season. Wanting to get her real-life children, Lucie and Desi Jr., involved she scrapped *The Lucy Show* and created a new comedy, *Here's Lucy.*

The Lucy Show was a huge hit with audiences—it was ranked among the top eight series on television for its entire run. Lucille Ball picked up two Emmys as Best Actress in a comedy series (the same number she won for *I Love Lucy*).

---

36. *Night Court*

Broadcast History:

Wednesday	9:30–10:00	January 1984–March 1984	NBC
Thursday	9:30–10:00	May 1984–March 1987	NBC
Wednesday	9:00–9:30	March 1987–June 1987	NBC
Wednesday	9:30–10:00	June 1987–July 1987	NBC
Wednesday	9:00–9:30	July 1987–August 1987	NBC
Thursday	9:30–10:00	August 1987–March 1988	NBC
Friday	9:00–9:30	March 1988–April 1988	NBC
Thursday	9:30–10:00	May 1988–September 1988	NBC
Wednesday	9:00–9:30	October 1988–August 1990	NBC
Friday	9:00–9:30	September 1990–January 1991	NBC
Wednesday	9:00–9:30	January 1991–November 1991	NBC
Wednesday	9:30–10:00	December 1991–May 1992	NBC

| Sunday | 9:30–10:00 | May 1992–June 1992 | NBC |
| Wednesday | 9:30–10:00 | June 1992–July 1992 | NBC |

#20 rated series in 1984–85
#11 rated series in 1985–86
#7 rated series in 1986–87

#7 rated series in 1987–88
#21 rated series in 1988–89
#29 rated series in 1989–90

4 Major Emmy Awards (12 nominations):
No Emmy Awards for Best Series (3 nominations)
No Emmy Awards for Best Actor (3 nominations)
4 Emmy Award for Best Supporting Actor (4 nominations)
No Emmy Awards for Best Supporting Actress (2 nominations

Cast: Harry Anderson; Karen Austin (1984); Selma Diamond (1984–85); Richard Moll; John Larroquette; Paula Kelly (1984); Charlie Robinson; Ellen Foley (1984–85); Markie Post (1985–92); Florence Halop (1985–86); Marsha Warfield (1986–92); S. Marc Jordan (1990–91); Joleen Lutz (1990–92).

Night Court was where you would expect to find the low level miscreants arrested on *Barney Miller*. This was not a coincidence. Creator Reinhold Weege was a former writer/producer on *Barney Miller*. Harry Anderson presided from the bench as Judge Harry Stone, who performed his own brand of legal system triage while dealing with low level offenses such as street walking, jay walking and diners who tried to run out of a restaurant without paying their check. Flippant, irreverent and an amateur magician, Judge Stone's rulings were guided by common sense and compassion and often had little relationship to enforcing laws as intended. Not that he cared. Anderson probably got a leg up on landing the role from guest appearances on *Cheers* as flimflam artist Harry the Hat, who also was adept at magic.

Not coincidentally, *Night Court* benefitted from a *Cheers* lead-in for its first four full seasons when it was a bottom-of-the-hour fixture. At that point, NBC felt the series had put down deep enough roots with the audience to lead off an hour on its own. *Night Court* had little in common with reality and it devolved toward broad farce in its later seasons. Episodes featured a two-part *Phantom of the Opera* spoof, a complaint against Wile E. Coyote for harassing the Road Runner, a ventriloquist's dummy, who freaked out everyone in the courthouse by talking on its own, and a diplomat from an obscure fictional country, which became a nuclear power as payback for allowing the United States to use it as a base for spying on Switzerland.

Anderson, Emmy-nominated three times as best comedic lead actor, had top billing but John Larroquette became the show stealer as prosecutor Dan Fielding. A self-infatuated skirt-chaser, Dan couldn't accept that any woman could find him less than irresistible. Although his character was usually the one viewers would root against and he often uttered mean-spirited putdowns of the down-on-their luck, Dan was not really a bad guy. Every now and then he would do something that would ingratiate himself to the other characters and the audience. The Television Academy loved him, too. Larroquette won a supporting actor Emmy four consecutive years. The streak might have continued if he hadn't chosen to take himself out of the running to give others a chance. His contributions also were a major factor in *Night Court* being nominated three times as outstanding comedy series.

Judge Stone had a succession of love interests until Markie Post became a regular as public defender Christine Sullivan for season three. Post was the first choice from the start but she was committed to *The Fall Guy* during *Night Court*'s first two seasons. However, she did make one guest appearance in season two. Christine and the judge were often in denial about their passionate feelings for one another but they had a difficult time keeping their hands off each other.

Paula Kelly, as public defender Liz Williams, was the first woman to capture Judge Stone's romantic interest but she was let go after season one. She was replaced the following season by Ellen Foley as Billie Young. But once the cancellation of *The Fall Guy* made Post available, she was Harry's main squeeze the rest of the way. Dan Fielding also had an interest in her, as he did for every woman to cross his path, but Christine unmercifully rejected his advances.

The bailiffs in Judge Stone's courtroom also had an atypical turnover rate but this was a matter of tragic necessity. Selma Diamond was in the original cast as Selma Hatchett but the actress died after the second season. Florence Halop took over as Florence Kleiner in the third year but she died after that season. Marsha Warfield next appeared on the scene as caustic, humorless Roz Russell and stayed with the series to the end.

While female bailiffs came and went, Richard Moll was a constant as Bull Shannon, a jolly white giant whose intellectual elevator didn't make it to the top floor. Bull might have appeared to be menacing but he was emotionally fragile and always assumed the best of people. Serving as Judge Stone's confidante and sounding board was his court clerk Mac Robinson, played by Charles Robinson. *Night Court* might have set the television record for most actors who retained either their first name or surname on the show.

37. *The Office*

Broadcast History:

Tuesday	9:30–10:00	March 2005–April 2005	NBC
Tuesday	9:30–10:00	August 2005–December 2005	NBC
Thursday	9:30–10:00	January 2006–July 2006	NBC
Thursday	8:30–9:00	May 2006–May 2007	NBC
Thursday	9:00–9:30	May 2007–May 2013	NBC

3 Major Emmy Awards (27 nominations):
1 Emmy Award for Best Series (6 nominations)
No Emmy Awards for Best Actor (6 nominations)
No Emmy Awards for Best Supporting Actor (3 nominations)
No Emmy Awards for Best Supporting Actress (1 nomination)
1 Emmy Award for Best Writing (7 nominations)
1 Emmy Award for Best Direction (4 nominations)

Cast: Steve Carell; Rainn Wilson; Jenna Fischer; John Krasinski; B.J. Novak; Leslie David Baker; Phyllis Smith; Angela Kinsey; Brian Baumgartner; Oscar Nunez; Kate Flannery; Mindy Kaling; Paul Lieberstein; Creed Bratton; Melora Hardin; David Denman; Ed Helms (2006–13); Rashida Jones (2006–11); Amy Ryan (2007–11); Ellie Kemper (2008–13); Kathy Bates (2009–11); Zach Woods (2009–13); James Spader (2010–12); Timothy Olyphant (2010–11).

The British invasion wasn't exclusive to music. Some of television's biggest hits and most influential series—most notably *All in the Family* and *American Idol*—have come to the United States from the other side of the Atlantic. *The Office* doesn't fit into the stratosphere reached by those two shows but its longevity and award recognition, including the 2006 Emmy for Best Comedy Series, make it worthy of a lofty position in U.S. television history. The premise and pilot episode were direct lifts from the British version starring Ricky Gervais, who had an executive producer's credit in the United States. Gervais also wrote and appeared in a few episodes. Both shows were shot as if they were documentaries on life in a typical office setting. Under the guise of speaking to the filmmaker, characters broke the fourth wall and spoke directly to the audience.

The American edition quickly had to go its own way as, per custom, the British show produced only 14 episodes over three seasons. NBC's *The Office* went on for nine seasons and 201 episodes. Ratings were mediocre in the big picture but this was largely due to *The Office* airing during one of NBC's darkest ratings eras—the network had very few highly rated series with which to surround and boost ratings for other series. While it didn't measure up to hits on rival networks, *The Office* usually was the highest rated series on NBC.

Steve Carell assumed the daunting task of taking over the lead role created by Gervais, which was fresh and familiar to many American viewers because of the BBC America cable network. Gervais's character was named David Brent. Carell's was Michael Scott. Each was the manager of a small paper company, which was being overwhelmed by larger rivals. This made the threat of downsizing and loss of jobs a Sword of Damocles over everyone's head.

The series was set in the Dunder Mifflin branch in Scranton, Pennsylvania. Michael was a well meaning boss, who took a paternalistic interest in the lives of his staff. However, as a result of his practical jokes, hare-brained schemes to bolster business and often unwelcome and clumsy insinuations into their lives, the staff thought of him more as a crazy uncle. Michael would never intentionally hurt anyone's feelings but his tendency to utter insensitive and politically incorrect remarks about someone's race, gender or sexual lifestyle frequently offended and got him into trouble with corporate.

Frequent targets were Stanley Hudson (Leslie David Baker), an African American man who just wanted to be left alone to do his job and resented Michael's condescending attempts at camaraderie, and Oscar Martinez (Oscar Nunez), who, as a gay Hispanic, was in double jeopardy when it came to Michael's ham-fisted attempts to appear prejudice free. An episode dealing with Michael being forced to lead a sensitivity training session and making matters worse might have been one of the series best.

Carell was well known from his work on Jon Stewart's *The Daily Show* on the Comedy Central network. For most of the rest of the regular cast, *The Office* was a career maker. Rainn Wilson, as Dwight Schrute, sycophantic assistant to the regional manager (he preferred to omit "to the" because it made the minor position sound more important), became a breakout character to the extent that an attempt was made to spin him off into his own series but it didn't pass network muster. Dwight had a colorful and bizarre life away from the office. He lived on a family beet farm, which he turned into a bed-and-breakfast, so unappealing that a colleague dubbed it "The Beets Motel."

Dwight's dim-witted cousin Mose (a rarely seen character played by executive producer Michael Schur, Regis Philbin's son-in-law) ran the farm while Dwight was working at Dunder Mifflin. Dwight developed an infatuation, which evolved into a romance, with co-worker Angela Martin (Angela Kinsey), a cold fish. They foolishly thought their relationship was an office secret but it was giggled about by one and all. It ended the first of many times when Dwight mistakenly thought he was doing a good deed by putting Angela's sick pet cat out of his misery. But these two couldn't stay apart, even when she was involved with other men, including co-worker Andy Martin (Ed Helms) and a senator she married.

Another office romance, between Jim Halpert and Pam Beesly, became a viewer favorite and the centerpiece of numerous episodes. Jim (John Krasinski) was an Everyman, whose facial expressions and comments were designed to mirror what viewers were thinking about the latest strange turn of events. Jim also lived to torment the self-important Dwight with pranks and put-downs, that always evoked an extreme reaction, just what Jim was seeking. Pam (Jenna Fisher), the office receptionist and later a graphic artist, was engaged to a warehouse worker, Roy, when Jim came into her life. However, it was inevitable that their flirtations would evolve into something bigger. She eventually broke it off with Roy, and, after a lot of fits and starts, married Jim and had two children.

Michael also had a couple of office romances. A relationship with Jan Levinson (Melora Hardin), a former boss who had been fired, practically broke him. A second fling with Holly Flax (Amy Ryan), a childlike free spirit, became the catalyst for Carell's exit after season seven. It was explained he was moving with her to Colorado, where she had family.

Actors sometimes become writers on long running series. On *The Office*, it worked the other way. B.J. Novak and Mindy Kaling were staff writers, who took on the additional duties of playing Ryan Howard and Kelly Kapoor. Ryan and Kelly also became an office item, although she was more into him than he was into her. Kelly stopped at nothing to land Ryan, including faking a pregnancy. Ryan started as a Dunder Mifflin temp. He got promoted to the home office in New York, where his duties included overseeing the Scranton branch, a source of resentment for many back in Pennsylvania. Ryan fell victim to the temptations of the Big Apple and was fired for cooking the books to cover up his failings. He wound up back in Scranton as a temp again.

Carell's departure opened the way for a succession of new leaders in Scranton. Will Farrell checked in for a brief period, as did James Spader. However, *The Office* didn't have the same zing without Carell at the helm.

38. Three's Company

Broadcast History:

Thursday	9:30–10:00	March 1977–April 1977	ABC
Thursday	9:30–10:00	August 1977–September 1977	ABC
Tuesday	9:00–9:30	September 1977–May 1984	ABC
Tuesday	8:30–9:00	May 1984–September 1984	ABC

#11 rated series in 1976–77   #8 rated series in 1980–81
#3 rated series in 1977–78   #4 rated series in 1981–82
#2 rated series in 1978–79   #6 rated series in 1982–83
#1 rated series in 1979–80

1 Major Emmy Award (3 nominations):
1 Emmy Award for Best Actor (3 nominations)

Cast: John Ritter; Joyce DeWitt; Suzanne Somers (1977–81); Audra Lindley (1977–79); Norman Fell (1977–79); Richard Kline (1978–84); Don Knotts (1979–84); Ann Wedgeworth (1979–80); Jennilee Harrison (1980–82); Priscilla Barnes (1981–84).

Three's Company was television's version of burlesque or carnival sideshows. Indeed, the series was often put down as a pioneer for jiggle-vision. The come-ons were alluring but the reality was one big tease. The adaptation of a British comedy, *Man About the House*, was a series for its time. The basic premise, a straight guy sharing an apartment with two hot women, was risqué in the 1970s and 1980s, but would pass unnoticed in 21st century society. The series was also rife with insensitive gay references, which would not be tolerated in the era of political correctness.

The series saving grace was the deft physical humor and comedic timing of John Ritter. Ritter played Jack Tripper, a would-be chef, who jumped at the chance to leave the YMCA and move into an apartment near Santa Monica Beach with Chrissy Snow and Janet Wood, who needed a third person to chip in on the rent. Suzanne Somers rocketed to fame as Chrissy, a stereotypical dumb blonde, who occasionally would surprise everyone by saying something smart. These rare events surprised even Chrissy. Joyce DeWitt, a brunette, was the sensible roommate, who was overshadowed by Jack's antics and Chrissy's blondness and physical attributes, which were accentuated by tight outfits.

Although both women were attractive, neither had a steady boyfriend, leaving the creative door open to a cavalcade of scenarios driven by sexual innuendo and one of the women jumping to the mistaken conclusion that

Jack, who was recognized by both to be a bit of a horndog, was involved with the other behind her back. It never happened, never even got close.

While Jack and the girls were excited about their new living arrangement, their landlord, Stanley Roper (Norman Fell), was an old fashioned moralist. He was adamant that roommates of the opposite sex were not welcome in his building. To circumvent this objection, Jack and the girls convinced Mr. Roper that Jack was gay, so there would be no sexual hi-jinx. Maintaining this charade often cost Jack relationships with women he was attempting to court. In spite of constant slip-ups and telltale clues, Mr. Roper never figured out that he was being played as a fool. His wife, Helen (Audra Lindley), caught on to Jack's ruse almost immediately but she enjoyed being in on the joke. It was pretty much the only excitement in her life since she confided to the roommates that there was no more hanky-panky between her and Mr. Roper than there was supposed to be between Jack and his roommates.

The often caustic repartee between the Ropers was so well received by the audience that they were spun off into their own series. The void that their departure left was filled by Don Knotts as Ralph Furley, the brother of the owner of the building. Mr. Furley was essentially Barney Fife—the same character Knotts portrayed in *The Andy Griffith Show*—without the uniform and gun. He considered himself smarter than most, while the opposite was true, and fancied himself, without justification, as a ladies man. He also was just as steadfast against co-ed living as Stanley Roper. So Jack had to remain gay, taunted as "Tippytoes" by Mr. Furley, who was sure that if Jack would give him the opportunity, he could convert Jack into being straight. The only other regular male cast member was Richard Kline as Larry Dallas, Jack's closest friend and fellow wingman in pursuit of the opposite sex.

Three's Company was a ratings smash. It was ranked just outside the top 10 (at number 11) in its brief first season and then ranked in the top 10 for the next six seasons—it was the number one series in the 1979–80 season. While the series enjoyed much success with the audience, it did not duplicate that success with critics or the Emmy voters. The series only received three major nominations during its run—all for lead actor, John Ritter.

The series was put into jeopardy after its fifth season when Somers, at the urging of her husband/manager, staged a one-person strike in pursuit of a huge pay bump. The producers and ABC held their ground as well as holding Somers to her contract. They made her appear in every episode in humiliating circumstances, talking to her co-stars by long distance phone call, while under the guise of tending for her sick mother. Her scenes were shot without her co-stars present.

The following season Somers was replaced by Jenilee Harrison as Chrissy's cousin Cindy. In season seven, Priscilla Barnes was added to the cast as aspiring veterinarian Terry Alden. However, the magic of the original threesome was never reestablished. An attempt was made to keep the concept going by spinning off Ritter into a similar series, *Three's a Crowd*, but the magic was gone and so was the new show after one season.

---

39. *The Wonder Years*

Broadcast History:

Tuesday	8:30–9:00	March 1988–April 1988	ABC
Wednesday	9:00–9:30	October 1988–February 1989	ABC
Tuesday	8:30–9:00	February 1989–August 1990	ABC
Wednesday	8:00–8:30	August 1990–August 1991	ABC
Wednesday	8:30–9:00	August 1991–February 1992	ABC
Wednesday	8:00–8:30	March 1992–September 1993	ABC

#10 rated series in 1987–88	#8 rated series in 1989–90
#22 rated series in 1988–89	#30 rated series in 1990–91

4 Major Emmy Awards (20 nominations):
1 Emmy Award for Best Series (4 nominations)
No Emmy Award for Best Actor (2 nominations)
No Emmy Award for Best Guest Actor/Actress (3 nominations)
1 Emmy Award for Best Writing (6 nominations)
2 Emmy Awards for Best Direction (5 nominations)

Cast: Fred Savage; Daniel Stern (voice); Jason Hervey; Olivia d'Abo (1988–92); Alley Mills; Dan Lauria; Josh Saviano; Danica McKellar; Ben Stein (1988–91); Scott Nemes (1991–93); Giovanni Ribisi (1992–93); David Schwimmer (1992).

There is a moment in every boy's life when a switch flips in his head and other body parts and he begins the process of becoming a young man. Kevin Arnold's came on his first day at Robert Kennedy Junior High in suburban Long Island. Kevin (Fred Savage) and his pals were waiting for the school bus when walking down the block came Winnie Cooper, a girl they had seen every day of their lives but never the way they saw her on this day. Overnight, Winnie (Danica McKellar) had crossed the threshold from tomboy playmate to blossoming young lady. Before the pilot ended, Kevin and Winnie had shared their first kiss, as sweet, yet innocent an embrace as was ever depicted on television, as Percy Sledge's "When a Man Loves a Woman" played in the background. Unfortunately it came under tragic circumstances, news of the death of Winnie's brother in Vietnam. It was one of those moments that puts lumps in throats and brings tears to the eyes of viewers, a poignant final act to an almost perfect pilot.

It was received so enthusiastically by television critics, who had it screened for them on a lunch break during one of the semiannual press tours to Hollywood, that ABC announced later in the day that *The Wonder Years* would premiere in the coveted slot after the 1988 Super Bowl. This faith was rewarded. The first season had only a six-episode order but the Television Academy recognized it with a nomination for outstanding comedy series even though many of the episodes were steeped more in drama than humor. After all, it was a half-hour show, so that made it a comedy as far as the Emmys were concerned.

Savage, 13, also became the youngest actor nominated for the top prize in his field. *The Wonder Years* was a new way to tell a coming of age story with the on-again, off-again relationship of Kevin and Winnie at its core. In a twist, adult actor Daniel Stern was heard voicing the adult thoughts of the adolescent Kevin.

Typical teenage angst issues fueled the plots but the turbulent events unfolding outside their small town America cocoon were insinuated into the narratives. Kevin and his school buddies planned a protest against the war in Vietnam. They held their breath with the rest of America as the fate of Apollo 13 and its crew hung in the balance. In a "tear down paradise, put up a parking lot scenario," Kevin and his contemporaries tried to stop the destruction of the park that was their childhood playground—the place where Kevin and Winnie shared that first kiss—to build a mall.

There also were family elements reminiscent of the softer domestic sitcoms of the past. Kevin's older brother Wayne (Jason Hervey) seemed to exist solely to torment and embarrass the baby of the family. The oldest of the Arnold children, Karen (Olivia D'Abo), was into the social rebellion of the era and didn't appear in dozens of episodes. She finally exited the show for good when she broke the news to her family that she was moving to Alaska with her boyfriend (played by a barely recognizable David Schwimmer), a heart-rending turn for her folks.

Kevin's dad Jack Arnold (Dan Lauria), a World War II veteran, worked for a defense firm, NORCOM, at a mundane desk job he hated. This explained his arriving home each night in a cranky mood. Kevin came to understand this after a visit to his father's workplace when he saw what his father had to swallow to bring home a paycheck to support the family. Jack's discontent eventually led him to quit and build his own furniture business, which, when his time came, he passed down to Wayne.

Mom, Norma (Alley Mills), was a homemaker, not far removed from June Cleaver, as the series began. However, she eventually tiptoed into the work force, including a job at Kevin's school, which became an aggravating circumstance for his social standing. Before the curtain came down, Norma had implausibly evolved into a prosperous businesswoman.

Paul Pfeiffer (Josh Savino) was Kevin's closest friend. They remained tight in spite of obstacles such as Paul opting for a different high school and briefly dating Winnie. Kevin and Winnie each had several other romantic interests, almost a new one each season. One of Kevin's was Becky Slater, an aggressive teenager played by Crystal McKellar, Danica's sister, who reportedly was the second choice to play Winnie. Despite the romantic detours, Kevin and Winnie always seemed to rebound back to each other. Even when Winnie went abroad to study art history, they wrote each other regularly.

The exception came in the series finale. Stern's voiceover explained what had happened in the subsequent years to each of the characters. The key reveal came when Stern disclosed that the day Winnie came home from France, Kevin predictably met her at the airport … with his wife and child. This was a heartbreaker for many fans, who had been led to assume throughout the series run that somehow Kevin and Winnie would live happily ever after. *The Wonder Years* failed to enjoy the success in syndication that might have been expected of a show with its popularity and there has been speculation that the unhappy ending might be the cause.

40. *The Jeffersons*

Broadcast History:

Saturday	8:30–9:00	January 1975–August 1975	CBS
Saturday	8:00–8:30	September 1975–October 1976	CBS
Wednesday	8:00–8:30	November 1976–January 1977	CBS
Monday	8:00–8:30	January 1977–August 1977	CBS
Saturday	9:00–9:30	September 1977–March 1978	CBS
Saturday	8:00–8:30	April 1978–May 1978	CBS
Monday	8:00–8:30	June 1978–September 1978	CBS
Wednesday	8:00–8:30	September 1978–January 1979	CBS
Wednesday	9:30–10:00	January 1979–March 1979	CBS
Wednesday	8:00–8:30	March 1979–June 1979	CBS
Sunday	9:30–10:00	June 1979–September 1982	CBS
Sunday	9:00–9:30	September 1982–December 1984	CBS
Tuesday	8:00–8:30	January 1985–March 1985	CBS

Tuesday	8:30–9:00	April 1985–June 1985	CBS
Tuesday	8:00–8:30	June 1985–July 1985	CBS

#4 rated series in 1974–75	#6 rated series in 1980–81
#21 rated series in 1975–76	#3 rated series in 1981–82
#24 rated series in 1976–77	#12 rated series in 1982–83
#8 rated series in 1979–80	#19 rated series in 1983–84

1 Major Emmy Award (13 nominations):
No Emmy Awards for Best Actor (1 nomination)
1 Emmy Award for Best Actress (7 nominations)
No Emmy Awards for Best Supporting Actress (5 nominations)

Cast: Sherman Hensley; Isabel Sanford; Mike Evans (1975, 1979–81); Damon Evans (1975–78); Roxie Roker; Franklin Cover; Berlinda Tolbert; Paul Benedict (1975–81, 1983–85); Zara Cully (1975–78); Ned Wertimer; Marla Gibbs; Ernest Harden, Jr. (1977–79); Jay Hammer (1978–79); Ebonie Smith (1984–85); Danny Wells (1984–85).

The Jeffersons was a spinoff of *All in the Family,* one of the most prolific producers of second- and third-generation series in television history. The Jeffersons were Archie Bunker's next-door neighbors in Queens, New York. Lionel Jefferson was the best friend of Archie's son-in-law, Michael "Meathead" Stivic. As a result, Archie frequently crossed swords with Lionel's feisty father George (Sherman Hemsley), who was every bit the black bigot that Archie was the white bigot. George, a high school dropout, had his life changed forever when he was injured in an auto mishap. The insurance settlement provided the funds for George to open a dry cleaning store. When the business exploded to a string of stores, suddenly wealthy George and his family moved to a luxury apartment in Manhattan's Upper East Side.

Success didn't temper the short-tempered George's attitudes. If anything it sharpened them. George added those less prosperous than him to others he looked down upon. This included but was not exclusive to people of different races, religions and gender. Short of stature and self-esteem, George yearned to climb the social ladder in the same way he had moved up financially. He claimed to be a distant descendent of Thomas Jefferson and Sally Hemmings and courted media attention of any kind at every opportunity, almost always making a fool of himself.

Just as Edith Bunker was a neutralizing factor for Archie, George's wife Louise (Isabel Sanford)—"Weezie" was his affectionate name for her—was George's admirable opposite in tolerance and not judging people. She wasn't as loud as her spouse but she had the ability to cut the full-of-himself George down to size with a sharp retort to one of his tactless outbursts.

The Jeffersons was nominated for seven acting Emmys but Sanford's win in 1981 was the only time one of the regulars was called to the stage to accept the golden statue. For all his insensitivity and bluster, George had a good and generous heart, although he tried to keep it secret from everyone but Weezie. The Jeffersons supported what they thought was a foster child for many years and reacted well when they learned that all wasn't what they were sold. He also wrote sizable checks to a group of maids when the investment he made for them went bust, a reality he never let on to them.

George engaged in verbal battles on a daily basis with the family's housekeeper, Florence Johnston (Marla Gibbs), but when she came up $100 short (a goodly sum in that era) of being able to fulfill a dream, he took a C-note out of his pocket and gave it to her. Gibbs became a breakout character in her own right and was spun off into her own series, *Checking In*. Alas, it was a short-lived ratings bomb and she bounced right back to *The Jeffersons*. When *The Jeffersons* was canceled, Gibbs segued right into another new sitcom, *227*.

George's bigotry was provided ideal foils in his neighbors, Tom (Franklin Cover) and Helen Willis (Roxie Roker), an interracial couple, a rarity on television series in that era. Tom was an affable fellow who did his best to get close to George. Helen was his opposite. She was tight with Weezie but missed no opportunity to antagonize George. George mocked the Willis children as zebras, then had to learn to live with the fact that Lionel was in love with one of the Willis daughters, Jenny (Belinda Tolbert). Mike Evans reprised his role as Lionel in the first season after which the role was taken over by Damon Evans (no relation) for the next three seasons. Mike Evans returned in the role for the 1979–80 and 1980–81 seasons. To George's chagrin, Lionel and Jenny married. They had a daughter of their own, Jessica. However, the marriage ended in divorce and they ceased to be regulars, although they did make occasional guest appearances.

George also had issues with another neighbor, Harry Bentley (Paul Benedict), a Brit who worked at the United Nations. Bentley and George had the common bond of painful back ailments. This didn't keep George from being relentlessly rude, often refusing to allow Bentley to enter the apartment, slamming the door in his face. After 11 seasons, *The Jeffersons* was canceled without warning at the end of the 1985 season, denying the cast and writers the opportunity to create a farewell episode they felt their longevity had earned.

Despite the show being constantly moved around CBS' prime time schedule, *The Jeffersons'* audience seemed to find it regardless of the frequent night and time slot shifts. The series was among the ten highest rated series on television for four seasons, and ranked among the top 25 for eight of its 11 seasons.

41. *Sanford and Son*

Broadcast History:

Friday   8:00–8:30   January 1972–September 1977   NBC

#6 rated series in 1971–72   #2 rated series in 1974–75
#2 rated series in 1972–73   #7 rated series in 1975–76
#3 rated series in 1973–74   #27 rated series in 1976–77

No Major Emmy Awards (6 nominations):
No Emmy Awards for Best Series (3 nominations)
No Emmy Awards for Best Actor (3 nominations)

Cast: Redd Foxx; Demond Wilson; Slappy White (1972); Don Bexley; Noam Pitlik (1972); Hal Williams (1972–76); Beah Richards (1972); Gregory Sierra (1972–75); Nathaniel Taylor; LaWanda Page (1973–77); Whitman Mayo (1973–77); Lynn Hamilton; Howard Platt (1972–76); Pat Morita (1974–75); Marlene Clark (1976–77); Raymond Allen (1976–77); Edward Crawford (1976–77).

Sanford and Son wasn't among the many spinoffs from *All in the Family* but it owed its existence to Archie Bunker as much as any of *All in the Family's* offspring. One year after *All in the Family* hit the Nielsen mother lode for CBS, NBC responded with Redd Foxx as a black counterpart to Archie's WASP bigotry. Also like *All in the Family*, *Sanford and Son* was an adaptation of a British comedy, *Steptoe and Son*, from prolific hit-maker Norman Lear.

Foxx, known for his "dirty" standup comedy act and raunchy party records, made his television debut as Fred Sanford, the owner of a junkyard in Los Angeles' South Central neighborhood. The junkyard did less commerce than a Victoria's Secret in Saudi Arabia. Like Archie, Fred was cantankerous and mouthy. He had nothing good to say about anyone who wasn't like him. Much of the dialog that passed muster as a result of America's embrace of Archie would be redlined by the network Standards & Practices office in the 21st century era of political correctness. Among other offenses, Fred made frequent use of the "N" word. It wasn't only the word, it was the context. Protesting a traffic citation from a white policeman, Fred pleaded to the judge that he and other blacks were being discriminated against. "Look around this courtroom. There are enough 'n------s' to make a Tarzan movie."

Demond Wilson co-starred as widower Fred's only child Lamont, who served the same purpose as Archie's son-in-law Michael, "the Meathead," a neutralizing force to Fred's insensitivity and intolerance. Lamont disregarded ethnicity in accepting other people. To the chagrin of Fred, a Puerto Rican neighbor, Julio Fuentes (Gregory Sierra), became one of Lamont's closest friends. Even more disconcerting to Fred, Lamont became engaged in a serious romantic relationship with Julio's sister Marie.

Fred and Lamont battled verbally like husband and wife. Lamont chafed that Fred relentlessly labeled him a "big dummy" and treated him like a child. "Don't tell me what to do, I'm a grownup," he would complain. However, like spouses, it was obvious there was a lot of love between them. They also shared a yearning to improve their lots in life by getting out of the junk business. However, their means to this end usually involved playing fast and loose with ethics and the law and were unfailingly thwarted.

Fred, fearing he might be left alone, did his best to serve as an impediment to any attempt by Lamont to find a steady girlfriend. Lamont reciprocated by trying to come between Fred and his girlfriend, a nurse named Donna Harris (Lynn Hamilton), who he feared would take the place of his late mother. Eventually Lamont came around and accepted Donna.

Lamont had a quick temper and often warned he was going to move out. Every now and then he made good on this threat. But no matter how angry he got, he always came back and forgave his father. When things got really intense, Fred would fall back on his ailment for all occasions, clutching his supposedly ailing heart and crying out, "This is the big one. I'm coming to join you, Elizabeth" (his deceased wife). In a sadly ironic turn of events, Foxx did die suddenly of a heart attack in 1991 while performing in a CBS comedy, *The Royal Family.*

Fred's arguments with Lamont were tame compared to his jousts with Aunt Esther (Lawanda Page), the Bible-quoting sister of Fred's late wife who joined the series in the second season. She called him "a heathen," and "a stain on the family." He called her Esther Kong and said she made King Kong look like John Boy (of *The Waltons*). Fred warned that if she took her clothes off for a physical examination she would be arrested for causing blindness. Heading to Hawaii for a vacation, Fred set up Esther by offering to bring home a grass skirt for her. "What would I do with a grass skirt?" she asked, falling into his trap. "Graze," Fred retorted.

Fred's closest contemporary friend was Grady Wilson (Whitman Mayo), a slow on the uptake quiet contrast to Fred's boisterousness. Fred's halo effect on Grady encouraged NBC to attempt a spinoff (*Grady*), which failed to catch on. Grady also took center stage with Lamont when Foxx staged a salary strike during the 1973–74 season, skipping several episodes. His absence was explained as Fred being on a trip to St. Louis. Grady and Lamont tried to service the ruse by talking with him on the phone. But without Foxx, the magic was gone. NBC capitulated and Foxx returned for three more seasons, two in Nielsen's Top 10. Four years after *Sanford and Son* left NBC, Foxx attempted a revival without Wilson but its time had come and passed.

Sanford and Son was a ratings smash, having placed among the ten highest rated series on television for its first five seasons. However, the Emmy voters weren't as enamored. While the series and Redd Foxx were each nominated three times, *Sanford and Son* never won a major Emmy award during its six-year run.

42. *Maude*

Broadcast History:

Tuesday	8:00–8:30	September 1972–September 1974	CBS
Monday	9:00–9:30	September 1974–September 1975	CBS
Monday	9:30–10:00	September 1975–September 1976	CBS
Monday	9:00–9:30	September 1976–September 1977	CBS
Monday	9:30–10:00	September 1977–November 1977	CBS
Monday	9:00–9:30	December 1977–January 1978	CBS
Saturday	9:30–10:00	January 1978–April 1978	CBS

#4 rated series in 1972–73   #9 rated series in 1974–75
#6 rated series in 1973–74   #4 rated series in 1975–76

1 Major Emmy Award (10 nominations):
No Emmy Awards for Best Series (2 nominations)
1 Emmy Award for Best Actress (5 nominations)
No Emmy Awards for Best Writing (1 nomination)
No Emmy Awards for Best Direction (2 nominations)

Cast: Beatrice Arthur; Bill Macy; Adrienne Barbeau; Brian Morrison (1972–77); Kraig Metzinger (1977–78); Conrad Bain; Rue McClanahan; Esther Rolle (1972–74); John Amos (1973–74); Fred Grandy (1973–74); Hermoine Baddeley (1975–77); Marlene Warfield (1977–78).

Maude was Edith Bunker's cousin and Archie Bunker's nemesis. It took only two guest shots by Beatrice Arthur as Maude Findlay on *All in the Family* for prolific hit-maker Norman Lear to realize the character was comedy gold. Maude was unlike any female comedic lead America had ever seen. She was loud, abrasive, socially active, partisan, often mean-spirited and intolerant of anyone who didn't share her viewpoint of tolerance. In essence, she was Archie Bunker on the left. Her pet phrase whenever someone disagreed with her was, "God will get you for that."

All in the Family might have pioneered injecting topical political issues into situation comedy but Lear's first spinoff from the landmark series took it to the next level. Nothing was off limits, no matter how uncomfortable it might have made the audience and the network. A two-part episode pre–*Roe v. Wade* in which Maude, age 47, learned she was pregnant and decided to abort the child, stirred nationwide protests and some station boycotts. *Maude* also tackled gay rights before it became a prominent cause. Other hot button issues rarely discussed in television comedies included adultery, tranquilizer addiction, alcoholism, emotional breakdowns, menopause and sexual assault. A November sweeps episode in season four was a one-woman tour-de-force for Arthur, who poured out her heart to her analyst. Rare were the episodes that didn't involve something heavy.

Maude was not an easy person to get along with. Walter Findlay (Bill Macy) was her fourth husband, a mild mannered guy, who nevertheless was able to stand up to his more forceful spouse. The couple lived in Tuckahoe, New York, a bedroom community just north of the Bronx and about 30 miles from the Bunkers in Queens. Maude put aside her social activism from time to time to dabble in working outside the home but Walter, who owned an appliance store, was the couple's primary source of income. When his business hit the skids, he overdosed on sleeping pills but survived.

Because of Maude's overbearing ways, she went through housekeepers as much as she did husbands. Anxious to demonstrate how strongly she was down for the civil rights cause, Maude was frequently patronizing to Florida Evans (Esther Rolle), a strong black woman who didn't back down from Maude. This made Florida an audience favorite and she was spun off into her own domestic comedy, *Good Times*. Her successor, Nell Naugatuck (Hermione Baddeley), a heavy drinker, failed to click in the same way and was written out, ostensibly to return to her native British Isles. She was replaced for the final season with Victoria Butterfield (Marlene Warfield).

Maude's daughter Carol Traynor (Adrienne Barbeau) was a strident feminist like her mother and also had problems maintaining relationships. Twice divorced in her twenties, she was the single parent of a son, Phillip (Brian Morrison), age 9 when the series started. Undeterred, Carol had a succession of lovers and was a cougar before that term was coined to represent an older woman courting a younger mate. Only one of Carol's suitors, Chris (Fred Grandy), stuck around for long.

Arthur and Vivian Harmon were the Findlays' closest friends. Arthur, a service buddy of Walter, was a widower and Vivian, a recent divorcee, was a college friend of Maude. The Findlays introduced them and they married during the second season. Arthur (Conrad Bain) served as a surrogate for Archie, an opinionated but well-spoken conservative, whose politics were a wedge issue between him and Maude. Vivian (Rue McClanahan) was apolitical and went along to get along.

Maude was solidly entrenched in Nielsen's Top 10 shows for its first four seasons but dropped precipitously in seasons five and six. In an effort to resuscitate the series, a change in approach was adopted for season six. Maude was appointed to a seat in Congress, creating a necessity for her and Walter to relocate to Washington. This was justification to jettison the entire supporting cast. Almost a decade later, Arthur and McClanahan would reunite on *The Golden Girls*. Arthur was not satisfied with the new direction of the show and decided she had had enough. Without Arthur, there could be no *Maude*, so the show was canceled.

43. *Laverne & Shirley*

Broadcast History:

Tuesday	8:30–9:00	January 1976–July 1979	ABC
Thursday	8:00–8:30	August 1979–December 1979	ABC
Monday	8:00–8:30	December 1979–February 1980	ABC
Tuesday	8:30–9:00	February 1980–May 1983	ABC

#3 rated series in 1975–76   #21 rated series in 1980–81
#2 rated series in 1976–77   #20 rated series in 1981–82
#1 rated series in 1977–78   #25 rated series in 1982–83
#1 rated series in 1978–79

No Major Emmy Awards (No nominations)

Cast: Penny Marshall; Cindy Williams (1976–82); Eddie Mekka; Phil Foster; David L. Lander; Michael McKean; Betty Garrett (1976–81); Carole Ita White (1976–77); Ed Marinaro (1980–81); Leslie Easterbrook (1980–83).

Any discussion of *Laverne & Shirley* has to begin with the opening two words of the series' signature theme, because they are what come to mind first in reminiscences of the *Happy Days* spinoff. By one standard *Laverne & Shirley* is the most successful spinoff in history. It is one of only two second-generation comedies to top the Nielsen season-long rankings. *The Andy Griffith*

Show did it once. *Laverne & Shirley* was the number one rated show twice. Artistically, the lightweight exploits of the two young women would rarely be mentioned as among the finest of the genre. In eight seasons on the air, it pulled only one minor Emmy nomination, for costume design. Its success was largely the product of being the right comedy in the right place at the right time. *Happy Days* capitalized on the nostalgic appeal of *American Graffiti*, and *Laverne & Shirley* piggybacked on the success of *Happy Days*.

The girls were introduced as friends of The Fonz on an episode of *Happy Days*. When the spinoff premiered, it was in the half-hour time slot following *Happy Days*. The logical explanation for the two series swapping numbers one and two in the Nielsen rankings by *Laverne & Shirley*'s second season is the number of homes watching television is higher at 8:30 than 8:00 p.m. and there was no reason for viewers already in place for *Happy Days* to stray. (This was in the three-network era before cable began to become a programming presence.)

Laverne DeFazio (Penny Marshall) and Shirley Feeney (Cindy Williams) were blue collar goofballs working in a dead end job on the assembly line of a Milwaukee brewery. They were hopeless romantics but hopeless when it came to actual romance. In one off-the-wall episode, they thought they had met a couple of Mr. Rights in a park only to be busted for solicitation. Laverne was gregarious and pessimistic and retained the sharp accent of her native Brooklyn. Her trademark was a script letter "L" on almost every top in her wardrobe. Shirley was quieter and loved animals. She adopted the optimistic ditty "High Hopes" as her anthem. They shared a basement level apartment near the brewery for the first five seasons then moved to California when they were laid off at the brewery.

Their upstairs neighbors, Lenny and Squiggy (another L&S), were a couple of ne'er-do-wells with good hearts and big dreams, which always went unfulfilled because they couldn't do anything right. Lenny Kosnowski (Michael McKean) boasted that he was 89th in line to the Polish throne (which no longer existed). Andrew "Squiggy" Squigman (David L. Lander) adopted the greased hair and motorcycle jacket look of tough guys but it was all for effect; he was a timid pushover. The guys might have had crushes on the girls but these were never reciprocated.

Carmine "The Big Ragu" Ragusa (Eddie Mekka) was Shirley's high school sweetheart and they still had a soft spot for each other but pretty much had moved on to others (at least in Carmine's case). Carmine, a former boxer, operated a dance studio in Milwaukee and trailed the girls to Hollywood in search of show business fame and fortune. Laverne's father Frank (Phil Foster) owned a nearby bowling alley, which was a hangout for the regulars. He was fiercely protective of his daughter and, by extension, Shirley. He also moved to California and opened another hangout, Cowboy Bill's. He courted and eventually married oft-wed Edna Babish (Betty Garrett). She wound up leaving Frank, too, when Garrett opted out of the series for another opportunity.

Typical episodes bordered on the farcical: The girls becoming 10 cents-a-dance partners; Shirley obsessing to a ridiculous extent over her pet canary; a hypnotist causing Laverne to behave like a chicken; Squiggy being mistaken for a defecting Russian ballet dancer and Laverne becoming convinced she had a curse on her for discarding a chain letter. Occasionally, heavier story lines were attempted and they worked better than might be expected from such a slight production. Unwanted pregnancies were explored in an episode in which Laverne feared she might have been pregnant even though she had no memory of doing what it takes, which the girls dubbed "Fo-de-oh-doh." In another show, the girls took a neighbor's special needs daughter under their wing. Shirley got a lesson in alcoholism when her hard-drinking brother Bobby came for a visit.

The most poignant episode of the series arguably was one in which Laverne had trouble coping with the death of a serious boyfriend, a fireman (played by a pre–*Cheers* Ted Danson) killed in the line of duty. When Shirley finally found the guy who would be her spouse it was a matter of writing room expediency. Williams, pregnant in real life, got into a dispute with the producers and negotiated her way out of the series at the start of season eight. Art imitated life as Shirley married a soldier named Walter Meany, which made her Shirley Feeny Meany, and became pregnant. The explanation for her leaving the show was she was moving to join her husband. This proved to be the beginning of the end for the series.

44. *Curb Your Enthusiasm*

Broadcast History:

Sunday	10:00–10:30	October 2000–December 2000	HBO
Sunday	10:30–11:00	September 2001–November 2001	HBO
Sunday	10:00–10:30	September 2002–November 2002	HBO
Sunday	9:30–10:00	January 2004–March 2004	HBO
Sunday	10:00–10:30	September 2005–December 2005	HBO
Sunday	10:00–10:30	September 2007–November 2007	HBO
Sunday	10:00–10:30	September 2009–November 2009	HBO
Sunday	10:00–10:30	July 2011–September 2011	HBO

1 Major Emmy Award (25 nominations):
No Emmy Awards for Best Series (7 nominations)
No Emmy Awards for Best Actor (5 nominations)
No Emmy Awards for Best Supporting Actress (2 nominations)
No Emmy Awards for Best Guest Actor/Actress (2 nomination)
1 Emmy Award for Best Direction (9 nominations)

Cast: Larry David; Cheryl Hines; Jeff Garlin; Susie Essman; Richard Lewis; Bob Einstein; Shelly Berman.

Larry David gave away one of the great characters in sitcom history. The co-creator of *Seinfeld* fashioned George Costanza after himself. Unlike his creative partner Jerry Seinfeld, who chose to play himself in the landmark series, David opted to remain behind the scenes and handed off the part to Jason Alexander. David essentially retook the character in *Curb Your Enthusiasm*.

David kept his own identity as a selfish narcissist. He acknowledged the riches Seinfeld had brought. Instead of a cramped Manhattan apartment, David lived in a Beverly Hills mansion. In contrast to the star struck George, Larry hobnobbed with a constellation of stars. He also had a beautiful, smart wife, Cheryl (Cheryl Hines). However, like his alter ego, he remained miserly and insensitive. When his friend Marty Funkhouser's father died, Larry asked the grieving Marty (Bob Einstein) what he intended to do with the deceased's prize Dodgers tickets. In another sorry faux pas, Larry was caught pilfering flowers from the roadside memorial marking the location where Marty's wheelchair bound mother was struck and killed by a car. At a Seder dinner, Larry unjustly accused a prominent surgeon of stealing his *New York Times*.

Jeff Garlin had a featured role as Larry's uncouth best friend and agent Jeff, who once snuck away from a dinner party and masturbated on the bed covers in Larry's guest bedroom. Jeff's wife Susie (Susie Essman) was a shrill, foul-mouthed woman, who blamed Larry for many of her husband's outrages. She seemed incapable of addressing Larry without throwing in the F-word.

David crafted *Curb Your Enthusiasm* in a unique way. He drew up a story outline for each episode then asked the performers to improvise how they felt their characters would react to each situation. David's reputation and standing in Hollywood enabled him to attract an array of A-list stars to appear, the majority playing slightly fictionalized versions of themselves. Ted Danson and his wife Mary Steenburgen were semi-regulars. In one story arc, they and Larry became partners in a top-end restaurant. True to form, Larry sabotaged the place when he got into a beef with the chef on the eve of the opening.

Richard Lewis appeared often as himself. In season five he revealed to

Larry that he was desperately in need of a kidney transplant. It turned out Larry was a match, so he promised Lewis that if he couldn't find anyone else, he would donate a kidney. Larry spent the rest of the season searching for another donor to get him off the hook. Mel Brooks also appeared as himself, recruiting Larry to star in a Broadway revival of *The Producers*. This took the show from its Hollywood base to New York. U.S. Senator Barbara Boxer had a cameo as herself in an episode in which Larry badgered her to do something about his dry cleaner losing a favorite shirt.

The entire cast of *Seinfeld*, including some prominent recurring characters, reassembled in a four-episode arc in what all said was as close to a reunion of the series as will ever be staged. Critics and fans of *Seinfeld* felt that these episodes served as a more fitting ending to *Seinfeld* than its original two-part finale.

Others who made appearances included Dustin Hoffman, Martin Scorsese, Ricky Gervais, Martin Short, Hugh Hefner and Shaquille O'Neill. In one episode, Larry nearly ended the career of Shaq when the basketball giant tripped over Larry's feet at courtside for a Lakers game. As with *Seinfeld*, episodes tended to be based on small scenarios that complicate everyday life. They usually turned into theater of the absurd. Mistaking a friend's request to bring a "Survivor" to a social event, Larry invited a Holocaust survivor. His friend's guest turned out to be Colby Donaldson, who was on the reality television show *Survivor*.

In another classic episode, hoping to beat traffic and get to a Dodgers game on time, he picked up a sidewalk prostitute to ride alongside him so he could use the high occupancy vehicle lane. She turned out to be easier to get into the car than out of his life. This episode inadvertently cleared a man of capital murder. The suspect used footage from the show, taken at an actual Dodgers game, to show he was there, miles away from the crime scene.

Social activists, Larry and Cheryl invited a family from Louisiana, rendered homeless by Hurricane Katrina, to live with them. The family took full advantage and then some. The fact that Cheryl was more dedicated to progressive causes caused a rift in the marriage, with Cheryl leaving Larry. This mirrored real life, where Larry's wife, an environmental warrior, left him.

The last 10-episode (never more, never less) season of *Curb* aired on HBO in 2011. However, the door was left open for the series to return. HBO executives said they had an open-ended understanding with David. They would call and ask if he was ready to do another season. He would usually say, "Let me think about it." When he was ready, he would call back. HBO anxiously awaited those calls.

45. *Newhart*

Broadcast History:

Monday	9:30–10:00	October 1982–February 1983	CBS
Sunday	9:30–10:00	March 1983–April 1983	CBS
Sunday	8:30–9:00	April 1983–May 1983	CBS
Sunday	9:30–10:00	June 1983–August 1983	CBS
Monday	9:30–10:00	August 1983–September 1986	CBS
Monday	9:00–9:30	September 1986–August 1988	CBS
Monday	8:00–8:30	August 1988–March 1989	CBS
Monday	10:00–10:30	March 1989–August 1989	CBS
Monday	10:30–11:00	August 1989–October 1989	CBS
Monday	10:00–10:30	November 1989–April 1990	CBS
Monday	8:30–9:00	April 1990–May 1990	CBS
Monday	10:00–10:30	May 1990–July 1990	CBS
Friday	9:00–9:30	July 1990–August 1990	CBS

#12 rated series in 1982–83　　#16 rated series in 1985–86
#23 rated series in 1983–84　　#12 rated series in 1986–87
#16 rated series in 1984–85　　#25 rated series in 1987–88

No Major Emmy Awards (21 nominations):
No Emmy Awards for Best Series (2 nominations)
No Emmy Awards for Best Actor (3 nominations)
No Emmy Awards for Best Supporting Actor (6 nominations)
No Emmy Awards for Best Supporting Actress (7 nominations)
No Emmy Awards for Best Guest Acting (1 nomination)
No Emmy Awards for Best Writing (2 nominations)

Cast: Bob Newhart; Mary Frann; Steven Kampmann (1982–84); Tom Poston; Jennifer Holmes (1982–83); Julia Duffy (1983–90); William Sanderson; Tony Papenfuss; John Volstad; Rebecca York (1984); Peter Scolari (1984–90); Lee Wilkof (1984–85); Todd Sussman (1985–89).

Newhart is best approached by working backward. The series finale in 1990 is widely viewed as the finest wrap up in the history of television. Indeed, *Entertainment Weekly* put it atop its list of the 20 Best television series finales ever. Bob Newhart was a beloved performer for his standup routines, comedy albums and, most of all, his six seasons on the eponymous *The Bob Newhart Show.* The final scene of *Newhart* had him in bed with his *Bob Newhart Show* wife, played by Suzanne Pleshette. The studio audience roared its approval as it began to realize what was happening. Recovering from a blow to the head by a golf ball, Newhart recounts how he had this strange dream. He was a guy named Dick Loudon, who owned an inn in Vermont, which attracted an array of really strange characters.

Really strange is understatement, which played perfectly into the low-key reactive style of the star. Dick Loudon was a New York–based author of "How To..." books. Able to do his writing anywhere and wanting a simpler life, he and his wife Joanna (Mary Frann) bought a 200-plus-year-old hotel, the Stratford Inn, in rural Vermont. The hotel rarely had guests but somehow this never was an issue.

Along with the hotel, came handyman George Utley (Tom Poston), whose family had been maintaining the Stratford going back a couple of centuries. George was a little slow on the draw but otherwise a salt of the earth type. He knew everyone in the area and didn't have a judgmental bone in his body. He didn't see anything odd about anyone, no matter how they presented themselves.

No one was more peculiar than a trio of woodsmen, Larry, Darryl and Darryl. Larry introduced them at every entrance with "Hi, I'm Larry. This is my brother Darryl and this is my other brother Darryl." The two Darryls (Tony Papenfuss and John Volstad) never uttered a sound until the final episode. However, apparently through ESP, Larry (William Sanderson) could interpret at length what they were thinking. They would merely nod their assent to his take on their thoughts. Some of Larry's tales were too tall to be plausible but an uncanny number turned out to be fact. Among them was the boast that Johnny Carson paid their utility bills. With everyone disbelieving this, Carson made a guest appearance to confirm Larry's claim.

The brothers owned the adjoining Minuteman Café, a place unlikely to ever merit a mention—unless it was a warning—in Zagat's. Road kill was regarded as a delicacy and dirty dishes were cleaned by wiping them on the shirt of one of the guys. Don't want powdered sugar on your donut? No problem. Larry or one of the Darryls would blow it off. The brothers, whose last name was not revealed, bought the restaurant in year three and became regulars after sporadic appearances during the first two seasons.

The previous owner, Kirk Devane (Steven Kampmann), was a compulsive liar, who would tell a lie, then immediately apologize and acknowledge he was not telling the truth. He left the series after two seasons, written out with the explanation that he married a woman who played a clown, and they moved away. The Stratford's first housekeeper for the Loudons, Leslie Vanderkellen (Jennifer Holmes), was a rich, snooty student at nearby Dartmouth College. She took the job, she said, to find out what it was like to be an average person. She must have been a quick learner, since she left after one season.

Leslie's departure opened the door for her sister Stephanie (Julia Duffy) to succeed her. Not that Stephanie did anything more than show up. Stephanie considered herself a flawless flower. The thought of breaking a sweat or even breaking a nail was not something she even wanted to ponder. Stephanie found a mate, Michael Harris (Peter Scolari), who shared her assessment of herself. Michael doted on Stephanie's every whim and came through on cue whenever she needed reassurance about how irresistible she was. Lost in their own world, Stephanie and Michael giggled their days away.

Michael's entrée was as the producer of a television program, *Vermont Today*, which the town's station cajoled Dick to host. In their part of Vermont, Dick qualified as a celebrity. Michael was in charge of lining up guests and he came through with a wide array of oddballs, including off-the-wall mayor Chester Wanamaker (William Lanteau) and man-hungry librarian Prudence Goddard (Kathy Kinney). But he also landed the likes of Senator and presidential candidate George McGovern and newsman turned cult favorite Edwin Newman.

Todd Sussman was a frequent presence as self important town constable, Officer Shifflett, who carried himself like Dirty Harry even though no one took him seriously. When Michael hit a dry spell producing guests, he got fired and had to take some menial jobs. Without what Stephanie considered a prestigious position, she told Michael she couldn't be his girlfriend anymore. When Michael landed back on his feet, she reconsidered. They got married and had a daughter.

The town went through a drastic transition when a Japanese company made the citizens an offer they couldn't refuse, paying each of them a fortune for their property in order to build a golf course. Everyone but Dick jumped at the life-changing offer. Undaunted, the foreign entrepreneurs built the country club around the Stratford. Dick stepped outside one day and was struck in the head and knocked unconscious by an errant golf ball. Next thing he knew, he was awakening from one of the strangest and most delightfully entertaining dreams in the history of television.

Newhart was popular with the audience, having ranked among the 25 highest rated series for each of its first six seasons. The series was also a darling of the Emmy voters, receiving 21 major nominations, while failing to win even once.

46. *Kate & Allie*

Broadcast History:

Monday	9:30–10:00	March 1984–September 1986	CBS
Monday	8:00–8:30	September 1986–September 1987	CBS
Monday	8:30–9:00	September 1987–November 1987	CBS
Monday	8:00–8:30	December 1987–June 1988	CBS
Saturday	8:00–8:30	July 1988–August 1988	CBS
Monday	9:00–9:30	August 1988–September 1988	CBS
Monday	8:30–9:00	December 1988–March 1989	CBS
Monday	10:30–11:00	March 1989–June 1989	CBS
Monday	8:00–8:30	June 1989–September 1989	

#8 rated series in 1983–84   #14 rated series in 1985–86
#17 rated series in 1984–85   #19 rated series in 1986–87

3 Major Emmy Awards (11 nominations):
No Emmy Awards for Best Program (3 nominations)
2 Emmy Awards for Best Actress (5 nominations)
1 Emmy Award for Best Directing (3 nominations)

Cast: Susan Saint James; Jane Curtin; Ari Meyers (1984–88); Frederick Koehler; Allison Smith; Paul Hecht (1984–86); Gregory Salata (1984–85, 1987–88); Sam Freed (1987–89); Peter Onorati (1988–89).

Kate and Allie put a twist on blended families. As the title suggests, the heads of this household and the only adults were two women, long-time friends. After each became divorced they decided to share expenses by moving with their children into a Manhattan apartment. This was a bold departure for television in the 1980s. Divorce was still a touchy subject for lead series characters. The fact that the protagonists were women raised additional issues. A primary one was the concern by CBS that the audience might wonder whether Kate and Allie were in a lesbian relationship. In the new millennium this might be considered an inspired idea for a television series. In the third quarter of the 20th century, it was regarded as a potential turnoff to viewers and anathema to sponsors. To combat this, each episode showed the two mothers with children from previous marriages retreating to separate bedrooms.

Although they carried emotional scars from their failed marriages, they frequently expressed an interest in the opposite sex, sometimes the same man, and frequently dated. However, when Susan Saint James, married in real life to NBC sports executive Dick Ebersol, became pregnant in season four, her condition was not written into the show and her baby bump was hidden from the audience by various creative devices. One of them was a flashback episode to how the two women met and became friends.

CBS took the bold creative risk for this series because of the individual familiarity and popularity of the two leads. Saint James, who played Kate McArdle, sparkled as the spunky spouse in *McMillan and Wife*. (Most of the public was unaware at the time that her television husband, hunky Rock Hudson, was gay.) Jane Curtin, who played Allie Lowell, was part of the original cast of *Saturday Night Live*. She and Dan Aykroyd succeeded Chevy Chase as co-anchors of the "Weekend Update" segment. Aykroyd made Curtin a sympathetic figure by regularly flaunting his self assessed superior sophistication and knowledge with "Jane, you ignorant slut..."

Curtin won a couple of Emmys as Allie. The series, which cracked Nielsen's Top 20 for each of its first four seasons—season one consisted of only six episodes—was Emmy-nominated three times, as was Saint James. However, neither got to take home a single golden trophy.

Kate, who had feminist leanings, worked outside the home as a travel agent. Allie was a traditional stay-at-home mom and homemaker. By the fifth season, Kate had left her job and joined with Allie in establishing a catering business. Allie had two children, Chip (Frederick Koehler) and Jennie (Allison Smith). Kate had only a daughter, Emma (Ari Myers). The kids were usually only peripherally involved in story lines. When they became the focus of an episode, such as Jenny and Emma competing for the same role in a school play or, as the kids grew older, dealing with teen sex, it was viewed through the prism of how it impacted the lives of the mothers.

Kate and Allie had occasional issues of their own. Allie resented Kate's advice that she was making a mistake in trying to reignite the flame with her former husband Charles (Paul Hecht) during a down period in his new relationship. Allie also became miffed over Kate's re-telling to friends of how Allie had been fired from a part-time job. At one tense point in their friendship, they resorted to couples counseling to put their relationship back on track. However, most of the time, the two were there for each other.

Allie gradually became more self assured and assertive. Feeling unappreciated by Kate and the kids for all she did around the house she went on strike. She also decided to go to college and successfully earned a degree. When she felt Charles and his new wife Claire (Wendie Malick) weren't giving Chip and Jennie the attention they deserved, she went to their home and challenged them to do the right thing.

Before she and Kate embarked on their catering business, she went to work for a struggling public television station, which was absurdly misman-aged. At the end of season five, Allie became engaged to a former football player turned sportscaster, Bob Barsky, who she met at a supermarket in season four. Sam Freed, who played Bob, had appeared twice earlier in the show as different characters. Allie and Bob married and moved into their own place at the start of season six. In an attempt to keep the concept intact, Bob's job put him on the road so often that Kate moved in with Allie to keep her company. This contrivance failed to strike a chord with the audience. Ratings plunged and CBS canceled the series at season's end.

47. *Malcolm in the Middle*

Broadcast History:

Sunday	8:30–9:00	January 2000–June 2002	FOX
Sunday	9:00–9:30	July 2002–September 2002	FOX
Sunday	9:30–10:00	July 2002–September 2002	FOX
Sunday	9:00–9:30	November 2002–July 2004	FOX
Sunday	7:30–8:00	July 2004–May 2005	FOX
Sunday	7:00–7:30	June 2005–September 2005	FOX
Friday	8:30–9:00	September 2005–January 2006	FOX
Sunday	7:00–7:30	January 2006–August 2006	FOX

#18 rated series in 1999–2000
#22 rated series in 2000–01
#25 rated series in 2001–02

6 Major Emmy Awards (27 nominations):
No Emmy Awards for Best Program (1 nomination)
No Emmy Awards for Best Actor (1 nomination)
No Emmy Awards for Best Actress (7 nominations)
No Emmy Awards for Best Supporting Actor (3 nominations)
2 Emmy Award for Best Guest Actor/Actress (9 nominations)
2 Emmy Awards for Best Writing (2 nominations)
2 Emmy Awards for Best Directing (4 nominations)

Cast: Jane Kaczmarek; Bryan Cranston; Frankie Muniz; Christopher Kennedy Masterson; Justin Berfield; Erik Per Sullivan; Craig Lamar Traylor; Daniel von Bargen (2000–01); Karim Prince (2000); Eric Nenninger (2000–02); Kasan Butcher (2000–01); Catherine Lloyd Burns (2000); Sandy Ward (2001–02); John Ennis (2002); Kenneth Mars (2002–04); Cloris Leachman (2003–06); James Rodriguez (2005–06); Lukas Rodriguez (2005–06).

Life often isn't pretty for a middle child. It can get really ugly when you're a middle child with an IQ higher than the rest of your dysfunctional family combined. Such was the plight of the title character of *Malcolm in the Middle*. Frankie Muniz brought an ideal mix of appreciation for his gift of genius and typical adolescent angst to the role of Malcolm Wilkerson (the family surname was mentioned only in the pilot).

Muniz courted approval and sympathy from the audience by breaking down the fourth wall and speaking directly to viewers about his predicament du jour. A continuing annoyance for the amazingly well rounded youngster was the fact that his superior intelligence caused him to be sentenced to a class for similarly gifted students, every one of whom was a nerd. Schoolmates dubbed this group the Krelboynes, a derogatory reference to Seymour Krelboyne, a geeky character from the Broadway play *Little Shop of Horrors*.

Malcolm defied the laws of genetics. His parents, Lois and Hal, were dumb and dumber, characters superlatively portrayed by Jane Kaczmarek and Bryan Cranston. Kaczmarek was nominated as outstanding lead actress in a comedy all seven seasons the series was on the air. Cranston was nominated three times as best supporting actor. (He would go on to win four best actor drama Emmys from six nominations for acclaimed drama series *Breaking Bad*.)

Interestingly, given the series title and emphasis, Muniz was nominated only once. The only acting Emmys won by the series were the two that went to Cloris Leachman for guest roles as daffy Grandma Ida. In addition to her lack of smarts, Lois was a control freak, who strove in vain to be a disciplinarian. Somebody had to attempt to maintain at least a semblance of control over her brood, lest they destroy the neighborhood and each other.

Hal didn't have the emotional maturity of his boys, so he was incapable of exercising parental responsibility. Hal was as cowed as the kids by Lois's assertive personality. He loved her passionately, and she him, but he was a constant source of frustration for her for his lack of support in controlling the family. To the contrary, he was often as bad as they were. On a trip to a casino, he used Malcolm to count cards at blackjack and got the two of them into a jackpot with some nasty looking people. He also habitually forgot significant occasions, such as Lois's birthday and their anniversary. Just as well. One year when he did remember their anniversary, his gift was a piece of second-hand furniture, which turned out to be infested by bats.

Malcolm's three brothers (a fourth was born in season four) were dim bulbs, whose lack of smarts was compounded by an absence of couth and common sense. Oldest son Francis (Christopher Kennedy Masterson) was so uncontrollable that Lois and Hal exiled him to military school, where his rebellious streak got him into hot water more often than lobsters at a seafood restaurant. As soon as he was old enough Francis got himself emancipated and took off for Alaska, where he met and married a native woman named Piama (Emy Coligado). Francis, who later took a job at a Wild West ranch, became an infrequent presence after season five.

Reese (Justin Barfield), Lois and Hal's next born, was incapable of clear thinking. Once gifted with a hand grenade, he immediately pulled the pin creating a panic situation. He walked away from the army when he decided it wasn't for him. He also was a bully, pounding Malcolm and others unmercifully whenever the opportunity arose. Inadvertently it was discovered that he had a remarkable gift for cooking.

Dewey (Erik Per Sullivan), a few years younger than Malcolm, was a cavalcade of mischief in his early years, although much of what he did went under the radar because his older brothers were guilty of more serious offenses. As he grew older, it was discovered that he had a flair for music as well as being almost as intelligent at Malcolm. However, due to a mix-up at school, he was relegated to a class for slower learners, the Buseys (not hard to guess who that is named for) and wound up being smarter than the teacher.

The series failed to win an Emmy from its only nomination but it did garner the arguably more prestigious Peabody Award. Also, the theme song, "(You're Not) The Boss of Me" by They Might Be Giants, won a Grammy. Unlike most family comedies, *Malcolm in the Middle* never offered socially responsible resolutions and moral lessons to its nonsense. Viewers loved it for a while, driving the series into Nielsen's top 25 its first three seasons. Alas, by the time the final episode of 151 wrapped, it had plunged out of the top 100.

48. *Coach*

Broadcast History:

Wednesday	9:00–9:30	March 1989–June 1989	ABC
Tuesday	9:30–10:00	June 1989–August 1989	ABC
Wednesday	9:30–10:00	August 1989–September 1989	ABC
Tuesday	9:30–10:00	November 1989–November 1992	ABC
Wednesday	9:30–10:00	November 1992–July 1993	ABC
Tuesday	9:30–10:00	July 1993–July 1994	ABC
Monday	8:00–8:30	August 1994–March 1995	ABC
Wednesday	9:30–10:00	March 1995–May 1995	ABC
Tuesday	9:30–10:00	June 1995–January 1996	ABC
Tuesday	8:30–9:00	February 1996–May 1996	ABC
Tuesday	9:30–10:00	May 1996–September 1996	ABC

| Saturday | 9:00–9:30 | September 1996–October 1996 | ABC |
| Wednesday | 8:30–9:00 | December 1996–August 1997 | ABC |

#18 rated series in 1989–90	#6 rated series in 1992–93
#18 rated series in 1990–91	#6 rated series in 1993–94
#10 rated series in 1991–92	#15 rated series in 1995–96

2 Major Emmy Awards (11 nominations):
1 Emmy Award for Best Actor (3 nominations)
No Emmy Awards for Best Supporting Actor (4 nominations)
No Emmy Awards for Best Supporting Actress (2 nominations)
1 Emmy Award for Guest Actor/Actress (2 nominations)

Cast: Craig T. Nelson; Jerry Van Dyke; Shelley Fabares; Bill Fagerbakke; Clare Carey (1989–93); Kris Kamm (1989–91); Pam Stone (1989–95); Ken Kimmons; Travis McKenna (1989–90); Georgia Engel (1991–97); Katherine Helmond (1995–97); Rita Taggart (1994–95); Vicki Juditz (1995–97); Shashawnee Hall (1995–97); John Valdetero (1995–97); Julio Oscar Mechoso (1995–96); Brennan Felker (1996–97); Brian Felker (1996–97).

Coach was a decided underdog when it debuted in the fall of 1989. Comedies with a sports motif have a horrendous history of failure, whether they are as praiseworthy as Aaron Sorkin's *Sports Night* or pathetic as *The Waverly Wonders*, an exploitation of the celebrity of Joe Namath. *Coach* beat the odds and ran for nine seasons thanks to a stellar performance by Craig T. Nelson and a smartly crafted supporting ensemble as well as an astute decision to downplay football in favor of typical workplace comedic vignettes.

Nelson won the show's only performing Emmy from the regular cast as Hayden Fox, coach of the initially under-achieving Minnesota State University Screaming Eagles. The team's success gradually improved to the extent they played for a national championship in season 7. This led to Hayden being recruited to coach a fictional NFL expansion team in Orlando in seasons 8 and 9. The team's owner, Doris Sherman (Katherine Helmond), knew nothing about the game and wasn't bothered by this.

What made the popularity of the series even more improbable was Hayden's stadium full of distasteful personal traits. A narcissist, he was shamelessly selfish and unfailingly insensitive. Tunnel-visioned toward football, his worldliness was astonishingly shallow. Remarkably, Nelson made this character someone with whom the audience could root for and embrace. *Coach* ranked in Nielsen's top 20 six times with three of those seasons in the top 10.

Some of the credit has to go to long time sitcom veteran Shelley Fabares, who was twice Emmy nominated as the steadying influence in Hayden's life, his girlfriend and eventual wife Christine Armstrong, a television newswoman. She was often chagrined by his child-like behavior and they had their rocky moments, including a brief split. But Christine was uniquely able to recognize his redeeming qualities and gradually smooth out his rough spots. She didn't get close to the screen time Nelson did but without her patience, Hayden might not have been as acceptable to viewers. Fabares is one of those actresses who never got top billing for her many roles but always was integral to the success of series as a child star on *Fury* and *Annie Oakley*, as a teen singing idol with "Johnny Angel," which was introduced on *The Donna Reed Show*, to recurring adult turns in hit series such as *Love American Style, Fantasy Island, One Day at a Time* and *The Practice*. The highlight of her career might have been a poignant tour de force as the spouse of the titular character in *Brian's Song*, regarded by many as the finest made-for-television movie ever.

Hayden had a pair of loyal assistant coaches, who blindly idolized him, Luther Van Dam (Jerry Van Dyke) and Michael "Dauber" Dubinski (Bill Fagerbakke). Neither was a candidate for the academic College Bowl. The easily befuddled Van Dam, Hayden's defensive coordinator, who had sub-zero self esteem, was reminiscent of Yogi Berra. At one high point for the team, he blurted out, "I could die right now and be happy for the rest of my life." Van Dyke was nominated four times for a best supporting actor Emmy.

In addition to coaching Minnesota State's special teams, Dauber was a career student, oblivious to his classroom progress until he was surprised to learn he had earned multiple degrees. His unwavering support of Hayden extended to taking the coach's side even when Dauber dated women's basketball coach Judy Watkins (Pam Stone), Hayden's nemesis. His problem with her, beyond the fact that she was a better poker player than him, was her winning record made her a threat to his position as the most important coach on campus.

Hayden allowed nothing and no one, including his nominal boss, wimpy Athletic Director Howard Burleigh (Kenneth Kimmins), who was intimidated by Hayden, to challenge that. When NBA Hall of Famer Rick Barry showed up to interview for the men's basketball head coaching position, Hayden did everything he could to sabotage Barry's candidacy. Hayden adopted similar tactics when a hotshot coach from Boston was up for the job.

Thanks to the sports setting of *Coach*, Barry was only one of a parade of legendary athletes, who walked through the show as themselves. Among them were Dick Butkus, Mike Ditka, Bob Griese and Troy Aikman. The ABC tie to the series also produced *Monday Night Football* broadcasters Al Michaels, Frank Gifford and Joe Theismann. The stars also called on family members for guest roles. Nanette Fabray made multiple appearances in a role that fit her perfectly, Christine's mother (in real life, she was Shelley's aunt). Dick Van Dyke also agreed to a guest shot.

As much as Hayden strove to filter out distractions from football, one he couldn't escape was his daughter Kelly (Clare Carey). She grew up living with Hayden's estranged wife, so she decided to enroll at Minnesota State to get to know her father better. He did his best to keep her at arm's length, especially after she fell in love with and married a geeky mime, Stuart Rosebrock (Kris Kamm). Hayden tried to keep it from Kelly but he was ecstatic when their marriage broke up after about a year. Not long after, Kelly was essentially written out of the series with the explanation she had taken a job in New York. A replacement of sorts appeared when Hayden and Christine, after years of unsuccessfully trying to conceive a child, adopted a baby named Timmy. This was a game changer for Hayden. Two years in the NFL was enough for him. He decided that he missed his cabin in the woods in Minnesota and wanted that to be the place where Timmy should be raised.

NBC decided to air a sequel/spin-off, also called *Coach*, starring Craig T. Nelson as coach Hayden Fox for the 2015–16 television season.

---

49. *Entourage*

Broadcast History:

Sunday	10:00–10:30	July 2004–September 2004	HBO
Sunday	10:00–10:30	June 2005–September 2005	HBO
Sunday	10:00–10:30	June 2006–August 2006	HBO
Sunday	10:00–10:30	April 2007–September 2007	HBO
Sunday	10:00–10:30	September 2008–November 2008	HBO
Sunday	10:30–11:00	July 2009–October 2009	HBO
Sunday	10:30–11:00	June 2010–September 2010	HBO
Sunday	10:30–11:00	July 2011–September 2011	HBO

3 Major Emmy Awards (18 nominations):
No Emmy Awards for Best Series (3 nominations)
3 Emmy Awards for Best Supporting Actor (7 nominations)
No Emmy Awards for Best Guest Actor/Actress (1 nomination)
No Emmy Awards for Best Writing (1 nomination)
No Emmy Awards for Best Direction (6 nominations)

Cast: Adrian Grenier; Kevin Connolly; Kevin Dillon; Jerry Ferrara; Jeremy Piven; Debi Mazar; Perrey Reeves; Rex Lee; Emmanuelle Chriqui (2005–11); Rhys Coiro (2007; 2010–11); Gary Cole (2008–10); Scott Caan (2009–11).

Lots of people think their life is rich fodder for a TV series. Mark Wahlberg had the wherewithal and connections to make this happen. Wahlberg dropped out of New Kids on the Block then created his own act, Marky Mark and the Funky Bunch, before turning to acting, where he emerged as an Oscar nominated leading man and producer. The highs (in more ways than one) and lows of his experiences in Hollywood became the basis for *Entourage*. In season six, he appeared as himself in an episode.

Vincent Chase, played by Adrian Grenier, was Wahlberg's alter ego, a hunk whose looks and physique brought him show business fame and fortune before he was ready to handle it. To help him cope in Hollywood, he dragged along three buddies from Queens, New York, creating make-work jobs for them. Vince's career became a series of bad decisions. (This also mirrored Wahlberg's history.) Vincent made millions starring in big box office flicks such as *Aquaman* and *Smoke Jumpers* but yearned to be an artiste doing independent art house films. When he couldn't get a studio to back him, he produced them himself. These choices wound up almost bankrupting him and killing his career. His personal life could have sustained years of tabloid front pages. A party animal he bedded a harem of starlets but ultimately fell hardest for a porno queen.

Eric Murphy (Kevin Connolly), the brains of Vincent's support group—not a sterling compliment—became Vince's manager despite having no experience beyond managing a pizza parlor. However, "E," as the guys referred to him, was a quick study. He learned to hold his own in the ferociously backstabbing show business shark tank and became a valuable asset for Vince. Nevertheless, they did have their stormy periods, including a brief breakup.

While Vince had women throwing themselves at him, Eric was smooth and handsome enough to fare well in this area, too. But the mate he coveted most, Sloan McQuewick (Emmanuelle Chriqui), the daughter of a Hollywood power player, proved hard to get. Salvatore "Turtle" Assante (Jerry Ferrara) was a street hustler, who officially was Vince's driver. He was in fact more a go-fer, who could handle chores like scoring marijuana and groupies. He used his connection to Vince, which he shamelessly embellished whenever it suited his purpose, to launch side businesses such as a car service and promoting a brand of tequila. His greatest feat, however, might have been seducing Jamie Lynn Sigler, playing herself post–*Sopranos*. He almost blew this by bragging about it to the guys, who didn't believe him anyway.

Wahlberg's brother Donnie preceded him into stardom, only to be eventually outshone by Mark. Vincent's younger brother (Kevin Dillon) also aspired to make it big in the business, adopting the screen name Johnny

Drama. However, he was always in Vince's shadow and deeply resented it even though he used the family ties to get roles. His star never rose to the heights of Vince's but after many low periods in the business, he did land a part in a hit television series, only to put that into jeopardy by openly looking for bigger and better opportunities. During his down periods, he earned his keep as the group's cook and Vincent's bodyguard. The latter was a farce. Johnny talked a tough game but had nothing to back it up.

Jeremy Piven broke out as Ari Gold, Vince's amoral, insensitive, foul-mouthed, politically incorrect agent. Other than that, he was a charming guy. Ari clashed constantly with "E" as they scrimmaged for credit for Vince's successes and blamed the failures on each other. Ari's unscrupulous behavior cost him his job and jeopardized his marriage but he was a survivor who always found a way to land on his feet, even if it entailed stepping on someone else. Piven was Emmy-nominated four times as outstanding supporting actor in a comedy and won the trophy all but once. These were the only Emmys taken by a cast member from the series 18 major nominations, including three for outstanding comedy, none of which got the gold.

Ari was particularly cruel to his assistant Lloyd (Rex Lee), an openly gay Asian. Ari screamed and berated him and mocked his sexual orientation without regard to who heard him. Lloyd put up with the humiliations because he hoped his work with Ari would move him upward on the show business representation ladder. This aspiration came to fruition when Johnny Drama agreed to become one of his first clients.

The show business milieu and popularity of the series attracted a battalion of guest stars, including late night hosts Jay Leno and Jimmy Kimmel, television stars Sofia Vergara, Bob Saget and Anna Faris, pop music's Kanye West and Mary J. Blige and sports superstars LeBron James and Tom Brady. Even before *Entourage* left HBO there were negotiations for a big screen feature. Rancorous negotiations over salaries, etc., put this plan on hold for some time until 2014 when production finally began.

50. *Alice*

Broadcast History:

Wednesday	9:30–10:00	September 1976–October 1976	CBS
Saturday	9:30–10:00	November 1976–September 1977	CBS
Sunday	9:30–10:00	October 1977–October 1978	CBS
Sunday	8:30–9:00	October 1978–February 1979	CBS

Sunday	9:00–9:30	March 1979–September 1982	CBS
Wednesday	9:00–9:30	October 1982–November 1982	CBS
Monday	9:00–9:30	March 1983–April 1983	CBS
Sunday	9:30–10:00	April 1983–May 1983	CBS
Sunday	8:00–8:30	June 1983–January 1984	CBS
Sunday	9:30–10:00	January 1984–December 1984	CBS
Tuesday	8:30–9:00	January 1985–March 1985	CBS
Tuesday	8:30–9:00	June 1985–July 1985	CBS

#30 rated series in 1976–77	#7 rated series in 1980–81
#8 rated series in 1977–78	#5 rated series in 1981–82
#13 rated series in 1978–79	#27 rated series in 1983–84
#4 rated series in 1979–80	

No Major Emmy Awards (5 nominations):
No Emmy Awards for Best Actress (1 nomination)
No Emmy Awards for Best Supporting Actor (1 nomination)
No Emmy Awards for Best Supporting Actress (3 nominations)

Cast: Linda Lavin; Philip McKeon; Vic Tayback; Polly Holliday (1976–80); Beth Howland; Marvin Kaplan (1977–85); Pat Cranshaw (1976–78); Dave Madden (1978–85); Patrick J. Cronin (1978–79); Bob McClurg (1978–79); Duane Campbell (1978–85); Victoria Carroll (1978–80); Michael Ballard (1979–80); Alan Haufrect (1979–80); Ted Gehring (1979–81); Michael Alldredge (1979–81); Raleigh Bond (1979–81); Diane Ladd (1980–81); Celia Weston (1981–85); Phillip R. Allen (1981–82); Martha Raye (1982–84); Jerry Potter (1982); Tony Longo (1982–85); Charles Levin (1983–85); Michael Durrell (1984–85); Jonathan Prince (1984–85); Doug Robinson (1984–85).

Alice was loosely based on the theatrical feature *Alice Doesn't Live Here Anymore.* However, the relationship between the CBS comedy and the Martin Scorsese movie was more like very distant cousins than close kin. The names and situations of the core characters were the same and the scenario that set the plots into motion were similar but that's where the connection ended.

Widowed Alice Hyatt, relieved to be out of what had become a loveless marriage, was driving cross country with her pre-adolescent son Tommy in the hopes of starting a new life and career as a singer in California. Car trouble led to a pit stop in Arizona. In need of cash to pay for the repairs, she took a waitress job she considered temporary at Mel's Diner. It wound up becoming more than temporary and she settled down in Arizona. However, the television show exorcised an intermediate stop in which she became involved in a torrid adulterous affair with a violent lover. Soft, unsophisticated comedy drove the small screen adaptation, although the series occasionally ventured into controversial areas for the era, such as discriminatory attitudes toward gays. Most of the time, the primary plots focused on the personality traits and quirks of the staff and customers at the greasy spoon eatery.

The practical, down-to-earth Alice was a career-making role for Linda Lavin, who was Emmy nominated as outstanding lead actress in a comedy. In addition to the title character, plots were concocted that allowed her to stretch and vamp as extraneous characters of both genders. In spite of the fact that she was the newest employee at Mel's, the others welcomed her as a confidante and shoulder to lean on and adopted Tommy and his growing pains as if he was their own son. Phillip McKeon took on the part of Tommy, replacing Alfred Lutter, who reprised his movie role in the pilot.

While Alice was the center of the show's universe, Polly Holliday became the breakout character as loud, loose moraled Flo Castleberry, "an aggressive extrovert with an overactive libido." Her trademark putdown, "Kiss my grits!" became the series trademark phrase. Holliday was Emmy-nominated three times in the best supporting actress category. Encouraged by the appeal of her character, CBS decided to spin her off to her own series, *Flo*. She left Mel's with the explanation a customer of the diner hired her at a fabulous salary to run his restaurant in Houston. However, she never got that far. She made a stop in Fort Worth and wound up buying a honky tonk she named Flo's Yellow Rose, which became the setting for her series. *Flo* failed to duplicate the popularity of *Alice* and was canceled after its second season. However, except for flashback scenes in the finale, she never returned to *Alice*.

The middle ground between low key Alice and boisterous Flo was occupied by sweet, naïve Vera Goodman (Beth Howland). Not very worldly, Vera looked for the best in everyone and took everything at face value, which made her emotionally vulnerable. Mel (Vic Tayback) adopted the persona of a gruff, impatient taskmaster. He and Flo were constantly at each other's throats and he regularly put down Vera as a "dinghy." However, scratch the surface and Mel was a softie, protective and supportive of his waitresses. When Flo made her exit, Mel wasn't embarrassed to shed some tears. (The parade of men who had made Flo's mobile home a local hotspot cried, too.) Mel's Achilles heel was his penchant for gambling. His lack of success sometimes put him and the diner at risk to shady characters but the women always helped him find a way to bail out of jams. Tayback also was Emmy nominated in the supporting actor field.

Flo's departure led to an imaginative retooling of the show. Diane Ladd, who was Oscar nominated as Flo in the movie, joined the cast as Belle Dupree, who had a romantic history with Mel. This didn't turn out to be as inspired in practice as it seemed in theory. Ladd was not a good mix with the others and she left after one season. Next up was a new character, a former truck driver named Jolene Hunnicut (Celia Weston). Like Ladd's Belle, she didn't enjoy the prominence or popularity of Flo.

In another storyline, Vera was courted, fell in love with and married a police officer named Elliot. Alice also found true romance with a country singer, Travis Marsh (played by Lavin's real life husband Charles "Kip" Levin), who convinced her to leave for Nashville and pursue her lifelong dream to become a country singer. Everything was tied up with a neat bow in the final episode. Alice won a recording contract and came back to Arizona to clear out her home. Vera announced she was pregnant and was leaving the diner to become a stay-at-home mom. Mel was bowled over by a lucrative offer from a real estate developer to buy the diner for the land it sat upon. In a final gesture to show his true feelings toward his employees, Mel gave each of them a $5,000 bonus—a tidy sum for the time—from the proceeds of the sale.

While *Alice* was never considered a critical success, the series did prove popular with audiences. The show ranked among the 30 highest rated series for seven of its nine seasons—ranking among the top 10 for four of its seasons.

51. *Hogan's Heroes*

Broadcast History:

Friday	8:30–9:00	September 1965–September 1967	CBS
Saturday	9:00–9:30	September 1967–September 1969	CBS
Friday	8:30–9:00	September 1969–September 1970	CBS
Sunday	7:30–8:00	September 1970–July 1971	CBS

#9 rated series in 1965–66
#17 rated series in 1966–67

2 Major Emmy Awards (11 nominations):
No Emmy Awards for Best Series (3 nominations)
No Emmy Award for Best Actor (2 nominations)
2 Emmy Awards for Best Supporting Actor (5 nominations)
No Emmy Awards for Best Supporting Actress (1 nomination)

Cast: Bob Crane; Werner Klemperer; John Banner; Robert Clary; Richard Dawson; Ivan Dixon (1965–70); Kenneth Washington (1970–71); Larry Hovis; Cynthia Lynn (1965–66); Sigrid Valdis (1966–70).

A Nazi prisoner of war camp was an unlikely setting for a broad comedy but *Hogan's Heroes* made it work for six seasons. It probably helped that the show's World War II was bloodless and atrocity free. Lots of things, mostly German roads, bridges and armaments, went boom. However, no human was shown dying. Not a hint of the Holocaust was heard. This differentiated it from the dark 1953 prisoner-of-war film *Stalag 17,* which was likely an inspiration. The good guys, allied soldiers who used their incarceration to thwart the Germans, unfailingly prevailed and made fools of the enemy. The Television Academy took no issue with the subject matter, nominating *Hogan's Heroes* as television's outstanding comedy three times.

Col. Robert Hogan (Robert Crane) was the ranking POW officer at Stalag 13, a prison camp from which there had never been a reported escape, even though the resourceful Hogan moved fleeing allied forces in and out of the camp as if it were a ride at Disneyland. In many ways, Hogan was a wartime version of Sgt. Ernie Bilko (see *The Phil Silvers Show*). Hogan's men constructed more tunnels than an ant farm under the nose of their captors. Somehow they managed to transform the supposedly vicious German shepherd guard dogs into friendly pussycats. Under the less than watchful eyes of the Nazis, Crane and his men turned flagpoles into radio antennae and built landbased periscopes, which allowed monitoring of Nazi activities.

Hogan had an unwitting ally in camp commandant Col. Wilhelm Klink (Werner Klemperer), a bumbling incompetent, who had never seen combat and was determined to maintain this status. Lest the Germans reassign Klink and bring in a tougher, smarter commandant, Hogan made sure Klink's blemish-free record remained intact. If need be to cover up a genuine escape, Hogan would stage a faux breakout and tip it off to Klink, who would then revel in his efficiency and make sure the upper command knew about it. In return, Klink allowed Hogan almost free run of the camp, including his office. There were times when they were even drinking buddies.

Hogan took advantage of his access to eavesdrop on German strategy. As a bonus, the dashing American got to romance Klink's knockout secretaries, Helga (Cynthia Lynn) and Hilda (Sigrid Valdis), who repaid his attention by slipping him bits of intelligence. Klemperer, who made an almost lovable figure of the Nazi Klink, was Emmy-nominated five times and won twice as best supporting actor in a comedy. Crane was twice nominated as lead actor but failed to take home the gold.

Klink's inept right-hand man, Sgt. Hanz Schultz (John Banner), made the colonel look like Field Marshall Rommel. The portly Schultz, who feared being sent to the Russian front more than Klink, had a signature expression to cover his backside: "I know nothing," stretching out the final word for emphasis. Hogan made certain there was no evidence of the comrades he moved through the camp and kept all the registered prisoners under him from attempting to escape. This enabled him to manipulate Klink into unknowingly doing whatever was necessary to facilitate Hogan's latest mission.

Under the guise of Klink brown-nosing Berlin, Hogan encouraged a celebration for Hitler's birthday. While the Nazi officers frolicked with comely frauleins, Hogan and his men sabotaged an artillery battery installed to fend off an incursion by allied troops. Determined to blow up a key bridge used to ferry German troops and supplies, Hogan snuck a bomb into a courier's motorcycle, then cajoled Klink to change the messenger's route so that he would be on the bridge when the explosive detonated. If it took an avalanche to curtail German troop movements, Hogan and his men were adept at making that happen.

Hogan had at his immediate disposal a barracks full of POWs, each seemingly boasting a useful skill, to facilitate sabotage. James Kinchloe (Ivan Dixon) was a communications whiz responsible for Hogan being in constant touch with the allied command. Peter Newkirk was skilled at picking locks and pockets. Richard Dawson, who played Newkirk, would go on to greater fame and fortune as the kissy-face host of *Family Feud*. Frenchman Louis LeBeau (Robert Clary) was a masterful chef, a talent that was drafted by Klink for dinners attended by Nazi officers. This afforded LeBeau opportunities to listen to what was being said. Sgt. Andrew Carter (Larry Hovis) was a crack bomb-maker, although he wasn't always able to get them to explode exactly when planned. It would have been fitting to have the final episode coincide with the end of the war but this did not happen. Apparently the producers were not aware that the end was upon them. (Spoiler alert: the good guys won!)

52. *3rd Rock from the Sun*

Broadcast History:

Tuesday	8:30–9:00	January 1996–April 1996	NBC
Tuesday	8:00–8:30	April 1996–July 1996	NBC
Thursday	9:30–10:00	July 1996–August 1996	NBC
Sunday	8:00–8:30	August 1996–September 1997	NBC
Wednesday	9:00–9:30	September 1997–May 1998	NBC
Wednesday	8:00–8:30	May 1998–June 1998	NBC
Wednesday	9:00–9:30	June 1998–December 1998	NBC
Tuesday	8:00–8:30	December 1998–July 1999	NBC
Tuesday	8:30–9:00	July 1999–February 2000	NBC

Tuesday	8:00–8:30	February 2000–May 2000	NBC
Thursday	8:30–9:00	June 2000	NBC
Tuesday	8:00–8:30	July 2000–September 2000	NBC
Tuesday	8:30–9:00	October 2000–January 2001	NBC
Tuesday	8:00–8:30	January 2001–February 2001	NBC
Tuesday	8:30–9:00	April 2001–May 2001	NBC

#22 rated series in 1995–96
#28 rated series in 1996–97

5 Major Emmy Awards (18 nominations):
No Emmy Awards for Best Series (2 nominations)
3 Emmy Awards for Best Actor (6 nominations)
2 Emmy Awards for Best Supporting Actress (3 nominations)
No Emmy Awards for Best Guest Actor/Actress (5 nominations)
No Emmy Awards for Best Direction (2 nominations)

Cast: John Lithgow; Kristen Johnson; French Stewart; Joseph Gordon-Levitt; Jane Curtin; Simbi Khali; Elmarie Wendel; Shay Astor (1995–98); Ron West (1996–2001); Jan Hooks (1996–2000); Wayne Knight (1997–2001); Larisa Oleynik (1998–2000).

People are strange is both the title of a 1968 hit by rock group The Doors and the thematic underpinning of *3rd Rock from the Sun*. The NBC comedy shared a similar approach to Robin Williams' manic *Mork & Mindy*. Both series used space aliens to put the behavior of the human race—at least that part of it based in Middle America—under a microscope. It's a tribute to Williams' brilliance that it took four times as many characters on *3rd Rock* to make the point.

John Lithgow was the most equal of the ensemble, assuming the human identity of Dick Solomon, the commander of the mission from an unnamed planet populated by beings of superior intelligence to Earthlings (insert snide observation here). Dick wasn't the brightest star in his home planet's constellation but at the college in Ohio where he took a position as a professor of physics he was Stephen Hawking squared.

Subtlety and sophistication were not hallmarks of the broad comedy, which was twice Emmy nominated as outstanding comedy. The theatrically trained Lithgow tended to loudly project his lines as if he were trying to reach the back rows of the balcony. It was an off-putting habit in the intimate arena of television. However, his peers loved him. He was Emmy-nominated as best comedic actor all six seasons the show was on the air and took home the gold three times. The audience wasn't as enamored. The series enjoyed moderate success in its first two seasons, landing among Nielsen's 30 highest rated series, but by the final three seasons it went virtually ignored, plunging out of the top 75.

Kristen Johnson took on the identity of Sally, the lone "female" on the mission, who was sometimes introduced as Dick's sister. Large but well proportioned—the label Amazonian was sometimes used to describe her—Johnson was ideally cast, since back home she was of the same non-specific gender as the men. The mission's security officer became the woman of the crew on Earth because she lost some kind of bet. Johnson took home a couple of supporting actress Emmys from three nominations.

Joseph Gordon-Levitt, the brains of the group as information officer Tommy, was the oldest on their home planet but assigned to take on the persona of a 14-year-old high school student because it was felt he was the most emotionally capable of adapting to the stresses of being a teenager on Earth. He accepted the challenge with gusto, joining a rock band whose sole purpose was to attract girls. Like villages, planets need an idiot. French Stewart filled that role as Harry, who had no real purpose on the mission but tagged along because there was a vacancy on the space ship and he had nothing better to do that day.

Love and sex weren't issues back home but each of the main characters caught on quickly to its prominence on Earth. Dick developed an infatuation for anthropology professor Dr. Mary Albright (Jane Curtin), with whom he shared an office. His romantic ardor for her wasn't initially reciprocated. She was introduced as an ice queen although it was revealed she had a hyperactive history of sexual escapades, which earned her the nickname Dr. Slutbunny. Mary gradually let down her guard, charmed by Dick's quirks and oddball ways of expressing himself.

Dick and the others had a facile command of basic English but sometimes got into sensitivity trouble when they took idioms and slang literally. Mary finally agreed to date Dick by the end of the first season. He must have been a quick study. There was no such thing as sex back home but while Mary found many things odd about Dick, the way he performed romantically was not among them. She was quite pleased. By the outset of the third season, he asked her to marry him, a proposal that immediately hit a snag. Nevertheless they continued to be an on-again, off-again couple. Throughout the course of the series, he wooed or was wooed by a succession of women, including Roseanne, who was dispatched from his home planet to be his wife, a coupling he aggressively resisted. His only enduring relationship was with Mary.

Sally might have resented having to be the woman of the crew and frequently reminded the guys that she was tougher than they were but she came to crave the attention attractive women get on Earth and learned how to use her feminine wiles to manipulate the opposite sex. A Frenchman named

Michael was so taken with her that he proposed marriage, which she had no interest in. Because of a thing she had for authority figures, she wound up settling for a portly, self-important cop, Officer Don Orville (Wayne Knight).

Tommy was the first to explore Earth females, landing a date and his first kiss in the second episode. He had two regular girlfriends, August Leffler (Shay Astor) and Alissa Strudwick (Larissa Oleynik) whose father Vincent (Ron West) became an academic rival to Dick. Even Harry managed to occasionally score with women, including Vicki, the daughter of their busybody landlady Mrs. Dubcek (Elmarie Wendel).

Jan Hooks, who played Vicki, was among a sizable group to earn Emmy nominations as outstanding guest stars in a comedy series. Others who were afforded this honor were Kathy Bates, Laurie Metcalf, John Cleese and William Shatner, who finally showed up as The Big Head, the ruler of the home planet, who was only referred to in the first three seasons. The Big Head's command to end the mission brought down the curtain on the show in 2001.

---

53. *One Day at a Time*

Broadcast History:

Tuesday	9:30–10:00	December 1975–July 1976	CBS
Tuesday	9:30–10:00	September 1976–January 1978	CBS
Monday	9:30–10:00	January 1978–January 1979	CBS
Wednesday	9:00–9:30	January 1979–March 1979	CBS
Sunday	8:30–9:00	March 1979–September 1982	CBS
Sunday	9:30–10:00	September 1992–March 1983	CBS
Monday	9:30–10:00	March 1983–May 1983	CBS
Sunday	8:30–9:00	June 1983–February 1984	CBS
Wednesday	8:00–8:30	March 1984–May 1984	CBS
Monday	9:00–9:30	May 1984–August 1984	CBS
Sunday	8:00–8:30	August 1984–September 1984	CBS

#12 rated series in 1975–76	#10 rated series in 1979–80
#8 rated series in 1976–77	#11 rated series in 1980–81
#10 rated series in 1977–78	#10 rated series in 1981–82
#18 rated series in 1978–79	#16 rated series in 1982–83

2 Major Emmy Awards (3 nominations):
No Emmy Awards for Best Actress (1 nomination)
1 Emmy Award for Best Supporting Actor (1 nomination)
1 Emmy Award for Best Direction (1 nomination)

Cast: Bonnie Franklin; Mackenzie Phillips (1975–80, 1981–83); Valerie Bertinelli; Pat Harrington, Jr.; Richard Masur (1975–76); Mary Louise Wilson (1976–77); Charles Siebert (1976–79); Michael Lembeck (1979–80; 1981–84); Nanette Fabray (1979–84); Ron Rifkin (1980–81); Glenn Scarpelli (1980–83); Shelley Farabres (1981–84); Boyd Gaines (1981–84); Howard Hesseman (1982–84); Lauren Maloney (1983–84); Paige Maloney (1983–84).

One Day at a Time had one of television's most unintentionally double-edged titles. When what to call the series was being discussed, it is unlikely the powers-that-be considered how their ultimate decision would reflect not only the show's premise, a single mother's struggles to raise a family, but also one of the stars' constant real-life headline-producing battles to deal with drug addiction.

Bonnie Franklin starred as Ann Romano, a divorcee living in Indianapolis with her two daughters, Julie, 17, and Barbara Cooper, 15. (The girls kept their father's surname even though their mother didn't.) Barbara turned into a career launch pad for Valerie Bertinelli, whose sweet, girl-next-door image endured into the new millennium when she was old enough to be a grandmother. Meanwhile Mackenzie Phillips, as Julie, became a paradigm for everything that outsiders see as decadent in show business. Phillips had chronic issues with drug abuse, which she said started in her pre-teens, before she was cast in the CBS comedy.

She was arrested on a drug charge during the show's third season and her continued abuse became such a problem during the run of the series that she was twice written out of the show, including the entire season six. Her character was not a part of more than 80 of the show's 209 episodes. Years after the series left the air, an even more shocking revelation came to the fore. Trying to sell a biography, *High on Arrival*, Phillips told Oprah Winfrey she had a decade-long sexual relationship with her father, John Phillips of the popular 1960s singing group, The Mamas and Papas. It began at about the midpoint of the series run, when she was 18, Phillips said. Her father, who had passed away when she made the allegations, wanted them to seek a country where incest is legal so they could marry, she said.

The series delved into edgy material, including drug use, but never to the extent of what was going on in Phillips' life. Many of the heavier storylines were extended over multi-part episodes. Seasons two and three each opened with four-part story arcs. Every subsequent season had at least one two-parter. Season eight had a couple of two-parters and one three-parter.

Up to that point, few characters in long-running series ever evolved to the extent that Franklin's Ann Romano did. At the outset, she was newly single, living paycheck to paycheck without noteworthy career skills, and trying to cope with two young daughters at a sensitive, challenging time in their lives. Although Ann remained single for most of the series run, there was always at least one man prominent in her life, building superintendent, Dwayne Schneider (Pat Harrington, Jr.), who considered himself quite the ladies man. Ann was one of the few women with whom Schneider (he went by only his surname) was content to have a platonic relationship. He also served as a paternal overseer for the girls.

Harrington won the show's only acting Emmy as the off-the-wall character every successful comedy seems to have. Franklin was nominated once but did not win. The Television Academy might not have paid the series much respect but America loved it, propelling it into Nielsen's Top 20 for every season but the final one. This was a remarkable achievement inasmuch as the show had about a dozen different time periods.

As the series progressed, Ann established herself as a successful advertising executive, who eventually owned her own firm. She seriously dated a number of men, starting with Richard Masur as David Kane, who wanted her to marry him as early as episode five. She also fell in love with a business partner, Nick Handris (Ron Rifkin), a single dad, who, alas, was killed in a tragic accident. With the girls on their own, Ann resumed parental responsibilities raising Nick's son Alex (Glenn Scarpelli). She became a surrogate mother again when Julie and her husband Max Horvath (Michael Lembeck) moved in with their daughter Annie (played by twins Lauren and Paige Maloney). Julie then inexplicably disappeared (another drug sabbatical for Phillips) for a period.

The death of Nick was the catalyst to bring a former business adversary, Francine Webster (Shelley Fabares), back into Ann's life. Recognizing Ann's need for a new partner, she convinced her to put their old problems aside and go into business together. Fabares' aunt, Nanette Fabray (she changed the spelling of the family surname) also had a recurring role as Ann's mother, Grandma Romano. Just as in real life, Barbara was the more grounded daughter. She met and married a dental student, Mark Royer (Boyd Gaines). Ann got to know his father, Sam (Howard Hesseman) and they fell in love and married. Freed of parental responsibilities as the series wound toward its conclusion, Ann jumped at an alluring opportunity to live and work in England and she and Sam moved there in the final episode.

54. *Rhoda*

Broadcast History:

Monday	9:30–10:00	September 1974–September 1975	CBS
Monday	8:00–8:30	September 1975–January 1977	CBS
Sunday	8:00–8:30	January 1977–September 1978	CBS
Saturday	8:00–8:30	September 1978–December 1978	CBS

#6 rated series in 1974–75
#7 rated series in 1975–76
#25 rated series in 1977–78

2 Major Emmy Awards (16 nominations):
No Emmy Awards for Best Series (1 nomination)
1 Emmy Award for Best Actress (4 nominations)
1 Emmy Award for Best Supporting Actress (8 nominations)
No Emmy Awards for Guest Actor/Actress (2 nominations)
No Emmy Awards for Best Writing (1 nomination)

Cast: Valerie Harper; Julie Kavner; David Groh (1974–77); Nancy Walker (1974–76, 1977–78); Harold J. Gould (1974–76, 1977–78); Lorenzo Music (voice only); Cara Williams (1974–75); Candy Azzara (1974–75); Todd Turquand (1974); Barbara Sharma (1974–76); Richard Masur (1974–75); Scoey Mitchell (1975–76); Ron Silver (1976–78); Anne Meara (1976–77); Michael Delano (1977–78); Ray Buktenica (1977–78); Ken McMillan (1977–78); Rafael Campos (1977–78); Nancy Lane (1978).

Rhoda is one of television's prime examples of the old saying, "Be careful what you wish for. You might get it." Viewers who fell in love with self deprecating Rhoda Morgenstern during four seasons on *The Mary Tyler Moore Show* couldn't wait for Valerie Harper's second banana character to bust out in her own spinoff series. The pilot episode of *Rhoda* on September 9, 1974 was the highest rated premiere in Nielsen history. Fans yearned to see the multi-time loser at love find happiness and a suitable mate. *Rhoda* delivered, arguably too quickly.

The premise had Rhoda, now in her early 30s, relocating from Minneapolis to her former hometown, New York City. "She ran away from home at 24," in the words of her matchmaking mother Ida (Nancy Walker), who still lived in the Big Apple with Rhoda's father Martin (Harold J. Gould). Rhoda's younger sister Brenda (Julie Kavner), who had even lower self-esteem when it came to romance than Rhoda, had a place of her own.

When she left the Twin Cities, Rhoda thought she was going home for a two-week visit. Before it was time to pack for the return trip to the Midwest,

Brenda introduced Rhoda to a divorcee with a young son, Joe Gerard (David Groh), for whom Brenda occasionally babysat. Rhoda and Joe hit if off to such an extent that when it was time for her to leave, Joe pleaded with her to stay. If she was going to stay, Rhoda told Joe, she needed a commitment. The one she got wasn't quite the one she hoped for; Joe asked her to move in with him (not yet fully acceptable on a network television program). While it wasn't a full-fledged proposal, Rhoda hadn't gotten many overtures like that, so it was an appealing offer. However, before they got to consummate their new living arrangement, Rhoda had second thoughts. If Joe wanted her to move in, she wanted a ring on her finger. He agreed, although it would turn out later, reluctantly.

Rather than tease the audience along by extending the engagement, the producers had them at the altar by the eighth episode. The biggest delay came when Rhoda's Minneapolis nemesis, Phyllis Lindstrom (Cloris Leachman), failed to provide the transportation she promised. Rhoda had to race through the streets of New York in her wedding dress in an attempt to get to the church on time as guests anxiously checked their watches. Among those in attendance were former *Mary Tyler Moore Show* characters, Mary, Lou Grant (Ed Asner), Murray Slaughter (Gavin McLeod) and Georgette Franklin (Georgia Engel). America swooned. About 52 million viewers tuned in for the hour-length episode. The birth of Little Ricky on *I Love Lucy* in 1953 was the only series episode to that point to draw more viewers.

Harper won an Emmy in 1975 as outstanding lead actress in a comedy series. Kavner would join her for her supporting role in 1978. The question became "Now what?" Viewers got what they wanted but married life for the long desperate Rhoda wasn't nearly as interesting. The producers and writers scrambled to sustain interest. Rhoda was given a career as a window dresser, working alongside an old friend, Myrna (Barbara Sharma). However, by the time the third season had to be plotted, the producers and the audience arrived at the same conclusion: Rhoda had become boring. The show tried to put the aerosol back in the can by having Rhoda and Joe split, returning her to single life. The breakup came fast, in the season-opening episode. Joe confessed that he never really wanted to be married to Rhoda and agreed only because she pressured him.

Some episodes offered half-hearted attempts at reconciliation but Joe was seen in only nine shows before he disappeared for good. The audience revolted, deluging the network and the show with hate letters. A series that regularly resided among the top 10 most watched series in its first two seasons, *Rhoda* tumbled out of Nielsen's top 30. Rhoda jumped back into the dating pool with results as unsatisfactory as they had been back in *The Mary Tyler Moore Show* days. The first to hit on her was a lounge lizard named Johnny Venture (Michael Delano) but Rhoda had little interest in him.

Anne Meara was brought to the series as Rhoda's new best friend, Sally Gallagher, but she was written out after one season. The only real breakout character on the series turned out to be heard-but-never-fully-seen Carlton the Doorman (Lorenzo Music), who later got his own animated series *Carlton Your Doorman*. Brenda's romantic adventures also were moved more to the fore. Her roster of suitors included Nick Lobo (Richard Masur), the accordionist at Rhoda and Joe's wedding, her neighbor Gary Levy (Ron Silver), who seemed to have more of an interest in Rhoda, and a toll collector, Benny Goodwin (Ray Buktenica). None turned out to be Mr. Right or even Mr. I'll Settle for Him.

Further detracting from what viewers had initially taken to heart, Ida and Martin were dispatched on a long vacation touring America in the third season, as Walker and Gould each departed to star in what turned out to be short-lived series' of their own; the eponymous *Nancy Walker Show* and *Blansky's Beauties* for her and *The Feather and Father Gang* for Gould. The quick cancellations of those shows cleared the way for Walker and Gould to return to *Rhoda* but the magic was gone. They eventually separated, too.

By its fifth and last season *Rhoda* had dropped out of the Nielsen top 40. With no further ideas how to resuscitate the concept, CBS didn't even allow the once blockbuster hit to complete its final season, pulling the plug in early December.

55. *The George Burns & Gracie Allen Show*

Broadcast History:

Thursday	8:00–8:30	October 1950–March 1953	CBS
Monday	8:00–8:30	March 1953–September 1958	CBS

#20 rated series in 1953–54   #27 rated series in 1955–56
#26 rated series in 1954–55   #28 rated series in 1956–57

No Major Emmy Awards (12 nominations):
No Emmy Awards for Best Series (4 nominations)
No Emmy Awards for Best Actress (6 nominations)
No Emmy Award for Best Supporting Actress (2 nominations)

Cast: George Burns; Gracie Allen; Bea Benaderet; Hal March (1950–51); John Brown (1951); Fred Clark (1951–53); Larry Keating (1953–58); Bill Goodwin (1950–51); Harry Von Zell (1951–58); Rolfe Sedan; Ronnie Burns (1955–58); Judi Meredith (1957–58).

George Burns and Gracie Allen followed a well traveled path in the early days of television. The married couple made their name in vaudeville. Their popularity brought Hollywood calling. Their next stop was radio, where *The Adventures of Gracie* and later *The George Burns & Gracie Allen Show* became what passed for radio situation comedy. Like so many other major players in radio, they merely adapted this to television in the infancy of the medium. Television was feeling its way through what might work or not and the optimum way to present it.

When *The George Burns & Gracie Allen Show* debuted in 1950, not all series were shown on a weekly basis. *Burns & Allen* aired every other week in its first two seasons, sharing a half-hour with *The Garry Moore Show*. They served as the lead-in for *Amos 'n' Andy*, which subsequently became so vilified that it is the only known series considered so objectionable that CBS locked the episodes away in a vault and took legal action against those who tried to market bootleg copies, an effort which experienced spotty success. It wasn't until the third season that *The George Burns & Gracie Allen Show* became a weekly regular and was scheduled as part of a Monday night lineup, including *I Love Lucy*, which built dominance on the night that endured almost uninterrupted into the 21st century.

George was a generous straight man given to self-deprecation—"I had to go to night school to learn to tie my shoes." At the midpoint of the 20th century, this was a knee-slapper. In other signs of the times, George might have been one of the last people on television to use the terms "ice box" and "necking." However, scatter-brained Gracie was the show-stealer. No one could jump to erroneous conclusions faster and more hilariously than Gracie. Episodes were built around her reacting farcically to simple misunderstandings. When a female staff member told Gracie she had won a trip for two to Hawaii, Gracie took it upon herself to find a mate for her, oblivious to the fact that the woman was happily married.

Gracie had a unique way of dealing with life that made a snippet of sense while causing others to shake their heads in bewilderment. She dealt with spelling errors by refusing to use the word again. "That way I never make the same mistake twice." Gracie would send strangers, from tax assessors to traffic cops, fleeing from her non-sequiturs and cockeyed sense of logic. She wanted a fireproof house, she said, because if it burned down, it wouldn't be her fault.

George and her friends panicked when Gracie was summoned for jury duty and was determined to do her civic duty.

George and especially Gracie, who was Emmy-nominated six times, carried the show, which garnered four best comedy Emmy nominations. They received support from their neighbors the Mortons and their friend Harry Von Zell. Bea Benaderet, who went back to the radio days of *Burns & Allen*, reprised her role as Blanche Morton—the Ethel Mertz to Gracie's Lucy—and was twice Emmy nominated. Her curmudgeonly husband Harry was portrayed through the years by four different actors. Hal March, who would go on to become embroiled in the quiz show scandals as the host of the *$64,000 Question*, was the first Harry. March was followed, in order, by John Brown, Fred Clark and ultimately Larry Keating.

Harry Von Zell played himself as George's buddy and the personality who did commercials for Carnation Milk ("The milk from contented cows") at the top and bottom of the show. Carnation also received regular plugs during the show's vignettes, which was not unusual during television's early days. George and Gracie's real life son Ronnie was a recurring presence as he pursued a show business career. Gracie doted on him to the extent that when he adopted a stage name, she decided to change her name, too, as a gesture of support.

In another sign of the times in which the show aired, CBS was still giving meaning to the saying that television was a guest in viewers' homes and was compelled to behave appropriately. Men in the cast mostly wore coats and ties and the women favored modest dresses. Suggestive one-liners were never heard. Sex was not acknowledged to be a fact of life. Staging was rudimentary. Most scenes were set in George and Gracie's living room and the audience was allowed to see that it was a sound stage set. In some episodes, curtains would go up and down, as if it were live theater, which, in a way, it was.

George, curling a trademark cigar, would stand out front setting up the plot, then commenting on it between acts. At episode's end, George and Gracie would stand in front of a curtain and do a brief monologue, which usually ended with George cueing his wife, who had just blurted out something silly, "Say goodnight, Gracie." Gracie said "goodnight" for the final time at the end of the 1958 season. George tried to keep the momentum going with a new series, *The George Burns Show*. Without Gracie, it wasn't the same and CBS canceled the new program after one season.

56. *Soap*

Broadcast History:

Tuesday	9:30–10:00	September 1977–March 1978	ABC
Thursday	9:30–10:00	September 1978–March 1979	ABC
Thursday	9:30–10:00	September 1979–March 1980	ABC
Wednesday	9:30–10:00	October 1980–January 1981	ABC
Monday	10:00–11:00	March 1981–April 1981	ABC

#13 rated series in 1977–78
#19 rated series in 1978–79
#25 rated series in 1979–80

3 Major Emmy Awards (15 nominations):
No Emmy Awards for Best Program (3 nominations)
1 Emmy Award for Best Actor (2 nominations)
1 Emmy Award for Best Actress (7 nominations)
1 Emmy Award for Best Supporting Actor (1 nomination)
No Emmy Awards for Best Directing (2 nominations)

Cast: Robert Mandan; Katherine Helmond; Diana Canova (1977–80); Jennifer Salt; Jimmy Baio; Robert Guillaume (1977–79); Arthur Peterson; Cathryn Damon; Richard Mulligan; Billy Crystal; Ted Wass; Richard Libertini (1977–78); Kathryn Reynolds (1977–78); Robert Urich; Jay Johnson; Bob Seagren (1978); Sal Viscuso (1978–79); Rebecca Balding (1978–81); Dinah Manoff (1978–79); Donnelly Rhodes (1978–81); Caroline McWilliams (1978–79); John Byner (1978–80); Eugene Roche (1978–81); Randee Heller (1979); Peggy Pope (1979–81); Candace Azzara (1979); Marla Pennington (1979–81); Lynne Moody (1979–81); Roscoe Lee Browne (1980–81); Allan Miller (1980–81); Gregory Sierra (1978–81); Barbara Rhoades (1980–81); Jesse Welles (1980–81).

Broadcast television has been a juicy target for protests over content since the invention of the cathode ray tube. It exists with an inviting bullseye on it because it comes into people's homes, is subject to Federal Communications Commission oversight and is supported by sponsors sensitive to the threat of product boycotts. But the medium had never seen anything like the howls of outrage that greeted the announcement of *Soap*, an ABC spoof on daytime dramas.

The previous benchmark was *All in the Family* in 1971. But the uproar over Archie Bunker was nothing like what happened during the summer of 1977 in advance of *Soap*. The National Council of Churches and several religious denominations objected to the heavy emphasis, albeit in a comical manner which would be tame by 21st century norms, on sex. The Catholic Church was particularly perturbed because one of the female characters seduced a priest in the confessional. Conservative activists, many of whom hid behind misleading letterheads, which suggested they were motivated only by trying to protect children, were apoplectic. Gay groups expressed concern with how a homosexual character, a breakthrough for television, would be depicted. Interestingly, the first major event of the series was a murder. This bothered no one.

A largely erroneous preview in *Newsweek* magazine helped whip up the frenzy. The reality, almost as hilarious as *Soap* turned out to be, was that none of these people, including the *Newsweek* critic, had seen the show. Nevertheless, ABC was bombarded with tens of thousands of cards and letters (email did not yet exist) demanding that *Soap* be canceled before anyone got to see it. About twenty ABC affiliates declined to carry the series. Others delayed its airing to late night instead of its intended 9:30–10:00 p.m. time slot. To his credit, then ABC programming chief Fred Silverman refused to be bullied and held his ground. However, when the show premiered, it was preceded by what is believed to be the first disclaimer in broadcast network history.

As often is the case, the controversy turned out to be asset. The debut of *Soap* attracted almost 40 percent of the audience watching television that night. According to a poll, 76 percent of those who watched didn't find the show offensive. Of those who did, half indicated they would watch again. Soap was Emmy-nominated for Best Comedy Series three times. While the series never won the award, Richard Mulligan, Cathryn Damon and Robert Guillaume all won acting Emmys.

Soap masterfully captured the convoluted, risqué storytelling of the daytime shows it was spoofing. The lives of dozens of characters regularly intersected in improbable scenarios. Bed hopping ran rampant. The series was presented as the saga of two sisters, Jessica Tate and Mary Campbell, and their extended families. Jessica (Katherine Helmond) was married to a horndog contractor Chester (Robert Mandan), who would sleep with any woman who could draw a breath. Initially, Jessica was in denial about her husband's serial philandering. When she finally came to grips with what she had known all along, she became as promiscuous as her husband, who she divorced in season four.

Among Jessica's many mates was a Latin American revolutionary, El Puerco (Gregory Sierra). Jessica became implicated in the death of Mary's son, tennis pro Peter Campbell (Robert Urich), and was convicted for the crime. The season one cliffhanger revealed that she was innocent and offered five different possible perpetrators. It turned out Chester did the deed.

Chester went to prison but escaped with a career criminal named Dutch (Donnelly Rhodes).

Chester's sexual conquests included his sister-in-law-to-be Mary (Cathryn Damon) before he married Jessica. Years later, he would learn that this tryst produced a son, Danny (Ted Wass), who grew up believing he was the biological son of a mobster named Johnny Dallas, Mary's first husband. Following his father's career path, Danny was ordered by a mob boss to assassinate his stepfather Burt (Richard Mulligan), who was thought to have killed Johnny. Danny refused, not wanting to destroy his mother's happiness and had to go on the lam. Danny saved himself by agreeing to marry the godfather's obnoxious daughter (Dinah Manoff).

Burt and Mary each had a child from a previous marriage. Mary's son Jodie (a career launch pad for Billy Crystal) was one of television's first openly gay regular characters. But he went over to the other side when he fell for an attorney named Carol (Rebecca Balding). They had a child and then Carol abandoned them. The confused Jodie underwent hypnotherapy and came out of it believing he was an elderly Jewish man, Julius Kassendorf. This was a precursor to a character later fully developed by Crystal.

Burt had a son named Chuck (Jay Johnson), a mild mannered ventriloquist who revealed a darker side by expressing his thoughts through his vicious-tongued dummy Bob, best described as what could be the result of a child conceived by Don Rickles and Kathy Griffin. Burt eventually lost it, thinking he could make himself disappear with the snap of his fingers. He did disappear when he was kidnapped by space aliens. To cover what they had done, the aliens substituted a lookalike, who had an insatiable sexual attitude. Mary didn't understand what had happened but she was thrilled.

Jessica and Chester had three other children. Their adopted daughter Corinne (Diana Canova) made Chester seem like a model of morality. She teased and married a priest, Father Tim Flotsky (Sal Viscuso). Their child, Timmy turned out to be possessed by the devil. Eunice Tate (Jennifer Salt) carried on an affair with a married congressman then fell in love with and married Dutch. Billy Tate (Jimmy Baio) was a well-adjusted teen when he was introduced but went off the rails and joined a cult called the Sunnies. He also had a fling with one of his teachers, Carol (Rebecca Balding) who launched a campaign to kill him when he broke off their relationship.

Jessica's father, The Major (Arthur Peterson), who suffered from dementia, also lived with them. He got his nickname from his penchant for skulking around the house in his military uniform convinced he was still fighting World War II. The Tate's sarcastic butler, Benson, looked with disdain on most of the family, although he sympathized with Jessica. Robert Guillaume made it a breakthrough role, which led to his character, Benson, being spun off into his own series (appropriately titled *Benson*). At the outset of each episode, announcer Rod Roddy would recap what had happened previously then ask, "Confused?" Why would anyone be confused?

57. *Family Affair*

Broadcast History:

Monday	9:30–10:00	September 1966–September 1969	CBS
Thursday	7:30–8:00	September 1969–September 1971	CBS

#15 rated series in 1966–67	#5 rated series in 1968–69
#5 rated series in 1967–68	#5 rated series in 1969–70

No Major Emmy Awards (8 nominations):
No Emmy Awards for Best Series (2 nominations)
No Emmy Awards for Best Actor (4 nominations)
No Emmy Awards for Best Writing (1 nomination)
No Emmy Awards for Best Directing (1 nomination)

Cast: Brian Keith; Sebastian Cabot; Anissa Jones; Johnnie Whitaker; Kathy Garver; Nancy Walker (1970–71).

Family Affair epitomized the television "If at first you do succeed, try, try again—until it stops succeeding." Producer Don Fedderson had a huge hit, starting in 1961, with *My Three Sons*. The tale of a single father, assisted by his father-in-law, was still going strong when Fedderson came back in 1966 with *Family Affair*, which had essentially the same premise. A bachelor raising three children—two nieces and a nephew, orphaned by a tragic accident— with the help of an English manservant. After *Family Affair* also hit big, Fedderson took a third swing in 1971 with *The Smith Family*, another comedy (starring Henry Fonda, and a pre–*Happy Days* Ron Howard) with only a slight variation. This time a couple of natural parents were raising three kids. Maybe it was the wife, maybe it was audience fatigue, but the series bombed out in one season. Fedderson never produced another series.

Brian Keith starred in *Family Affair* as Bill Davis—Uncle Bill to the kids—a handsome, wealthy building engineer with an active social life and an elegant Manhattan penthouse. Everything changed about a year after his brother and sister-in-law perished in an auto accident. Their children, ado- lescent Cissy and the barely school age twins, Jody and Buffy, were scattered among three sets of relatives, none of whom were thrilled by the new burden thrust upon them. The kids were miserable, too, at being separated. Low-key, soft-spoken Uncle Bill stepped up and took them all in. The instant family signaled the end of his former free-wheeling lifestyle. He became fully devoted to his new responsibilities.

Work took second position and he greatly curtailed his bachelor ways to be there for them as much as possible. He even considered moving out of the city to the country because he felt it might have been a better place to raise the children. Bill had a prim and proper butler, Mr. Giles French (Sebastian Cabot), to ride herd on the youngsters while he was at work or trying to maintain a semblance of his former social life.

Mr. French, who cherished order and tidiness, did not greet the new responsibilities enthusiastically. Over time his resistance melted as the children worked their way into his heart. He began to regard them as if they were his own. A moment of truth came in season three when his former English employer, a nobleman with a massive castle, pleaded with him to return to Britain to run the household. There was even a sweetener—the pitch included a reunion with a woman with whom Mr. French once had a strong romantic attachment. He was packed and ready to go when he realized he couldn't leave the children. He was still fastidious but he learned to tone it down. Mr. French should have seen his inability to separate himself from the children coming. The first year he and Uncle Bill had the kids they became miserable and lonely when the children went to sleep away camp. The two adults couldn't wait for the kids to get home.

Uncle Bill still dated, though less frequently. One relationship reached the serious stage until the woman made it clear she wasn't ready or willing to become a surrogate parent. She issued an ultimatum: it was either her or the children. She actually thought she had a shot at winning. She didn't know Uncle Bill as well as she thought she did.

As Jody and Buffy got older, they began to realize there was a vacancy in Uncle Bill's life and tried to play matchmaker without success. The show's humor was gentle and not complex. Controversial social issues were virtually non-existent. Most plots revolved around the twins learning about life and Uncle Bill guiding them how to do the right thing. In one episode, Bill was confronted by a dilemma faced by many parents. The twins each became convinced that he liked the other one better. In another, Jody and Buffy befriended a fellow orphan and sheltered him in the apartment when he ran away.

Although the roles were designed to be equal, Jody (Johnny Whitaker) and Cissy (Kathy Garver) were often outshone by the precious Buffy (Anissa Jones). Cissy especially was cast into the background as the writers moved the precocious twins to the forefront, especially in the first couple of seasons. It wasn't until Cissy was finally of acceptable dating age that vignettes were written for her, including one in which an Austrian of royal birth proposed marriage. Cissy was flattered but, of course, declined. The tables were turned in another plot when she fell hard for a rock musician, who broke her heart when he cheated behind her back.

Buffy had a favorite doll, Mrs. Beasley, who she used as a confidante. This keyed a merchandizing bonanza. Young girls everywhere wanted their own Mrs. Beasley. Unfortunately, Jones didn't share the carefree life of her character. She died of a massive drug overdose at the age of 18. (Keith also took his own life in 1997 but he was 75.)

Despite the series simplicity and lack of sophistication—it was twice Emmy nominated as outstanding comedy series. Keith was thrice nominated as lead actor and Cabot also received a nomination in the lead actor category. The viewing audience was more enamored. *Family Affair* cracked Nielsen's top 15 in its premiere season then ranked in the top 5 for the next three years. When it crashed out of the top 30 in season 5, it was canceled.

---

58. *Designing Women*

Broadcast History:

Monday	9:30–10:00	September 1986–November 1986	CBS
Thursday	9:30–10:00	December 1986–January 1987	CBS
Sunday	9:00–9:30	February 1987	CBS
Monday	9:30–10:00	March 1987–February 1988	CBS
Monday	8:30–9:00	February 1988–June 1988	CBS
Monday	9:30–10:00	June 1988–September 1989	CBS
Monday	10:00–10:30	September 1989–October 1989	CBS
Monday	9:30–10:00	November 1989–September 1992	CBS
Friday	9:00–9:30	September 1992–May 1993	CBS

#23 rated series in 1989–90
#10 rated series in 1990–91
#6 rated series in 1991–92

No Major Emmy Awards (10 nominations):
No Emmy Awards for Best Series (3 nominations)
No Emmy Award for Best Actress (2 nominations)
No Emmy Awards for Best Supporting Actor (1 nomination)

No Emmy Awards for Best Supporting Actress (1 nomination)
No Emmy Awards for Best Writing (1 nomination)
No Emmy Awards for Best Directing (2 nominations)

Cast: Delta Burke (1986–91); Dixie Carter; Jean Smart (1986–91); Annie Potts; Meshach Taylor; Alice Ghostley (1987–93); Julia Duffy (1991–92); Jan Hooks (1991–93); Judith Ivey (1992–93); Sheryl Lee Ralph (1992–93)

The South rose again as the home of sharp, entrepreneurial, outspoken and sexy woman in this stereotype-destroying comedy. A counterpoint to the jigglevision era of *Charlie's Angels*, the focus was on four Atlanta women in the interior decorator business. Julia Sugarbaker (Dixie Carter) was the co-founder with her sister Suzanne (Delta Burke) of the eponymous Sugarbaker's Designs. Julia had the business smarts. The flighty Suzanne, a former beauty queen, contributed financing. Mary Jo Shively (Annie Potts), a divorced single mother of two, was a designer and Charlene Stillfield (Jean Smart), a sweetheart who was incapable of harboring negative thoughts about anyone, was the office manager. Anthony Bouvier (Meshach Taylor), who had been convicted of a crime he didn't commit and sent to prison, was putting his life back together as a do-it-all man around the office.

By the time the show left the air after seven seasons, Anthony had graduated college and become a partner in the business. *Designing Women* leaned on situation comedy staples—farcical misunderstandings, physical comedy and characters finding themselves in bizarre circumstances. It also frequently delved into political and social issues, such as racial prejudice, homophobia, AIDS, substance abuse, domestic violence, immigration and regional snobbery against people from the South. Each of these provided Linda Bloodworth-Thomason, who co-created the show with her husband Harry and wrote many of the episodes, an opportunity to sound off.

Few things riled her as much as the stereotype of Southerners as uneducated hicks. Linda and Harry were close friends of Bill and Hillary Clinton and episodes made mention of Bill's 1992 campaign for the presidency, in which the Thomasons were heavily involved. They choreographed significant parts of the Democratic national convention at which Bill was nominated. Bill's predecessor as a President from the South, Jimmy Carter, also was positively referenced. Many of Linda's political screeds came out of the mouth of Julia, the most politically motivated of the regular characters. In a way, Julia was Linda's alter ego. The irony was Carter was a strong Republican, who didn't subscribe to almost anything her character said. Legend has it that Carter struck a deal. Whenever Julia had to launch a political diatribe with which Carter, an accomplished singer, didn't agree, the Thomasons would concoct a scenario in which Julia got to sing a tune.

But the emphasis was comedy, some of it laugh out loud, other times poignant, and a lot steeped in romance. Each of the women found, or almost found, Mr. Right. Julia was devastated when her longtime main man, Reese (real life spouse Hal Holbrook), died suddenly. Suzanne had more lovers and ex-husbands, most of who cheated on her, than a Kardashian. Mary Jo was badly burned by her former husband Ted (Scott Bakula), who remained on the fringes of her life because of their children. This made her reluctant to jump back into the dating pool. When she finally did, she had a litany of unsuccessful attempts to find a new spouse, until she connected with a guy named J.D. (Richard Gilliland).

Charlene, a hopeless romantic, finally found the love of her life, a military man named Bill (Doug Barr), in season four. They married and had a child. At the end of the fifth season, she informed the Thomasons and CBS that she wanted out. So in the first episode of season six, she said her goodbyes to the others and left for England to be with Bill, who had been deployed overseas. Anthony almost married the wealthy daughter of a hotel baron. When that romance went wrong, he wound up wed to a Las Vegas showgirl named Etienne (Sheryl Lee Ralph).

Burke launched a very public feud with the Thomasons when she complained about working conditions on the set during a Barbara Walters interview. At the same time, Burke's noticeable weight gain, estimated at 50 pounds, also became an issue. Burke, a former Miss Florida, no longer looked like the vain beauty queen Suzanne was supposed to be. The battling back and forth in the media resulted in Burke either skipping or being written out of several episodes in seasons four and five and her departure from the series at the start of season six. In one of those only in Hollywood developments, the Thomasons buried the hatchet in 1994 and created a new series for Burke, *Woman of the House*, which was canceled after one season. The actresses hired to replace Burke and Smart produced mixed results. Julia Duffy, coming off a long run on *Newhart*, stepped in as Suzanne's sister, Allison, who alienated the other characters with her controlling ways. Research indicated the character also was a turn off to fans and she was sent packing after one season.

The final season, Judith Ivey was brought in as B.J. Poteet, a larger than life Texan with a colorful background. *Saturday Night Live* alumna Jan Hooks was more warmly received as Smart's replacement, Carlene Dobber, younger sister of Charlene. Alice Ghostley also was a frequent presence as a woman in her dotage, who kept patronizing Sugarbaker's because she enjoyed being around the women. They came to enjoy her company as well, as did the audience.

Designing Women hit the peak of its popularity in its sixth season, ranking as the sixth most watched series on television—helped by the presences of a strong lead-in series, *Murphy Brown*. The series never won a major Emmy award, though it was nominated ten times.

---

59. *The Bob Cummings Show (Love That Bob)*

Broadcast History:

Sunday	10:30–11:00	January 1955–September 1955	NBC
Thursday	8:00–8:30	July 1955–September 1957	CBS
Tuesday	9:30–10:00	September 1957–September 1959	NBC

2 Major Emmy Awards (14 nominations):
No Emmy Awards for Best Series (3 nominations)
No Emmy Awards for Best Actor (4 nominations)
2 Emmy Awards for Best Supporting Actress (5 nominations)
No Emmy Awards for Best Writing (1 nomination)
No Emmy Awards for Best Directing (1 nomination)

Cast: Bob Cummings; Rosemary DeCamp; Ann B. Davis; Dwayne Hickman; Nancy Kulp; Lyle Talbot; Lisa Gaye; Diane Jergens (1955–56); King Donovan (1955–58); Mary Lawrence (1956–58); Gloria Marshall (1956–57); Joi Lansing (1956–59); Carol Henning (1956–57); Ingrid Goude (1957–58); Tammy Johnson (1959).

Bob Cummings was the on-screen Charlie Sheen of the 1950s, a debonair, charming womanizer. Cummings starred in the eponymous series as Bob Collins, a photographer of Hollywood actresses and fashion models, who yearned to bed the bevy of beauties in front of his lens. Alas Bob Collins—Cummings played a character with the same name in the theatrical *You Came Along*—prowled during the innocent Eisenhower years when even married couples weren't allowed to be seen sharing a bed and pregnant was "the 'p' word" on television. But Cummings, like other series headliners, was asked to serve in character as a huckster for the sponsors' products, in this case Winston cigarettes.

The times dictated that the series be primarily theater of the mind. Sex existed only in the imagination of the viewer. Bikinis were more heard of than seen. The buxom knockouts Bob got to shoot were generally seen in demure one-piece swimsuits. Bob was allowed to talk a good game but rarely got so much as a chaste kiss. Many of his subjects fell for Bob's smooth talking ways but something almost always happened to thwart his amorous schemes. That "something" was usually driven by the people around Bob.

His super efficient, plainish secretary Schultzy (Ann B. Davis) had her own designs on Bob, so she did her best to sabotage his romantic conspiracies. Gracie Allen and Bea Benaderet made a guest appearance in their *Burns and Allen* characters to get Bob to take a romantic interest in Schultzy but it was a quixotic mission. Bob appreciated her as a secretary, particularly after he replaced her in one episode with a ditzy blond, but that was all.

Pamela Livingstone (Nancy Kulp), a bird watcher intentionally crafted to be unappealing physically, with a personality to match, also aggressively pursued Bob, oblivious to the reality that if she were the last woman on Earth, Bob would choose to maintain celibacy.

His nephew Chuck (Dwayne Hickman) idolized Bob or more precisely the bacchanal lifestyle Chuck was convinced Bob led. Chuck's mother, Bob's widowed sister Margaret (Rosemary DeCamp), was a buzz-kill determined to have Bob settle down to a life of monogamy, preferably with Schultzy. Bob loved her nonetheless and reciprocated by setting up Margaret with dates.

It's no wonder Bob had no interest in marriage. Whenever the series depicted a married man, he was always hen-pecked by a stereotypical domineering wife. Cummings, who like Sheen maintained his boyish good looks into his fifties, doubled as his grandfather Josh Collins, who shared his yen for gorgeous women and flying. Both characters were accomplished pilots, an interest Cummings had in real life. Bob Collins was a member of the Air Force Reserve, a device used to drive some plots. In one, he tried to use his military connection to ace Peter Lawford, who made a cameo playing himself, out of being a judge at a beauty contest sponsored by the Air Force.

Cummings was Emmy-nominated four times for lead actor in a comedy and continued to have a thriving career after the show wrapped. However, he never managed to land in another long-running series. This included the one-and-done *New Bob Cummings Show*, which debuted two years after the demise of the original *Bob Cummings Show*, which was redubbed *Love That Bob* in syndication.

Meanwhile Cummings supporting players went on to greater fame in long-running series. Ann B. Davis, who won a pair of Emmys from four nominations as Schultzy, built even greater audience affection as Alice Nelson, the beloved housekeeper for *The Brady Bunch*. DeCamp landed recurring character roles as Aunt Helen in *Petticoat Junction*, Helen Marie in *That Girl* and Grandma Amanda in *The Partridge Family*. Pamela Livingstone was just a warmup for Nancy Kulp, who played basically the same character as Miss Hathaway on *The Beverly Hillbillies*. Pamela drove a broken down jalopy that looked like something the Clampetts might have traded in to move up to the primitive truck they drove from West Virginia to California. Dwayne Hickman also transitioned from Chuck into a new role with the same girls crazy persona. He left the series in its final season to become the titular character in *The Many Loves of Dobie Gillis*.

The Bob Cummings Show was recognized with three Emmy nominations as best comedy. The show was never a Nielsen sensation, failing to ever crack the season-long Top 30. Nevertheless, it was sufficiently popular in the entertainment community to draw then A-list guest stars such as George Burns, Alan Ladd, Charles Coburn, Zsa Zsa Gabor and Steve Allen. The series had a fascinating network history. It premiered on NBC as a midseason replacement, moved to CBS for its next two seasons, then returned to NBC, which canceled it after two more seasons.

60. *The Odd Couple*

Broadcast History:

Thursday	9:30–10:00	September 1970–January 1971	ABC
Friday	9:30–10:00	January 1971–June 1973	ABC
Friday	8:30–9:00	June 1973–January 1974	ABC
Friday	9:30–10:00	January 1974–September 1974	ABC
Thursday	8:00–8:30	September 1974–January 1975	ABC
Friday	9:30–10:00	January 1975–July 1975	ABC

3 Major Emmy Awards (14 nominations):
No Emmy Awards for Best Series (4 nominations)
3 Emmy Awards for Best Actor (10 nominations)

Cast: Tony Randall; Jack Klugman; Al Molinaro; Garry Walberg (1970–74); Larry Gelman; Archie Hahn (1973–74); Ryan McDonald (1970–71); Monica Evans (1970–71); Carol Shelly (1970–71); Joan Hotchkis (1970–72); Janis Hansen (1971–75); Brett Somers; Penny Marshall (1971–75); Elinor Donahue (1972–74).

A discussion of *The Odd Couple* demands specificity. There was really only one television adaptation of the Neil Simon play about mismatched roommates that mattered. It ran on ABC from 1970 to 1975. But there have been two other direct adaptations for television. *The New Odd Couple*, created as a stop-gap during a writers strike in 1982, featured African American lead actors Ron Glass and Demond Wilson. Another *Odd Couple* in 2015 starred Matthew Perry and Thomas Lennon. The gold standard is the edition starring Tony Randall as fastidious Felix Unger and Jack Klugman as slovenly Oscar Madison. Jack Lemmon and Walter Matthau set a stratospheric bar in the 1968 theatrical version but Randall and Klugman came close to matching it over 114 episodes.

Alas, in spite of critical raves and peer recognition, the series failed to achieve noteworthy ratings, never cracking Nielsen's top 25 rated series. It was saved from cancellation only because viewing ticked upward during the summer when viewers caught up with the much praised series rather than watch reruns of their in-season favorites. This same phenomenon was the salvation of *Miami Vice* in the 1980s after its maiden season, which was scheduled against the *Dallas* juggernaut.

The Television Academy was more attentive. Randall and Klugman were both nominated for an Emmy for each of the five seasons. Klugman won twice, Randall once. The series was nominated as best comedy four times.

The setup was two men, who couldn't be less alike in lifestyles and temperaments, sharing a Manhattan apartment. Both were divorcees, who had driven their former spouses crazy with their egocentricities. Felix (Randall) was a neat freak, more than a touch effeminate, with obsessive compulsive disorder tendencies. His wardrobe hung in the closet in alphabetical order. Although a hypochondriac, he did suffer from genuine maladies such as chronic sinusitis, which caused suffering he had no compunctions about sharing. He enjoyed the finer things in life such as a gourmet meal, vintage wine, opera and the ballet.

Oscar (Klugman) was a sports columnist, loud and abrasive. His clothes wound up wherever he threw them as he took them off. His apartment resembled a frat house on the Sunday morning after homecoming celebrations. His idea of a gourmet meal was steak, fried onion rings and beer. The only museum he had any interest in was the baseball Hall of Fame. Oscar was long divorced when Felix's wife Gloria decided she could no longer tolerate his overbearing neatness and grating petty critiques. She demanded he leave. With no other place to go, Felix shows up at Oscar's door, ostensibly for temporary lodging.

The original opening narration for the series described Felix and Oscar as friends from childhood. This was dropped after the fourth episode, which was keyed around them meeting for the first time when both served on the same jury. The original explanation made more sense. Only someone who knew Felix since they were kids could put up with him. Felix made everyone in the jury room so crazy with his nit-picking and contrariness that Oscar as a stranger would have crossed the street to avoid him in the future.

Felix's saving grace was his good heart. His attempts to insinuate himself into Oscar's professional and personal lives almost always produced calamitous results. His meddling once cost Oscar his job. He also got Oscar into hot water with the Internal Revenue Service. But as frustrated as Oscar got, he knew Felix meant well and would do anything for him. This included taking a haymaker from a hockey goon mad at Oscar for a nasty column about him.

Oscar's patience did have limits. Following Gloria's lead, he occasionally demanded Felix get out and stay out. It wasn't only Oscar. During one of Felix's exiles, he crashed with their friend Murray the cop (Al Molinaro), only to be tossed from there, too. His next stop was the Pigeon Sisters, Cicely (Monica Evans) and Gwendolyn (Carole Shelly), who lived upstairs from Oscar. They couldn't take him for very long, either. Fortunately for Felix, Oscar always relented and invited him back.

The former wives appeared infrequently. Janis Hansen played Felix's Gloria, the woman who remained first in his heart. Klugman's real-life spouse, Brett Somers, appeared as his ex-wife Blanche, who shared a mutual loathing with Oscar. The Pigeon Sisters were among several women with whom Felix and Oscar became involved. Oscar also dated Dr. Nancy Cunningham during the first season. Afterward, he made reference to the never seen Crazy Rhonda Zimmerman. Elinor Donahue arrived in season two as Felix's girlfriend Miriam.

Somers was not the only example of casting nepotism. Penny Marshall, the sister of executive producer Garry Marshall, recurred as Oscar's secretary Myrna Turner. Garry Marshall also later cast her in her career-making role on *Laverne & Shirley*. In an episode in which Myrna got married, the groom was played by Rob Reiner, then Marshall's husband.

The roommates did have their memorable moments, including appearing on *Password* and *Let's Make a Deal*. Felix also pulled strings to get Oscar a job working with Howard Cosell, who made a guest appearance. On another occasion, Felix agreed to fake it as the leader of a country band in order to make good on one of Oscar's gambling debts.

The quick audible in the opening about how long the two had known each other was symptomatic of the series' attitude about continuity. Felix was the father of two children, Leonard and Edna. Each was played by two actors. Willie Aames and Leif Garrett appeared as Leonard. Pamelyn Ferdin and Doney Oatman shared the role of Edna. Richard Stahl appeared as nine different characters and Herbie Faye made guest appearances in five different roles. In the series finale, Felix's begging and pleading for Gloria to take him back paid off and the two were remarried. Oscar had his peace back at last.

61. *Room 222*

Broadcast History:

Wednesday	8:30–9:00	September 1969–January 1971	ABC
Wednesday	8:00–8:30	January 1971–September 1971	ABC
Friday	9:00–9:30	September 1971–January 1974	ABC

#28 rated series in 1971–72

3 Major Emmy Awards (7 nominations):
1 Emmy Award for Best Series (2 nominations)
No Emmy Award for Best Actor (1 nomination)
1 Emmy Award for Best Supporting Actor (2 nominations)
1 Emmy Award for Best Supporting Actress (2 nominations)

Cast: Lloyd Haynes; Denise Nicholas; Michael Constantine; Karen Valentine; Howard Rice (1969–71); Judy Strangis; Heshimu; Pendrant Netherly (1969–71); David Jolliffe (1970–74); Ta-Tanisha (1970–72); Eric Laneauville (1971–73).

Room 222 was a departure from most situation comedies set in a high school environment. The primary focus was the teachers. It's not that the kids weren't prominent. But when student-teacher contretemps arose, the plots focused on how the faculty reacted to the young people rather than vice versa.

Reflecting this emphasis, the four leading players were all faculty members. Lloyd Hanes was indisputably the dominant figure as Pete Dixon. His official role was history teacher but he also was the go-to guy for both teachers and students when conflicts or problems arose. Colleagues loved him for his calm, reasoned demeanor. They even drafted him to lead them in a strike. He was a favorite of the students because he was cooler than the Polar Vortex. The only people around Walt Whitman High School who didn't revere him were up-tight faculty members, who adhered to the old school, my-way-or-the-highway techniques of classroom protocol.

Denise Nicholas played Liz McIntyre, Whitman's guidance counselor and Pete's love interest. She also was popular with the teens because she made an effort to speak to them in their jargon and understand the personal and real world pressures that often had a negative impact on academic performance. It didn't hurt that she also was the girlfriend of the exceedingly popular Mr. Dixon.

Karen Valentine became a breakout star as Alice Johnson, a perky student teacher in the series' first season and a full-fledged faculty member thereafter. Her upbeat, eager-to-please persona led Whitman's principal, Seymour Kauffman, to nickname her Mary Poppins. Michael Constantine played Principal Kauffman, whose crafting also was a step away from the stereotypical tyrannical, aloof administrator. Kauffman made it clear that high school is not a democracy and he was in charge. But he tempered his authority with a dry sense of humor and actually enjoyed the company of the teachers—most of them. Everyone at Whitman failed to appreciate how much Principal Kauffman's approach meant to them until they faced the possibility of him leaving and being replaced by an autocrat.

The fact that Hanes and Nicholas were African Americans with top billing in a racially mixed cast on a series that achieved longevity was a noteworthy development for its time. The Emmys rewarded the show's quality with the award for best new series (a category that since has been discontinued) in 1970. The same year it also was nominated as outstanding comedy series. Valentine and Constantine each won an Emmy from two nominations and Haynes garnered a single nomination.

The lead characters had to address typical high school issues: problem students who challenged authority; troubled kids as a result of tumultuous home lives; under-achievers who refused to make an effort to elevate their grades; students who really weren't college material but refused to accept it; and others who should have been preparing for higher learning but weren't motivated to do so.

They occasionally had to insinuate themselves into the love-lives of their students, such as persuading a young couple intent on eloping to Mexico that they were throwing away promising futures. The faculty members' own romantic entanglements also came into play. Alice got involved with the widowed father of one of her students and Kauffman became infatuated by a former nun, who had left the convent. Some students became love struck toward their teachers. One was so enamored by Pete and Liz that he became a constant, annoying presence in their personal lives.

Room 222 was in the vanguard of hybrid comedies, which leavened their light approach with substantial dollops of drama, some of it topical. Issues such as the civil rights movement, homosexuality, the Vietnam War, ageism, sexism and unfairly judging others because of their appearance drove plots. The laugh track generally was toned down to mild chuckles.

The high school setting allowed for an eclectic mix of youthful guest stars, many unknowns at the time of their appearance. Pre–*Star Wars* Mark Hamill was in a pair of episodes. Cindy Williams, who would become half of *Laverne & Shirley*, had three guest shots. Rob Reiner showed up at Whitman before he became "The Meathead" on *All in the Family*. Larry Linville and Jamie Farr were in separate episodes before they became cast-mates on *M*A*S*H*. Chuck Norris played himself in an episode.

Room 222 is on a short list of series saved by strong Emmy support. Legend has it that ABC was set to pull the plug because of low ratings after the initial season but reconsidered thanks to the laurels tossed its way by the Television Academy. Alas ratings never substantially improved and the show was canceled midway through its fifth season.

---

62. *December Bride*

Broadcast History:

Monday	9:30–10:00	October 1954–June 1958	CBS
Thursday	8:00–8:30	October 1958–September 1959	CBS

#10 rated series in 1954–55	#5 rated series in 1956–57
#6 rated series in 1955–56	#9 rated series in 1957–58

No Major Emmy Awards (5 nominations):
No Emmy Awards for Best Actress (2 nominations)
No Emmy Awards for Best Supporting Actor (1 nomination)
No Emmy Awards for Best Supporting Actress (2 nominations)

Cast: Spring Byington; Frances Rafferty; Dean Miller; Verna Felton; Harry Morgan.

December Bride's lofty ranking in situation comedy history is a product of being in the right place at the right time. In an era when some people were fascinated to see anything on their television screen, it followed *I Love Lucy* on Monday night on CBS. A test pattern could have become one of the top rated shows, as *December Bride* did. When *December Bride* premiered in 1954, most homes received only three or four channels. Competition included *Junior Press Conference* on ABC and *Boxing from St. Nicholas Arena* on Dumont.

Like many series in the infancy of television, *December Bride* was a radio transplant. On CBS's powerhouse Monday, it didn't have to be much to become a Top 10 fixture. Simplistic vignettes played out by a pleasant cast with a charisma deficiency was all it took.

Spring Byington, an appealing if not particularly memorable actress, had the title role as Lily Ruskin, a widow on the prowl for a new husband in the December of her life. She came close to fulfilling the complete title in the pilot. Traveling via train from her native Philadelphia to Los Angeles to move in with her daughter, Ruth Henshaw (Frances Rafferty) and son-in-law Matt Henshaw (Dean Miller), she was courted and eventually proposed to by a man at the same stage of life. A series of misunderstandings (forever a staple of situation comedies) led Ruth and Matt to believe Lily's fiancée was a shady character at best, a big-time crook at worst. Actually, he was a wealthy business tycoon. When he discovered what they thought of him, he called off the engagement and fled.

Lily was a charming extrovert, considerate and helpful to others. She worked with neighborhood children trying to master musical instruments and ballet, tutored a newlywed wife, who was inept in the kitchen, how to make tasty meals for her husband and always had a pot of coffee on the burner for local police officers in need of a pick-me-up. Lily even vowed to write shorter letters to lighten the burden her favorite mailman had to carry.

To Lily's chagrin, Matt and Ruth tended to be over-protective and doted on her as if she was incompetent. When they mistook Lily's fatigue, traceable to all the good deeds she did on a daily basis, for an illness, they summoned a doctor. Assured this wasn't the case, they jumped to the conclusion—an exercise they regularly committed—that she was bored. They coaxed everyone from a square dancing buff to a portly female off-road adventurer to an illusionist to drop by to enliven her already filled-to-the-brim daily agenda.

Matt was a rarity for television comedy, a son-in-law who cherished his wife's mother and said she was welcome in his home for as long as she wanted to stay. He even screened her dates to heighten the chances she wouldn't fall into the clutches of Mr. Wrong. Ruth was the dutiful wife, anxious to please her spouse and often seen in an apron covering a fashionable dress. Matt also wore the uniform of the day for situation comedies, a jacket and tie, even when lounging around the house.

If *December Bride* had been a one-woman show starring Byington, and Matt and Ruth were merely reference points in the script, it wouldn't have been appreciably different than the CBS version. In fact, a key character was merely a reference point. Harry Morgan, in one of the first major roles of his career, brought a spark to the series as Matt's neighbor and best friend Pete Porter. Matt's affection for Lily drove Pete crazy. Pete was the comedy stereotype, a wise-cracking, sarcastic cynic, who didn't have a lot good to say about his wife Gladys and only terrible things to say about her mother.

The extent to which Pete was the show-stealer was indicated by CBS's decision to spin him off into his own comedy, *Pete and Gladys*, even though Gladys was never seen in *December Bride*. Cara Williams was cast in the part in one of television's earliest spinoffs.

Lily made friends easily but she was particularly close with Hilda Crocker (Verna Felton), a woman roughly her age, who also was husband hunting. Hilda tried much too hard to be a firecracker, who loved Las Vegas and any place else where a good time could be had. She boasted she was in show business way back when and would burst into song at the slightest prompting.

As soon as *December Bride* stopped getting the lift supplied by *I Love Lucy* in its first four seasons and had to depend on *The Danny Thomas Show* for a lead-in, ratings began to slip. When it was shifted to Thursday in the fall of 1958, its Nielsen ratings went into a free fall, which could not be stemmed by CBS scheduling *I Love Lucy* reruns in front of it. CBS called a halt to the production of original episodes, although the network continued to air reruns in prime time and daytime.

December Bride received five major Emmy nominations, winning none. Spring Byington was twice nominated for lead actress in a comedy series. Verna Felton (twice) and Harry Morgan (once) were also nominated in the supporting character categories.

---

63. *Hazel*

Broadcast History:

Thursday	9:30–10:00	September 1961–September 1965	NBC
Monday	9:30–10:00	September 1965–September 1966	CBS

#4 rated series in 1961–62   #22 rated series in 1963–64
#15 rated series in 1962–63

2 Major Emmy Awards (4 nominations):
No Emmy Awards for Best Series (1 nomination)
2 Emmy Awards for Actress (3 nominations)

Cast: Shirley Booth; Don DeFore (1961–65); Whitney Blake (1961–65); Maudie Prickett; Howard Smith; Bobby Buntrock; Norma Varden (1961–65); Donald Foster (1961–65); Cathy Lewis (1961–65); Robert P. Lieb (1961–65); Mala Powers (1965–66); Ann Jillian (1965–66); Ray Fulmer (1965–66); Lynn Borden (1965–66); Julia Benjamin (1965–66).

Shirley Booth was a major get when NBC was able to convince her to make the jump to episodic television as the star of *Hazel*, a fluffy series based on a popular comic strip by Ted Kay. The relatively new medium, which was looked down upon by many in film and theater, wasn't used to attracting actors or actresses who had won both Oscars and Tony awards, as Booth had for *Come Back, Little Sheba*. Booth's television debut might have come sooner but for an unsatisfactory audition. She was up for the starring role in the radio version of *Our Miss Brooks* but was judged not right for the part. It went to Eve Arden, who stayed with it when it transitioned from radio to television.

Hazel, which allowed Booth to complete the show business golden trifecta by capturing a pair of Emmys, took full advantage of her talent. Her character, a maid named Hazel Burke, dominated her universe to such an extent, she was the sun and her supporting cast was relegated to the equivalent of planets orbiting the sun.

Hazel technically worked for attorney George Baxter and his family. However, Don DeFore, who played male lead George, was as much a second banana as he was as Ozzie's malt shop buddy Thorny on *The Adventures of Ozzie & Harriet*. Hazel only let George occasionally believe he was in charge. Hazel had the complete bag of tricks to get her way.

Plots were soft and simplistic. An episode in which Hazel greatly annoyed a man who had nodded off in church by flicking his ear, only to have him turn out to be one of George's most important clients, was as complex as it got. Most of the time, Hazel was an eager-to-please chatterbox and busybody. But when it served her purposes, she could be flirty or feisty and deviously manipulative. George quipped in an admiring tone that she had a diabolical mind.

She generally used her skills for good. When she discovered a school teacher she liked was pining to meet the right man for marriage, Hazel went into full match-making mode to set up the teacher with a widower from across the street, even though George had a different woman in mind for his neighbor. Predictably, Hazel's instincts were more astute. George's choice was a cunning gold-digger, who intended to exile the neighbor's children to boarding school as soon as she got a ring on her finger.

Episodes always dissolved into the satisfactory resolutions the audience craved. George had a client who was anxious to transform a canoe pond into an industrial park. Hazel, who had fond memories of being courted there, went into full community organizer mode to stop the development. She feared the old gent, who for years had run the canoe rental shack, would be put out to pasture. She was heart-broken when George prevailed for his client. But it turned out the canoe guy was looking for a way out of a business that had gone sour and had landed a better job in the new industrial park.

Hazel had a couple of crucial allies in her control of the Baxter home. George's wife Dorothy (Whitney Blake) was a co-conspirator in many of Hazel's schemes to thwart George. Otherwise, Dorothy, an interior designer, was a typical situation comedy wife, down to earth and practical but primarily an accessory to her more featured husband. Hazel was nominally deferential to the prim and proper George, addressing him as Mr. B, but she affectionately nicknamed Dorothy, who she had known since Dorothy was a little girl, "Missy."

The Burke's only child, Harold (Bobby Buntrock), might as well have been Hazel's son. She treated him as such and nicknamed him "Sport." Hazel helped with his schoolwork and taught him how to kick a football. Whenever a family controversy arose, with Hazel at odds with George, there was never a question on which side Sport would come down.

Hazel had an interesting history. It started on NBC in black and white but by its second season had converted to color. (Parent company RCA was ahead of its rivals in producing shows in color because it wanted to sell new color television sets.) After four seasons, the first two of which landed among the 15 highest rated series on television, *Hazel* was picked up by CBS. George and Dorothy were written out of the series, ostensibly to travel the world on business. Harold was left behind in the care of Hazel. Hazel became the housekeeper for George's brother Steve (Ray Fulmer), a real estate agent, his wife Barbara (Lynn Borden) and their daughter Susie (Julia Benjamin). The audience did not embrace the reworked cast as they had the original and the revamp was canceled after one season on its new network.

64. *Who's the Boss?*

Broadcast History:

Tuesday	8:30–9:00	October 1984–April 1985	ABC
Tuesday	9:00–9:30	April 1985–July 1985	ABC
Tuesday	8:00–8:30	August 1985–August 1991	ABC
Tuesday	8:30–9:00	August 1991–September 1991	ABC
Saturday	8:00–8:30	September 1991–January 1992	ABC
Saturday	8:30–9:00	February 1992–March 1992	ABC
Saturday	8:00–8:30	March 1992–June 1992	ABC
Wednesday	9:30–10:00	June 1992–July 1992	ABC
Thursday	8:00–8:30	July 1992–September 1992	ABC

#30 rated series in 1984–85   #8 rated series in 1988–89
#10 rated series in 1985–86   #12 rated series in 1989–90

#10 rated series in 1986–87   #23 rated series in 1990–91
#6 rated series in 1987–88

No Major Emmy Awards (2 nominations):
No Emmy Awards for Best Supporting Actress (2 nominations)

Cast: Judith Light; Tony Danza; Alyssa Milano; Danny Pintauro; Katherine Helmond; Jonathan Halyalkar (1990–91); Curnal Achilles Aulisio (1992).

Who's the Boss? was comedy comfort food, a sweet, predictable series. The audience could anticipate what was going to happen each week from the opening scene. These expectations were never disappointed. No matter how dire some scenarios might have seemed in mid-episode they were always resolved by episode's end in a crowd-pleasing way. The personal appeal and winning chemistry of the lead players contributed to the longevity of the ABC series.

Tony Danza, coming off an extended run in *Taxi* as washed up boxer Tony Banta, co-starred as a similar character, Tony Miceli. The pleasingly self deprecating Danza joked that the reason his characters retained his first name was so he always knew people on the set were referring to him when they called "Tony." Tony Miceli was a former major league baseball player, driven into retirement prematurely by an injury, which apparently had no effect on the other facets of his life. An easy-going widower, he wanted to take his daughter Samantha (Alyssa Milano) out of his native Brooklyn to a less hectic environment.

Judith Light, familiar to many from a long-running, Daytime Emmy winning role on *One Life to Live*, co-starred as Angela Bower, a divorced, type-A advertising executive living in Fairfield, Connecticut. She was in need of a live-in housekeeper and babysitter for her son Jonathan (Danny Pintauro), a few years younger than Samantha. Tony answered a want ad for the job and, with no other viable candidate Angela hired him despite the awkwardness of having a virile male living platonically under her roof.

Tony and Angela had their small clashes, as any couple living together would, but Angela appreciated that she had lucked into the ideal person in Tony, a jovial, good natured guy with a great sense of humor, even if he was a klutz performing some of his household duties. It was a bonus that Tony also served as the male role model absent from Jonathan's life. In turn, Angela became a maternal figure for Samantha. The emotional bonds and sexual tension that formed between Tony and Angela quickly came to the fore. However, they strove mightily to ignore this elephant in their living room. They even maintained separate social lives, dating others. But these outside interests never were enduring because Tony and Angela knew deep down that they were the right person for each other.

Tony and Angela might have kept their libidos in check but Angela's randy, sharp-tongued mother Mona—a show-stealing turn by Katharine Helmond—was a sexually voracious cougar before the term came into vogue. The younger the better was Mona's dating philosophy, although the closest she came to the altar was an engagement to someone closer to her age, a guy named Max, played by Leslie Nielsen. Nielsen was one of many A-list stars to visit the show. The topper was an appearance by Frank Sinatra. Ray Charles, Mike Tyson, Betty White and a pre–*Friends* Matthew Perry, playing a college friend of Samantha, also made guest shots.

Having Tony and Angela maintain a semblance of separate lives created options for the writing staff, which wasn't confronted by the necessity to find new ways to advance the romantic relationship on a weekly basis. Storylines were devised in several ways. Tony's domestic chores didn't demand his full-time attention, especially as Samantha and Jonathan got older. To keep busy, Tony sought outside work, such as managing the fast food joint that was not only the hangout for the in crowd at Samantha's high school but the place where she also had a part-time job. When Tony's meddling almost wrecked Samantha's social standing, Tony segued to door-to-door Avon sales. Tony eventually decided to further his education, enrolling in the college that also would become Samantha's alma mater.

At the outset, Angela worked for a large firm but after three seasons, she opened her own company, fueling new workplace headaches as plot fodder. The typical adolescent angst of Samantha and Jonathan as they matured and became more independent also drove episodes. Even though her father and Angela never married, Samantha eventually found her Mr. Right, a medical student who decided he preferred to become a puppeteer.

The fact that in the end Angela and Tony didn't formalize their relationship by marrying was the only time viewers' hopes and expectations weren't realized. Their romance was left open-ended so that the audience could come to its own conclusion as to what happened after the curtain came down for the final time. This creative choice was largely motivated by the hope that it would bolster syndication sales, which turned out to be lucrative.

Who's the Boss? was very popular with audiences, if not with the Emmy voters. The series ranked in Nielsen's top 10 for four of its first five seasons. The only Emmy consideration the show received was for supporting actress in a comedy—nominated twice (Katherine Helmond).

65. *My Three Sons*

Broadcast History:

Thursday	9:00–9:30	September 1960–September 1963	ABC
Thursday	8:30–9:00	September 1963–September 1965	ABC
Thursday	8:30–9:00	September 1965–August 1967	CBS
Saturday	8:30–9:00	September 1967–September 1971	CBS
Monday	10:00–10:30	September 1971–December 1971	CBS
Thursday	8:30–9:00	January 1972–August 1972	CBS

#13 rated series in 1960–61
#11 rated series in 1961–62
#28 rated series in 1962–63
#27 rated series in 1963–64
#13 rated series in 1964–65
#15 rated series in 1965–66
#29 rated series in 1966–67
#24 rated series in 1967–68
#14 rated series in 1968–69
#25 rated series in 1969–70
#19 rated series in 1970–71

No Major Emmy Awards (3 nominations):
No Emmy Awards for Best Supporting Actor (1 nomination)
No Emmy Awards for Best Supporting Actress (1 nomination)
No Emmy Awards for Best Direction (1 nomination)

Cast: Fred MacMurray; Tim Considine (1960–65); Don Grady (1960–71); Stanley Livingston; William Frawley (1960–65); William Demarest (1965–72); Cynthia Pepper (1960–61); Robert P. Lieb (1960–61); Florence MacMichael (1960–61); Peter Brooks (1961–63); Ricky Allen (1961–63); Olive Dunbar (1961–63); Olan Soule (1961–63); Meredith MacRae (1963–65); Barry Livingston (1963–72); Tina Cole (1967–1972); John Howard (1965–67); Dawn Lyn (1969–72); Beverly Garland (1969–72); Joseph Todd (1970–72); Michael Todd (1970–72); Daniel Todd (1970–72); Anne Francis (1971–72); Ronne Troup (1970–72)

By one standard, *My Three Sons* is the second most successful live action situation comedy in television history. The 12 seasons produced is exceeded by only the 14 seasons of *The Adventures of Ozzie & Harriet*. In an example of knowing the cost of everything and the value of nothing, ABC let the series slip away to CBS after the 1964–65 season because it didn't want to cover the cost of shooting the episodes, which had been in black and white on ABC, in color. Five of the seven remaining seasons landed the show among Nielsen's 25 highest rated series, two in the Top 15.

Its longevity was the only thing remarkable about the series. From 380 episodes, it garnered only two performing Emmy nominations, one for a guest shot by Irene Hervey, the other in the supporting player category for William Demarest. A single nomination for directing filled out the show's entire Emmy history.

My Three Sons was a throwback to the innocent era of shows like *The Adventures of Ozzie & Harriet* and *The Donna Reed Show*. The plots were simplistic and linear. Topical and dark issues were totally absent, as was anything controversial. Men and women engaged only in chaste kisses and embraces. They were never seen in a bedroom together. A family crisis was four people trying to get out of the house to work and school at the same time or teenage brothers liking the same girl.

McMurray transited the same gentle persona that had made him a big screen favorite in Disney flicks like *The Shaggy Dog* to television as Steven Douglas, an aeronautical engineer left with the task of raising three boys when his wife died at an early age. In order to get MacMurray to agree to star in the series, the producers had to agree on a unique shooting plan which stipulated that all of MacMurray's scenes were to be shot in a limited number of days, not necessarily at the same time of the year. This unique shooting schedule produced some serious problems. At times, guest stars had to return months later to finish filming an episode. Another way that writers worked around MacMurray's unorthodox schedule was to include many instances that had MacMurray's character out of town and he would appear communicating with family members on the telephone.

Tim Considine played Steve's oldest, Mike, an athlete and social butterfly. Although he played a few years younger in the series, Considine was already 20 when *My Three Sons* premiered in 1960 and he looked it. He stayed with the show only through the first episode on CBS, which was built around his marriage to a girl named Sally, played by Meredith McRae. His departure was reportedly triggered by a contract dispute. He was treated like a prodigal son in subsequent seasons with his name rarely even mentioned in the Douglas household.

Don Grady, 16 when the show debuted, played closer to his actual age as Robbie Douglas. He and Mike had a close relationship although they often became embroiled in typical teenage contretemps. Grady stayed with the series through season 11 when he married a girl named Katie, played by Tina Cole. At the end of the season, Grady was written out of the show, ostensibly to help build a bridge in South America. Before he left, he and Tina had triplets. Unlike McRae, who was jettisoned when her on-screen husband left, Cole was retained, bringing three new sons to the Douglas household. An attempt was made to spin off Grady, Cole and the triplets into their own series but the pilot didn't impress the CBS brass sufficiently to earn a berth on the schedule.

The baby of the family, precocious Chip (Stanley Livingston), was little more than half his older brother's show ages and resented always being left out of their adventurous activities. In the beginning, like most boys his age, he was girl phobic. Of course, he grew out of this and eventually took a teen bride of his own, Polly (Ronnie Troup), who married at a tender age to escape a troubled home.

When Mike's departure left the series one son short, a plot scenario was concocted in which Chip befriends another boy his age, Ernie, who is waiting to be adopted. When Steve learns of Ernie's plight, he steps up and adopts him, bringing a third male child into the fold. Keeping it all in the family in real life, Stanley Livingston's brother Barry was cast as Ernie.

Although a widower, Steve didn't have to raise the children by himself. His wife's father, Bub O'Casey, moved in to keep house and ride herd on the boys when Steve wasn't around. William Frawley, familiar to television audiences as *I Love Lucy*'s Fred Mertz, played Bub. When he became too ill to continue during the 1964–65 season, his uncle Charlie moved into the Douglas's home to fill his role. William Demarest, who played Charlie, was the lone regular to gain an Emmy nomination.

Another significant change occurred in 1967. The Douglas clan left their home in the fictional Midwest town of Bryant Park and relocated to the Los Angeles area. Steve's status as single and handsome with a good job made him a potential prize catch for husband-seekers. An episode or two a season was devoted to Steve meeting and occasionally becoming infatuated or trying to escape the clutches of an attractive woman. Until the show's 11th season, something always happened to his relationships before they got close to the altar.

It wasn't until his original sons had grown into young adults and taken wives of their own that Steve finally fell for and married a woman named Barbara (Beverly Garland). Barbara brought a 5-year-old daughter from a previous marriage, Dodie (Dawn Lynn).

By the time *My Three Sons* reached its 12th season, MacMurray was the only original cast member left. When the show slipped out of the Nielsen top 30 for only the second time in its history in 1971–72, CBS decided it had run its course and canceled it.

66. *The Real McCoys*

Broadcast History:

Thursday	8:30–9:00	October 1957–September 1962	ABC
Sunday	9:00–9:30	September 1962–September 1963	CBS

#30 rated series in 1957–58	#5 rated series in 1960–61
#8 rated series in 1958–59	#14 rated series in 1961–62
#11 rated series in 1959–60	

No Major Emmy Awards (5 nominations):
No Emmy Awards for Best Actor (1 nomination)
No Emmy Award for Best Supporting Actor (1 nomination)
No Emmy Awards for Best Supporting Actress (1 nomination)
No Emmy Awards for Best Writing (1 nomination)
No Emmy Awards for Best Direction (1 nomination)

Cast: Walter Brennan; Richard Crenna; Kathy Nolan (1957–62); Lydia Reed; Michael Winkelman (1957–62); Tony Martinez; Andy Clyde; Madge Blake; Betty Garde (1959–60); Janet DeGore (1963); Butch Patrick (1963); Joan Blondell (1963).

The Real McCoys were the Clampetts without oil money. They moved to California from the hills of West Virginia. Just like *The Beverly Hillbillies*.

Walter Brennan, a four-time Oscar nominee and three-time winner for supporting roles in big screen Westerns, moved to television to head the ensemble as Grandpa Amos McCoy, a cantankerous but big-hearted farmer, who had difficulty adapting to modern ways. Grandpa took giddy pleasure in showing the old ways were sometimes still best. His shining moment came when his divining rod located underground water where modern scientific techniques had failed. In spite of his ornery nature, Grandpa was a marvelous role model for the younger members of the clan, instilling strong family values and ethics in his grandchildren on a regular basis. He became particularly close to Little Luke McCoy (Michael Winkleman), who idolized him.

Virtue and doing the right thing were always rewarded. An unscrupulous land speculator tried to buy a seemingly worthless piece of the McCoy farm, because he knew the state would pay a premium for it to clear the way for a freeway. Amos thought the man was a fool and substituted a seemingly more valuable parcel into the bill of sale, unwittingly foiling the scheme to cheat him.

Richard Crenna, previously known for his role as Walter Denton, a teen with a high-pitched voice on both the radio and television versions of *Our Miss Brooks*, stepped up to an adult role as Luke. He and his younger brother Little Luke shared the same first name, he explained, because his late parents were so excited when Little Luke was born that they forgot they had a son named Luke.

Just before they left Smokey Corners, Luke took a bride, Kate (Kathy Nolan), whose lack of farm skills and advanced age—she had just entered her twenties, ancient for an unmarried woman by Appalachian standards—

perturbed Grandpa. He got over this quickly and came to love her like a daughter.

Brennan, Crenna and Nolan were each nominated for an Emmy. Kate enthusiastically stepped into the role of surrogate mother for Little Luke and his teenage sister Hassie (Lydia Reed). As the show progressed, Little Luke and Hassie evolved into young adults. When the series shifted to CBS, Little Luke was written out as joining the military and Hassie went away to college.

Amos inherited the land in the San Fernando Valley from his uncle Ben. When the McCoys arrived neighbors were few and miles apart. This area is now one of the most densely populated in the United States. The only neighbors the McCoys had regular interaction with were George and Flora MacMichael, who raised sheep on their adjoining spread. Grandpa got off to a bad start with them. He chased Flora (Madge Blake) and her livestock off his land for no reason other than it was his land. She retaliated by shutting off the water from her land, which supplied the McCoy farm.

Chastened, Amos made his peace with her to get the water turned back on. A spinster, Flora came to have her eye on Amos but he wanted none of it. Amos did become pals with her brother George (Andy Clyde), although the two set-in-their-ways senior citizens were constantly at each other's throats, even over innocuous issues such as arm wrestling and checkers.

In addition to willing Amos the land, Uncle Ben also left him his foreman, Mexican-American Pepino (Tony Martinez), who initially came across as a caricature but proved to be wise and indispensible in running the farm. He became Amos's best friend and addressed him as "Senor Grandpa." When Pepino became an American citizen he paid tribute to Amos and the family by adopting the surname McCoy.

The Real McCoys is credited with being the inspiration for CBS's subsequent rural dominated lineup, keyed by *The Beverly Hillbillies, The Andy Griffith Show* and their several spinoffs. Irene Ryan, who gained fame as Granny Clampett, and Nancy Kulp, who went on to play Miss Hathaway on *The Beverly Hillbillies*, each had a guest role on *The Real McCoys*.

Other young actors, who paid visits to the McCoys en route to major stardom, included Beau Bridges, Ellen Burstyn, Adam "Batman" West, Alan Hale, Jr., and Tina Louise prior to their three-hour cruise to *Gilligan's Island* and Lucille Ball's recurring sidekick Gale Gordon.

The Real McCoys was a surprise success story during its five seasons on ABC. From seasons two through five, it was a fixture in Nielsen's top 20 and twice cracked the top 10.

A sixth season on CBS had an entirely different thrust. In addition to

Little Luke and Hassie departing, Luke became a widower. The family nature was abandoned in favor of Luke's pursuit, with the unsolicited meddling of Grandpa, of a new wife. The combination of the revised concept, the cast defections and the transition to a new network, almost always a ratings killer, didn't play well with America and the series was canceled.

---

67. A Different World

Broadcast History:

Thursday	8:30–9:00	September 1987–June 1992	NBC
Thursday	8:00–8:30	July 1992–November 1992	NBC
Thursday	8:30–9:00	November 1992–January 1993	NBC
Thursday	8:00–8:30	May 1993–June 1993	NBC
Friday	8:00–8:30	July 1993	NBC

#2 rated series in 1987–88   #4 rated series in 1990–91
#3 rated series in 1988–89   #17 rated series in 1991–92
#4 rated series in 1989–90

No Major Emmy Awards (2 nominations):
No Emmy Award for Best Guest Actor/Actress (2 nominations)

Cast: Lisa Bonet (1987–88); Jasmine Guy; Dawnn Lewis (1987–92); Kadeem Hardison; Darryl Bell; Marisa Tomei (1987–88); Marie-Alise Recanser (1987–88); Loretta Devine (1987–88); Amir Williams (1987–88); Bee-be Smith (1987–88); Kim Wayans (1987–88); Sinbad (1987–91); Mary Alice (1988–89); Glynn Turman (1988–93); Cree Summer (1988–93); Charnele Brown (1988–93); Lou Myeres (1988–93); Reuben Grundy (1989–90); Jada Pinkett (1991–93); Ajai Sanders (1991–92); Joe Morton (1991); Karen Malina White (1992–93); Gary Dourdan (1992); Michael Ralph (1992).

The Cosby Show was in all likelihood television's last mega-hit series. Multi-channel cable and satellite television makes the extraordinary audience magnetism of *The Cosby Show*—more than half the country watching television typically tuned in—unattainable in the 21st century. *The Cosby Show* propelled NBC from a cellar-dwelling network to an unbeatable juggernaut. Adhering to the credo that if something works do it more, a spinoff became inevitable. Cosby's plan was to set it at a traditionally black college since he regretted that they were falling out of favor as full integration made mainstream universities welcoming to African American students. Cosby wanted to revitalize the black college's appeal. *A Different World* succeeded on all counts. Ratings were huge and young African Americans said they started to give traditionally black schools a second look after watching the NBC comedy.

A bonus for Cosby was the opportunity to exile an increasingly difficult Lisa Bonet, who played his daughter Denise, to another series. The premise had Denise opting to attend fictional Hillman College in Virginia, where she would interact primarily with other young African Americans. Members of the Huxtable clan crossed over to visit Denise at school. Lest the series be an all–African American show Marissa Tomei was cast as Maggie Lauton, who connected with Denise and became a close friend. This scenario survived only one season.

Cosby was infuriated by Bonet using her free time in the offseason to star in a risqué movie, *Angel Heart*, which featured nudity and explicit sexual situations. Bonet also did a nude layout for a magazine. The final straw came when she became pregnant. Bonet might have been married to singer Lenny Kravitz in real life but Denise Huxtable was still a single girl. No daughter of Cliff Huxtable was going to be seen as an unwed teenage mother. This might be amusing given some of the sexual assault allegations made against Cosby by a succession of women over the course of his career but in the late 1980s, Cosby was Mr. Wholesome, America's model parent.

There were other issues with Bonet, who was often tardy or a no show on the set. Denise was called back to New York and *The Cosby Show* but a storyline was concocted that had her leaving home to tour Africa, which would cover her gestation period. Also after the first season, Tomei asked to be released from the series so that she could pursue her film career, which soon led to an Oscar for *My Cousin Vinny*.

A Different World became a vastly different world in its second season. With Bonet out of the picture, supporting characters stepped to center stage. Whitley Gilbert (Jasmine Guy), originally depicted as a flighty dilettante who became Denise's closest friend, and her boyfriend Dwayne Wayne (Kadeem Hardison), who dated Denise but eventually courted and married Whitley, became the focal point of plots. The tone of the series also changed under the direction of Debbie Allen, sister of Phylicia Rashad, who played Clair Huxtable on *The Cosby Show*. What had been a non-controversial, soft sitcom morphed into a series which regularly tackled social issues, especially those of particular urgency to college students and young African Americans.

The Cosby Show had been criticized for "not being black enough." *A Different World* became the antidote to such charges. It was one of the first comedies to seriously treat the AIDS epidemic, which was roiling black communities. Racial profiling, reverse discrimination, voting drives, segregated clubs, the Clarence Thomas-Anita Hill hearings and the civil disturbances that followed the Rodney King verdict were among topics that drove episodes. Students were seen wearing dreadlocks, jerry curls and the colors of the black liberation flag. Civil rights leader Jesse Jackson made a guest appearance in season two. Lena Horne and Gladys Knight each were Emmy nominated for guest roles, the only performing Emmy nominations the series garnered. Tupac Shakur made a rare television appearance.

The series also had its share of frivolity as the relationship of Whitley and Dwayne progressed until they faced the same hassles and arguments of all young people in love. Whitley developed a new best female friend, Kimberly Reese (Charnele Brown), a pre-med student who was squeamish around blood. Her boyfriend Ron Johnson (Darryl Bell) was a free-spirit, who was Dwayne's best friend and more of a presence in the life of Whitley and Dwayne than they would have preferred. Kim shared an apartment with vain, flirtatious Winifred "Freddie" Brooks, whose fling with Ron drove a wedge between him and Kim.

Jaleesa Vinson (Dawnn Lewis), Denise's first college roommate, was more mature than the others and became the dorm monitor, which occasionally put her in an awkward role enforcing rules to friends. She had been married and divorced and her former spouse Walter was always on the fringe of her new life. In addition to its gilded pedigree as a *Cosby Show* offspring *A Different World* was blessed with the almost foolproof half-hour hammock between *The Cosby Show* and *Cheers*. Largely as a result of this, it was a Nielsen Top 5 fixture for its first four seasons. It slipped slightly in season five but remained in the Top 20. However, season six, with The *Cosby Show* gone as a lead-in, it plunged out of the Top 70 and the plug was pulled.

---

68. *The Life of Riley*

Broadcast History:

Friday	8:30–9:00	January 1953–September 1956	NBC
Friday	8:00–8:30	October 1956–December 1956	NBC
Friday	8:30–9:00	January 1957–August 1958	NBC

#16 rated series in 1952–53	#21 rated series in 1954–55
#13 rated series in 1953–54	#21 rated series in 1955–56

No Major Emmy Awards (No nominations)

Cast: William Bendix; Marjorie Reynolds; Wesley Morgan; Lugene Sanders; Tom D'Andrea (1953–55, 1956–58); Gloria Blondell (1953–55, 1956–58); Gregory

Marshall (1953–55); Douglas Dumbrille; Robert Sweeney; Emory Parnell; Sterling Holloway; Henry Kulky; George O'Hanlon (1955–56); Florence Sundstrom (1955–56); Martin Milner (1957–58).

The Life of Riley has been misappropriated over the years to signify having it made. Its precise origin is a matter of debate but in its television incarnation, it stood for anything but the good life. Chester A. Riley was a lovable but bumbling lug, whose daily routine had only one certainty. No matter what Riley did and how well intentioned it was, it was going to turn out disastrously, evoking his signature phrase of frustration, "What a revoltin' development this is!" which also has been widely appropriated, including by Eve Arden in *Our Miss Brooks*.

Like many television series of the early 1950s, *The Life of Riley* was an adaptation of a popular radio series. In fact, it was a multi-media format. In addition to its radio life (which included an identically titled but unrelated series in the 1940s), the concept was adapted into a 1949 theatrical feature. *A Life of Riley* comic book also was published.

Moreover, there were a couple of distinct *The Life of Riley* television series. The first starred Jackie Gleason as Chester A. Riley but it lasted only one season due to a dispute between the producers and sponsor. William Bendix, who played Riley on radio and the big screen, assumed the role for the second incarnation, which ran for six seasons, four of them placing among Nielsen's 25 highest rated series for the season. While the series was somewhat popular with audiences, it was not popular with the Emmy voters, never receiving a nomination for a major Emmy award.

Bendix was unavailable contractually when the Gleason edition launched. Riley—he was rarely addressed by his first name—was a blue collar, lunch pail carrying riveter at Cunningham Aircraft and a devoted family man. He and his wife Peg (Marjorie Reynolds) had two children Babs (Lugene Sanders) and Junior (Wesley Morgan). It's not unfair to say Riley had two kids but Peg had three—Babs, Junior and Riley. He was a large man but a big baby in need of regular supervision. An appointment to have the routine procedure of having his tonsils removed sent him into a tizzy of fearful apprehension and end-of-life preparations.

The connection between Gleason and Bendix extended beyond playing the same role. The similarities between Riley and Gleason's iconic Ralph Kramden are unmistakable. Both were portly, middle class guys with extremely understanding and patient spouses. Also, each was a dreamer, who repeatedly came up with unconventional ideas, which inevitably backfired, to improve his family's lot in life. The most significant difference between the characters was Riley had kids, Ralph didn't. Riley also had a sunnier disposition.

Another similarity was each had an off-kilter best friend, who encouraged off-the-wall activities then bailed out when things went awry. For Ralph Kramden, it was Ed Norton. For Riley it was his co-worker Jim Gillis (Tom D'Andrea). Riley wasn't as self centered as Ralph. His efforts were often geared to helping others. Eager to deliver on a promise of a boat, which he didn't have, for a long planned group fishing trip, Riley improvised. He built one—in his living room.

In an attempt to help Babs win school office, Riley went overboard and promised a date with his daughter to the prom to any guy who voted for her. Babs got the votes to win but Riley wound up with a riot in his living room as a battalion of guys, each of whom thought they were the one who was going to escort Babs to the dance, turned unruly.

Matchmaking Babs was a relentless pursuit for Riley, with several episodes built around his clumsy and ultimately unsuccessful efforts. It's not as if Babs needed his help. She had no trouble finding a husband on her own. Riley never learned his lesson when it came to matchmaking. His promise to his boss that he would get a big man on campus to escort the boss' unattractive daughter to a dance also turned into a revoltin' development.

Junior also came in for unwanted assistance. When his scout troop needed a leader, Riley stepped forward even though he knew nothing about what it entailed. Despite working with his hands on an assembly line, Riley also knew nothing about building a car, even a soapbox derby type. But this didn't stop him from throwing himself into Junior's efforts to build one.

There was almost nothing Riley wouldn't do for his family. To please Peg, he signed up for dance instructions in spite of being as nimble on his feet as a three-legged rhino. When Babs married and was expecting her first child, the good father enlisted in a class on nursing babies, thinking it meant child care not breast feeding. What a revoltin' development that turned out to be.

---

69. *Our Miss Brooks*

Broadcast History:

Friday	9:30–10:00	October 1952–June 1955	CBS
Friday	8:30–9:00	October 1955–September 1956	CBS

#22 rated series in 1952–53
#14 rated series in 1953–54

1 Major Emmy Award (9 nominations):
No Emmy Awards for Best Program (3 nominations)
1 Emmy Award for Best Actress (5 nominations)
No Emmy Awards for Best Supporting Actor (1 nomination)

Cast: Eve Arden; Gale Gordon; Robert Rockwell; Richard Crenna (1952–55); Jane Morgan; Gloria McMillan (1952–55); Leonard Smith (1952–55); Mary Jane Croft (1952–54); Virginia Gordon (1952–53); Paula Winslowe (1953–56); Joseph Kearnes (1953–55); Jesslyn Fax (1954–56); Ricky Vera (1954–56); Bob Sweeney (1955–56); Nana Bryant (1955); Isabel Randolph (1955–56); Gene Barry (1955–56); William Ching (1955–56); Hy Averback (1956).

Our Miss Brooks was a mold-breaker. The Madison High School English teacher played by Eve Arden was a rare female lead in the 1950s. Unlike the most prominent one, Lucille Ball, Arden's Connie Brooks had a forceful personality, a quick wit and a sharp tongue and was not dependent on men. On a faculty dominated by men, she was a leader and outspoken activist.

Arden's work, which included some double duty as her twin sister, was recognized with one Emmy from five nominations. Despite being only a modest ratings success, cracking the Nielsen top 25 twice in four seasons, the series, another adaptation of a popular radio program, also was thrice nominated for Emmys.

Miss Brooks' admirable personal traits and refusal to back down made her the bane of Principal Osgood Conklin, a self important bully, who felt his position entitled him to unquestioning loyalty and obedience. Gale Gordon's portrayal of Mr. Conklin, which garnered an Emmy nomination, was the first of many similar roles for him and set the stage for his subsequent rocket ride to fame when he hitched his wagon to Lucy's star as her favorite foil.

It drove Mr. Conkin crazy that Miss Brooks not only could not be intimidated but more often than not got the best of him. She wasn't a one-woman army. She had many allies among the faculty and student body. Foremost was a mischievous student with a high-pitched voice, Walter Denton (Richard Crenna), who enlisted in all his favorite teacher's campaigns against Mr. Conklin. Walter also was her chauffeur to and from school. Richard Crenna did a masterful job in his breakthrough role as goofy Walter in spite of the fact that he was absurdly miscast as a high school student. He was 26 (and looked it) when *Our Miss Brooks* premiered.

Miss Brooks and Walter often made a fool of Mr. Conklin. For example, when he tried to engineer favorable publicity for himself by leaping from the school roof into a firemen's net as part of a life-saving demonstration. The cowardly Mr. Conklin had no intention of performing the stunt. He planned to force Miss Brooks to disguise herself to resemble him and take the leap. Walter thwarted this scheme by faking an actual fire from which the only escape was to jump. Mr. Conklin summoned what little courage he had and Miss Brooks and Walter enjoyed a hearty laugh.

Even when his intentions were noble, Walter had a way of ruining things for Mr. Conklin. In one episode he was enlisted to house sit for the principal, who had a living room full of pricy new bamboo furniture. Walter misinterpreted an alert on short wave radio that a killer storm was approaching. He dutifully followed instructions to break up any available bamboo to board up the windows. Alas, the report was coming from Bombay, India.

Connie's wrangling with Mr. Conklin went beyond the grounds of Madison High. In one episode, she had to intercede when Mr. Conklin tried to swindle Connie's kindly but not tightly wrapped landlady Margaret Davis (Jane Morgan) in a house sale. Connie's activism knew no bounds. When she heard an old horse might be headed toward the glue factory, she organized a campaign to save him.

If aligning with Miss Brooks wasn't enough to rile Mr. Conklin against him, Walter had the nerve to hit on Mr. Conklin's daughter Harriet (Gloria McMillan). Their relationship didn't go far in spite of Walter's best efforts. Although Walter spent most of his time around Miss Brooks, he did have one close friend, Stretch Snodgrass (Leonard Smith), an athlete whose lack of academic prowess made Walter look like a genius.

Connie also had to get aggressive to pursue her romantic interest, obsessively shy faculty mate Philip Boynton (Robert Rockwell). The one-sided courtship, which was complicated by English teacher Daisy Enright (Mary Jane Croft) also putting in a bid for Mr. Boynton's attentions, went nowhere during the series run on television. However, to satisfy the wishes of fans, he finally proposed and married her in a theatrical spinoff.

In the interim, Connie had another suitor. Madison High School was bulldozed to make way for a highway in 1955, so she took another teaching position at Mrs. Nestor's Private Elementary School for the 1955–56 television season. The physical education teacher there, Gene Talbot (Gene Barry), was as ardent in his overtures toward Connie as she had been with Mr. Boynton, who was hastily brought back when the audience didn't seem to approve of Talbot as Connie's new main man. In an only-on-television scenario, Mr. Conklin was hired as the new principal at Mrs. Nestor's school, resuming the contentious relationship between him and Miss Brooks. These improbable developments failed to strike a chord with the audience, ratings nose-dived and CBS dropped the show after one season with the new format.

70. *Mama*

Broadcast History:

Friday	8:00–8:30	July 1949–July 1956	CBS
Sunday	5:00–5:30	December 1956–March 1957	CBS

#10 rated series in 1949–50   #18 rated series in 1952–53
#10 rated series in 1950–51   #26 rated series in 1953–54
#11 rated series in 1951–52

No Major Emmy Awards (3 nominations):
No Emmy Awards for Best Series (1 nomination)
No Emmy Awards for Best Actress (2 nominations)

Cast: Peggy Wood; Judson Laire; Dick Van Patten; Rosemary Rice; Iris Mann (1949); Ruth Gates; Carl Frank; Alice Frost; Malcolm Keen (1949–51); Robin Morgan (1950–56); Roland Winters (1951–52); Kevin Coughlin (1952–56); Patty McCormack (1953–56).

Mama was one of television's earliest family viewing habits. It was an easy habit to fall into, given the quantity and quality of the competition. Moreover, it was an ideal show for a time when entire families and their neighbors gathered around tiny screens, marveling as much at the concept of television as the programs on it. Each episode was a warm mini-morality play with a pleasing resolution relatable in some way to everyone from impressionable youngsters to grandparents.

Sets were rudimentary. Landscapes and neighboring homes were obviously painted on canvas. It's probably revealing that *Mama's* rankings declined annually as the appeal of programs across the dial increased.

Peggy Wood transited from a career in legitimate theater to play the titular lynchpin of the series, Marta Hansen, matriarch of a Norwegian immigrant clan in San Francisco early in the 20th century. The series was based on the book *Mama's Bank Account* by Kathryn Forbes and preceded by a 1948 film, *I Remember Mama*.

Each episode began with Marta's teenage daughter Katrin (Rosemary Rice) perusing a family photo album, reminiscing about the people in it, a subtle way to introduce the various characters. The tagline, which led into the episode, was, "Most of all, I remember Mama."

Marta was a saintly woman, totally selfless and dedicated to her family. She would awaken well before the other family members to make sure her spouse Lars (Judson Laire) and their children, Katrin, Nels (Dick Van Patten) and Dagmar (Robin Morgan) had a hearty breakfast before they embarked on their day. When they were finally out of the house, Marta would go to market in search of bargains to put on their table. She balked at paying the outrageous 14 cents per pound for steak. Then she would spend as much as five hours preparing the evening meal. She never complained, although she would become perturbed on the rare occasions when her efforts weren't appreciated. Wood was honored twice with the only Emmy nominations for a performer, although the series was once nominated.

Lars was a soft-spoken, hard-working carpenter, fiercely proud of his family. He was a man with no vices but when a co-worker boasted that his son could out-spell Dagmar, he uncharacteristically gambled crucially needed family dollars that Dagmar would win a spelling bee. Scene-stealing Dagmar, about 11, was Daddy's little girl and Lars wouldn't abide someone putting her down in any way.

A Christmas episode, in which Lars related to Dagmar about how animals were gifted with the ability to speak for a short time on Christmas Eve as a reward for guarding the Baby Jesus in the manger, became an audience favorite. Unfortunately for future generations, *Mama* was presented live so only a few episodes were preserved on kinescope. Most were lost for all time.

Katrin, the middle child, was a typical teen. She abhorred having to take music lessons then practice at the expense of her fun time but she acceded to the wishes of Mama. She was a little jealous of the attention the high spirited Dagmar received but not to the extent that it became a divisive issue in the house. Nels, the oldest, was more proficient in sports than in school. As a defense mechanism, he made self deprecating fun of his academic deficiencies.

Marta's best friend, Aunt Jenny (Ruth Gates), was a gossipy meddler with a backward attitude reflective of the times. Education for girls, she opined, was a waste. All they need to learn is how to read a recipe and sign their name on a marriage license. Marta paid her little heed.

Mama premiered at a time when it was the norm for one sponsor to underwrite the entire series and for the product to be presented favorably either within the show or during the opening and closing credits. In the case of *Mama*, Maxwell House Coffee was the presenting sponsor. At some point, the Hansens would gather round the kitchen to enjoy a cup of "good to the last drop" coffee.

The sponsor, who made the show possible, was also responsible for its demise. Maxwell House reportedly became convinced that its sponsorship of *Mama* was not resulting in increased sales and withdrew its support, leading to a cancellation notice from CBS. In the 1980s, *Cagney & Lacey* was renowned for being resuscitated from cancellation by an outpouring of viewer mail protesting its cancellation. *Mama* was decades ahead. Outraged fans bombarded the network with letters of protest. CBS reacted by bringing back *Mama* but not in its familiar Friday night 8:00–8:30 time period, which had been reassigned. Instead, Mama was scheduled on Sunday afternoon. In the less desirable time slot, *Mama* floundered. Within three months it was canceled for good.

71. *Evening Shade*

Broadcast History:

Friday	8:00–8:30	September 1990–November 1990	CBS
Monday	8:00–8:30	November 1990–May 1994	CBS

#15 rated series in 1991–92
#19 rated series in 1992–93
#27 rated series in 1993–94

2 Major Emmy Awards (9 nominations):
1 Emmy Award for Best Actor (2 nominations)
1 Emmy Award for Best Supporting Actor (5 nominations)
No Emmy Awards for Best Supporting Actress (1 nomination)
No Emmy Awards for Best Guest Actor/Actress (1 nomination)

Cast: Burt Reynolds; Marilu Henner; Hal Holbrook; Ossie Davis; Charles Durning; Elizabeth Ashley; Michael Jeter; Jay R. Ferguson; Melissa Martin (1990–91); Jacob Parker; Ann Wedgeworth; Linda Gehringer; Burton Gilliam; Charlie Dell; Candace Hutson (1991–94); Hilary Swank (1991–92); Ari Meyers (1992–93); Alice Ghostley (1992–94); Wanda Jones (1993–94); Alexa Vega (1993–94); Leah Remini (1993).

Linda Bloodworth-Thomason dedicated her professional life to proving that a southern accent doesn't come at the cost of IQ points. Linda, a prolific writer, and her husband, producer Harry Thomason, did it with *Designing Women* then doubled down with *Evening Shade*. The title was the name of a fictional small town in Arkansas, home state of the Thomasons. Good friends with fellow Arkansans Bill and Hillary Clinton, they choreographed the 1992 Democratic National Convention at Madison Square Garden in which Bill was nominated for President.

Evening Shade was well populated with colorful characters but they were nobody's fool—well, most of them weren't. Burt Reynolds headed an A-list ensemble as Wood Newton. He grew up in Evening Shade, became a celebrated football player at the local high school, then went on to star in college and in the National Football League with the Pittsburgh Steelers. Retired from pro football, Wood went back home and took the head coaching position at the school for which he became a local hero. To his dismay, he learned playing at a high level was easier than coaching. His team didn't win a game in two and a half seasons. This can be lethal to a coach in the South but Wood was such a legendary figure in Evening Shade the town's people continued to give him their support, at least to his face.

Their patience was partially a product of the realization that Wood didn't have a lot with which to work. His best player was his oldest son, Taylor (Jay R. Ferguson), who wanted to give up the game lest he damage his looks, which he hoped would be his ticket to Hollywood. Wood couldn't imagine somebody would prefer Hollywood over football (just as Reynolds, who played for Florida State University, did).

Wood's staff, such as it was, consisted of nerdish Herman Stiles (Michael Jeter), a math teacher who knew nothing about football. The first thing he did when he got the coaching job was to buy a helmet and a canteen, which he carried around town filled with Gatorade. Herman was the only one who would work all the hours demanded for the $400 annual stipend.

Wood's wife Ava (Marilu Henner), the mother of their four children, had her own career as *Evening Shade*'s prosecuting attorney. Married at 18 to Wood, who was 30, she was the mother of three children when she threw her hat into the political ring. She discovered she was pregnant during the campaign. It was quite a jolt, as Wood had undergone a vasectomy. Their love was strong enough that Wood never considered the ugly potential explanation. Wood went right to the source of the problem, his fishing buddy, Dr. Harlan Eldridge (Charles Durning), who did the procedure. Wood knew Harlan was never very good at tying knots.

One of the few people in Evening Shade who wasn't a big Wood Newton booster was Ava's father, Evan Evans (Hal Holbrook), publisher of the local newspaper. He never forgave his son-in-law for what he considered cradle-robbing. "You ruined my life," he told Wood at every opportunity. Evan epitomized old fashioned. To the delight of his grandchildren, he had no idea what Granola was, saw nothing wrong with a kids' diet dominated by sugar-rich products and railed against modern educational practices, which included art and music at the expense of the three R's. He wasn't totally out-of-touch, so to speak, with younger generations. He dated brash stripper Fontana Beausoleil. A side benefit was this drove his nagging former wife Frieda crazy. Holbrook was written out of *Designing Women* by the Thomasons so he could play Evan Evans in *Evening Shade*. Elizabeth Ashley played the difficult Frieda and Linda Gehringer was the larger than life Fontana.

Every village on television has to have an idiot. Nub Oliver (Charlie Dell) filled this role in *Evening Shade*. Nub delivered Evan's newspapers from his home-built wagon, which he propelled like a skateboard, one knee inside it, the other leg pushing it forward. When he wasn't delivering the printed news, he was the self-appointed town crier. Around Evening Shade he was known as "Geraldo Rivera on wheels." Ponder Blue (Ossie Davis), proprietor of the local barbecue joint, was Wood's closest confidante and doubled as the series' narrator, setting up and closing each episode.

Evening Shade struck a chord with both viewers and the industry. It finished among the 20 highest rated series twice during its four seasons and was out of the top 30 only in its first season, when it ranked 32nd.

Reynolds won an Emmy from two nominations and Jeter won one from three nominations. Durning was honored with a pair of nominations and Ashley was nominated once. Ruby Dee also garnered a nomination in the guest category. The strength of the cast proved to be the show's undoing. The cumulative salaries they commanded became more than CBS was willing to pay and led to a cancellation notice while the series was still a hit.

---

72. *Here's Lucy*

Broadcast History:

Monday	8:30–9:00	September 1968–September 1971	CBS
Monday	9:00–9:30	September 1971–September 1974	CBS

#9 rated series in 1968–69   #10 rated series in 1971–72
#6 rated series in 1969–70   #15 rated series in 1972–73
#3 rated series in 1970–71   #29 rated series in 1973–74

No Major Emmy Awards (2 nominations):
No Emmy Awards for Best Supporting Actor (1 nomination)
No Emmy Awards for Best Writing (1 nomination)

Cast: Lucille Ball; Gale Gordon; Mary Jane Croft; Lucie Arnaz; Desi Arnaz, Jr.

Rank has its privilege and in the third quarter of the 20th century no one outranked Lucille Ball in television comedy. Thus, when Lucy decided in 1968 that if she was going to continue in situation comedy it would be with her own children, Lucie and Desi Jr., as co-stars, *The Lucy Show* was ended and *Here's Lucy* was created to take its place.

The backing of their mom was a blessing for the kids. Neither had noteworthy acting credentials. Desi Jr.'s biggest claim to fame was he was featured as an infant on the cover of the first *TV Guide*. He owed that to his mother, too, who cradled him in the shot. As a teen, he had some hit records as part of the pop music group Dino, Desi and Billy. As an actor he was an okay pop singing idol. Improbable premises had to be concocted to give him anything meaningful to do—Buddy Rich giving him a drum lesson; his mom getting him a gig in Wayne Newton's band; Joe Namath coaxing him to play football. Lucie was sweet and personable and credible enough as an actress to essentially play herself in an appealing manner. She was sufficiently likeable that a potential spinoff was devised for her, although CBS ultimately opted not to pick it up.

But, as always, *Here's Lucy* was a star vehicle for their mother. Lucy played Lucy Carter, a widower with two children, Kim (Lucie) and Craig (Desi Jr.). The title and players were different but Lucy was up to her characteristic slapstick and pratfall comedy in spite of her advancing age. She was 57 when the series premiered and eligible for Social Security by the time it wrapped six years later. An attempt to continue in this vein as an even older woman contributed to the demise of what would be her final series, *Life with Lucy*, in 1986.

In one episode of *Here's Lucy*, she climbed aboard a sliding library ladder to search for a book she had returned inadvertently with a $100 bill inside. The studio audience—this was the first time Lucy shot a series before a live crowd—loved it. The exact same scenario a couple of decades later produced an entirely different response, according to prolific producer Aaron Spelling. "When the audience saw Lucy careening around on that ladder, there were gasps," Spelling said. "They were afraid she was going to hurt herself." *Life with Lucy* didn't get past its first season. Coincidentally, Lucie did suffer a serious injury in an off-camera skiing mishap in 1972 and it had to be incorporated into that season's episodes.

Lucy was savvy enough to realign herself with old friends Gale Gordon and Vivian Vance to cover the shortcomings of her kids. Gordon, who also resurfaced in *Life with Lucy*, was cast as Lucy's brother-in-law and boss Harry Carter, a crank and tightwad who owned an employment agency. Harry had little use for the incompetent Lucy around the office but couldn't fire her because she was family. Vance, who showed up only sporadically, returned to familiar terrain as Lucy's best friend, Vivian Jones. Together, they got into the same kinds of ridiculous misunderstandings and foolhardy capers they originated on *I Love Lucy* and *The Lucy Show*.

Another sign of Lucy's status was her ability to cajole a cavalcade of A-list guest stars to appear in gauze-thin vignettes. Jackie Gleason appeared as *Honeymooners* icon Ralph Kramden. Jack Benny, playing his characteristic cheapskate, opened his home as a hotel to Lucy. Milton Berle was coaxed to liven up one of Lucy's parties. Lucy performed jury duty with Joan Rivers. Lucy meddled in the marriage of Steve Lawrence and Eydie Gorme. Richard Burton and Elizabeth Taylor—the Brad Pitt and Angelina Jolie couple of the day—appeared in an episode in which Lucy got to try on Liz's famous zillion karat diamond ring, then couldn't get it off her finger.

The most inspired stunt casting was when Lucy Carter got to meet Lucille Ball. America's enduring affection for Lucy kept *Here's Lucy*, which earned only two Emmy nominations, neither of which it won, in Nielsen's top 10 for its first four seasons. It dropped to number 15 in season five, the first time any series starring Lucy wasn't in the Nielsen top 10. A year later it slid to number 29 and the plug was pulled.

---

73. *Empty Nest*

Broadcast History:

Saturday	9:30–10:00	October 1988–July 1991	NBC
Saturday	9:00–9:30	August 1991–July 1994	NBC
Saturday	8:30–9:00	August 1994–October 1994	NBC
Saturday	8:00–8:30	October 1994–March 1995	NBC
Saturday	8:00–8:30	June 1995–July 1995	NBC
Saturday	8:30–9:00	June 1995–July 1995	NBC

#9 rated series in 1988–89   #7 rated series in 1990–91
#9 rated series in 1989–90   #23 rated series in 1991–92

1 Major Emmy Award (4 nominations):
1 Emmy Award for Best Actor (3 nominations)
No Emmy Awards for Best Guest Actor/Actress (1 nomination)

Cast: Richard Mulligan; Kristy McNichol (1988–93); Dinah Manoff; Park Overall; David Leisure; Paul Provenza (1992–93); Lisa Rieffel (1993); Marsha Warfield (1993–95); Estelle Getty (1993–95).

Empty Nest was unique in the realm of spinoffs. The series, which grew out of *The Golden Girls*, didn't depend on characters introduced on the first generation show. The binding between the two series was a neighborhood.

NBC couldn't get enough of Miami in the 1980s. *Miami Vice* was the network's hottest drama and *The Golden Girls* was one of its prize comedies. Doing what comes naturally for networks, it looked to push its luck with another Miami-based comedy featuring characters who were neighbors of *The Golden Girls* (which was shot entirely in Hollywood).

The first attempt in 1987 was underwhelming. A *Golden Girls* episode, which was an unofficial pilot, starred Paul Dooley and Rita Moreno, who were both learning to cope after their children, who had been the focus of their lives, moved out. NBC didn't like the way it turned out but still was fond enough of the concept to try again with some tinkering to the set-up.

Richard Mulligan, who was much praised for his work on *Soap*, was cast as Dr. Harry Weston, a recently widowed pediatrician, an ultimate nice guy beloved by his patients and their parents. One asked him to be the father of her child. Another pleaded with him to be her prom date. When he retired from his private practice after season six, he segued into volunteer work at a free clinic run by tough Dr. Maxine Douglas (Marsha Warfield). Mulligan was Emmy nominated three times, winning once.

Soap creator Susan Harris also was responsible for *The Golden Girls*, *Empty Nest* and its spinoff *Nurses*. On some Saturday nights, Harris concocted over-lapping storylines, which brought about crossover appearances from the characters on her three comedies. When another *Golden Girls* spinoff (*The Golden Palace*) fizzled, Estelle Getty became a regular on *Empty Nest* for its final two seasons, reprising her character Sophia Petrillo.

Empty Nest was a misnomer, since two of Harry's daughters, Barbara (Kristy McNichol) and Carol (Dinah Manoff), shared his home. Manoff also had a history with Harris. She played Mulligan's daughter-in-law on *Soap*. Barbara, an undercover cop, was an independent woman, confident, perky and upbeat. At least this is what she tried to project. In fact, she was wracked by insecurities. Carol was a basket case. A friend remarked that he had never seen her happy. This would have included her first wedding day when her fiancée mistakenly inserted a previous girlfriend's name into his wedding vows. Not surprisingly, the union ended in divorce, which propelled Carol back to her father's place. Undaunted, she continued to look for her soul mate, a search that uncovered a succession of losers. Her luck didn't change until the final episodes when she married again to a guy named Kevin (D. David Morin).

Barbara loved to torment Carol over her neuroses, doing little things like slanting pictures on the wall, because she knew this would drive her sister crazy. The sisters did have one common bond. Both were distressed that approaching their 30s they were still living at home. Meanwhile, Harry was thrilled to have them around. When they decided jointly to move out and get their own places, Harry went into a funk. He was thrilled when they changed their mind.

A third daughter, Emily (Lisa Rieffel), who was said to be away at college during the show's early seasons, moved back home when McNichol left the series after the fifth season to deal with health issues. However, Emily was written out after one season.

There was another important woman in Harry's life, his assertive nurse/receptionist LaVerne Todd (Park Overall), who ran his office and, as much as he allowed, his life. This included playing matchmaker. She set him up on one date with her pal from Arkansas, Barbara Mandrell. Although Harry was often intimidated by her, he appreciated how loyal LaVerne was and brought her along when he moved to the clinic.

Filling the duties of the obligatory wacky neighbor was David Leisure as next-door neighbor Charley Dietz, who worked for a cruise line. Judging from how often he popped unannounced and uninvited into the Weston home to mooch food or inject himself into a conversation by saying something wildly inappropriate, he didn't work much. Leisure was the sole survivor from the rejected pilot, although he played a different character. Charley was a lecher, who kept his black book of women on a computer, a big step forward at the time. Carol called him "the first high tech Neanderthal." But he did have redeeming qualities. Even though he hit on Harry's daughters, he was protective of them to the extent that he risked a beating by interceding when a bigger, tougher guy tried to force his affections on Carol.

There was one additional important member of the ensemble, Harry's dog Dreyfuss (Bear), who was an involuntary sounding board for each of the Westons. The pairing with *The Golden Girls* made *Empty Nest* one of television's most popular series, launching it into the Nielsen top 10 for its first three seasons. Once the shows were separated, *Empty Nest* began an irreversible slide first out of the top 20, then the top 40 until it hit rock bottom, out of the top 100 in its final season.

74. *Petticoat Junction*

Broadcast History:

Tuesday	9:00–9:30	September 1963–September 1964	CBS
Tuesday	9:30–10:00	September 1964–August 1967	CBS
Saturday	9:30–10:00	September 1967–September 1970	CBS

#3 rated series in 1963–64   #23 rated series in 1966–67
#10 rated series in 1964–65   #29 rated series in 1967–68
#15 rated series in 1965–66

No Major Emmy Awards (No nominations)

Cast: Bea Benadaret (1963–68); Edgar Buchanan; Jeannine Riley (1963–65); Pat Woodell (1963–65); Linda Kaye Henning; Smiley Burnette (1963–67); Rufe Davis (1963–68); Charles Lane (1963–68); Frank Cady; Roy Roberts (1963–64); Kay E. Kuter (1964–70); Virginia Sale (1964–65); Gunilla Hutton (1965–66); Lori Saunders (1965–70); Elvia Allman (1965–70); Susan Walther (1965–66); Meredith MacRae (1966–70); Lynette Winter (1966–70); Mike Minor (1966–70); Tom Lester (1966–70); Regis Toomey (1968–69); June Lockhart (1968–70); Byron Foulger (1968–70); Paul Hartman (1968–69); Elna Hubbell (1968–70); Geoff Edwards (1968); Jonathan Daly (1969–70).

Almost simultaneous to the British invasion of pop music in the early 1960s came the rural invasion of the CBS network. *The Andy Griffith Show* pioneered the trend, just ahead of *The Beverly Hillbillies* then *Petticoat Junction* and its spinoff *Green Acres*. *Petticoat Junction* was more related thematically to *The Andy Griffith Show* in that it presented country folks in their natural habitat—fish in water—rather than under the extraordinary fish out of water milieu of the Clampett clan in Beverly Hills.

Bea Benadaret, who recurred as fringe character Aunt Pearl on *The Beverly Hillbillies*, stepped into the center ring as Kate Bradley, owner/operator of the Shady Rest Hotel, a bed and breakfast type establishment, in the off-the-map burg of Hooterville. (This was before the chicken wing joint attached a different connotation to a town with this name—well, not exactly different.) Hooterville also became the setting for *Green Acres*, which was launched two years later. Crossovers between the characters was commonplace, including by canine scene-stealer Dog. Higgins, who played him, would gain greater fame as "Benji."

Irene Ryan, Granny on *The Beverly Hillbillies*, also contributed a couple of guest appearances in her familiar character. Hooterville was so far off the beaten track that when the train line that once served it struck it from its routes, years passed before its operators realized that one of its trains was still making regular runs between Hooterville and nearby Pixley with a pensioned engineer, Charley Pratt (Smiley Burnette) at the throttle of the Hooterville Cannonball and former conductor Floyd Smoot (Rufe Davis) handling all the other chores. Regular runs is actually an exaggeration—the Hooterville Cannonball's schedule was more along the line of "When do you want to leave?" and "We'll get there when we get there because we might stop to pick apples for Kate's mouth watering pies."

A recurring storyline had Kate wrangling with a crusty executive of the railroad, Homer Bedloe (Charles Lane), who wanted to shut down the Hooterville-Pixley run and recover his company's property. Through manipulation and chicanery Kate managed to thwart Mr. Bedloe's mission.

Kate, a widow, had more help than she needed in running the Shady Rest, which had a lower occupancy rate than the Bates Motel. Uncle Joe (Edgar Buchanan) had the title of manager although all he managed was to screw up things. Nevertheless, Kate allowed him to think she couldn't get along without him. Three knockout daughters, Betty Jo, Bobbie Jo and Billie Jo, also pitched in, serving as the series titillation factors. It was regularly mentioned that they liked to skinny dip in the railroad water tower. Betty Jo was a redhead, Bobbie Jo was a brunette and Billie Jo was a blonde, although the distinction was largely lost during the first two seasons, which were in black and white.

Over its seven-year run, the series underwent more changes than Bruce Jenner, starting with the transition to color in season three. That season also marked two significant cast changes. Lori Sanders replaced Pat Woodell as Bobbie Jo and Gunilla Hutton took over for Jeannine Riley as Billie Jo. Hutton lasted only one season before being replaced by Meredith McRae.

The personality of the characters also changed over the years. Bobbie Jo was introduced as a bookish dullard but morphed into a scatterbrain. Billie Jo was the boy crazy sister. As she matured, her self-confidence and self-esteem grew and she measured herself by her own accomplishments, not what men thought of her. Betty Jo (Linda Henning) grew up as a tomboy with no interest in the opposite sex. Her big kick in life was to step in for Charley and highball the Cannonball around Dead Man's Curve. Her priorities shifted when a pilot, Steve Elliott (Mike Minor), landed in town. They fell in love, married and had a daughter, Kathy Jo. This conveniently coincided with Kaye and Minor falling in love and marrying in real life. Art (in a manner of speaking) imitating life was arranged by the show's creator, Paul Henning, Linda's father.

Mortality also took its toll. Benadaret was stricken with cancer in season five and had to take a sabbatical. She tried to return but her illness limited her to only sporadic appearances before she died in 1968. Rosemary DeCamp temporarily stepped in as the girls surrogate mom, Aunt Helen, when it was still hoped that Benaderet might recover and rejoin the show. When Benaderet died, June Lockhart was hired to play Dr. Janet Craig, the new maternal character. But the show just wasn't the same. Burnette died in 1967 but as colorful as his character was, Charley's absence didn't have as great an impact. Floyd just stepped up his duties, adding engineer to his role as conductor.

Although *Petticoat Junction* was not nominated for any major Emmy award, it was a fan favorite. It was the third most popular series in the Nielsen rankings for its first season. It stayed in the top 30 through season five. But its audience base mirrored the show's setting, small town America. This didn't please Madison Avenue, which preferred people who bought their clothes rather than made them and patronized supermarkets instead of growing their own fruits and vegetables. This hastened its demise in 1970, a year before CBS purged the network of all its rural series.

---

75. Gomer Pyle, U.S.M.C.

Broadcast History:

Friday	9:30–10:00	September 1964–June 1965	CBS
Friday	9:00–9:30	September 1965–September 1966	CBS
Wednesday	9:30–10:00	September 1966–August 1967	CBS
Friday	8:30–9:00	September 1967–September 1969	CBS

#3 rated series in 1964–65   #3 rated series in 1967–68
#2 rated series in 1965–66   #2 rated series in 1968–69
#10 rated series in 1966–67

No Major Emmy Awards (No nominations)

Cast: Jim Nabors; Frank Sutton; Ronnie Schell; Barbara Stuart; Tommy Leonetti (1964–65); Larry Hovis (1964–65); Roy Stuart (1965–68); Ted Bessell (1965–68); William Christopher (1965–68); Forrest Compton; Allan Melvin (1965–69); Elizabeth MacRae (1967–69).

Jim Nabors is on a short list of actors who parlayed minor characters on established series into their own hit shows. Nabors' signature alter ego, Gomer Pyle, was created to fill a small void on *The Andy Griffith Show* necessitated by illness of Howard McNear, who played Floyd the barber. The good natured, not very bright or worldly filling station attendant in fictional Mayberry, North Carolina, was an outgrowth of characters Nabors, a bright guy with a degree from the University of Alabama, introduced in comedy clubs. Gomer was written into only 23 episodes over two seasons on *The Andy Griffith Show*. However, he made sufficient impact to encourage a spinoff, *Gomer Pyle, U.S.M.C.*, which enjoyed a five-season run of its own.

The series helped launch another facet of Nabors' repertoire, a rich baritone singing voice, which garnered him regular invitations to appear on variety series such as *The Carol Burnett Show* (she returned the favor appearing in two episodes of his show) and *The Tonight Show Starring Johnny Carson*. He also became an annual fixture belting out "Back Home in Indiana" in advance of the Indianapolis 500 auto race.

Gomer Pyle, U.S.M.C. took the hick Nabors created out of grease-stained overalls into Marine Corps fatigues. The series didn't earn any significant awards, or even nominations, but the public loved it. In its first season, in spite of a weak lead-in and having a bottom of the hour (9:30–10:00 p.m.) time period, it finished third among all series, one slot above *Andy Griffith*. The next year, with another military comedy, *Hogan's Heroes*, as a more compatible lead-in and a 9:00–9:30 p.m. time period, it vaulted to the second highest rated series. It remained in the Nielsen top 10 throughout its run.

Gomer Pyle, U.S.M.C. was essentially a two-character lead show. Nabors was the inept but eager-to-please young Marine, whose goodwill and congeniality was unflappable even under the worst duress. Frank Sutton was tough career solider Sgt. Carter, who first encountered Gomer as his drill instructor. The only other regular to appear in more than half the 150 episodes was Ronnie Schell as a fellow Marine named Duke Slater.

Gomer's relentless foul-ups so frustrated Sgt. Carter, who took pride in turning out nothing but honor platoons, that he drove the recruit mercilessly, hoping he would muster out. At the urging of fellow drill instructors, Sgt. Carter did everything he could think of to get Gomer to hate his guts. But no matter how brutal and tyrannical Sgt. Carter became, Gomer turned "I really like you" into a mantra. As a drill instructor, Carter felt "it's a terrible thing to be loved."

As a last resort, Sgt. Carter went to a shrink for advice and was told it might be time to think about transferring from being a drill instructor to a new assignment. He requested a transfer to advanced infantry training at Camp Henderson in California. Lo and behold, who showed up but Gomer, fresh out of basic training and assigned to advanced infantry training. Gomer's missteps were a relentless headache to Sgt. Carter. Indeed, marines to this day who can't do anything right are referred to as Gomer Pyles.

The situation was exacerbated by Gomer often emerging as the hero and Sgt. Carter the heavy. Typical was an episode in which Sgt. Carter had to press Gomer into temporary service as a military policeman. Obeying his sergeant's commands, Gomer denied entrance to the base to a VIP from Washington, who didn't have the proper credentials but vowed all sorts of recriminations for the slight. Sgt. Carter dressed down Gomer to his superiors only to be chastised that Gomer did exactly what he should have done. His task was to safeguard the base from intruders without proper identification without exception. For all the grief Gomer caused him, even the hard-nosed Sgt. Carter had moments when he couldn't help liking the hayseed kid.

Gomer didn't go back to Mayberry until a reunion television movie in 1986 but Mayberry often came to the spinoff. Griffith, along with Ron Howard as Opie, crossed over in a pair of episodes in which the youngster, feeling he had disappointed his father by not doing well at school, ran away from home and improbably made it all the way from Mayberry to the West Coast to join Gomer in the Marines.

Frances Bavier, as Aunt Bea, also did a two-parter in which she used a portion of a California vacation to visit her old friend from back home. Disappointed that Gomer couldn't get a pass because of base duty, she helped him spruce up the barracks with a woman's touch, setting off the fury of Sgt. Carter. This rage, too, backfired when a broadcast personality stopped Aunt Bee for a person on the street interview and she related how mean Sgt. Carter had been to a kindly old woman.

George Lindsey, as Goober, who took over for Gomer at the filling station on *The Andy Griffith Show*, also had a guest shot. Three actors who would go on to stardom in *M*A*S*H* also showed up at Camp Henderson. William Christopher, later better known as Father Mulcahy, was in 15 episodes. Wayne Rogers, who would become the television Trapper John, and Jamie "Klinger" Farr also made appearances.

Gomer Pyle, U.S.M.C., was a television rarity in that it ended after five seasons while still among Nielsen's top 10 series, so that Nabors could headline his own variety series, which turned out to be short-lived.

76. Veep

Broadcast History:

Sunday	10:00–10:30	April 2012–June 2012	HBO
Sunday	10:00–10:30	April 2013–June 2013	HBO
Sunday	10:30–11:00	April 2014–June 2014	HBO
Sunday	10:30–11:00	April 2015–June 2015	HBO

4 Major Emmy Awards (12 nominations):
No Emmy Award for Best Series (3 nominations)
3 Emmy Awards for Best Actress (3 nominations)
1 Emmy Award for Best Supporting Actor (2 nominations)
No Emmy Awards for Best Supporting Actress (2 nominations)
No Emmy Awards for Best Guest Actor/Actress (1 nomination)
No Emmy Awards for Best Writing (1 nomination)

Cast: Julia Louis-Dreyfus; Anna Chlumsky; Tony Hale; Matt Walsh; Reid Scott; Sufe Bradshaw; Timothy Simons; Dan Bakkedahl; Randall Park; Phil Reeves; Sarah Sutherland; Brian Huskey; Andy Buckley (2012); Kate Burton (2012) William L. Thomas; Peter Grosz (2012–13, 2015); Nelson Franklin (2012–13); Kevin Dunn (2013–15); Gary Cole (2013–15); Isiah Whitlock, Jr. (2013–15); David Pasquesi (2013–15); Sally Phillips (2013–14); Zach Woods (2013–15); Walid Amani (2013); David Rasche (2013, 2015); Jessica St. Clair (2013); Sam Richardson (2014–15); Kathy Najimy (2014–15); Christopher Meloni (2014); Glenn Wrage (2014); Diedrich Bader (2014–15); Paul Fitzgerald (2014–15); Patton Oswalt (2015); Jessie Ennis (2015); Hugh Laurie (2015).

Veep was the anti–*West Wing*. *The West Wing*—the uplifting Aaron Sorkin drama—deified a White House staff devoted to selflessly serving their country. Politics was relegated to the background as the welfare of America always took priority. Politics and "what's in it for me?" was the sole concern of the characters in the cynical *Veep*. If something they did advanced the interests of the nation, it was a happy accident. The only unifying thread between the characters in the two series was life at the highest levels of government was all consuming.

Selina Meyer was a former U.S. Senator from Maryland, who ran for president and failed to get the nomination. Her consolation was the second slot for the gender balance she brought to the national ticket. Her running mate, who was elected president, had no regard, nor did he have any real use for her. The vice presidency was the do-nothing job everyone warned Selena it would be. Nevertheless she initially embraced it energetically. She created a pet project, the Clean Jobs Commission, only to discover that she was the only one to pay it much heed. A filibuster reform effort met the same fate. The most attention she got from the media came when she waffled about the breed of dog she was going to choose. She was relegated to the customary vice presidential duties; photo ops, showing up at ceremonial events, such as pig roasts, entertaining school kids and handling foreign trips the never seen President shunned.

She became a subject of ridicule on *Saturday Night Live*. However, she was afforded the trappings of high office; fancy digs, a sizable support staff and a farcical motorcade of SUVs, limos and motorcycles every time she hit the street, even if it was just to get lunch, a recurring sight gag.

"Television makes stars, stars don't make television" is a familiar show business credo, which has repeatedly proven to be astute, as A-list stars bombed as they ventured with much hype into television. Julia Louis-Dreyfus, who starred as Selina, is an exception. Everything she became involved in, from *Saturday Night Live* through *Seinfeld*, *The New Adventures of Old Chris-*

tine and recurring roles in *Arrested Development* and *Curb Your Enthusiasm*, benefitted from her presence. She brought the same verve and vitality to *Veep*, which might not have had the same level of success without her. She won an Emmy for each of the show's first three seasons and the series was Emmy nominated for best comedy each of those years, too.

But *Veep* was not a one-woman show. Louis-Dreyfus was surrounded by a brilliant entourage of quirky characters that were smartly executed. Anna Chlumsky shone as Selina's ferociously loyal and controlling chief of staff, Amy Brookheimer, who was so soiled by the D.C. scene that she considered honesty a dirty trick. Tony Hale, who worked with Louis-Dreyfus on *Arrested Development*, brought his characteristic timidity to the role of Gary Walsh, Selena's obsequious personal assistant. Chlumsky and Hale were each twice Emmy-nominated in the supporting actor category and Hale won the Emmy for *Veep*'s second season.

Gary Cole, who joined the series in the second season as Kent Davison, a humorless, poll-obsessed senior strategist for the president, was Emmy nominated for a guest role in the third season even though he had essentially become a regular on the show. Matt Walsh played Mike McClintock, Selena's director of communications, who reveled in being close to power but not so much that he didn't do anything he could, including saying he needed to tend to his non-existent pet dog, to get out of work. His marriage to an aggressive reporter brought additional headaches to Selena.

Reid Scott portrayed Deputy Communications Director Dan Egan, who was not above romancing women who could help him climb the career ladder. But a panic attack brought about a brief hiatus in his service to Selena and raised doubts about his dependability. There were never any doubts about the dependability of Sue Wilson (Sufe Bradshaw), Selina's personal assistant. Every office has someone like her, efficient, self confident and impatient with those who don't share those traits. Jonah Bryan (Timothy Simons) was a liaison to the president, a position he lorded over people, although he was disliked by both the White House and Selina's staff.

Christopher Meloni made a series of appearances in the third season as Selina's personal trainer, who became a romantic interest. The relationship came to an abrupt end when he became a political liability after it was discovered he had authored blogs that put down fat people.

Kevin Dunn was another season two addition as Ben Cafferty, the White House Chief of Staff, who appeared to be suffering from a severe case of burnout. He took a liking to Selina and vowed that someday he would get her elected president. This became more than an idle promise when the president announced toward the end of the third season that he would not run for re-election and stepped down from the office. Selina became president and immediately threw her hat into the ring. The fourth season began with her as president and ended with election night results—a tie.

---

77. Nurse Jackie

Broadcast History:

Monday	10:30–11:00	June 2009–August 2009	SHOWTIME
Monday	10:00–10:30	March 2010–June 2010	SHOWTIME
Monday	10:00–10:30	March 2011–June 2011	SHOWTIME
Sunday	9:00–9:30	April 2012–June 2012	SHOWTIME
Sunday	9:00–9:30	April 2013–June 2013	SHOWTIME
Sunday	9:00–9:30	April 2014–June 2014	SHOWTIME
Sunday	9:00–9:30	April 2015–June 2015	SHOWTIME

2 Major Emmy Awards (12 nominations):
No Emmy Awards for Best Series (1 nomination)
1 Emmy Award for Best Actress (5 nominations)
1 Emmy Award for Best Supporting Actress (2 nominations)
No Emmy Awards for Best Guest Actor/Actress (3 nominations)
No Emmy Awards for Best Directing (1 nomination)

Cast: Edie Falco; Merritt Wever; Anna Deavere Smith; Peter Facinelli; Paul Schulze; Dominic Fumusa; Stephen Wallem; Ruby Jerins; Eve Best (2009–13); Haaz Sleiman (2009); Mackenzie Aladjem (2010–14); Adam Ferrara (2013–14); Betty Gilpin (2013–14).

The ingredients for a winning comedy should be obvious. Foremost, the material must be funny. At the very least the plot scenarios should make the viewer grin. The characters should be capable of eliciting at least smiles. As self-evident as these factors might be, they totally eluded the Television Academy in the case of *Nurse Jackie*. To the people who dispense the Emmy Awards and the producers who decided the category to enter, a comedy is any show that is a half-hour in length. There was nothing humorous about *Nurse Jackie*, a heavy piece about a terrific nurse with a horrid pharmaceutical dependency, which destroyed an otherwise blissful marriage and alienated her from her children. Nevertheless, the Showtime series captured comedy Emmys for its star, Edie Falco, and one of its supporting characters, Merritt Wever.

Count Falco, coming off a bravura stint in HBO's *The Sopranos*, among those who feel *Nurse Jackie* was wrongly categorized. In her Emmy acceptance speech she led with, "I am not funny." Her moving portrayal of Jackie Peyton,

R.N., was Emmy worthy, just not as a comedy. Jackie's road to becoming a pathetic junkie was driven by chronic back pains. Working at a busy New York City hospital, Jackie was afforded uncommon access to painkillers. That she was willing to lower herself to trade her body for pills with the resident pharmacist, Eddie Walzer (Paul Schulze), made her plight all the more distressing.

As despicable as it might have been for Eddie to take advantage of her, he was hopelessly infatuated with her and would have done anything he could to ease her pain without sexual payback. What's more, while he was having sex with her, Eddie had no idea Jackie was a married woman with two kids. In spite of working at Manhattan's All Saints Hospital for years, Jackie was successful in keeping her marital status secret from even her closest colleagues. Likewise, she was able to keep her drug dependency, which degenerated to more than a dozen pills daily, and what she did to score them from her husband Kevin (Dominic Fumusa), who operated a neighborhood tavern.

Jackie's ruse began to unravel when Eddie discovered she was married and began to frequent Kevin's place to see who his competition for Jackie was. It became really bizarre when Eddie and Kevin became pals and Eddie received invitations from Kevin to social events at the Peyton home. Eventually, a despondent Eddie, who survived a suicide attempt, revealed his relationship with Jackie to Kevin and the Peytons divorced.

In season six, Kevin found a new love and put closure on his relationship with Jackie by marrying for the second time. Even after Eddie lost his job and the pharmacy became automated, complicating Jackie's access to pain killers, she found other ways to service her habits, including pilfering the prescriptions of patients.

Jackie's issues spilled over into her family's life. Her adolescent daughter Grace (Ruby Jerins) was afflicted with anxiety disorder and panic attacks and became a pill popper, too. In one humiliating episode, mother and daughter discovered they had the same street dealer. Through this, Jackie maintained the respect of her colleagues by carrying out her hospital duties with extraordinary efficiency and dedication. However, she was prone to dispensing her own brand of emergency room justice to thugs who she feared were getting away with violent crimes. When colleagues learned Jackie's secret, they attempted an intervention. It seemed to them they had achieved success but Jackie was so clever in hiding her dependency and scoring pills that they came to realize she had them fooled.

Merritt Wever, as eager beaver young nurse Zoey Barkow, initially idolized Jackie, who served as her mentor, confidante and friend until even she became disillusioned. Dr. Fitch Cooper (Peter Facinelli), commonly known as "Coop," also had a crush on Jackie, which went nowhere. Among other things, the older Jackie was turned off by Coop's inability to keep his hands off women's breasts, which he claimed was caused by some mysterious affliction.

Dr. Eleanor O'Hara (Eve Best), a single professional woman who more than anything wanted to be a mother, was Jackie's closest friend. Hospital administrator Gloria Akalitus (Anna Deavere Smith) suspected something was amiss in Jackie's life but Jackie's superlative work encouraged her not to probe too deeply until a change in hospital ownership forced her to be more diligent in riding herd over the staff.

Her marriage was not the only relationship destroyed by Jackie's drug abuse. After splitting with Kevin, she connected with a kindly cop named Frank (Adam Ferrara), who was aware of her problems and did his best to clean her up. But in spite of a stint in rehab and Frank attempting to monitor her activities, Jackie relapsed again and a heartbroken Frank kissed her off, too. Sounds like a barrel of laughs, no?

---

78. *Dream On*

Broadcast History:

Tuesday	10:30–11:00	November 1990–January 1991	HBO
Sunday	10:00–10:30	July 1991–October 1991	HBO
Saturday	10:00–10:30	June 1992–November 1992	HBO
Wednesday	10:00–10:30	June 1993–March 1994	HBO
Wednesday	10:00–10:30	June 1994–September 1994	HBO
Sunday	9:30–10:00	January 1995–April 1995	FOX
Monday	9:00–10:00	June 1995–July 1995	FOX
Wednesday	10:00–10:30	July 1995–March 1996	HBO

2 Major Emmy Awards (7 nominations):
1 Emmy Award for Best Guest Actor/Actress (4 nominations)
No Emmy Awards for Best Writing (1 nomination)
1 Emmy Award for Best Direction (2 nominations)

Cast: Brian Benben; Chris Demetral; Denny Dillon; Wendie Malick; Jeff Joseph (1990–91); Dorien Wilson (1991–96); Michael McKean (1991–96); Renee Taylor (1992–94).

Martin Tupper was a child of television. This was made clear in the opening credits of HBO's *Dream On.* When he was a toddler, barely able to sit up on his own, his mother habitually plopped him in front of the set—it was black and white during his childhood—and used it as his babysitter. Almost all the formative lessons he learned came from the tube. The things he saw and heard exhibited a strong influence on his adult persona. From moments of suffocating stress to the throes of passion, Martin's actions and reactions were shaped by what he had seen on television.

The creators of _Dream On_, Marta Kauffman and David Crane, devised a creative means to reveal his thought process, interrupting the plots to inject black-and-white snippets from old movies and television shows to illustrate the way Martin was feeling at that given moment. Everyone from Groucho Marx to Ronald Reagan; Jack Benny to Ozzie Nelson; Emmett Kelly to Lou Costello; even some cartoon characters, lived rent free in Martin's psyche.

Kauffman and Crane followed _Dream On_ by collaborating to create _Friends._ Kevin Bright, an executive producer of the HBO series, served in the same capacity on the comedy that eventually became the cornerstone of NBC's dominant Thursday night. _Dream On_ was cleverly conceived and executed but it was more than laughs that brought viewers to it. It was one of the earliest premium cable series to effectively meld explicit sex and nudity with standard story telling.

Martin (Brian Benben) was at a lowpoint in his life as the series began. Even though he was estranged from his wife Judith (Wendie Malick) for two years, he was in denial about the inevitability of a divorce. Harboring unfounded hopes for reconciliation, he vigorously resisted signing the papers until she figuratively put a gun to his head. Martin's ego was further bruised by the fact that Judith was anxious to shed him so she could marry a doctor, Richard Stone, who could have been a role model for Mother Theresa. Considered a miracle man healer, he also was a globally renowned philanthropist. Martin's feelings of inadequacy were compounded by his pre-adolescent son Jeremy (Chris Demetral) looking at Dr. Stone as a combination rock star/world class athlete. Every word of praise for Dr. Stone hit Martin like a punch in the gut, illustrated by old boxing footage.

Shared custody of Jeremy was the adhesive that kept Martin and Judith connected over the years. Martin cherished the times with his son but they did create problems, especially when Jeremy became old enough to have a sex life of his own. When Jeremy decided he wanted to become an author, he pushed away his father in order to be edited (among other activities) by one of Martin's attractive assistants.

Martin's post–Judith years would be a fantasy come true for most guys. A hot young woman was anxious to tear off her clothes and jump in the sack with him in almost every episode. But his amorous escapades usually turned into nightmarish events. A tryst with an NYU student still not old enough to drink legally wound up putting him in the emergency ward with an anxiety attack. Another bedmate turned out to be more interested in seducing Judith.

Some women were interested in Martin merely as an inroad to having their book published and turned hostile when it didn't happen.

Martin's lifelong friend Eddie, a lecherous talk show host based in the Ed Sullivan Theater (later home to *The Late Show with David Letterman*), was his primary enabler when it came to one-night stands. Eddie's celebrity from television facilitated his womanizing and he made sure there was always a friend for Martin. Jeff Joseph played Eddie in the first season. Dorien Wilson took over the role in season two and stayed with the series to the end.

Martin's professional life at a publishing house was one ordeal after another. His mouthy secretary, Toby Pedalbee (Denny Dillon), was insolent and disrespectful. She took every opportunity to taunt him during distressing times in his life, which was most of the time. Nevertheless, Martin remained loyal to her and even was foolish enough to go into a phone sex business with her.

His boss, Gibby Fiske (Michael McKean), was a tyrannical Aussie, who reviled in relentlessly mocking and tormenting him and threatening to fire him. Although none of the regular cast was nominated for Emmy consideration, a parade of guest stars, including Jason Alexander, Paul Dooley, Gwen Verdon and David Clennon, had their work recognized by the Television Academy, with only Clennon getting to take home the prize.

During *Dream On*'s six seasons on HBO many viewers said they would enjoy it for the humor even without the sex and nudity. They lied. The producers heard the praise and sanitized the episodes for a transition to the Fox broadcast network. It was canned after one low rated season. An attempt to syndicate the series for late night on basic cable was no more successful. However, the show endures in one small way. The screen static that is part of the introduction to all HBO series comes from the credits sequence of *Dream On*.

79. Benson

Broadcast History:

Thursday	8:30–9:00	September 1979–July 1980	ABC
Friday	8:00–8:30	August 1980–March 1983	ABC
Thursday	8:00–8:30	March 1983–April 1983	ABC

Friday	8:00–8:30	May 1983–March 1985	ABC
Friday	9:00–9:30	March 1985–September 1985	ABC
Friday	9:30–10:00	October 1985–January 1986	ABC
Saturday	8:30–9:00	January 1986–August 1986	ABC

#23 rated series in 1979–80

1 Major Emmy Award (9 nominations):
1 Emmy Award for Best Actor (5 nominations)
No Emmy Awards for Best Supporting Actor (1 nomination)
No Emmy Awards for Best Supporting Actress (3 nominations)

Cast: Robert Guillaume; James Noble; Missy Gold; Inga Swenson; Caroline McWilliams (1979–81); Lewis J. Stadlen (1979–80); Rene Auberjonois (1980–86); Ethan Phillips (1980–85); Jerry Seinfeld (1980–81); Didi Conn (1981–85); Billie Bird (1984–86); Donna LaBrie (1985–86).

Soap's zany Jessica Tate didn't have many cogent thoughts. However, one of them was a dandy. When her cousin James Gatling, the widowed governor of an unnamed state, needed someone to manage his household, Jessica suggested her butler Benson, who had done an incredible job under crazy conditions in the Tate home. If he could maintain his sanity and dignity amidst the chaotic looniness of the Tates and Campbells, how hard could keeping things under control in a state house be?

Robert Guillaume's character was more than up to the challenge of graduating from being one of many on *Soap* to being the main man on his spinoff. In fact, the new series endured almost twice as long as the parent show. Guillaume also earned five Emmy nominations and finally got to take home the trophy in his last opportunity in 1985. The character didn't change a bit. The insolent butler, who used to sneer when the doorbell in the Tate mansion rang, "You want me to get that?" was just as lippy and sarcastic in his new surroundings. An ambitious lieutenant governor warned that when he achieved higher office he would remember those who helped him out. Benson snapped, "I'll be happy to show you out." When the politician then began another statement with "God..." Benson interrupted with "You want his job, too?"

Like Jessica Tate, Governor Gatling (James Noble) was a well meaning, amenable sort. He just had a tendency not to think things all the way through. He liked to tell the story of when he managed and played on a baseball team and spent so much time pondering the ideal lineup that he forgot to include himself in it. He was the quintessential empty suit politician, who came to realize that Benson was able to maintain his cool in any crisis, which was an incalculable asset to him.

The rest of the governor's staff didn't look upon the newcomer with the same admiration. One of those who didn't particularly care for Benson was a delivery boy named Frankie, played by a then little known comedian, Jerry Seinfeld, whose gig lasted only three episodes in 1980. The governor's chief of staff John Taylor (Lewis J. Stadlen) also got off on the wrong foot with Benson by treating him life a glorified errand boy. Taylor left the show after the first season, replaced by Clayton Endicott III (Rene Auberjonois).

Benson's number one nemesis was the governor's cook Gretchen Krauss (Inga Swenson), who had a belligerent Teutonic persona and a superior attitude. A commanding, no nonsense individual, she wasn't used to being challenged and got irritated when Benson didn't kowtow to her as others on the staff did. However, Benson realized Krauss was good at her job and knew where the bodies were buried, thanks to her total access around the mansion and well-developed eavesdropping skills. So she and Benson eventually became mutually respectful allies.

Benson got off to a better start with the governor's secretary, Marcy Hill (Caroline McWilliams), an upbeat woman with an unfortunate knack for unthinkingly saying the inappropriate. Benson became reacquainted with an old flame, who had left him for a business tycoon. He explained to Marcy that she passed on love for wealth and power. "That wouldn't have happened if she had stayed with you," Marcy replied. McWilliams, who with Swenson shared a *Soap* history with Guillaume, left the series in 1981 and was replaced as the governor's gatekeeper by Didi Conn as Denise Stevens, who would become Denise Stevens Downey when she married press secretary Pete Downey (Ethan Phillips).

Benson's strongest bond was with the governor's young daughter Katie (Missy Gold) to whom he became a surrogate father figure. Even she wasn't immune to his irreverent wit. Helping her create a Native American village for a school project, Benson cracked that she shouldn't make it too nice because the government would then take it away from the Native Americans.

Benson's competence in an administration filled with nincompoops was recognized and he began an accelerated trip up the political ladder. He became the state's budget director then lieutenant governor. In the process, another aspect of Benson's backstory, his surname was revealed. There was probably a widespread perception that it was Benson but that turned out to be his first name. His full name was Benson DuBois.

Benson stayed on the air for seven seasons despite never really achieving major audience success. It ranked among the top 25 television series only once, in its first season. In the final season, Benson took the ultimate political step, throwing his hat into the ring for governor against the man he used to work for, Governor Gatling. This briefly created some bad blood but they eventually buried the hatchet. The last scene of the last show ended with the two of them watching the election returns. The curtain came down just before the outcome was revealed.

---

80. *Full House*

Broadcast History:

Friday	8:00–8:30	September 1987–February 1988	ABC
Friday	8:30–9:00	March 1988–July 1989	ABC
Friday	8:00–8:30	August 1989–August 1991	ABC
Tuesday	8:00–8:30	August 1991–August 1995	ABC

#27 rated series in 1988–89	#10 rated series in 1992–93
#23 rated series in 1989–90	#12 rated series in 1993–94
#15 rated series in 1990–91	#24 rated series in 1994–95
#8 rated series in 1991–92	

No Major Emmy Awards (No nominations)

Cast: Bob Saget; John Stamos; David Coulier; Candace Cameron; Jodie Sweetin; Mary Kate Olsen; Ashley Olsen; Andrea Barber; Lori Loughlin (1988–95); Gail Edwards (1991–94); Scott Weinger (1991–93); Blake Tuomy-Wilhoit (1992–95); Dylan Tuomy-Wilhoit (1992–95); Jurnee Smollett (1992–94); Marla Sokoloff (1993–95).

A trio of guys suddenly finding themselves raising children was a hot concept in the fall of 1987. *3 Men and a Baby* filled theater seats to such an extent that a sequel was quickly commissioned. The same season *Full House* debuted on ABC en route to a highly rated eight-year run. In a rarity, the television series actually arrived first, premiering in September, two months ahead of the theatrical. But the ABC comedy wasn't the instant crowd-pleaser the movie was.

Asked to open Friday night, a tough chore for a new series, *Full House* languished outside the Nielsen Top 50. A year later, scheduled behind the more established *Perfect Strangers*, *Full House* was discovered by the masses. It became a dependable Top 30 performer, peaking at number eight in season five and number 10 the following year. However, while it remained a viewer favorite, the Hollywood crowd barely paid attention, snubbing it entirely in Emmy nomination voting. However, this series is undoubtedly the entry on ABC's popular TGIF Friday night lineup most remembered by an entire generation.

Life was good for Danny Tanner. He was a popular television sportscaster, had a wife, Pamela, he adored and three beautiful daughters, D.J., Stephanie and Michelle. Everything changed in a flash when Pam, who mothered the kids while Danny supported the family, was killed in an auto mishap. Danny was overwhelmed, uncertain how he could juggle his career and the demands of being a single parent. His brother-in-law Jesse, an exterminator aspiring to be a rock star, and lifelong pal Joey, a standup comedian waiting to be discovered, stepped up. They volunteered to put their careers and social lives in second position to move in with Danny and help with the kids.

Bob Saget seemed an odd choice as wholesome Danny. His standup comedy act was known as one of the raunchiest in show business and he continued to turn red brick walls blue in comedy clubs after getting the role. It could be said it is a tribute to his ability that he could balance the two personas so deftly. He almost had to pass on the part due to a commitment to CBS. But after a pilot, that never made the air, was shot Saget was able to free himself of the CBS obligation and took over the role.

John Stamos also seemed to be taking a career detour as Uncle Jesse Cochran. Prior to *Full House*, he was best known as ladies man Blackie Parish in the soap opera *General Hospital*. In an early episode, Jesse made veiled reference to this, lamenting, "My life has become a G-rated movie." As a tribute to his Greek heritage, he got the producers to change his character's surname to Katsopolis after the first season. Jesse, who fronted his own band, finally found romance again thanks to Danny, who was reassigned by his television station from covering sports to co-hosting a morning talk show. His on-air partner was Rebecca "Becky" Donaldson (Lori Loughlin). Danny introduced her to Jesse and they had instant chemistry. By season four, they were married and, in season five, she gave birth to twins, Nicky and Alex (Blake and Dylan Tuomy-Wilhoit). Rather than get a place of their own, Jesse and Becky built an apartment in the attic, making the house even fuller.

Dave Coulier was in a comfort zone as Joey Gladstone. Coulier had a long credit sheet of young people's shows (some of it voice work), including *Scooby-Doo and Scrappy-Doo*, *The New Mickey Mouse Club*, *Muppet Babies* and *Slimer and the Real Ghostbusters*. His character, Joey, made use of this array of voices as he chased the show business rainbow.

The guys were the nominal stars but the cutesy little girls regularly stole the show. Their ages were spaced by about three years each to provide a vast reservoir of issues from changing diapers to managing an adolescent's first puppy love. Candace Cameron—sister of *Growing Pains* Kirk Cameron—got the most to do initially as the oldest Tanner daughter D.J. She was basically a good kid. However, in trying to deal with peer pressure, especially as she reached her teens, she got into typical young people's scrapes. Issues such as her attempts to deal with teen drinking and how far to go with a boy turned many episodes into mini-homilies.

Stephanie (Jodie Sweetin) had a serious case of middle child syndrome. She also was the Tanner child most troubled by the absence of her mother. Becky filled some of the void but she was not Stephanie's real mom. Stephanie was the most mischievous of the kids, insinuating herself into the lives of all her other housemates, especially D.J.'s. Hollywood work rules for minors resulted in Michelle being played by twins Mary Kate and Ashley Olsen, although the audience at first was led to believe it was only one young actress. As Michelle became a scene-stealer and the truth about who was playing her became widely known, the Olsen twins became the breakout stars and were able to maintain superstar careers into young adulthood.

In 2015, Netflix decided to bring the original cast together (except for the Olsen twins) in order to produce new episodes under the title *Fuller House*.

---

81. *Weeds*

Broadcast History:

Monday	10:00–10:30	August 2005–October 2005	SHOWTIME
Monday	10:00–10:30	August 2006–October 2006	SHOWTIME
Monday	10:30–11:00	August 2007–November 2007	SHOWTIME
Monday	10:00–10:30	June 2008–September 2008	SHOWTIME
Monday	10:00–10:30	June 2009–August 2009	SHOWTIME
Tuesday	10:00–10:30	August 2010–November 2010	SHOWTIME
Monday	10:00–10:30	June 2011–September 2011	SHOWTIME
Sunday	10:00–10:30	July 2012–September 2012	SHOWTIME

No Major Emmy Awards (7 nominations):
No Emmy Awards for Best Series (1 nomination)
No Emmy Award for Best Actress (3 nominations)
No Emmy Awards for Best Supporting Actress (3 nominations)

Cast: Mary-Louise Parker; Hunter Parrish; Alexander Gould; Kevin Nealon; Justin Kirk; Elizabeth Perkins (2005–09); Allie Grant (2005–09); Andy Milder; Tonye Patano (2005–11); Romany Malco; Maulik Pancholy; Indigo (2005–07); Renee Victor; Shoshannah Stern; Martin Donovan (2005–06); Becky Thyre; Jack Stehlin (2006–09); Fatso-Fasano (2006–12); Page Kennedy (2006–07); Guillermo Diaz (2007–12); Matthew Modine (2007); Demian Bichir (2008–10); Enrique Castillo (2008–10); Hemky Madera (2008–10); Jennifer Jason Leigh (2009–12); Amanda Pace (2009–12); Michael Harney (2011–12); Bruce Nozick (2011–12); Ethan Kent (2011–12); Gavin Kent (2011–12).

The liberties of cable television, particularly premium cable, are generally categorized as being in the areas of sex, nudity and language. Freedom of subject matter might be more crucial to the creative process than any of them. At its time, *Weeds* could never have been made for broadcast television. The premise, a young suburban mother of two making ends meet by becoming a marijuana dealer, could not have passed muster with any network standards and practices department. In one way, *Weeds* was the next generation of the *Cheech & Chong* features, at least at the outset when there was a lot of humor, and it could be argued that the Showtime series paved the way for the lavishly praised *Breaking Bad*. The setups were identical: a law abiding person suddenly in difficult financial circumstances and desperate to provide for her or his family becomes involved in the commerce of narcotics and winds up in deeper and darker territory, including murder.

Mary-Louise Parker starred as Nancy Botwin, whose fiscal circumstances went south when her husband suddenly dropped dead. Her solution was to make ends meet by becoming a pot dealer in the suburban subdivision of Agrestic, California. The cookie-cutter, antiseptic nature of Agrestic and other communities just like it was mocked in the catchy theme song "Little Boxes." The warm reception to the ditty, sung exclusively during the first season by Malvina Reynolds, led to covers by an eclectic mix of artists including Elvis Costello, Joan Baez, Engelbert Humperdinck, Billy Bob Thornton and Donovan. It was almost a status symbol to be asked to interpret it at the top of each episode and fans looked forward to seeing whom the artist of the week would be.

Nancy's new means to make a living started modestly, selling small quantities of pot to friends and neighbors. Demand grew like, well, weeds. To increase her supply, she threw in with a family of growers and wholesalers, Heylia James (Tonye Patano) and her offspring, Conrad (Romany Malco) and Vaneeta (Indigo). Conrad developed a strain he dubbed MILF, which became Nancy's best seller.

The number of those in Nancy's inner circle anxious to be part of her business also increased exponentially. Doug Wilson (Kevin Nealon), an accountant and shady local politician, volunteered to be Nancy's first financial advisor. Among other things he suggested that she open a bakeshop as a front. Nancy's ne'er-do-well brother-in-law Andy (Justin Kirk) showed up and wanted in, too. Doug and Andy became permanent members of Nancy's entourage, trailing her around the country and the world, getting into precarious predicaments of their own along the way. Andy also revealed that he had a secret romantic crush on his sister-in-law. Nancy immediately squelched any hopes he might have had along those lines and he reluctantly accepted her lack of feelings for him.

Nancy got an unwanted ally in her older son Silas (Hunter Parrish). Like any mother, she recoiled at the thought of her child becoming involved in the illicit trade. When she realized her protests were futile, she accepted him into the family business. Her younger son Shane (Alexander Gould) had the most interesting life odyssey of all. He was most seriously impacted by the sudden death of his father. As a child he continued to engage in one-way conversations with his late dad. His language turned vulgar and he became an alcoholic. But he remained a staunch defender of his mother, to the extent when he sensed her life in danger he murdered the person threatening her. As he became a young adult, he adopted a police officer as his new father figure and by show's end, he became a cop.

Nancy did not mourn her husband for an extended period. Over the course of the series she became intimately involved with a DEA agent (unknowingly at first), a Mexican drug cartel king, with whom she had a third child, Stevie, and a rabbi. Also constantly on the fringes of Nancy's life was her Agrestic neighbor Celia Hodes (Elizabeth Perkins), with whom Nancy had a love-hate relationship. Celia was unhappily married and was just as unhappy as a parent. She banished her daughter Quinn (Haley Hudson) to military school and was embarrassed by her other daughter Celia (Allie Grant) because she was morbidly obese. Ironically, Celia's weight problems became a boon as she was hired as a highly paid plus-size model.

Perkins matched Parker's three Emmy nominations, the only ones for performers, and the series was nominated once for best comedy. At the end of season three, Agrestic literally went up in smoke and the Botwins relocated to a seaside community near San Diego, where she fell in with international drug traders. Before the series ended, she did three years in prison while the rest of the family went on the lam to Denmark. When she was released to a halfway house in New York City, her posse returned from overseas and picked up where they left off. Eventually they wound up back where they started, doing what they did best. However, this time they were on the right side of the law, operating a medical marijuana dispensary.

Weeds became the most watched series in Showtime's history to that point and the season four opener drew more than a million viewers, a milepost for the network. The series finally ended after eight seasons.

82. *Growing Pains*

Broadcast History:

Tuesday	8:30–9:00	September 1985–March 1988	ABC
Wednesday	8:00–8:30	March 1988–August 1990	ABC
Wednesday	8:30–9:00	August 1990–August 1991	ABC
Friday	9:30–10:00	August 1991–September 1991	ABC
Saturday	8:30–9:00	September 1991–January 1992	ABC
Saturday	9:30–10:00	February 1992–April 1992	ABC
Wednesday	8:30–9:00	May 1992–July 1992	ABC
Thursday	8:30–9:00	July 1992–August 1992	ABC

#18 rated series in 1985–86	#14 rated series in 1988–89
#8 rated series in 1986–87	#21 rated series in 1989–90
#8 rated series in 1987–88	#27 rated series in 1990–91

No Major Emmy Awards (No nominations)

Cast: Alan Thicke; Joanna Kerns; Kirk Cameron; Tracey Gold; Jeremy Miller; Josh Andrew Koenig (1985–89); K.C. Martel; Lisa Capps (1987–88); Rachel Jacobs (1987–88); Bill Kirchenbauer (1987–88); Kristen Dohring (1988–90); Kelsey Dohring (1988–90); Jane Powell (1988–90); Robert Rockwell (1988–90); Gordon Jump (1989–91); Betty McGuire (1989–91); Julie McCullough (1989–90); Chelsea Noble (1989–92); Jamie Abbot (1989–91); Ashley Johnson (1990–92); Leonardo DiCaprio (1991–92).

Growing Pains was a light comedy on the screen. Behind the scenes there was lots of intense drama. The ABC series was a throwback to the era of edge-free family comedies. It occasionally delved into weighty issues, such as drug abuse, drunk driving and racism, but for the most part, episodes weren't any heavier than *The Adventures of Ozzie and Harriet* and *The Donna Reed Show*. Like those series, *Growing Pains* had the adults in the title but the success of the series came to hinge on its younger characters evolving into teen magazine heartthrobs.

Alan Thicke (who would become better known as the father of singer Robin Thicke, who appeared as an extra in three episodes) starred as patriarch Dr. Jason Seaver. A psychiatrist, Jason worked out of his home so he could tend their children, Mike (Kirk Cameron), 15, Carol (Tracey Gold), 14, and 9-year-old Ben (Jeremy Miller), while his wife Maggie (Joanna Kerns) returned to work as a journalist. At the end of the third season, Maggie became pregnant with another child, Chrissy, who zoomed from infant to 6-year-old in two seasons.

The family surname apparently wasn't picked out of a hat. Someone with influence must have been a fan of the New York Mets. *Growing Pains* was set in Long Island, not far from Shea Stadium, and Tom Seaver was the Mets' golden boy. The Seavers had a neighboring family, the Koosmans. Jerry Koosman was another Mets pitching ace.

Jason could have been the Mr. Mom of the Year every year. Patient and understanding to a fault thanks to his belief in the innate goodness of people, Jason always was able to come up with the enlightened solution to family crises. He even fit in well with the Mothers Club at his children's school. Sometimes he fit in too well for Maggie as women fawned all over him. One of Jason's few faults was a jealous streak of his own about Maggie working closely with good-looking men at the office.

Maggie didn't need this pressure. She already had severe guilt pangs about not being home when the kids needed her. The children often unintentionally fed this remorse with reminders that they could have used her help or guidance but she wasn't there. As the show progressed, Mike emerged as the breakout character. It became obvious young female viewers couldn't get enough of him, so his screen time was enhanced and episodes were built around him. His parents had to deal with Mike's sudden yen for gambling; his desire to take karate lessons and later to join the drama club to impress girls; his nomination for class president, etc.

However, Cameron became an Excedrin headache backstage. Shortly after he turned 17, he had a religious epiphany and became a fervent Evangelical Christian. He refused to do scenes that he viewed as even slightly racy. He red-lined any dialog that could have been considered double entendres. His sanctimoniousness alienated fellow cast members and he accused the producers of being pornographers. Incensed, some of them quit. The nadir of his intolerance came when he demanded Julie McCullough, who played Mike's fiancée Julie, be fired when he discovered she had once posed for *Playboy*. A script had to be developed in which Julie left him standing at the altar. What's more, Cameron insisted that the series hire his real-life girlfriend, Chelsea Noble, to play Mike's new squeeze, Kate McDonald. Cameron had met Noble while visiting his sister Candace on the set of *Full House*, in which she played D.J. Tanner. Cameron and Noble married in real life in 1991 and have six children.

Carol was a sweet young lady with a winning personality, who really missed having her mother around. She took it upon herself to serve as surrogate mother, helping with the cooking and other chores. Like most girls her age, she was boy crazy. One of the guys she fell for was played by a young

Brad Pitt. Another romance with a superstar-to-be led to the series most heart-breaking episode. A boyfriend named Sandy, played by pre–*Friends* Matthew Perry, drove his car after drinking, got into an accident and died.

Gold, whose sister Missy was a regular on *Benson*, almost died in real life during the series. She had been overly concerned about her weight since adolescence. As she matured and filled out, jokes were written in which the other Seavers poked gentle fun at her increased poundage. Unbeknownst to them, she took the teasing to heart. She went on severe diets, essentially starving herself until she was suffering from anorexia. Her weight plunged from 130 pounds to 79 pounds, putting her life into jeopardy. She had to take a leave, which extended from the middle of season six to the series' final two episodes, to be treated. Carol's absence was explained as her being overseas studying.

Pitt and Perry weren't the only future superstars to appear on the series. Then unknown Leonardo DiCaprio became a regular during the final season as Luke Brower, a homeless youngster, who was a star student in a class taught by Mike, by then an adult and a teacher. When the Seavers learned of Luke's plight they took him into their home. Through no fault of DiCaprio, this turned out to be the series lowest rated season. After never being out of Nielsen's top 30 and a top 10 show twice, *Growing Pains* plunged into the 70s, which spelled the end of the road.

83. *Arrested Development*

Broadcast History:

Sunday	9:30–10:00	November 2003–April 2004	FOX
Sunday	8:30–9:00	June 2004–April 2005	FOX
Monday	8:00–8:30	September 2005–October 2005	FOX
Monday	8:00–9:00	December 2005–January 2006	FOX
Friday	8:00–10:00	February 2006	FOX
On Demand	May 2013	NETFLIX	

4 Major Emmy Awards (15 nominations):
1 Emmy Award for Best Series (3 nominations)
No Emmy Awards for Best Actor (2 nominations)
No Emmy Awards for Best Supporting Actor (3 nominations)
No Emmy Awards for Best Supporting Actress (1 nomination)
2 Emmy Awards for Best Writing (5 nominations)
1 Emmy Award for Best Direction (1 nomination)

Cast: Jason Bateman; Michael Cera; Jeffrey Tambor; Jessica Walter; Will Arnett; Tony Hale; Portia de Rossi; David Cross; Alia Shawkat; Liza Minnelli (2003–05);

Judy Greer (2003–05); Henry Winkler (2003–05); Justin Lee (2004–06); Amy Poehler (2004–05); Mae Whitman (2004–06); Mo Collins (2004–05); Justin Grant Wade (2004–05); Charlize Theron (2005); Bob Einstein (2005–06).

Arrested Development was a ratings failure fans wouldn't allow to die. Despite being from Hollywood hitmaker Ron ("Opie") Howard and having a sterling cast, it never found a viable audience for Fox and was canceled after three seasons. It probably wouldn't have lasted that long but for its surprisingly high DVD sales and a relatively small coterie of fans, who supported it with an unrelenting fervor rarely seen outside the realm of science fiction series. After keeping it on Fox longer than ratings dictated, fans continued to lobby for its return. Seven years after the series left broadcast television, the new Netflix streaming delivery system revived it for 15 episodes, the first off-network series to be resuscitated as a webcast.

Steeped in sarcasm and irony, *Arrested Development* is one of those series that can be categorized as "too smart for broadcast television." Too many viewers take everything they see literally and don't get spoofs. Nothing in *Arrested Development* was intended to be taken seriously. The focus was the off-the-wall Bluth family of Southern California. Patriarch George Bluth (Jeffrey Tambor) ran a booming real estate and construction business. This allowed his family to live la dolce vita to the hilt. It turned out the bottom line was substantially fortified by investor fraud and other financial shenanigans. George was busted by the Securities and Exchange Commission as he celebrated his retirement aboard a yacht. He went to prison and his family's holdings were seized.

The Bluths were suddenly broke. Most of them would have been homeless if they weren't able to move into the company's lone remaining model home. The strength of the series was that every character in the extended family was sufficiently interesting and/or zany to be the pivotal character in a series of his or her own. Tambor and Jason Bateman, who played favorite son Michael Bluth, were nominated twice each for Emmys. Will Arnett as Michael's brother GOB (George Oscar Bluth) and Jessica Walter as matriarch Lucille Bluth also were Emmy nominated and the series was named best comedy in 2004, one of three years in which it was nominated.

Michael was the adult in the room, the only level-headed Bluth. Michael expected that his father would name him the successor to run the family business. He was crestfallen when his mother, a manipulative, controlling drunk, was tapped instead. Michael's disappointment diminished when his father subsequently explained he saw the trouble with the feds coming and didn't want to put Michael under the gun.

A single father, Michael threw almost all his energies into raising his only son, George Michael (Michael Cera), who wasn't the ripest banana in the bunch. Indeed, the teen ran the family frozen banana stand, which he managed to run down and burn down. Otherwise, he was a good kid. Part of George Michael's problems were traceable to his infatuation with his cousin Maeby Funke (Alia Shawkat), who teased him into making out with her just to tick off her parents. She might have learned this from her mother, Lindsay Bluth Funke (Portia de Rossi), Michael's spoiled rotten twin sister, who married a defrocked psychiatrist, Tobias Funke (David Cross), to spite her parents. Tobias was oblivious to the fact that many of his ways led even family members to wonder if he was gay. This speculation was further fueled when a book he wrote before he lost his medical license became a sensation in the gay community.

GOB had the illusion that he was a magician but any hopes that he would be accepted in the field vanished when he committed the profession's unforgivable sin. He inadvertently revealed the secrets behind a trick. To give him something to do, Lucille made him the head of the family business, or what little was left of it.

Another Bluth offspring, Buster (Tony Hale), was an educated idiot, who had been overly protected by his smothering mother. To avoid facing adult life, he studied everything from Indian lore to cartography, all of which prepared him to do nothing. Never having had to face the real world, he also was prone to panic attacks.

George actually enjoyed his incarceration, confiding to Michael that it was like a vacation. However, when the opportunity presented itself, he broke out by fooling an identical twin (also Tambor) to take his place. Michael was then burdened by helping his father stay on the loose.

In spite of its audience shortfall, *Arrested Development* became a cool thing to do in Hollywood. Henry Winkler recurred as the Bluth's disreputable attorney Barry Zuckerhorn. Liza Minelli signed on to play Lucille Austero, a friend and rival of Lucille's and a lover of GOB and Buster. Charlize Theron appeared in a series of episodes as one of Michael's lovers. Julia Louis-Dreyfus had a stint as another of Michael's girlfriends. Mae Whitman portrayed Ann Veal, a strident Christian who replaced Maeby in George Michael's heart. Ben Stiller appeared as Tony Wonder, a nemesis of GOB. Amy Poehler was cast as GOB's unnamed wife. Judy Greer was prominent as Kitty Sanchez, George's assistant and partner in crime, who also was his lover. Jane Lynch played the colorfully named Cindi Lightballoon, who was introduced as an undercover fed trying to uncover dirt on George only to fall in love with him.

Netflix held out hope in 2015 that it would underwrite a fifth season of *Arrested Development* and rumors of a theatrical adaptation, many of them generated by cast members, persisted.

84. *Ellen* (*These Friends of Mine*)

Broadcast History:

Wednesday	9:30–10:00	March 1994–May 1994	ABC
Tuesday	9:30–10:00	August 1994–September 1994	ABC
Wednesday	9:30–10:00	September 1994–March 1995	ABC
Wednesday	8:30–9:00	March 1995–September 1995	ABC
Wednesday	8:00–8:30	September 1995–November 1996	ABC
Wednesday	9:30–10:00	December 1996–February 1997	ABC
Tuesday	8:30–9:00	March 1997–April 1997	ABC
Wednesday	9:30–10:00	April 1997–July 1998	ABC

#13 rated series in 1994–95
#30 rated series in 1996–97

2 Major Emmy Awards (9 nominations):
No Emmy Awards for Best Actress (4 nominations)
1 Emmy Award for Best Guest Actor/Actress (2 nominations)
1 Emmy Award for Best Writing (2 nominations)
No Emmy Awards for Best Directing (1 nomination)

Cast: Ellen DeGeneres; David Anthony Higgins; Joely Fisher; Alice Hirson; Steven Gilborn; Patrick Bristow; Holly Fulger (1994); Maggie Wheeler (1994); Arye Gross (1994–96); Clea Lewis (1995–98); Jeremy Piven (1995–98); Jack Plotnick (1996–98).

Ellen was a nondescript series of no great artistic or ratings merit that made television history on April 30, 1997, with the innocuously titled "Puppy Episode." In the two-parter, which wrapped up the show's fourth season, Ellen DeGeneres became the first series headliner to come out as gay, personally and in character. This was an historic milestone for television but not a shocking revelation. Ellen's sexual orientation was known in show business circles for some time and it became gradually known to the general public.

By the time "The Puppy Episode" aired what was going to happen had been thoroughly reported. Nevertheless, ABC insisted upon the unprecedented step of demanding a viewer advisory even though there was nothing daring or explicit in the episode. By 21st century standards, it was Disney Channel fare. Controversy rarely harms any production and it certainly didn't hurt *Ellen.* The episode, which won an Emmy for writing, drew the largest audience in the show's history with an estimated 42 million people tuning in.

Ellen Morgan (DeGeneres) arranged to get together with an old college buddy named Richard (Steven Eckholdt), who had become a television personality and was in town shooting a story. Ellen told friends she considered the meeting a date. During dinner they were joined by one of Richard's co-workers, a producer named Susan, a role that won a guest star Emmy nomination for Laura Dern. Interestingly, DeGeneres was nominated, one of four times for this series, but did not get the prize.

After Susan excused herself, Ellen went up to Richard's hotel room for what seemed about to become doing what comes naturally. But the situation turned inexplicably awkward for Ellen. She quickly excused herself, only to run into Susan in the hallway. Susan invited her into her room and told Ellen matter-of-factly that she was gay. Ellen, in deep denial of her own sexuality, freaked and ran back to Richard, determined to prove to herself that she was straight. She lied to her friends the next day that she and Richard had wild and crazy sex. However, she admitted to her therapist, a guest appearance by Oprah Winfrey, that nothing happened because Richard had no physical appeal to her.

With Richard due to fly back home, Ellen hurried to the airport, ostensibly to say goodbye to him. In fact, she was hoping to see Susan again. Susan sensed what was troubling Ellen and urged her to be honest to herself. Ellen hemmed and hawed before finally blurting out, "I'm gay!" She inadvertently did it in front of an open airline microphone, so her honesty wasn't only to herself and Susan but to scores of people waiting for their flights.

This was an abrupt course correction for the series. At its outset, *Ellen* was one of several comedies that adhered closely to the *Seinfeld* blueprint. Titled in its first season *These Friends of Mine,* the series was built around a small circle of young adults, who spent an implausibly large portion of their lives in each other's company. Ellen, who ran, then bought a Los Angeles bookstore, was the center of this circle. Although she had self-esteem issues, she joked that she was "charming, funny and irresistible." She wasn't off the mark. She also was flirtatious and aggressively in pursuit of Mr. Right. However, it might have been a subtle hint that she had no interest in men who were available to her.

Joe Farrell (David Anthony Higgins), the bookstore's barista with an inflated sense of self worth, threw himself at her and allowed himself the delusion that she wanted him despite her best efforts to discourage this notion. At home, she had a handsome, straight male roommate, Adam Green (Ayre Gross). He also was desperately searching for romance, so much so that he would try to keep up a conversation with a woman who had dialed the wrong number. But Ellen and Adam had no romantic appeal to each other.

When Adam moved out, still before Ellen came out, another straight guy, Spence Kovak (Jeremy Piven) became Ellen's new roomie. But he was Ellen's cousin. Spence, a doctor wannabe, became involved in an affair with Ellen's friend Paige (Joely Fisher), who was engaged at the time, a relationship terminated by her dalliance with him. This was in character for the vain, pretentious and promiscuous Paige. Although she and Ellen were close, Paige always tried to one-up her friend.

Also in Ellen's orbit was Audrey Penney (Clea Lewis), an extrovert and busybody with a high-pitched voice that would give dogs a headache. Even after Ellen came out, there was never a hint that Ellen's relationships with the regular female characters were anything but platonic. However, once Ellen was out the fifth season became dominated by her dealing with her homosexuality and gay issues.

She was celebrated by gay rights activists but in an affirmation of the saying that the pioneers always take the most arrows, the general public recoiled. Ratings plunged and the series was canceled.

---

85. *The Donna Reed Show*

Broadcast History:

Wednesday	9:00–9:30	September 1958–September 1959	ABC
Thursday	8:00–8:30	October 1959–January 1966	ABC
Saturday	8:00–8:30	January 1966–September 1966	ABC

#30 rated series in 1961–62
#16 rated series in 1963–64

No Major Emmy Awards (4 nominations):
No Emmy Award for Best Actress (4 nominations)

Cast: Donna Reed; Carl Betz; Shelley Fabares (1958–63); Paul Petersen; Patty Petersen (1963–66); Bob Crane (1963–65); Ann McCrea (1963–66); Janet Langard (1964–65); Darryl Richard (1965–66).

The Donna Reed Show was a typical 1950s family situation comedy—sweet, bland and family friendly. Lassie was a guest star. You don't get any more wholesome. Simplistic vignettes were played out by an appealing ensemble built around a beloved and still vibrantly youthful star.

More than a decade before she made the transition to television Reed had the iconic role of Mary Hatch Bailey in *It's a Wonderful Life*. She followed with an Oscar winning turn as best supporting actress in the 1953 film *From Here to Eternity*. So there was a fan base in place for her television debut as Donna Stone in the eponymous ABC series. Donna Stone, a trained nurse who put her career on hold to be a homemaker, was the hub of a traditional nuclear family, a rarity in an era when male leads dominated family comedies.

Smart and charming, she was a candidate for Mother of the Year every year. The series could have been dubbed *Mother Knows Best*. Reed's status as the glue that held the series together was recognized with four consecutive Emmy nominations. Her husband Alex (Carl Betz), a pediatrician, maintained an office in their suburban two-story house. However, an episode rarely passed without him being summoned to make an unexpected house or hospital call.

Spats between the two were rare and mild. Neither ever left the house—or sometimes a room—without giving the other an affectionate kiss. Nevertheless, Donna would fret that they weren't as romantic as they used to be, especially after they had been in the company of newlyweds. Although it was kept low key, the feeling prevailed that this couple enjoyed a rich love life, another rarity for this period when twin beds separated by a piece of furniture were still the rule.

Every now and then, Donna would rebel against her image as the perfect wife and homemaker and yearn for a "me" day but she always quickly snapped back and embraced her role. As the kids got older, she ventured outside the home more often to assist in community events and charities.

A crisis for Alex was being asked to judge a beautiful baby contest in which the entrants included his patients and the offspring of Donna's friends. The closest he and Donna came to a dispute was a decision over whether a new set of golf clubs for him or a new washing machine for her should be the priority of the family budget.

The Stones had two children, Mary (Shelley Fabares), 14 at the start of the show, and her slightly younger brother Jeff (Paul Petersen). The kids were well behaved but not angelic. They bickered with each other and their parents but never turned insolent or disrespectful. The usual adolescent mischief and contretemps rarely turned serious. Mary would overbook dates for a dance. Jeff got into funks because his folks wouldn't spring for a new football uniform. He sometimes assumed they liked Mary better. This must have been a guy thing in the Stone household since Alex occasionally chafed at his conviction that the kids liked their mother better.

All things considered they were a model American family, almost clones of the Nelsons of *The Adventures of Ozzie and Harriet* or the Cleavers of *Leave It to Beaver*. The Stones had something else in common with the Nelsons. Once Ricky Nelson used his series to break out as a teen-idol singing star, the producers had Fabares and Petersen do likewise. Fabares had a million-selling single, "Johnny Angel," in early 1962. Later that year, Petersen released a novelty tune, "She Can't Find Her Keys," which didn't hit as big. A year later, he enjoyed greater success with a sappy ballad, "My Dad," which was keyed to an episode in which he and Alex were unable to find father-son time together.

The elevated profiles with younger viewers of Mary and Jeff on a series built around its titular adult star provided a booster shot to the show, which was never a Nielsen smash. It cracked the top 20 only once.

Fabares left the series in 1963 to pursue an adult career. Her departure was explained as Mary going away to college. This afforded her the opportunity to return from time to time. To fill the void in the home, the Stones adopted a young orphan, Trisha, played by Petersen's real-life kid sister Patty. Jeff's presence also was expanded. A best friend named Smitty (Darryl Richard) was introduced as a regular.

After Mary's departure Donna and Alex also interacted more with their neighbors, Dr. Dave Kelsey (pre–*Hogan's Heroes* Bob Crane) and his spouse Midge (Ann McCrea). This allowed for more mature plotting although the program's non-edgy tradition was not breached. After a prodigious 275 episodes, Reed tired of the grind and allowed the series to come to an end.

86. *The Adventures of Ozzie & Harriet*

Broadcast History:

Friday	8:00–8:30	October 1952–June 1956	ABC
Wednesday	9:00–9:30	October 1956–September 1958	ABC
Wednesday	8:30–9:00	September 1958–September 1961	ABC
Thursday	7:30–8:00	September 1961–September 1963	ABC
Wednesday	7:30–8:00	September 1963–January 1966	ABC
Saturday	7:30–8:00	January 1966–September 1966	ABC

#29 rated series in 1963–64

No Major Emmy Awards (2 nominations):
No Emmy Awards for Best Series (1 nomination)
No Emmy Awards for Best Supporting Actor (1 nomination)

Cast: Ozzie Nelson; Harriet Nelson; David Nelson; Ricky Nelson; Don DeFore (1952–58); Frank Cady (1954–65); Parley Baer (1955–61); Lyle Talbot (1956–66); Mary Jane Croft (1956–66); Skip Young (1957–66); Gordon Jones (1958–60); James Stacy (1958–64); Joe Flynn (1960–62); Constance Harper (1960–66); June Blair (1961–66); Jack Wagner (1961–66); Charlene Salerno (1962–65); Kristin Harmon (1964–66); Ivan Bonar (1964–66); Greg Dawson (1965–66); Sean Morgan (1965–66).

The Adventures of Ozzie and Harriet never hit number one in the Nielsen ratings. In fact, it never cracked the top 25. But it likely will be able to lay claim forever to number one in another significant category. Its 14 years on ABC makes it the longest running live action situation comedy in the history of television. This longevity is more remarkable considering the concept was a popular radio program for eight years before it debuted on television. For a couple of years, there was a weekly *Adventures of Ozzie and Harriet* on both radio and television. There also was a theatrical feature film in 1952, *Here Comes the Nelsons*, which laid the groundwork for the television series.

All the Nelsons had to do was be themselves. They kept their own names. Their television home was a replica of their real home. When the children grew up and got married, their spouses joined the series playing themselves. All were minimalist actors, which explains their snub by the Television Academy. The only Emmy nomination for a performer went to supporting actor Don DeFore, who played Ozzie's pal Thorny. The series also received only one nomination.

Ozzie Nelson came to prominence as a bandleader. However, this was not a factor in the series in which he had no visible means of support. This became a source of humor among comedians and critics. Ozzie got up every day, put on a suit and tie but rarely left the house to go anywhere but the malt shop. Nevertheless, the Nelsons somehow lived a comfortable upper middle class life. Shortage of money was never an issue, unless it was used as a plot device, such as the family going into a dither because they thought David had been unable to make a car payment. (It turned out to be the situation comedy staple, a misunderstanding.)

Harriet was a former singer, another career that went unmentioned in the show. She was the quintessential stay-at-home wife, fashionably dressed even when making cookies for her boys and neighborhood kids or pancakes for Ozzie and a buddy who just dropped in. Her out-of-home activities were limited to shopping for groceries and staying active in a woman's club made up of peers in similar domestic situations.

Neither Ozzie nor Harriet was a bumbler or straight person for the other. Although they were presented as the ideal married couple, they were perhaps the least interesting pair ever to front a situation comedy. Their sons, David and Ricky, grew up in front of America. David was often relegated to second banana status to Ricky, who for a time when he was a mischievous adolescent was introduced in the opening credits as "...and the irrepressible Ricky."

When the brothers were in high school in real life, they were in high school on the show. Ditto, college. When David, four years older, met the woman he came to love and marry, June, their courtship and newlywed home life became fodder for plots.

The same thing happened when Ricky fell in love with his-wife-to-be Kristin, the daughter of Heisman Trophy–winning football player and later sportscaster Tom Harmon and sister of actor Mark Harmon. Their marriage, which ended in divorce, produced four children, three of who went into show business. Tracy Nelson co-starred in *The Father Dowling Mysteries* among numerous credits. Her younger brothers, Gunnar and Matthew, created the pop rock music duo Nelson.

Ricky's own entrance into the music business, a cover performance of Fats Domino's "I'm Walkin'" on an episode in April 1957, gave the television series a boost, especially among younger viewers. From this point on, numerous episodes found a way to feature a song by Ricky. When a plot couldn't be concocted to have a song fit in naturally, a stand-alone performance was tacked on to the end of the episode.

Ricky's emergence as a teen idol spurred other series with young stars (e.g., Shelley Fabares and Paul Peterson of *The Donna Reed Show* and Johnny Crawford of *The Rifleman*) to push them into pop music.

The series full title, *The Adventures of Ozzie and Harriet*, was a bit of an embellishment. An adventure for the Nelsons was Ozzie trying to cajole neighborhood 10-year-old boys into going to a dance with 10-year-old girls, which was arranged by Harriet's women's club. A family crisis was a dispute over which Nelson was more responsible for a traffic light being installed at a busy intersection: Ozzie for interceding with a politician; Harriet for the push from her women's club; David, who organized a petition drive at school; or Ricky for pleading with a friendly policeman to do something.

The series that was so charming in the 1950s fell out of step with the

more cynical, turmoil ridden America of the 1960s and ABC decided to end
the show in 1966.

---

87. *How I Met Your Mother*

Broadcast History:

Monday	8:30–9:00	September 2005–October 2006	CBS
Monday	8:00–8:30	October 2006–February 2008	CBS
Monday	8:30–9:00	March 2008–June 2009	CBS
Monday	8:00–8:30	July 2009–March 2014	CBS

#28 rated series in 2013–14

No Major Emmy Awards (6 nominations):
No Emmy Awards for Best Series (1 nomination)
No Emmy Awards for Best Supporting Actor (4 nominations)
No Emmy Awards for Best Direction (1 nomination)

Cast: Josh Radnor; Jason Segel; Cobie Smulders; Neil Patrick Harris; Alyson Hannigan; Cristin Milioti; Bob Saget (voice).

How I Met Your Mother was a nine-year tease to an unsatisfactory payoff.
There have been many disappointing final episodes—*Seinfeld, The Sopranos,
Lost,* to name just a few—but the negative reaction to them wasn't such that
the producers felt compelled to come up with an alternate ending after the
show left the air out of fear DVD sales would be severely impacted by fan
protests. The *How I Met Your Mother* base wasn't that strong that any fans
could afford to be alienated. The series exceeded a season's average of 10 million viewers and a breakthrough into Nielsen's Top 40 only once, in its final
season, which was bolstered by the promise of a resolution. So a new (hopefully) crowd-pleasing wrap was added to the box set.

The seeds were planted in the pilot. No doubt inspired by the phenomenal run of *Friends, How I Met Your Mother* was a slight fable of five friends
living in Manhattan, who spent an extraordinary amount of time in each
other's lives. The titular premise was told in flashback as Ted Mosby (Josh
Radnor), an architect and college professor, related to his adolescent children
in the year 2030 how he came to meet and marry their mother.

Ted's inner circle consisted of Marshall Erikson (Jason Segel) and Lily
Aldrin (Alyson Hannigan), a couple who met in college and became Ted's
apartment-mates until they married, Barney Stinson (Neil Patrick Harris), a
lecherous womanizer with an irresistible personality, and Robin Scherbatsky

(Cobie Smulders), who was introduced in the pilot as the first of Ted's potential mates. Bob Saget served as the unseen narrator of Ted's pursuit of Ms. Right.

From the moment she appeared on screen, Robin was the most likely future spouse for the instantly smitten Ted. However, the producers inexplicably opted to close the premiere with Saget, as Ted, revealing this was how he met "Aunt Robin," effectively eliminating her as the kids' mom. Cristin Miloti, who appeared throughout the series' run in different bit parts, was eventually cast as Mrs. Mosby, the former Tracy McConnell, in the final episode of season eight. However, in the season nine episode in which she and Ted finally recited their vows, it was revealed that their happiness was short-lived because she died three years later, leading Ted to resume his courtship of Aunt Robin. This was the catalyst for the fan resentment at being strung along to an event dismissed in a matter of seconds. The hastily released revised ending had Ted's narration shifting to, "When I think of how lucky I am to wake up next to your mom every morning, I can't help but be amazed at how easy it was."

Miloti was preceded as Ted's squeeze by a procession of attractive women, beginning with Robin, who had several runs as Ted's significant other, including a period in which they lived together. Ashley Williams had a double dip as Victoria, who got serious with Ted, left him for a job overseas then returned in season eight. Sarah Chalke came closest to exchanging rings with Ted as Stella, a single mother and dermatologist who met Ted when he went to her to remove an embarrassing tattoo. Although she was still appearing as a regular on *Scrubs*, Ted proposed to her character and she accepted. However, just before they could be pronounced Mr. and Mrs. Mosby, she backed out and returned to the man who fathered her child.

Rachel Bilson had a brief fling with Ted while one of his students but her significance turned out to be that she was Tracy's roommate. Jennifer Morrison got off to a rocky start as Zoey, a preservationist activist protesting against the demolition of a landmark building so that it could be replaced by one designed by Ted. She eventually crossed the thin line between hate and love even though she was married to a substantially older eccentric known as The Captain (Kyle McLachlin). Ted's final fling before Tracy was a brief one with an architecture groupie named Jeanette (Abby Elliott).

Although Ted was the pivotal character, Barney was arguably the most interesting of the group, only partially for his lechery. It was revealed Barney had an African American, gay half-brother, played by Wayne Brady. Barney was convinced that *The Price Is Right* legend Bob Barker was his biological father. In fact, it turned out to be a guy named Jerry, played by John Lithgow. Barney's womanizing was driven by his commitment phobia, a condition cured when he fell in love with and eventually married Robin. This, too, led to a revision of the finale. In order to make Robin available to Ted, the producers had Barney and Robin divorcing in the original. The alternative ending, in which Ted and Tracy lived happily ever after, eliminated the necessity of a divorce and the narration revealed that Barney and Robin had reconciled and presumably also lived happily ever after, conceiving three children.

Robin, a Canadian, aspired to be a respected television newswoman, a career path that saw her on an obscure cable news channel in the wee hours of the morning. This dalliance with television wasn't a first. It was revealed to her chagrin she had been a teen idol north of the border as Robin Sparkles, singer of a bouncy ditty titled "Let's Go to the Mall." Around her trysts with Ted and Barney, she had almost as full a roster of lovers as Ted, including characters played by Enrique Iglesias, Jr., and Kal Penn.

Marshall and Lily met in college and with only a few brief breaks maintained their romantic relationship through courtship, marriage and parenthood. Marshall, an attorney, and Barney, who worked in an undefined executive role for a bank, frequently clashed over who was Ted's best male friend. Lily was a teacher until she was able to fulfill her long-time dream to become an artist.

Hannigan, who had a following from *Buffy the Vampire Slayer*, and Harris, a child prodigy as *Doogie Hower, M.D.*, were the best known of the regulars. Harris became the only one to be Emmy nominated, garnering four nods as best supporting actor. The only other major nominations from 28 overall was one for the series as outstanding comedy and one for directing. All nine Emmys won came in technical categories.

88. *The Bob Newhart Show*

Broadcast History:

Saturday	9:30–10:00	September 1972–October 1976	CBS
Saturday	8:30–9:00	November 1976–September 1977	CBS
Saturday	8:00–8:30	September 1977–August 1978	CBS

#16 rated series in 1972–73   #17 rated series in 1974–75
#12 rated series in 1973–74   #26 rated series in 1975–76

No Major Emmy Awards (3 nominations):
No Emmy Awards for Best Series (1 nomination)
No Emmy Awards for Best Actress (2 nominations)

Cast: Bob Newhart; Suzanne Pleshette; Bill Daily; Peter Bonerz; Marcia Wallace; Patricia Smith (1972–73); Larry Gelman (1972–76); Pat Finley (1974–76); Will Mackenzie (1975–77); Jack Riley; Florida Friebus; Penny Marshall (1972–73); Noam Pitlik (1972–73); Renee Lippin (1973–76); John Fiedler (1973–78); Lucien Scott (1974–75); Oliver Clark (1976–77); Howard Hesseman (1977–78).

The Bob Newhart Show was the first of what became a trilogy of eponymous situation comedies built around the dry, reactive humor of the comedian. Newhart once joked to television critics that he didn't know what to make of the sequence of their titles. The first series he headlined was *The Bob Newhart Show*. Next came *Newhart*. The third was called *Bob*. He wondered if he would someday get to star in a series called just *The*.

Newhart's forte was playing straight man for his supporting ensemble. He didn't even need the other person to be present. His stage persona, major parts of which were incorporated into his television series, was built around hilarious phone exchanges in which only his end of the conversation was heard. It was all that was needed to produce laughs.

His *Bob Newhart Show* character, Chicago psychologist Dr. Bob Hartley, was an ideal vehicle to serve his style. He had an array of off-kilter patients, including a pitcher for the Cubs whose slump was mental, a minister thinking about abandoning his calling, a ventriloquist convinced his dummy was a real person, a woman (Florida Friebus), who knitted non-stop during most sessions, a gay man (Howard Hesseman), who needed support to come out, and several patients who developed a crush on Bob.

Bob's professional colleagues in his medical building also tended to be off-the-wall, as did his flighty receptionist. On the home front, a high-rise apartment, Bob had a needy neighbor. The voice of sanity in his life was his spouse, Emily, played masterfully by Suzanne Pleshette, who was twice nominated for an Emmy—the only cast member to be so honored. However, the series did pull one nomination as outstanding comedy.

As rich as his career was, Newhart personally did not win an Emmy until 2013 when he was honored for a guest shot on *The Big Bang Theory*. Blessed with a cushy time slot behind *The Mary Tyler Moore Show* on a Saturday night led off by *All in the Family* and *M*A*S*H*, *The Bob Newhart Show* cracked Nielsen's Top 20 for its first three seasons before beginning a gradual fade. When it was asked to lead off Saturday in its sixth season, ratings cratered and CBS put it out of its misery.

Bob and Emily, an educator who turned out to have a higher IQ than Bob, became such a cherished couple that a reunion in the finale of *Newhart* is often mentioned as the finest series-ending episode of all time. Newhart and Pleshette were seen in bed as he told her of this crazy dream he had of being the owner of an inn in Vermont. Still loving the old series, the audience went wild.

Bob fit the Midwesterner stereotype. He was friendly, low-key and old-fashioned. One of the few occasions when he felt he had to assert himself came when his sister Ellen (Pat Finley) announced she was going to move in with her boyfriend. It might have been slightly prudish but Bob felt he could not stand by and see his sister cohabit with a man who was not her husband. The situation wasn't helped by the fact that the man with whom she was about to live, Howard Borden (Bill Dailey), was Bob's flaky neighbor. An airline navigator, he spent almost as much time in the Hartleys' apartment as Bob and Emily, often seeking help or counsel regarding the latest petty hassle in his life. Nevertheless, Bob described Howard to others as his best friend, a distinction that bugged Bob's professional neighbor, Dr. Jerry Robinson (Peter Bonerz), a dentist whose office was on the same floor as Bob's. He thought he was Bob's BFF. This relationship became complicated when Jerry decided he needed help and went to Bob as a patient. It hit another ticklish spot when Jerry revealed to Bob that he had a crush on Emily.

Perhaps to keep things on an even keel, there was a time when Howard also joined Bob's therapy group. Howard and Jerry also once vied for the romantic attention of the same woman, played by Mariette Hartley, and both had flirtatious moments with Carol Kester (Marcia Wallace), the mouthy, free spirited receptionist Bob and Jerry shared. Jerry and Howard were among a long line of men who attracted Carol's attention. She was debating whether to move in with a guy in the premiere. After deciding not to take this step, she had flings with a much older man; a severely overweight suitor; one of Bob's regular patients, neurotic, contrarian Elliot Carlin (Jack Riley), and a poet. She finally married a guy, Larry Bondurant (Will Mackenzie), after one date. She missed an opportunity with Jerry, who inherited a fabulous amount of money in season four and decided it was time to give up dentistry and enjoy life.

In the series finale, Bob also decided it was time for a change. He closed his practice and he and Emily moved to Oregon where he took a teaching position at a small college.

89. *Diff'rent Strokes*

Broadcast History:

Friday	8:00–8:30	November 1978–October 1979	NBC
Wednesday	9:00–9:30	October 1979–October 1981	NBC
Thursday	9:00–9:30	October 1981–August 1982	NBC
Saturday	8:00–8:30	August 1982–August 1985	NBC
Friday	9:00–9:30	September 1985–March 1986	ABC
Saturday	8:00–8:30	June 1986–August 1986	ABC

#27 rated series in 1978–79
#26 rated series in 1979–80
#17 rated series in 1980–81

No Major Emmy Awards (No nominations)

Cast: Conrad Bain; Gary Coleman; Todd Bridges; Dana Plato (1978–84); Charlotte Rae (1978–79); Nedra Volz (1980–82); Dody Goodman (1981–82); Shavar Ross (1981–86); Le Tari (1981–85); Janet Jackson (1981–82); Mary Jo Catlett (1982–86); Rosalind Chao (1982–83); Steven Mond (1982–83); Nikki Swasey (1982–86); Danny Cooksey (1984–86); Dixie Carter (1984–85); Mary Ann Mobley (1985–86); Jason Hervey (1985–86).

Gary Coleman was a child star waiting to break out from his first appearance in commercials and one-shot guest roles on series such as *The Jeffersons* and *Good Times*. The camera loved the diminutive dynamo, who was under four-feet tall on the show and grew to only four-foot-seven as an adult. His slight stature was a result of lifelong kidney disease. His moon face, radiant smile, exuberant personality and perfect timing made him a comedy natural. *Diff'rent Strokes* was the ideal showcase to utilize his youthful charisma. A benevolent white corporate tycoon, keeping a promise to his late black housekeeper, adopted her two kids, ages 8 and 12, and introduced them to the finer things in life, including a luxurious Park Avenue townhouse.

Coleman starred as the younger of the two, Arnold Jackson. Todd Bridges played his older brother Willis. Conrad Bain was their benefactor, Phillip Drummond, a widower, who was the biological father of a 13-year-old daughter, Kimberly, played by Dana Plato. Charlotte Rae was the first of three Drummond housekeepers, Mrs. Garrett, whose popularity led to her being spun off into *The Facts of Life*. Nedra Volz and Mary Jo Catlett followed Rae, as the less prominent Adelaide Brubaker and Pearl Gallagher, respectively.

The premise, which was praised in its time for promoting tolerance and diversity but would likely be condemned in the 21st century as condescending, was almost irrelevant and the supporting cast was merely straight persons for Coleman. The series, at least in its early years, was little more than a cavalcade of set-up lines teed up for Coleman to knock out of the park as his cherubic face filled the screen. Drummond: "It's starting to snow." Arnold: "I thought you had a bad case of dandruff." Cast in a school play as the Great Emancipator, Arnold bellyached, "I'll be the only Abraham Lincoln in history shorter than his hat." Arnold developed a signature catch phrase, "What chu you talking about, Willis [or whoever else he was addressing]?" to display his incredulity about what was being said. So it went until later in the series eight-year run.

Cute has a limited shelf life, even with a prodigy such as Coleman. The producers tried to adapt by introducing a romantic element, a new wife for Drummond, Maggie McKinney, in season six. Dixie Carter originated the role but she opted to leave the series after season seven and was replaced as the same character by Mary Ann Mobley. Maggie conveniently had a young son, Sam, about the same age Coleman was at the show's outset. Danny Cooksey, as Sam, was also cute and could handle a clever-beyond-his-years retort but he was no Gary Coleman.

Heavier plots, which dealt with societal issues germane to young people also became part of the mix. Then First Lady Nancy Reagan made a cameo appearance to promote her "Just Say No" to drugs campaign. Other issues put under the microscope included child predators, eating disorders and racism. Working for his school newspaper, Arnold exposed the prevalence and perils of steroid abuse among young athletes. This put him more than a decade ahead of Major League Baseball and the National Football League.

An issue the series might have tackled but understandably didn't was the exploitation of child stars and their fate after their brief fling with fame and fortune. The young stars of *Diff'rent Strokes* have one of television's most distressing post-series histories. Coleman, who was 18 when the series ended, reportedly earned as much as $100,000 per episode. But when he became of legal age to handle his own money he discovered his parents and financial advisors had spent much of the estimated $18 million he earned. He successfully sued but recovered not much more than a million dollars. A good deal of what was left after attorney fees went to medical treatments, including regular dialysis.

He found life after stardom difficult to handle. He was arrested for punching a female fan seeking an autograph. His career descended into demeaning roles and appearances on talk shows where sometimes his size became the butt of jokes. When even those opportunities dried up, he took a job as a security guard. In 1999, he was forced to file for bankruptcy. His only known marriage, to an actress, Shannon Price, who was 17 years his junior, ended after less than a year and was marked by a series of domestic violence allegations. In an interview, he confessed to twice attempting suicide. He died in 2010 at 42.

Bridges fell into a crack addiction after the demise of *Diff'rent Strokes.* Within two years of the series ending he was charged with the attempted murder of a drug dealer. A vigorous and imaginative defense by future O.J. Simpson lawyer Johnnie Cochran won a not-guilty verdict. He also allegedly wrecked someone else's car by deliberately driving his own auto into it.

Plato's story might have been the saddest of all. Even while on the show and barely into her teens, she had drug and alcohol problems. She reportedly overdosed on Valium when she was 14. When she became pregnant in 1984, she was cut from the series because the producers didn't feel pregnancy fit with the wholesome image of the young stars they were trying to convey. However, she was allowed to return sporadically to her role as a guest. Her career spiraled downward to the point where B-movies led to soft-core porn flicks after she had breast augmentation surgery. She also claimed most of the money she made on *Diff'rent Strokes* was stolen by handlers. Desperate, she held up a Las Vegas video store. The clerk recognized her from television and she was arrested within an hour. A judge went easy on her and let her off with probation. She was later arrested again for forging a prescription for a painkiller. This time she went to jail for 30 days. In 1999, she died of an overdose of painkillers at 35.

In spite of the fact that *Diff'rent Strokes* was never a huge ratings hit (it did rank in the top 20 during its third season) and neither the series, nor any of the actors were ever nominated for a major award, ABC picked up the series after NBC dropped it at the end of the 1984–85 season. However, the relocation didn't revitalize the show and it was canceled after one season on its new network.

90. *Scrubs*

Broadcast History:

Tuesday	9:30–10:00	October 2001–August 2002	NBC
Thursday	8:30–9:00	June 2002–August 2003	NBC
Thursday	9:30–10:00	July 2003–January 2004	NBC

Tuesday	9:30–10:00	February 2004–May 2004	NBC
Thursday	9:30–10:00	May 2004–August 2004	NBC
Tuesday	9:30–10:00	September 2004–December 2004	NBC
Tuesday	9:00–9:30	January 2005–May 2005	NBC
Thursday	9:00–9:30	August 2005–September 2005	NBC
Thursday	9:30–10:00	August 2005–September 2005	NBC
Tuesday	9:00–9:30	January 2006–March 2006	NBC
Tuesday	9:30–10:00	January 2006–March 2006	NBC
Tuesday	8:30–9:00	March 2006–May 2006	NBC
Wednesday	9:00–9:30	August 2006–September 2006	NBC
Wednesday	9:30–10:00	August 2006–September 2006	NBC
Thursday	9:00–9:30	November 2006–March 2007	NBC
Thursday	9:30–10:00	April 2007–November 2007	NBC
Thursday	9:30–10:00	April 2008–May 2008	NBC
Tuesday	9:00–9:30	January 2009–February 2009	ABC
Tuesday	9:30–10:00	January 2009–February 2009	ABC
Wednesday	8:00–8:30	March 2009–May 2009	ABC
Tuesday	9:00–9:30	June 2009	ABC
Tuesday	9:30–10:00	July 2009	ABC
Tuesday	9:00–9:30	December 2009–January 2010	ABC

#14 rated series in 2002–03

No Major Emmy Awards (6 nominations):
No Emmy Awards for Best Series (2 nominations)
No Emmy Awards for Best Actor (1 nomination)
No Emmy Awards for Best Writing (1 nomination)
No Emmy Awards for Best Directing (2 nominations)

Cast: Zach Braff; Donald Faison; Sarah Chalke; Ken Jenkins; John C. McGinley; Judy Reyes (2001–09); Neil Flynn; Aloma Wright (2001–07); Robert Maschio; Sam Lloyd; Christa Miller; Travis Schuldt (2006–08); Eliza Coupe (2009–10); Kerry Bishe (2009–10); Michael Mosley (2009–10); Dave Franco (2009–10).

Scrubs was a clever, creative attempt to de-mythologize and humanize the medical profession. With occasional exceptions, medical series traditionally portray doctors and nurses as heroic figures with only minor, insignificant character flaws. *Scrubs* took a different, irreverent approach. While its protagonists were for the most part admirable characters, the underlying premise was that they were regular people with considerable flaws.

The series earned widespread critical acclaim and 6 major Emmy nominations, though it did win a couple of minor awards. However, viewer reception was illustrative of why doctor series take the tack they do. With the exception of season two, an outlier when it ranked number 14 in the Nielsen rankings, *Scrubs* never cracked Nielsen's top 40 and seasons four through eight ranked between 87th and 106th. The ninth and final season, a retooling of the show with a substantially new cast, bottomed out at number 116.

Clearly, people like to think that those in whose hands they place their lives are mythic figures. Zach Braff starred as the pivotal figure, Dr. John "J.D." Dorian, who was introduced as an intern at Sacred Heart Teaching Hospital. Over the course of the series, he evolved into a resident, then a full-fledged staff physician and a teacher at a medical college. J.D. also served as narrator of the off-the-wall events at Sacred Heart and in his randy personal life, which had him romantically involved with a procession of women, fathering children by two of them, only one of whom was his wife. His thoughts were played out through fantasy sequences interjected into the plots. Musical interludes also were integral with pop songs chosen whose lyrics mirrored the story lines. In season six, an entire episode was musically based. This episode earned one of the series' two Emmy directing nominations.

J.D.'s best buddy was Christopher Turk (Donald Faison), his roommate at William & Mary and medical school. They joined the staff of Sacred Heart together and advanced up the career ladder. Turk conquered initial self-confidence issues to become Sacred Heart's Chief of Surgery. He also had a lusty personal life. Carla Espinoza (Judy Reyes), Sacred Heart's chief nurse, was the primary object of his affections. A mouthy tease, she made him sweat and suffer before giving in to his attention. They married in season three and had two children but it wasn't all smooth sailing. Their relationship almost went on the rocks as a result of an indiscretion by her with J.D.

J.D. also had trysts with characters played by Christa Miller, the former wife of a colleague; Amy Smart; Tara Reid; Heather Graham and Elizabeth Banks, who became one of his baby mothers. However, a colleague, Dr. Elliot Reid (Sarah Chalke), was never far from his head and heart. They were off and on (literally as well as figuratively) throughout the series before finally wedding and having a child in season eight. (Chalke was also rumored as a prime candidate to be the titular spouse on *How I Met Your Mother*.)

Dr. Reid, who came from a family of male doctors, causing severe bouts of self doubt, did not sit around pining for J.D. during their off periods. She had flings with characters played by Rick Schroder, Scott Foley, Travis Schuldt and Tom Cavanaugh, as J.D.'s older brother Dan.

Between romps in the linen closet, the main characters had to deal with the challenges of healing and dealing with difficult co-workers. Dr. Perry Cox (John C. McGinley) was a tough love mentor to the younger members of the staff. He was especially hard on D.J., who he constantly put down with female nicknames like Zsa Zsa. But it was gradually revealed that this evolved from his belief in J.D.'s extraordinary potential as a healer. His support didn't waiver even after he discovered J.D. had a fling with his former wife, Jordan (Miller, spouse of *Scrubs* creator/executive producer Bill Lawrence), for whom he still had feelings and with whom he eventually had a reconciliation.

Dr. Cox, who had a prickly personality, also wrangled non-stop with Dr. Bob Kelso (Ken Jenkins), Sacred Heart's crusty Chief of Medicine over what Dr. Cox perceived to be Dr. Kelso putting the hospital's bottom line ahead of healing. Dr. Cox was so alienated by his boss that he punched him in the nose in season three. This led to one of the most farcical episodes of the series as Dr. Kelso's nose squeaked uncontrollably, serving like a bell on a cat. When Dr. Kelso resigned in season seven, Dr. Cox inherited his job after a short-lived successor, played by Courteney Cox, was fired.

J.D. had an additional tormentor in the hospital's janitor (Neil Flynn), whose name, Glenn Matthews, was mentioned only once. J.D. and the janitor got off to a rocky start in the premiere and J.D. was terrorized by him thereafter.

Scrubs ran on NBC for its first seven seasons. When the network announced its intentions to end the series, ABC, whose studio produced the show, stepped in to continue it. Most of the regulars signaled their intention to leave after one season on the new network, so ABC attempted to keep it going with a new ensemble, led by Eliza Coupe, Michael Mosley, Dave Franco and Kerry Bishe, who served as the new narrator. Out of loyalty to Lawrence, Braff agreed to appear in six episodes. Viewers wanted no part of the reworked show, whose characters had been introduced in a web series, and ABC ended it after one season.

91. *Green Acres*

Broadcast History:

Wednesday	9:00–9:30	September 1965–September 1968	CBS
Wednesday	9:30–10:00	September 1968–September 1969	CBS
Saturday	9:00–9:30	September 1969–September 1970	CBS
Tuesday	8:00–8:30	September 1970–September 1971	CBS

#11 rated series in 1965–66
#6 rated series in 1966–67
#15 rated series in 1967–68
#19 rated series in 1968–69

No Major Emmy Awards (No nominations)

Cast: Eddie Albert; Eva Gabor; Pat Buttram; Tom Lester; Alvy Moore; Hank Patterson; Barbara Pepper (1965–69); Frank Cady; Kay E. Kuter (1965–70: Sid Melton (1966–69); Mary Grace Canfield (1966–71); Fran Ryan (1969–70); Judy McConnell (1970–71).

Green Acres was spun off from *Petticoat Junction* but it wasn't spun very far. The two CBS comedies were set in the same backwoods locale, Hooterville, and characters regularly made crossover appearances. Thematically, *Green Acres* was also closely related to *The Beverly Hillbillies*. The fish-out-of-water premises of the two series were direct opposites. The Hillbillies had to learn to adapt their bumpkin ways to the big city. *Green Acres* relocated a couple of New York swells to the hick sticks.

Oliver Wendell Douglas (Eddie Albert), a prosperous corporate attorney, and his diva wife Lisa (Eva Gabor) had a comfortable lifestyle amidst the social whirl of Manhattan's Park Avenue. However, since his childhood on a farm near Saratoga, New York, Oliver had dreamed of becoming a man of the soil. His domineering father had a different vision. He groomed his son to follow him into the legal profession. The closest Oliver came to farming in his earlier years was tending plants on his penthouse balcony.

After a stint in the Air Force, Oliver came home to resume his legal career but never gave up on his dream. A want ad for a 160-acre spread near Hooterville hooked him, sight unseen. Just as well. The property was a local joke, previously owned by scoundrel and scam artist, Mr. Haney (scene stealing Pat Buttram). The land had been untended for years. The unfinished farmhouse needed upgrading to qualify as a shack. Nonetheless, to Oliver, it was the Taj Majal, even though the floor gave way and he had to climb a pole to make a phone call. Besides, Mr. Haney promised he could provide everything needed to spruce up the house and work the land—at outrageously inflated prices. This included a crop-duster plane Mr. Haney claimed was owned by the Wright Brothers—goggles, helmet and parachute extra.

Lisa, who, according to the theme song was allergic to hay, wasn't as enthralled as Oliver. Her reaction to the news Oliver had bought the place and was moving her to a burg that travel agents couldn't find was a shriek that could be heard from Manhattan to Hooterville. However, being a loving wife, she agreed to give it a try. The Douglases threw themselves into embracing the cultures and customs of the backwoods but they never fully abandoned their old ways and got fully with the program.

Oliver was a local joke for his penchant to do the chores and work the land atop his tractor in a three-piece suit and tie. There were no jeans or ging-ham for Lisa, either. Her uniform du jour was a formal gown, a feather boa and hats otherwise seen at the Kentucky Derby. She also gave the farm animals human names. The latter might have been her least odd behavior.

One of the town's most respected "citizens" was a pig named Arnold, who was addicted to western movies on television and communicated tele-pathically to everyone but Oliver. Arnold, a regular on both Hooterville-set series, also was the catalyst for Oliver going briefly back to practicing law. Arnold's owners, Fred (Hank Peterson) and Doris Ziffel (Barbara Pepper), who thought of themselves as Arnold's parents, turned to Oliver to take their case when Mr. Haney put a lien on Arnold to satisfy an unpaid debt. They were petrified that if Mr. Haney got his hands on Arnold their "child" was going to wind up on a plate next to a couple of eggs.

Unlike Mr. Haney, most of the residents of Hooterville while eccentric were good people anxious to lend a helping hand. The Douglases came to depend on Eb Dawson (Tom Lester), an eager beaver handyman who was nei-ther bright nor very handy, to get their place in working order. The socially awkward Eb somehow managed to land a date with Betty Jo Bradley of *Pet-ticoat Junction*.

Brother and sister carpenters Alf (Sid Melton) and Ralph Monroe (Mary Grace Canfield) also pitched in to lend a hand to Oliver and Lisa. Ralph adopted a masculine name because Alf figured that people wouldn't hire them if they knew half the team was female. There were other better reasons to look elsewhere for help. Among their projects was repairing the phone line at the general store run by Sam Drucker (Frank Cady), another regular on both series. They completed the task but not to Sam's satisfaction, since he had to hold the receiver upside down, speaking into the ear piece.

Green Acres was never popular with the Television Academy, failing to earn a single Emmy nomination. However, it was a people pleaser, landing in Nielsen's top 20 four times. Nevertheless, it became a victim of CBS's advertiser-encouraged purge of all the network's rural shows in 1971.

---

92. *The Facts of Life*

Broadcast History:

Friday	8:30–9:00	August 1979–September 1979	NBC
Friday	8:30–9:00	March 1980–May 1980	NBC
Wednesday	9:30–10:00	June 1980–July 1980	NBC

Friday	8:30–9:00	August 1980–October 1980	NBC
Wednesday	9:30–10:00	November 1980–October 1981	NBC
Wednesday	9:00–9:30	October 1981–August 1985	NBC
Saturday	8:30–9:00	September 1985–June 1986	NBC
Saturday	8:00–8:30	June 1986–May 1987	NBC
Wednesday	9:00–9:30	June 1987–July 1987	NBC
Saturday	8:00–8:30	July 1987–September 1988	NBC

#26 rated series in 1980–81   #24 rated series in 1984–85
#24 rated series in 1981–82   #27 rated series in 1985–86
#24 rated series in 1983–84

No Major Emmy Awards (1 nomination):
No Emmy Awards for Best Actress (1 nomination)

Cast: Charlotte Rae (1979–86); Lisa Whelchel; Kim Fields; Mindy Cohn; John Lawlor (1979–80); Jenny O'Hara (1979); Felice Schacter (1979–80); Julie Piekarski (1979–80); Julie Anne Haddock (1979–80); Molly Ringwald (1979–80); Nancy McKeon (1980–88); Hugh Gillin (1980–81); Roger Perry (1981–83); Geri Jewell (1981–84); Pamela Segall (1983–84); Woody Brown (1983–84); George Clooney (1985–86); MacKenzie Astin (1985–88); Cloris Leachman (1986–88); Sherrie Krenn (1987–88); Todd Hollowell (1987–88); Robert Romanus (1987–88); Paul Provenza (1987–88); Scott Bryce (1988).

The Facts of Life is one of the few spinoffs to outperform the series from which it sprung. Edna Garrett (Charlotte Rae) was the housekeeper for the Drummond clan of *Diff'rent Strokes*. The final episode of *Diff'rent Strokes'* first season was a backdoor pilot for the new series. Mrs. Garrett did a favor for Kimberly Drummond (Dana Plato), pitching in to help sew costumes for a play at the upstate New York girls' school Kimberly attended. Mrs. Garrett made such a positive impression at the school (as well as with viewers) she was offered the open job of housemother. She was reluctant to leave Manhattan and the Drummonds but was talked into the new opportunity. The transition from the good life at the Drummonds came with a price, she joked. In addition to losing her prestigious address, Mrs. Garrett also lost 25 pounds as a result of what she labeled her "inflation diet." She only ate what she could afford. Rae earned the only major Emmy nomination the series garnered.

The first season of *The Facts of Life*, the only one that didn't crack Nielsen's top 40, turned into a testing ground. One thing the producers realized was there were too many girls competing for screen time. For the second season, the core ensemble was reduced to three holdovers, Blair Warner (Lisa Whelchel), Tootie Ramsey (Kim Fields) and Natalie Green (Mindy Cohn), and one newcomer, Jo Polniaczek (Nancy McKeon). Among those dropped from regular status was Molly Ringwald as Molly Parker, although she did make subsequent sporadic appearances.

From then on, the show prospered in the ratings, breaking into Nielsen's top 30 five times. NBC also ordered a couple of movies of the week when those were in vogue in the 1980s: *The Facts of Life Goes to Paris* and *The Facts of Life Down Under*. There also was a *Facts of Life Reunion* telemovie in 2001.

Plato did not cross over into the new series. However, her *Diff'rent Strokes* co-star Gary Coleman did make a couple of guest appearances, including in the game changing season two opening episode. His *Diff'rent Strokes* brother Willis (Todd Bridges) also appeared twice.

The Facts of Life did tackle controversial issues—teen sex, drugs, hurtful gossip, etc.—in its maiden season but the addition of McKeon in season two spiced up the overall tone. Jo showed up riding a motorcycle with a chip on her shoulder and a biker chick attitude. She was bitter at becoming a victim of an ugly divorce and resented being exiled to Eastwood (changed from the initial season's East Lake). Jo especially resented the life of privilege Blair's wealthy family had provided her and they became almost instant adversaries, although they did have moments of détente. Before she had time to learn the lay of the land, Jo coaxed Blair to sneak off campus with her to check out a nearby college bar. Neither was of legal drinking age but Jo had a phony identification card and quickly produced one for Blair.

Tootie and Natalie trailed behind to see what was going to go down. They all went down when an undercover cop busted them for being in a bar under age. Their punishment included being yanked from their dorm rooms and sentenced to live together in an old storage room across the hall from Mrs. Garrett, who normally a pushover for the girls, vowed to monitor their every move.

Before Jo's arrival, the girls were essentially innocents, whose mischief-making was limited to silly adolescent stunts. Blair was the resident blonde beauty and very aware of it. She dressed fashionably and flirted with any attractive male, who found his way to the campus.

Natalie was Miss Congeniality, a personality kid with a portly physique, which she joked about in a self-deprecating manner. Late in the series run, Natalie became the first to lose her virginity. Legend has it that Blair was the writers' choice for this event but Whelchel had become very religious and didn't want to be a negative role model for her young fans.

Tootie was the youngest, 11 during the series' first season, so she tried super hard to act like one of the big kids. One of the ways she sought to ingratiate herself to the older girls was to serve as the conduit for gossip. Tootie was obsessed with Michael Jackson. The gloved one was unattainable for a guest shot but his brother Jermaine did make one. Teen idols of the time Fabian and Bobby Rydell also appeared.

Arguably the biggest casting coup, although it wasn't known at the time, was getting a relatively unknown George Clooney to appear in 17 episodes from 1985 to 1987 as George Burnett, a hunky carpenter, who did some work at the school. He had several recurring roles in series in the interim but it would be almost a decade until he became a global heartthrob as Dr. Doug Ross on *ER*.

Casting history was made when Geri Jewell became the first actor with cerebral palsy to be hired as a semi-regular on a series. Jewell's character, a student named Geri Tyler, appeared in a dozen episodes.

As with most series that endure as long as *The Facts of Life*, there were several changes over the years. Allowing for life's natural progression, Jo and Blair graduated from Eastland at the end of season four. To maintain the cast, Mrs. Garrett opened her own restaurant, "Edna's Edibles," and hired those two to work for her alongside Tootie and Natalie. When the eatery burned down in season seven, the girls collaborated on a new business, a gift shop, "Over Our Heads."

Rae, who gradually reduced her workload, left the series altogether at the start of season eight, ostensibly to move to Africa with her new husband. Cloris Leachman stepped in as Mrs. Garrett's sister Beverly, who agreed to serve as the new mentor for the younger women. NBC, which had a dearth of successful shows, would have commissioned a tenth season but the younger members of the cast decided nine was enough.

---

93. *The Wizards of Waverly Place*

Broadcast History:

Friday	8:00–8:30	October 2007–January 2008	DISNEY
Sunday	8:30–9:00	January 2008–May 2009	DISNEY
Friday	8:00–8:30	June 2009–August 2009	DISNEY
Friday	8:30–9:00	August 2009–January 2012	DISNEY

3 Major Emmy Awards (5 nominations):
3 Emmy Awards for Best Series (5 nominations)

Cast: Selena Gomez; David Henrie; Jake T. Austin; Jennifer Stone; Maria Canals Barrera; David DeLuise; Ian Abercrombie; Bill Chott; Dan Benson; Jeff Garlin (2007–10); Lucy Hale (2007–08); Amanda Tape (2007–09); Josh Sussman (207–08; 2010–12); Bridgit Mendler (2008–12); Gregg Sulkin (2009–12); Andy Kindler (2009–12); Gilland Jones (2009); Heidi Swedberg (2009); Kari Wahlgren (2010–12); Bailee Madison (2010–12); Frank Pacheco (2010–12); John Rubinstein (2010–12); Fred Stoller (2010–12); McKaley Miller (2010–12).

A series explicitly targeting teens and 'tweens on the youth-oriented Disney Channel is an unlikely candidate for a roster of the leading situation comedies of all time. *The Wizards of Waverly Place* earned this distinction by being nominated five times by the Prime Time Emmys as Outstanding Children's Television Program and winning three times; producing 106 episodes, the most ever for a Disney Channel series; and attracting more than 10 million viewers for its finale in 2012, the most ever for the Mickey Mouse network. A movie length episode in 2009 pulled in an audience in excess of 11 million, second all-time on The Disney Channel to *High School Musical*. After the series wrapped, The Disney Channel produced another telemovie, *The Wizards Return: Alex vs. Alex.*

The premise was homage to *Bewitched/I Dream of Jeannie* for the acne set. Indeed, a couple of minor characters, Mr. Laritate (Bill Chott) and Jenny Majorhealey (Gilland Jones and Heidi Swedberg), are takeoffs on Larry Tate of *Bewitched* and Major Healey of *I Dream of Jeannie*.

The series was a star vehicle for Selena Gomez, who played Alex Russo, one of three siblings in a unique family, which ran a sandwich shop in lower Manhattan. Along with her brothers Justin (David Henrie) and Max (Jake T. Austin), the Russos had magical powers. To be precise, the kids were apprentices in the wizardry game. Their father Jerry (David DeLuise) was a wizard, who was training his children to succeed him. The catch was, only one of them would qualify to be an adult wizard. This created a competition among the youngsters and the necessity for their parents to prepare all three for the eventuality that two of them would have to settle for living life as mere mortals. A secret room off the shop served as a warehouse for the instruments to make magic as well as a training facility in the tricks of the trade.

Vivacious Alex, a street smart, opinionated young lady, was the favorite of writers and the fans. She was as boy crazy as most teen girls but was generally cool about keeping her feelings in check. When she finally did fall hard for a guy, Mason Greyback (Greg Sulkin), he turned out to be a werewolf.

In addition to Alex's budding mystical powers she had a heightened sense of fashion and shone when given an internship in a design house. Her preference was to get by on her mortal talents. However, in a pinch, she wasn't averse to falling back on her otherworldly gifts, which included the ability to freeze the world around her while she rearranged situations to suit her goals.

Justin was a bit of a goofball and more than a bit of a geek. Among his quirks, he showered while still wearing his underwear. Approaching adulthood chronologically, he still played with toy action figures. He had a mastery of wizardry accouterments, such as a speed shirt, which facilitated moving at warp speed; a nightcap, which induced immediate sleep; and smarty pants, which made the wearer a genius. He wasn't as knowledgeable about their kryptonite-like qualities, the undesirable side effects that accompanied each of them. Justin fashioned himself a ladies man but was exceedingly awkward around the opposite sex. Off the set, according to fan magazines, Henrie and Gomez had a short-lived romance. However, her most celebrated relationship in the tabloids was with Justin Bieber.

Max was a few years younger than Alex and Justin but behaved and spoke beyond his years, as television children whose words are put into their mouths by adult writers tend to be. He was determined to beat out his siblings to become the new family wizard but was equally obsessed with getting rich.

While their father was their mentor, their down-to-earth mother, Theresa (Maria Canals Barrera) thought the whole concept of wizardry was ridiculous and constantly put it down. As with Elizabeth Montgomery's *Bewitched* character and Barbara Eden's Jeannie, one condition their father hammered home was the necessity to keep their powers a secret. This proved easier said than done. Alex's best friend, Harper Finkle (Jennifer Stone), figured it out by the second season. By the final season, Mason and Justin's closest pal, Zeke Beakerman (Don Benson), also were in on the secret.

Predictably, Alex wound up winning the competition to become the family's new wizard. To leave the audience with a happily-ever-after conclusion, Justin was appointed the new trainer of wizards and allowed to keep his magical powers. Max also wound up achieving a goal, potentially making a load of money as the new proprietor of the family sub shop.

---

94. iCarly

Broadcast History:

Saturday   8:00–8:30   September 2007–November 2012   NICKELODEON

94. *iCarly*

No Major Emmy Awards (5 nominations):
No Emmy Awards for Best Series (5 nominations)

Cast: Miranda Cosgrove; Jennette McCurdy; Nathan Kress; Jerry Trainor; Noah Munck; Reed Alexander.

The history of television is replete with comedies about television shows within the show. Reflecting the computer-obsessed generation, *iCarly* was the first to be about a webcast within a show. It might also be the greatest success story of extreme narrowcasting. *iCarly* made no effort to reach beyond the adolescent crowd it targeted. The openly stated attitude was if you were beyond your mid-twenties, Dude, you were an old person.

Five-times Emmy nominated as outstanding children's program, iCarly was a showcase for Miranda Cosgrove, who scored with tweens and teens as the younger sister on another popular Nickelodeon show, *Drake and Josh*. Cosgrove, who used the celebrity from being on television to launch a successful singing career, played the title character, Carly Shay, who was smart, cute and conscious of it. However, she managed to avoid conceit and had a winning personality.

Carly lived in a Seattle loft with her goofball brother Spencer, 26 (Jerry Trainor). A ne'er-do-well, he liked to describe himself as a law school dropout. Truth was he dropped out after three days. Spencer was supposed to be in charge of Carly while their single parent father was away on submarine duty but chronological age notwithstanding Carly was the adult in their home. Among Spencer's immature brainstorms was the installation of a tiny plot of grass in their living room, which he trimmed with a gas-powered lawn mower.

Carly and her girlfriend Sam Puckett (Jennette McCurdy) were goofing around at a high school talent show when their buddy Freddie Benson (Nathan Kress) recorded their antics and posted them online. The girls became instant sensations. Fans wanted more so Carly and Sam, with Freddie handling the technical end, created their own webcast, *iCarly*. Carly and Sam affected the personas of free spirited party animals. They jumped and giggled like the young girls they were and reveled in their lack of worldliness and sophistication. They played music and danced. Occasionally they would offer tips they regarded as hilarious, like how to make adult diapers out of newspaper.

Among the constant hassles confronting them was a caustic internet critic, Nevel Papperman (Reed Alexander), who blasted and ridiculed their webcast and even tried to knock it off the web. This dastardly figure turned out to be a lonesome 11-year-old geek, who had a crush on Carly and would have called off his campaign if she would just give him a kiss.

Although much of the series dealt with the girls planning their webcasts and pulling them off, the wafer-thin plots also delved into typical teen drama, mainly school and boys. Carly was courted by her share of guys, Freddie included, and she went out with several without getting serious. An oddball named Gibby (Noah Munck) also was infatuated with Carly but he had no shot, not even when he used an adorable puppy in a vain bid to win her affection. Nevertheless, he volunteered to serve as the go-fer for the webcast and the foil in their skits just to stay close to Carly in case she ever had a change of heart.

Sam, from a broken home with an oft-absent mother, presented herself as a tough, cold chick but it was a defense mechanism arising from a fear of revealing her emotional vulnerability. She had a love-hate relationship with Freddie, emphasis on the latter, through the early years of the series. It wasn't until a high tech gimmick outed her that she admitted she had romantic feelings for him. Perhaps from years of practice, the two of them still battled over every little thing to the exasperation of Carly.

Sam was so caught off guard by her own shift in attitude toward Freddie that she signed herself into a mental institution to deal with it. This led to a casting coup. Jim Parsons, at the height of his *Big Bang Theory* popularity, made a guest shot as a mentally disturbed guy, who thought he was a time traveler and shared many of the personality traits and quirks of Sheldon Cooper. Jimmy Fallon also took note of *iCarly* when the girls spoofed bits they saw on *The Tonight Show*. Fallon invited them to appear on the NBC late night program.

Parsons and Fallon weren't the biggest names to make an appearance. In an episode in which Carly was pining to be with her father on his birthday but he couldn't get home, Michelle Obama, who said she was a fan of the series, showed up to comfort Carly and remind her she was one of thousands of children in military families, who were forced to make sacrifices. The leading man in situation comedy, the host of the highest rated late night program and the First Lady of the United States made an impressive trifecta for a fluffy series, whose goal was to entertain viewers, many of whom were still wearing braces.

iCarly produced one spin-off series, *Sam & Cat*, which starred McCurdy and a young Ariana Grande (who had been appearing in the Nickelodeon series *Victorious*), who would go on to superstardom as a teen singing sensation after the spin-off ended after two seasons.

95. *Wings*

Broadcast History:

Thursday	9:30–10:00	April 1990–May 1990	NBC
Friday	9:30–10:00	September 1990–December 1990	NBC
Thursday	9:30–10:00	January 1991–March 1991	NBC
Thursday	9:30–10:00	June 1991–January 1993	NBC
Thursday	8:30–9:00	February 1993–August 1994	NBC
Tuesday	8:00–8:30	September 1994–April 1996	NBC
Tuesday	8:30–9:00	April 1996–June 1996	NBC
Tuesday	9:30–10:00	June 1996–July 1996	NBC
Wednesday	8:00–8:30	August 1996–February 1997	NBC
Wednesday	9:00–9:30	March 1997–July 1997	NBC
Monday	9:30–10:00	July 1997–August 1997	NBC

#19 rated series in 1991–92   #18 rated series in 1993–94
#30 rated series in 1992–93   #26 rated series in 1994–95

No Major Emmy Awards (2 nominations):
No Emmy Awards for Best Actor (1 nomination)
No Emmy Awards for Best Actress (1 nomination)

Cast: Tim Daly; Steven Weber; Crystal Bernard; David Schramm; Rebecca Schull; Thomas Haden Church (1990–95); Tony Shalhoub (1991–97); Farrah Forke (1992–94); Amy Yasbeck (1994–97).

David Lee, Peter Casey and David Angell (who died in one of the planes that crashed into the Twin Towers on September 11, 2001) gave NBC one of its biggest hits, *Cheers*. As networks often do, NBC asked if they could deliver another one just like it. They did—*Wings*. To clarify, *Wings* was just like *Cheers* in form but not in the same universe artistically. *Cheers* was a classic, a four-time Emmy winner as television's outstanding comedy. *Wings* was a serviceable facsimile. It was never Emmy nominated as best comedy but it fit perfectly into the half-hour after *Cheers*, which is where NBC scheduled it for part of its run. Characters from *Cheers* made cross-over appearances on *Wings*. Kelsey Grammer and Tyne Daly were Emmy nominated as best actor and actress for their guest appearances, an honor never afforded any of the *Wings* regulars.

The settings and premises were similar. *Cheers* was set in a small Boston bar. *Wings* was set off the coast of Boston at a small airport on Nantucket Island. *Cheers* infrequently left the bar. Almost all of the *Wings* episodes took place in the interior of the airport terminal. Both series were more character than plot driven. Both focused on a disparate array of offbeat personalities.

Joe and Brian Hackett operated a one-plane regional airline, Sandpiper Air. Joe (Tim Daly) was low-key, conservative and personally disciplined. He resisted spontaneity and hated change. He was the moral center of the operation. Brian (Steven Weber) was a free spirited, amoral narcissist. His irresponsibility led to him being bounced out of astronaut training. The Hacketts had been competitive throughout their lives. This included the pursuit of the same women.

Joe and Brian had a six-year estrangement when Brian stole Joe's fiancee Carol (Kim Johnson Ulrich) and married her. Carol eventually dumped Brian and Joe got a measure of revenge when she appeared in a two-part episode. Brian thought she had come to Nantucket to reconcile. Instead, in a private moment before she left, she told Joe she had made a mistake and should have stayed with him.

Although Brian preferred to play the field, the competition flared anew over Helen Chapel (Crystal Bernard), who worked in close proximity to the brothers at the airport. As with Carol, Joe had the inside track but Brian never gave up trying to woo her away. Helen worked the terminal lunch counter, a dubious job choice inasmuch as she had a lifelong compulsion to over-eat even after shedding countless pounds to regain a svelte figure. She convinced herself the serving job was just a stopgap until she achieved her dream of playing cello in a symphony orchestra, an ambition repeatedly frustrated at a procession of auditions.

Joe and Helen would eventually wed. Amidst myriad one-night stands, Brian got into a couple of serious relationships, one with a former Playboy model, Alex Lambert (Farrah Forke), in seasons four and five. She came to Nantucket to operate a helicopter business. She moved in with Brian but broke it off after she learned he was up to his old hedonistic ways. Foiled in his efforts to win Helen, Brian next wound up with her sister Casey (Amy Yasbeck), who was coming off a divorce and not anxious to become seriously involved with another man. (Her former husband was played by John Ritter, who was her real life husband at the time of his sudden death.) Casey eventually fell for Brian's charms at Helen's wedding. Like all of Brian's relationships, this one also went up in flames.

Before Helen married Joe she agreed to a platonic green card marriage to allow Italian immigrant taxi driver Antonio Scarpacci (Tony Shalhoub) to stay in the country. Antonio, who joined the series in season three, was good natured and strove so mightily to overcome his language issues and fit in with the crowd that he endeared himself to one and all, which is why Helen allowed herself to get talked into the sham marriage.

Situation comedy's obligatory village idiot character was filled by future Oscar nominee (*Sideways*) Thomas Haden Church as mechanic and all-around handyman Lowell Mather. His trains of thought often jumped the tracks shortly after leaving the station. He wasn't street smart or worldly but he had a bank of knowledge of the obscure.

Older demographics were served by polar opposites Fay Cochran (Rebecca Schull) and Roy Biggins (David Schramm). Fay, who worked the Sandpiper counter, was outgoing and kindly. She had been widowed three times, all to men named George, so she considered herself a kind of jinx. Roy ran Aeromass, Sandpiper's competition. Roy was ornery and insensitive and didn't really care that he wasn't well liked.

Wings was a protypical bottom of the hour series (i.e., a series that began at either 8:30 p.m. or 9:30 p.m.). When it had a strong lead-in from a show like *Cheers*, it was a strong ratings performer. The seasons that it had to make it on its own, ratings plunged. When its final two seasons failed to crack Nielsen's 30 highest rated series, NBC canceled it after eight years.

---

96. *Married ... with Children*

Broadcast History:

Sunday	8:00–8:30	April 1987–October 1987	Fox
Sunday	8:30–9:00	October 1987–July 1989	Fox
Sunday	9:00–9:30	July 1989–July 1996	Fox
Sunday	8:30–9:00	July 1996–August 1996	Fox
Sunday	9:00–9:30	September 1996–October 1996	Fox
Sunday	7:00–8:00	November 1996–December 1996	Fox
Monday	9:30–10:00	January 1997	Fox
Monday	9:00–9:30	February 1997–July 1997	Fox

No Major Emmy Awards (No Nominations)

Cast: Ed O'Neill; Katey Sagal; Christina Applegate; David Faustino; David Garrison (1987–90); Amanda Bearse; Ted McGinley (1991–97); Kevin Curran (1991–95); Shane Sweet (1992–93); Dan Tullis, Jr. (1993–97); Harold Sylvester (1994–97); Tom McCleister (1994–97); Pat Millicano (1994–95); E.E. Bell (1994–97); Kevin Curran (1995–96); Kathleen Freeman (1995); Tim Conway (1995–96); Janet Carroll (1995–97).

When Fox launched its first prime-time lineup in 1987, a single night, it needed series capable of making a splash by being vastly different from what the three more established networks were offering. While NBC was becoming dominant with tame, sophisticated comedies such as *The Cosby Show* and *Cheers*, Fox went as far in the other direction as possible without endangering the licenses of its affiliates. No show symbolized this wild and wooly approach more than *Married ... with Children*. It was the epitome of lowest common denominator television, a comedy that could be enjoyed by the masses as a guilty pleasure but primarily aimed at non-discriminating viewers of limited taste and intellect.

The Bundy family was rude, crude, raunchy and loud. The series plots were obsessed with all things sexual. Al Bundy (Ed O'Neill) was once a big man in town, a high school football hero. As a married man, he had to settle for a boring job as a women's shoe salesman. He hated the thought of getting up and going to work each day trying to shoehorn vain customers' size 8 feet into size 4 heels. The only thing he loathed more was going home to his dysfunctional family.

Al's wife Peg (Katey Sagal) opted to become a stay-at-home non-homemaker. She didn't cook and she didn't clean. Her routine, according to Al, was "loaf, nibble, snore." She deigned to go to work only in special circumstances, such as when Al wouldn't give her the money to buy the family's first VCR. Television, especially anything involving Oprah, was her passion—her new passion. An irresponsible high school night of passion with Al, which resulted in the birth of their daughter Kelly, was the catalyst for their marriage, apparently the only reason for it. Since then, conjugal passion had become something whose absence she constantly harped upon. There was nothing wrong with Al. He loved to ogle women at strip bars and collected skin magazines. However, he bellyached, Peg no longer did it for him.

Anyone of the opposite sex did it for teenage Kelly (Christina Applegate). She flaunted her availability with revealing outfits, which unfailingly ignited a cascade of catcalls from the frat boy–minded studio audience. Kelly's promiscuity resulted in Al regularly getting into physical confrontations with young men anxious to take advantage of his daughter. Bud, the Bundys' youngest, was equally oversexed but without the success rate of his sister. She cruelly reminded him of this. It wasn't for lack of effort. Among Bud's ploys to score were attempts to pass himself off as a talent agent, a producer of hot calendars and a rapper named Grandmaster B. But something always seemed to thwart him before the moment of truth. In one of the rare instances when things proceeded to their natural conclusion he learned that his vivacious partner had been born a man. The sad thing was, Bud was considered the brains of the family. This didn't take into consideration the family's pet canines, Buck and, when he died, Lucky. Each dog regularly injected catty observations about their masters via voiceovers of what they were thinking.

Al and Peg had committed allies. Next-door neighbor Marcy (Amanda Bearse) had a scornful attitude toward Al, which he returned in kind. An activist feminist, Marcy formed an organization called FANG (Feminists Against Neanderthal Guys), whose poster child was Al. Al got back at Marcy by befriending and doing his best to turn husbands Steve Rhoades (David Garrison) and Jefferson D'Arcy (Ted McGinley) against her. (The Marcy D'Arcy alliteration must not have occurred to the writers until the series was in progress.) Steve was a bland, hen-pecked guy who got vicarious thrills hanging around with the uninhibited Al. Jeff was a scam artist with an intellect on a par with Kelly, so he was a willing partner in Al's schemes against their wives.

That O'Neill, Sagal and Applegate went on to successful, respected careers in more high-minded projects is indicative of the fact that you have to be really talented to salvage horrid material. Nonetheless, they often complained about the total snub of *Married ... with Childen* by the Television Academy when it came to the series and acting Emmy nominations. This was like a street corner purveyor of mystery meat bellyaching about not being recognized by Zagat.

---

97. Perfect Strangers

Broadcast History:

Tuesday	8:30–9:00	March 1986–April 1986	ABC
Wednesday	8:00–8:30	August 1986–February 1988	ABC
Friday	8:00–8:30	March 1988–July 1989	ABC
Friday	9:00–9:30	August 1989–April 1991	ABC
Friday	9:30–10:00	April 1991–May 1991	ABC
Friday	9:00–9:30	May 1991–December 1991	ABC
Friday	9:30–10:00	January 1992	ABC
Saturday	9:00–9:30	February 1992–April 1992	ABC
Saturday	9:30–10:00	May 1992–June 1992	ABC
Saturday	9:00–9:30	June 1992–July 1992	ABC
Friday	9:30–10:00	July 1992–September 1992	ABC
Friday	9:30–10:00	July 1993–August 1993	ABC

#13 rated series in 1985–86
#19 rated series in 1992–93

No Major Emmy Awards (2 nominations):

No Emmy Awards for Best Actor (1 nomination)
No Emmy Awards for Best Guest Actor/Actress (1 nomination)

Cast: Mark Linn-Baker; Bronson Pinchot; Ernie Sabella (1986–87); Belita Moreno (1986–92); Lise Cutter (1986); Rebecca Arthur; Melanie Wilson; Jo Marie Payton-France (1987–89); Eugene Roche (1987–88); Sam Anderson (1987–92); F.J. O'Neill (1989–92); Alisan Porter (1990).

The Odd Couple has had so many variations and knockoffs it qualifies for sub-divisions. *Perfect Strangers* comes from the *Mork & Mindy* category. (*Perfect Strangers* had the same creative team as *Mork & Mindy*.) The character of Balki Bartokomous, who suddenly dropped into the world of Larry Appleton, was so alien to the culture of the United States he might as well have been from another planet. Larry, who grew up in a large family in Wisconsin, was enjoying the solitary life of a bachelor in Chicago when a knock on his door set his life into turmoil. An elated Balki told him he had been searching for Larry because they were distant cousins; so distant Larry quipped they were "sort of related by rumor."

Balki, who had migrated from the mythical island nation of Mypos, needed a place to crash for a few days until he found a job. Prospects weren't bright, Larry deduced, as Balki's line of work was professional sheepherder. Nevertheless, Larry let him stay. Balki had a way of ingratiating himself with his sad puppy dog expression. If that didn't work, he would just start bawling. Conversely, when he was happy, he would launch into his silly but irresistibly appealing Dance of Joy. Balki's "few days" turned into the same "temporary" arrangement as Alan Harper's in his brother's beach house in *Two and a Half Men*—another variation of *The Odd Couple*. The cousins would move during the eight-season run of *Perfect Strangers* but Balki never moved out.

Perfect Strangers' success was virtually guaranteed when ABC scheduled its six-episode trial run in the platinum hammock between established hits *Who's the Boss?* and *Moonlighting*. The predictably strong welcome from viewers led ABC to reposition it as the leadoff show on Wednesday until the midpoint of season three when it shifted to Friday and became one of the anchor series of the popular TGIF segment—a two-hour block of situation comedies aimed at youngsters and tweens on Friday evenings.

Perfect Strangers was never a Nielsen smash but it performed solidly. It cracked the top 20 in its first and last seasons, interestingly both consisting of just six episodes. The latter came after the only season in which the show plunged out of the top 60 due to an ill-advised shift to Saturday, which had hemorrhaged viewers to the extent that it became the night with the lowest HUT (homes using television) levels of the week. By the new millennium, the broadcast networks had given up on programming original comedies and dramas on Saturday.

Bronson Pinchot, who earned *Perfect Strangers'* lone major Emmy nomination for a series regular (Doris Roberts garnered one for a guest role), carried the show as Balki, a character reminiscent of his role in *Beverly Hills Cop*. Whenever he became confused by a question because of his lack of familiarity with American ways, he would respond with an air of faux confidence, "Don't be ridiculous." This became the character's signature phrase. Mark Linn-Baker served primarily as the straight man as Larry, a role reportedly originally ticketed for comedian Louie Anderson.

With limited sheepherding opportunities in Chicagoland, Larry wangled a job for Balki in the Ritz discount store in which he worked. Their boss, Donald Twinkacetti (Ernie Sabella), was a mean spirited tightwad, who wasn't anxious to add to his payroll, but Larry sold his cousin under the false pretense that he was a whiz at fixing things. In fact, everything Balki touched turned out worse. However, this did help him get hired, since Twinkacetti figured the only way to recoup what Balki, who he nicknamed "Turnip," had cost him was to dock his pay.

By the third season, "Twinkie" was gone. Larry, who aspired to be a journalist, landed a job at the fictional Chicago Chronicle. Balki followed by getting hired in the mailroom. In a curious casting decision, Belita Moreno, who had played Twinkie's kindly spouse Edwina, assumed a new role as the newspaper's advice columnist, Lydia Markham. It was as if Edwina had never existed.

While working at the paper, Larry and Balki became acquainted with a mouthy elevator operator, Harriette Winslow (Jo Marie Payton-France). She and her husband Carl (Reginald VelJohnson), a policeman, moved into the cousins' building, setting the stage for them to be spun off into their own series, *Family Matters*, which also became a TGIF staple.

Larry had a platonic relationship with a neighbor, Susan Campbell (Lise Cutter), in the first season. By the second season, Susan was being gradually phased out as Larry and Balki began to romance different neighbors, airline flight attendants Jennifer Lyons (Melanie Wilson) and Mary Anne Spencer (Rebecca Arthur).

A well-intentioned plan, which backfired, led to Larry and Balki having to ineptly attempt to fill in for the women aboard a flight in one episode. Larry's relationship with Jennifer proceeded at a faster pace. They became engaged in season five and parents in season seven. Not even this important change in personal status caused a split between the cousins. Larry and Jennifer bought a house and quickly realized that the only way they could make the mortgage payments was to take in boarders—Balki and Mary Anne.

Balki's pursuit of Mary Anne had a rockier go of it and included a period when they split and dated others. However, they reconciled and married in season seven. At the start of the show's final season, Mary Anne and Jennifer both were pregnant. Before the final credits, both couples welcomed sons. Then they said goodbye.

---

98. *The King of Queens*

Broadcast History:

Monday	8:30–9:00	September 1998–July 1999	CBS
Monday	8:00–8:30	July 1999–July 2000	CBS
Monday	8:30–9:00	July 2000–September 2000	CBS
Monday	8:00–8:30	October 2000–June 2003	CBS
Monday	9:30–10:00	June 2003–September 2003	CBS
Wednesday	9:00–9:30	October 2003–July 2005	CBS
Monday	8:00–8:30	July 2005–July 2006	CBS
Wednesday	8:00–8:30	December 2006–January 2007	CBS
Monday	9:30–10:00	April 2007–August 2007	CBS

#26 rated series in 2000–01   #27 rated series in 2002–03
#21 rated series in 2001–02

No Major Emmy Awards (1 nomination):
No Emmy Awards for Best Actor (1 nomination)

Cast: Kevin James; Leah Remini; Jerry Stiller; Victor Williams; Patton Oswalt; Larry Romano (1998–2001); Lisa Rieffel (1998); Merrin Dungey (1999–2001, 2003–07); Nicole Sullivan (2001–05).

Mismatched couples, be they lovers or roommates, have always been a staple of television comedy. *The King of Queens* successfully mined this genre for nine seasons without noteworthy originality or award recognition. Despite its longevity, it was never high up in the Nielsen ratings and it garnered only a single Emmy-nomination (best actor in a comedy). But America embraced the show, thanks to advantageous scheduling and the crowd-pleasing appeal of lead players, Kevin James and Leah Remini, with a strong supporting turn from Jerry Stiller.

There will never be another series to match *The Honeymooners* but *The King of Queens* affected a similar vibe. It even did a *Honeymooners* homage in an episode filmed in black and white. James and Remini played Doug and

Carrie Heffernan, a middle class couple in one of the outer boroughs of New York City (Queens, instead of Brooklyn). He was overweight; she was slim and trim. Doug liked to think of himself as king of his castle but Carrie ruled the roost. Doug drove a delivery truck for a company that was UPS in every way but its name on the show.

James introduced the character in guest appearances on his long-time Long Island friend Ray Romano's series *Everybody Loves Raymond*. Romano and his cast mates reciprocated with occasional crossover appearances on James' series. Doug was a blue-collar stereotype, a good-natured lug who craved nothing more than to be left alone on the couch, munching out while watching sports. He rhapsodized over food, preferably junk food. He was proud that in his work review, he was called "an average worker." Other than on the job, the only exercise he got was bowling. He also was a bit of an arrested adolescent, who thought flatulence was hilarious, took selfies of his private parts and once lost a girlfriend because he shot the wrapping on a straw into her eye, damaging her cornea.

Carrie was controlling and intimidating with a sharp, cutting tongue. She relentlessly mocked her husband's poor eating habits and weight. She ran the house as if she was Doug's mother more than his spouse. On the rare occasions when she paid her husband a compliment, it was invariably followed by a zinger. Doug lived in fear of displeasing her. She yearned to live in Manhattan but he preferred Queens.

They often talked about starting a family but Carrie admitted she hated kids. She eventually relented and they attempted to adopt a child. How they got to become a couple was a mystery. How they stayed one wasn't. Their activities after the lights went out were amazing, both agreed. This is not to say l'amour was all that bound them together but without it, the rest might have paled into insignificance.

Stiller, coming off a brilliant secondary role as George Costanza's father on *Seinfeld*, was back in familiar territory as Arthur Spooner, Carrie's loud, meddlesome dad. A widower—he married a character played by his real life wife Anne Meara during the final season—he lived in the Heffernan's basement because he accidentally burned down his house. He generally got along better with Doug than his daughter, with whom he bickered over everything.

To protect Arthur from himself and keep him busy while they worked, the Heffernans got a dog walker friend of Carrie, Holly Shumpert (Nicole Sullivan), to let him tag along with her and her canine clients. Holly became fond of Arthur but was on the prowl for a younger man as all her attempts to find a romantic soul mate ended in disappointment. Her drinking problem might have been a factor.

Carrie was as critical of Doug's choice of friends as she was his sedentary lifestyle and voracious appetite. She tolerated his closest buddy, Deacon John Palmer (Victor Williams), a co-worker because Deacon's wife Kelly (Merrin Dungey) was a close friend. Deacon liked to encourage Doug's schemes to put something over on Carrie because he was even more dominated by his wife than Doug and would not dare to attempt such antics with her.

The Heffernans had a famous neighbor, Lou Ferrigno, but the friendship was strained because Doug and Carrie couldn't resist making *Incredible Hulk* references and jokes, which Ferrigno found belittling. Ferrigno was one of numerous show business figures who played themselves in guest shots. The eclectic roster included Kirstie Alley, Janeane Garofolo, Adam Sandler, Burt Reynolds, Huey Lewis, Eddie Money and Neil Sedaka.

Another of Doug's buddies, Spencer Olchin (Patton Oswalt), seemingly had nothing in common with others in the circle. A meek, nerdish science fiction geek and techie, he was more likely to be found at Comic-Con than a ball game. He lived by himself and was somewhat effeminate. Based on his viewing choices, his TiVo assumed he was gay, which he swore he was not. Indeed, it was revealed that he harbored a secret crush on Carrie. Arthur courted his domineering mother during the final season and the final episodes were dominated by the run up to their marriage.

99. *McHale's Navy*

Broadcast History:

Thursday	9:30–10:00	October 1962–September 1963	ABC
Tuesday	8:30–9:00	September 1963–August 1966	ABC

#22 rated series in 1963–64
#29 rated series in 1964–65

No Major Emmy Awards (5 nominations):
No Emmy Awards for Best Series (2 nominations)
No Emmy Awards for Best Actor (1 nomination)
No Emmy Award for Best Supporting Actor (1 nomination)
No Emmy Awards for Best Direction (1 nomination)

Cast: Ernest Borgnine; Joe Flynn; Tim Conway; Carl Ballantine; Gary Vinson; Billy Sands; Edson Stroll; Jane Dulo (1962–64); Gavin MacLeod (1962–64); Yoshio Yoda; Bob Hastings; John Wright (1964–66); Henry Beckman (1965–66); Simon

Scott (1965–66); Dick Wilson (1965–66); Jay Novello (1965–66); Peggy Mondo (1965–66).

You always spoof the one you love. Pre-Vietnam, the military was rich fodder for laughs. Four comedies lobbing affectionate barbs at life in uniform cracked the top 100—*The Phil Silvers Show* (*Sgt. Bilko*), *Hogan's Heroes, Gomer Pyle U.S.M.C.* and *McHale's Navy*. Post-Vietnam, there has been only one, *M*A*S*H*, which blended laughs with a serious dramatic tone. People died on *M*A*S*H*.

McHale's Navy originated in 1962 on the anthology series *Alcoa Premiere* as "Seven Against the Sea," starring Ernest Borgnine as Quinton McHale, a U.S. Navy officer marooned during World War II with a small band of sailors on the South Pacific island of Taratupa. With no escape option, they made the best of the situation, bonding with the native population to create a comfortable living environment. Eventually, they carried out a heroic act of creatively sinking a Japanese war ship.

The light-hearted elements of life on a South Pacific atoll, with war a distant nuisance, were picked up as the basis for the television series. In many ways, life on Taratupa mirrored that of Fort Baxter on *The Phil Silvers Show*. This was not coincidental. Edward J. Montagne was a producer on both series. Like Bilko, McHale was a fast-on-his-feet thinker and conniver constantly out to beat the system and outfox superiors, with commanding officer Captain Wally Binghamton (Joe Flynn) their most frequent foil.

McHale was less selfish than Bilko. Where Bilko was primarily out to enrich himself, many of McHale's schemes were to benefit his men. He created a virtual Club Med for them just across a small inlet from Taratupa. Their boat, the PT 73, didn't see much war action but it became the ideal vessel for leisure water sports.

One of McHale's most creative ruses blended all manner of rules-busting to arrange a forbidden wedding between one of his enlisted men, Christy Christopher (Gary Vinson), and a female officer on the verge of being deployed elsewhere. When word got back to Taratupa that the bride had become pregnant on her brief McHale-enabled honeymoon, McHale and his men organized a lottery to finance a gift for the baby. First prize was a date with a knockout played by a very young Claudine Longet. Out of gratitude, Christy and his wife gave their baby girl a name longer than a Spanish contessa, using female variations of every member of the squadron.

When the series' final season shifted war theaters from the South Pacific to a small town in Italy, McHale's men were assigned spartan accommodations.

He refused to let this stand. He stumbled upon a hidden wine cellar and set up comfortable lodging for one and all.

Tim Conway scored his breakout role as McHale's inept next in command, Ensign Charles Parker. Conway's characterization of the bumbling motor mouth with a knack for saying the wrong thing was a persona that served him well during a long and prosperous career. Parker was assigned to McHale's squadron as a by-the-book officer, whose assignment was to get the men to behave like well-disciplined sailors. In spite of noble intentions, he routinely screwed up everything he touched. He quickly turned and became an ally of McHale in their schemes against the Navy.

Binghamton was a reluctant warrior. He came to his position as a result of serving as the commodore of a yacht club before the war. Binghamton, like Bilko's Col. Hall, was haunted by a constant suspicion that McHale and his men were plotting to put one over on him. Like Col. Hall, Binghamton was right most of the time. He fretted that their misdeeds would become an obstacle to his aspirations to become an admiral. Binghamton, who was derided behind his back as "Old Leadbottom" because of a bullet he took in his backside, also harbored political ambitions. McHale attempted to serve his commanding officer's dream by staging a faux raid with his men dressed as German soldiers to impress a political kingmaker looking for a war hero to back for office. As usual, the plan backfired.

When the scene shifted to the European theater, Binghamton vowed that things would be different. He was going to run a tighter ship. Instead his headaches doubled when a local mayor, Mario Lugatto (Jay Novello), more devious than McHale, tried to scam him at every turn. Only McHale was a match for the crooked politician.

McHale's men included a couple of veterans of Sgt. Bilko. Billy Sands— Pvt. Paparelli at Camp Baxter—played mechanic James "Tinker" Bell. Bob Hastings, a lieutenant in the Army, had the same rank in the Navy as Elroy Carpenter, a lackey for Capt. Binghamton.

Other regulars included Carl Ballantine as Lester Gruber, who could get anything anyone wanted for a price and got himself a purple heart for cutting his finger while doing laundry; John Wright as Radioman Willy Moss and a pre–*Mary Tyler Moore Show/Love Boat* Gavin MacLeod as Happy Haines. The strangest regular of all might have been Fuji Kobiaji (Yoshio Yoda), the happiest prisoner of war this side of the *Hogan's Heroes* gang. Fuji, a Japanese deserter, relished becoming one of our guys and even found a way to stay with them when they were redeployed from the Pacific to Italy.

McHale's Navy was neither a ratings nor critical standout. It cracked the

Nielsen Top 25 only once and failed to win any Emmys, although it was nominated in the outstanding comedy field twice and Borgnine and Conway earned a nomination apiece. It did inspire a short-lived female version, *Broadside*, as well as a trio of spinoff movies, the final one in 1997 with Tom Arnold taking over the lead.

---

100. *Family Matters*

Broadcast History:

Friday	8:30–9:00	September 1989–April 1991	ABC
Friday	9:00–9:30	April 1991–May 1991	ABC
Friday	8:30–9:00	May 1991–August 1991	ABC
Friday	8:00–8:30	August 1991–May 1997	ABC
Saturday	8:00–8:30	June 1997–August 1997	ABC
Friday	8:00–8:30	September 1997–October 1997	CBS
Friday	9:00–9:30	November 1997–January 1998	CBS
Friday	9:00–9:30	June 1998–July 1998	CBS

#15 rated series in 1990–91   #30 rated series in 1992–93
#27 rated series in 1991–92   #30 rated series in 1993–94

No Major Emmy Awards (No nominations)

Cast: Jo Marie Payton; Reginald VelJohnson; Darius McCrary; Kellie Shanygne Williams; Jaimee Foxworth (1989–93); Rosetta LeNoire (1989–97); Telma Hopkins (1989–95); Joseph Wright (1989); Julius Wright (1989); Randy Josselyn (1989–91); Bryton McClure (1990–97); Jaleel White (1990–98); Barry Jenner (1990–92); Shawn Harrison (1991–96); Cherie Johnson (1992–98); Shavar Ross (1992–94); Michelle Thomas (1993–98); Orlando Brown (1996–98); Dick O'Neill (1997–98); Tammy Townsend (1997–98).

No comedy series in the history of television was more re-imagined from its original blueprint because of a late arriving, fringe character, who was supposed to appear only once, than *Family Matters*. The spinoff from *Perfect Strangers* was designed to focus on the Winslow family of Chicago. The parents, Harriette (Jo Marie Payton), then a mouthy elevator operator at the fictional Chicago Chronicle, and Carl (Reginald VelJohnson), a cop, had been introduced on *Perfect Strangers*.

The spinoff was to be boilerplate domestic family comedy. Three Winslow children were added to the mix. Eddie (Darius McCrary) was a conniving teenager always looking for ways to outsmart his parents or beat the system. Laura (Kellie Shanygne Williams) was a new teen on the cusp of blossoming into a cute young woman. Judy (Jaimee Foxworth) was the baby of the family, four years younger than Laura.

To infuse additional spice and expand potential story lines, Carl's controlling mom Estelle (Rosetta LeNoire), usually referred to as Mother Winslow, and Harriette's widowed sister Rachel (Telma Hopkins), who ran a small restaurant, and toddler son Richie moved in with the Winslows.

Through the first half of season one, the plots were nondescript familiar family comedy devices. The producers and ABC decided Eddie was the best bet for a breakout character with the targeted TGIF audience, so he was a pivotal figure in most of the early episodes. He maneuvered to get around Carl's edict that he couldn't go to a certain party. He was challenged to find a way to come up with the cash for a pair of sneakers that weren't in the family budget. He asked the wrong girl out for a date and wound up having to duck her very angry boyfriend.

Lightning struck in the 12th episode when Laura needed a date for a school dance. Well meaning family members set her up with three young men, one a geek from next door named Steve Urkel (Jaleel White). The clumsy adolescent with a high squeaky voice, pants pulled up to his chest and over-sized glasses stole the show. America became as instantly infatuated with him as his character was with Laura. Given the lead time between production and air, it would be more than a month before Urkel reappeared. Eddie figured prominently again. He cut a deal for Urkel to tutor him in math in exchange for arranging a date with Laura.

From then on, *Family Matters* essentially evolved into the Steve Urkel Show. The Winslows became accessories to the irresistible nerd's exploits. Payton wound up leaving the series because of this. At the start of the second season, White was promoted to regular status in the credits. With Urkel now the centerpiece, *Family Matters* soared from out of Nielsen's top 30 in season one to the top 15 in its second year.

Urkel was impossible not to like. He was willing to suffer being exiled to military school to cover for a misdeed committed by Eddie. But as good-hearted as he was, almost everything he touched turned into a disaster. He burned down a restaurant. A garage improvement project for which he volunteered to help Carl became a warning to Don't Do It Yourself. Given an opportunity to ride along with Carl on his patrol, Urkel managed to get the two of them locked in a railroad car. He drove a wedge between Harriette and Carl because she became jealous of the attention and acts of kindness Urkel showered on Laura.

Thanks to her relationship with Urkel, which was more a relationship in his mind than hers for most of the series run, Laura became the prominent Winslow offspring. With limited ways for her to interact with Urkel, Judy was written out of the series after season three and subsequently treated as if she never existed. At times, Urkel faced the reality that Laura wanted little to do with him. Both moved on to other people, although Laura always remained in Steve's heart. She finally realized that he was always in her heart, too. Late in the final season, she said the magic words to him: "I love you." The series ended with them locked in a passionate kiss.

The lengths the writers had to go to in order to service Urkel sometimes bordered on the absurd. Two new characters, Myrtle Urkel and Stefan Urquelle, were created, both played by White. An episode focused on Steve and Carl facing off on the *American Gladiators* reality show. In another, a screw up by amateur inventor Steve wound up with he and Carl in a wrestling ring against a couple of villains intent on taking them apart. Urkel won $1 million by making a half-court shot at an NBA game only to have to give the money back because, in his jubilation, he destroyed a pricey scoreboard.

Other shows centered around Carl inadvertently being turned into a clone of Steve when a personality transforming device, another of Urkel's inventions, went haywire. Other Urkel inventions transported the entire Winslow clan to Paris and Steve into outer space.

As dominant a character as Urkel was, his work was never recognized by his peers with an Emmy nomination. *Family Matters* earned only one technical nomination in its nine-year run, the last of which was on CBS after ABC let the aging series go. But for most of its run, the series was in or around Nielsen's top 30, thanks to a character who was supposed to appear only once.

Appendix A:
Ranked List of All Qualifying Situation Comedies

Rank	Program	Network	Aired	Seasons
1	All in the Family	CBS	1971–79	9
2	Cheers	NBC	1982–93	11
3	Frasier	NBC	1993–2004	11
4	M*A*S*H	CBS	1972–83	11
5	The Mary Tyler Moore Show	CBS	1970–77	7
6	Friends	NBC	1994–2004	10
7	Everybody Loves Raymond	CBS	1996–2005	9
8	I Love Lucy	CBS	1951–57	6
9	The Cosby Show	NBC	1984–2002	8
10	Seinfeld	NBC	1989–98	9
11	Modern Family	ABC	2009–15*	5
12	Murphy Brown	CBS	1988–98	10
13	Golden Girls	NBC	1985–92	7
14	The Danny Thomas Show	CBS	1953–64	11
15	The Dick Van Dyke Show	CBS	1961–66	5
16	30 Rock	NBC	2006–13	7
17	Will & Grace	NBC	1998–2006	8
18	The Andy Griffith Show	CBS	1960–68	8
19	Taxi	ABC	1978–83	5
20	Roseanne	ABC	1988–97	9
21	Barney Miller	ABC	1975–82	8
22	Mad About You	NBC	1992–99	7
23	The Big Bang Theory	CBS	2007–15*	8
24	The Phil Silvers Show	CBS	1955–59	4
25	Family Ties	NBC	1982–89	7
26	Bewitched	ABC	1964–72	8
27	Two and a Half Men	CBS	2003–15	12

Rank	Program	Network	Aired	Seasons
28	Happy Days	ABC	1974–84	11
29	Home Improvement	ABC	1991–99	8
30	Sex & the City	HBO	1998–2004	6
31	Get Smart	NBC	1965–70	5
32	The Beverly Hillbillies	CBS	1962–71	9
33	Father Knows Best	CBS	1954–60	6
34	The Larry Sanders Show	HBO	1992–98	6
35	The Lucy Show	CBS	1962–68	6
36	Night Court	NBC	1984–92	9
37	The Office	NBC	2005–13	9
38	Three's Company	ABC	1977–84	8
39	The Wonder Years	ABC	1988–93	6
40	The Jeffersons	CBS	1975–85	11
41	Sanford and Son	NBC	1972–77	6
42	Maude	CBS	1972–78	6
43	Laverne & Shirley	ABC	1976–83	8
44	Curb Your Enthusiasm	HBO	2000–15*	8
45	Newhart	CBS	1982–90	8
46	Kate & Allie	CBS	1984–89	6
47	Malcolm in the Middle	FOX	2000–06	7
48	Coach	ABC	1989–97	9
49	Entourage	HBO	2004–11	8
50	Alice	CBS	1976–85	9
51	Hogan's Heroes	CBS	1965–71	6
52	3rd Rock from the Sun	NBC	1996–2001	6
53	One Day at a Time	CBS	1975–84	9
54	Rhoda	CBS	1974–78	5
55	The George Burns & Gracie Allen Show	CBS	1950–58	8
56	Soap	ABC	1977–81	4
57	Family Affair	CBS	1966–71	5
58	Designing Women	CBS	1986–93	7
59	The Bob Cummings Show	NBC	1955–59	5
60	The Odd Couple	ABC	1970–75	5
61	Room 222	ABC	1969–74	5
62	December Bride	CBS	1954–59	5
63	Hazel	NBC	1961–66	5
64	Who's the Boss?	ABC	1984–92	8
65	My Three Sons	CBS	1960–72	12
66	The Real McCoys	ABC	1957–63	6
67	A Different World	NBC	1987–93	6
68	The Life of Riley	NBC	1953–58	6
69	Our Miss Brooks	CBS	1952–56	4
70	Mama	CBS	1949–57	8
71	Evening Shade	CBS	1990–94	4
72	Here's Lucy	CBS	1968–74	6

Rank	Program	Network	Aired	Seasons
73	Empty Nest	NBC	1988–95	7
74	Petticoat Junction	CBS	1963–70	7
75	Gomer Pyle, USMC	CBS	1964–69	5
76	Veep	HBO	2012–15*	4
77	Nurse Jackie	Showtime	2009–15	7
78	Dream On	HBO	1990–96	6
79	Benson	ABC	1979–86	7
80	Full House	ABC	1987–95	8
81	Weeds	Showtime	2005–12	8
82	Growing Pains	ABC	1985–92	7
83	Arrested Development	FOX	2008–13	4
84	Ellen	ABC	1994–98	5
85	The Donna Reed Show	ABC	1958–66	8
86	The Adventures of Ozzie & Harriet	ABC	1952–66	14
87	How I Met Your Mother	CBS	2005–14	9
88	The Bob Newhart Show	CBS	1972–78	6
89	Diff'rent Strokes	NBC	1978–86	8
90	Scrubs	NBC	2001–10	9
91	Green Acres	CBS	1965–71	6
92	The Facts of Life	NBC	1979–88	9
93	Wizards of Waverly Place	Disney	2007–12	4
94	iCarly	Nickelodeon	2007–12	6
95	Wings	NBC	1990–97	8
96	Married ... with Children	FOX	1987–97	11
97	Perfect Strangers	ABC	1986–93	8
98	King of Queens	CBS	1998–2007	9
99	McHale's Navy	ABC	1962–66	4
100	Family Matters	ABC	1989–98	9
101	Leave It to Beaver	ABC	1957–63	6
102	Love & War	CBS	1992–95	3
103	Private Secretary	CBS	1953–57	5
104	Louie	FX	2010–15*	5
105	Spin City	ABC	1996–2002	6
106	Archie Bunker's Place	CBS	1979–83	4
107	Grace Under Fire	ABC	1993–98	5
108	The Drew Carey Show	ABC	1995–2004	9
109	227	NBC	1985–90	5
110	Chico and the Man	NBC	1974–78	4
111	Just Shoot Me	NBC	1997–2003	7
112	Becker	CBS	1998–2004	6
113	That Girl	ABC	1966–71	5
114	Mr. Peepers	NBC	1952–55	3
115	My Name Is Earl	NBC	2005–09	4
116	Good Times	CBS	1974–79	6
117	WKRP in Cincinnati	CBS	1978–82	4

Rank	Program	Network	Aired	Seasons
118	Cybill	CBS	1995–98	4
119	The Monkees	NBC	1966–68	2
120	The Doris Day Show	CBS	1968–73	5
121	The Fresh Prince of Bel Air	NBC	1990–96	6
122	The Honeymooners	CBS	1955–56	1
123	The Nanny	CBS	1993–99	6
124	Extras	HBO	2005–07	2
125	Too Close for Comfort	ABC	1980–87	6
126	Tyler Perry's House of Payne	TBS	2006–12	8
127	The Ghost and Mrs. Muir	NBC	1968–70	2
128	Mike & Molly	CBS	2010–15*	5
129	Car 54, Where Are You?	NBC	1961–63	2
130	Gimme a Break	NBC	1981–87	6
131	Boy Meets World	ABC	1993–2000	7
132	Dharma & Greg	ABC	1997–2002	5
133	That '70s Show	FOX	1998–2006	8
134	Head of the Class	ABC	1986–91	5
135	Hannah Montana	Disney	2006–11	4
136	The Days & Nights of Molly Dodd	NBC	1987–91	5
137	Parks & Recreation	NBC	2009–15	7
138	My World and Welcome to It	NBC	1969–70	1
139	Welcome Back, Kotter	ABC	1975–79	4
140	The New Adventures of Old Christine	CBS	2006–10	5
141	Arli$$	HBO	1996–2002	7
142	ALF	NBC	1986–90	4
143	The Brady Bunch	ABC	1969–74	5
144	Dennis the Menace	CBS	1959–63	4
145	Julia	NBC	1968–71	3
146	Girlfriends	UPN	2000–08	8
147	Mister Ed	CBS	1961–66	6
148	I Dream of Jeannie	NBC	1965–70	5
149	It's Always Sunny in Philadelphia	FX	2005–15*	10
150	Step by Step	ABC	1991–98	7
151	According to Jim	ABC	2001–09	8
152	The Hogan Family	NBC	1986–91	6
153	The Goldbergs	CBS	1949–53	4
154	Dear John	NBC	1988–92	4
155	Girls	HBO	2012–15*	3
156	Mork & Mindy	ABC	1978–82	4
157	The John Larroquette Show	NBC	1993–96	4
158	The Bernie Mac Show	FOX	2001–06	5
159	Yes, Dear	CBS	2000–06	6
160	Bachelor Father	CBS	1957–62	5
161	United States of Tara	Showtime	2009–11	3

Rank	Program	Network	Aired	Seasons
162	The Gale Storm Show	CBS	1956–60	4
163	Sabrina, the Teenage Witch	ABC	1996–2003	7
164	Frank's Place	CBS	1987–88	1
165	That's So Raven	Disney	2003–07	4
166	It's Garry Shandling's Show	Showtime	1986–90	4
167	Rules of Engagement	CBS	2007–13	7
168	Amen	NBC	1986–91	5
169	The Partridge Family	ABC	1970–74	4
170	The Stu Erwin Show	ABC	1950–55	5
171	The Many Loves of Dobie Gillis	CBS	1959–63	4
172	The Farmer's Daughter	ABC	1963–66	3
173	He & She	CBS	1967–68	1
174	Blossom	NBC	1991–95	5
175	Private Benjamin	CBS	1981–83	3
176	Mr. Belvedere	ABC	1985–90	6
177	Webster	ABC	1983–89	6
178	Hangin' with Mr. Cooper	ABC	1992–97	5
179	Mayberry RFD	CBS	1968–71	3
180	Hot in Cleveland	TV Land	2010–15	6
181	Samantha Who?	NBC	2007–09	2
182	Californication	Showtime	2007–14	7
183	Moesha	UPN	1996–2001	6
184	The Famous Teddy Z	CBS	1989–90	1
185	Sports Night	ABC	1998–2000	2
186	Buffalo Bill	NBC	1983–84	2
187	The Patty Duke Show	ABC	1963–66	3
188	Meet Millie	CBS	1952–56	4
189	Major Dad	CBS	1989–93	4
190	House Calls	CBS	1979–82	3
191	The Aldrich Family	NBC	1949–53	4
192	George Lopez	ABC	2002–07	6
193	My Wife and Kids	ABC	2001–05	5
194	Amos 'n' Andy	CBS	1951–53	3
195	Hooperman	ABC	1987–89	2
196	Meet the Browns	TBS	2009–11	3
197	Davis Rules	CBS	1991–92	2
198	The Game	CW	2006–15	9
199	Hennesey	CBS	1959–62	3
200	Episodes	Showtime	2011–15*	4
201	The Middle	ABC	2009–15*	6
202	Veronica's Closet	NBC	1997–2000	3
203	The Joey Bishop Show	NBC	1961–65	4
204	Reba	WB	2001–07	6
205	My Little Margie	NBC	1952–55	4
206	Silver Spoons	NBC	1982–87	5
207	Sister, Sister	WB	1994–99	6

Rank	Program	Network	Aired	Seasons
208	Charles in Charge	Syndicated	1984–90	5
209	The Ann Sothern Show	CBS	1958–61	3
210	The Suite Life of Zach & Cody	Disney	2005–08	3
211	First and Ten	HBO	1984–91	6
212	The Steve Harvey Show	WB	1996–2002	6
213	My Favorite Martian	CBS	1963–66	3
214	Newsradio	NBC	1995–99	5
215	Good Luck, Charlie	Disney	2010–14	4
216	House of Lies	Showtime	2012–15*	4
217	Martin	FOX	1992–97	5
218	The Bill Cosby Show	NBC	1969–71	2
219	The Flight of the Conchords	HBO	2007–09	2
220	Suddenly Susan	NBC	1996–2000	4
221	Doogie Howser, M.D.	ABC	1989–1993	4
222	I Married Joan	NBC	1952–55	3
223	The Courtship of Eddie's Father	ABC	1969–72	3
224	Mom	CBS	2013–15*	2
225	Living Single	FOX	1993–98	5
226	Caroline in the City	NBC	1995–99	4
227	Gilligan's Island	CBS	1964–67	3
228	One on One	UPN	2001–06	5
229	Phyllis	CBS	1975–77	2
230	Flo	CBS	1980–81	2
231	Topper	CBS	1953–55	2
232	Victorious	Nickelodeon	2010–13	4
233	Community	NBC	2009–15*	6
234	Anything but Love	ABC	1989–92	4
235	Zoey 101	Nickelodeon	2005–08	4
236	The Wayans Bros.	WB	1995–99	5
237	Brooklyn Bridge	CBS	1991–93	2
238	The Jamie Foxx Show	WB	1996–2001	5
239	Unhappily Ever After	WB	1995–99	5
240	Lizzie McGuire	Disney	2001–04	4
241	The Parkers	UPN	1999–2004	5
242	Cosby	CBS	1996–2000	4
243	Love, Sidney	NBC	1981–83	2
244	The Flying Nun	ABC	1967–70	3
245	Jackson and Jill	Syndicated	1949–53	4
246	Cougar Town	ABC	2009–15	6
247	Dave's World	CBS	1993–97	4
248	Raising Hope	FOX	2010–14	4
249	Mr. Adams & Eve	CBS	1957–58	2
250	The Parent'hood	WB	1995–99	5
251	Still Standing	CBS	2002–06	4
252	Funny Face	CBS	1971–72	2
253	9 to 5	ABC	1982–83; 1986–88	3

Rank	Program	Network	Aired	Seasons
254	The Single Guy	NBC	1995–97	2
255	Grounded for Life	WB	2001–05	5
256	The League	FX	2009–15*	6
257	Jesse	NBC	1998–2000	2
258	Silicon Valley	HBO	2014–15*	2
259	The People's Choice	NBC	1955–58	3
260	Life with Bonnie	ABC	2002–04	2
261	New Girl	FOX	2011–15*	4
262	The New Dick Van Dyke Show	CBS	1971–74	3
263	Arnie	CBS	1970–72	2
264	Aftermash	CBS	1983–85	2
265	Pete and Gladys	CBS	1960–62	2
266	8 Simple Rules for Dating My Teenage Daughter	ABC	2002–05	3
267	Two Guys, a Girl and a Pizza Place	ABC	1998–2001	4
268	The Naked Truth	NBC	1995–98	3
269	The Bill Dana Show	NBC	1963–65	2
270	The Ruggles	ABC	1949–52	3
271	Two Broke Girls	CBS	2011–15*	4
272	The Comeback	HBO	2005; 2014–15*	2
273	What I Like About You	WB	2002–06	4
274	What's Happening!!	ABC	1976–79	3
275	F Troop	ABC	1965–67	2
276	Angie	ABC	1979–80	2
277	My Two Dads	NBC	1987–90	3
278	Beulah	ABC	1950–52	3
279	The Secret World of Alex Mack	Nickelodeon	1994–98	4
280	Hearts Afire	CBS	1992–95	3
281	The Hughleys	UPN	1998–2002	4
282	Day by Day	NBC	1988–89	2
283	For Your Love	WB	1998–2002	5
284	Out of Practice	CBS	2005–06	1
285	Kenan & Kel	Nickelodeon	1996–2000	4
286	The Munsters	CBS	1964–66	2
287	Half & Half	UPN	2002–06	4
288	Less Than Perfect	ABC	2002–06	4
289	Saved by the Bell	NBC	1989–93	5
290	The Sarah Silverman Program	Comedy Central	2007–10	3
291	Malcolm & Eddie	UPN	1996–2000	4
292	Drake & Josh	Nickelodeon	2004–07	4
293	Bridget Loves Bernie	CBS	1972–73	1
294	Eastbound & Down	HBO	2009–13	4
295	Fired Up	NBC	1997–98	2
296	The Gertrude Berg Show	CBS	1961–62	1

Rank	Program	Network	Aired	Seasons
297	Jonas L.A.	Disney	2009–10	2
298	Grand	NBC	1990	2
299	Let's Stay Together	BET	2011–14	4
300	Anger Management	FX	2012–14	3
301	Are We There Yet	TBS	2010–13	3
302	Everybody Hates Chris	UPN	2005–09	4
303	Romeo!	Nickelodeon	2003–06	3
304	All of Us	UPN	2003–07	4
305	Til Death	FOX	2006–10	4
306	Wilfred	FX	2011–14	4
307	My Boys	TBS	2006–10	4
308	In the House	UPN	1995–99	5
309	The Addams Family	ABC	1964–66	2
310	The Cavanaughs	CBS	1986–89	2
311	Hope & Gloria	ABC	1995–96	2
312	Room for Two	ABC	1992–93	2
313	Enlightened	HBO	2011–13	2
314	Boston Common	NBC	1996–97	2
315	The Eve Arden Show	CBS	1957–58	1
316	Sally	NBC	1957–58	1
317	Melissa & Joey	ABC Family	2010–15	4
318	Thunder Alley	ABC	1994–95	2
319	My Hero	NBC	1952–53	1
320	The Brian Keith Show	NBC	1972–74	2
321	Goodnight, Beantown	CBS	1983–84	2
322	Union Square	NBC	1997–98	1
323	The Ropers	ABC	1979–80	2
324	Stark Raving Mad	NBC	1999–2000	1
325	The Lot	AMC	1999–2001	2
326	The Associates	ABC	1979–80	1
327	Parker Lewis Can't Lose	FOX	1990–93	3
328	The Slap Maxwell Story	ABC	1987–88	1
329	Good Morning, Miami	NBC	2002–03	2
330	Life with Luigi	CBS	1952–53	1
331	The Suite Life on Deck	Disney	2008–11	3
332	Madman of the People	NBC	1994–95	1
333	You Again?	NBC	1986–87	2
334	Police Squad!	ABC	1982	1
335	Happy Endings	ABC	2011–13	3
336	Gloria	CBS	1982–83	1
337	Leap of Faith	NBC	2002	1
338	The Tony Randall Show	ABC	1976–78	2
339	Even Stevens	Disney	2000–03	3
340	Jessie	Disney	2011–15	4
341	The Jackie Thomas Show	ABC	1992–93	1
342	Roc	FOX	1991–94	3

Rank	Program	Network	Aired	Seasons
343	Baby Talk	ABC	1991–92	2
344	True Jackson, VP	Nickelodeon	2008–11	3
345	Chicken Soup	ABC	1989	1
346	Me & the Boys	ABC	1994–95	1
347	Duet	FOX	1987–89	3
348	Good Heavens	ABC	1976	1
349	Inside Schwartz	NBC	2001–02	1
350	High Society	CBS	1995–96	1
351	The Millers	CBS	2013–14	2
352	Fay	NBC	1975–76	1
353	The Exes	TV Land	2011–15*	4
354	Cursed	NBC	2000–01	1
355	Unfabulous	Nickelodeon	2004–07	3
356	Can't Hurry Love	CBS	1995–96	1
357	Eve	UPN	2003–06	3
358	Derek	Netflix	2012–14	2
359	Baby Bob	CBS	2002–03	2
360	The Bill Engvall Show	TBS	2007–09	3
361	The Soul Man	TV Land	2012–15*	4
362	Andy Richter Controls the Universe	FOX	2002–03	2
363	My Sister Sam	CBS	1986–88	2
364	Brooklyn 99	FOX	2013–15*	2
365	Phenom	ABC	1993–94	1
366	Sonny with a Chance	Disney	2009–11	2
367	Paul Sand in Friends and Lovers	CBS	1974–75	1
368	On Our Own	CBS	1994–95	1
369	The Crazy Ones	CBS	2013–14	1
370	Hiller and Diller	ABC	1997–98	1
371	Stockard Channing in Just Friends	CBS	1979	1
372	Rob	CBS	2012	1
373	Lucky	FX	2003	1
374	My Big Fat Greek Life	CBS	2003	1
375	The Martin Short Show	NBC	1994	1
376	Suburgatory	ABC	2011–14	3
377	Top of the Heap	FOX	1991	1

*still on air as of June 2015

Appendix B: Top 25 Situation Comedies by Decade

Top 25 Situation Comedies of the 1950s

Rank	Program	Network	Aired
8	I Love Lucy	CBS	1951–57
14	The Danny Thomas Show	CBS	1953–64
24	The Phil Silvers Show	CBS	1955–59
33	Father Knows Best	CBS	1954–60
55	The George Burns & Gracie Allen Show	CBS	1950–58
59	The Bob Cummings Show	NBC	1955–59
62	December Bride	CBS	1954–59
66	The Real McCoys	ABC	1957–63
68	The Life of Riley	NBC	1953–58
69	Our Miss Brooks	CBS	1952–56
70	Mama	CBS	1949–57
86	The Adventures of Ozzie & Harriet	ABC	1952–66
101	Leave It to Beaver	ABC	1957–63
103	Private Secretary	CBS	1953–57
114	Mr. Peepers	NBC	1952–55
122	The Honeymooners	CBS	1955–56
153	The Goldbergs	CBS	1949–53
160	Bachelor Father	CBS	1957–62
162	The Gale Storm Show	CBS	1956–60
170	The Stu Erwin Show	ABC	1950–55
188	Meet Millie	CBS	1952–56
191	The Aldrich Family	NBC	1949–53
194	Amos 'n' Andy	CBS	1951–53
205	My Little Margie	NBC	1952–55
209	The Ann Sothern Show	CBS	1958–61

Top 25 Situation Comedies of the 1960s

Rank	Program	Network	Aired
15	The Dick Van Dyke Show	CBS	1961–66
18	The Andy Griffith Show	CBS	1960–68
26	Bewitched	ABC	1964–72
31	Get Smart	NBC	1965–70
32	The Beverly Hillbillies	CBS	1962–71
35	The Lucy Show	CBS	1962–68
51	Hogan's Heroes	CBS	1965–71
57	Family Affair	CBS	1966–71
63	Hazel	NBC	1961–66
65	My Three Sons	CBS	1960–72
74	Petticoat Junction	CBS	1963–70
75	Gomer Pyle, USMC	CBS	1964–69
85	The Donna Reed Show	ABC	1958–66
91	Green Acres	CBS	1965–71
99	McHale's Navy	ABC	1962–66
113	That Girl	ABC	1966–71
119	The Monkees	NBC	1966–68
127	The Ghost and Mrs. Muir	NBC	1968–70
129	Car 54, Where Are You?	NBC	1961–63
138	My World and Welcome to It	NBC	1969–70
144	Dennis the Menace	CBS	1959–63
145	Julia	NBC	1968–71
147	Mister Ed	CBS	1961–66
148	I Dream of Jeannie	NBC	1965–70
171	The Many Loves of Dobie Gillis	CBS	1959–63

Top 25 Situation Comedies of the 1970s

Rank	Program	Network	Aired
1	All in the Family	CBS	1971–79
4	M*A*S*H	CBS	1972–83
5	The Mary Tyler Moore Show	CBS	1970–77
21	Barney Miller	ABC	1975–82
28	Happy Days	ABC	1974–84
38	Three's Company	ABC	1977–84
40	The Jeffersons	CBS	1975–85
41	Sanford and Son	NBC	1972–77
42	Maude	CBS	1972–78
43	Laverne & Shirley	ABC	1976–83
50	Alice	CBS	1976–85
53	One Day at a Time	CBS	1975–84
54	Rhoda	CBS	1974–78
56	Soap	ABC	1977–81
60	The Odd Couple	ABC	1970–75

Rank	Program	Network	Aired
61	Room 222	ABC	1969–74
72	Here's Lucy	CBS	1968–74
88	The Bob Newhart Show	CBS	1972–78
110	Chico and the Man	NBC	1974–78
116	Good Times	CBS	1974–79
117	WKRP in Cincinnati	CBS	1978–82
120	The Doris Day Show	CBS	1968–73
139	Welcome Back, Kotter	ABC	1975–79
143	The Brady Bunch	ABC	1969–74
156	Mork & Mindy	ABC	1978–82

Top 25 Situation Comedies of the 1980s

Rank	Program	Network	Aired
2	Cheers	NBC	1982–93
9	The Cosby Show	NBC	1984–2002
13	Golden Girls	NBC	1985–92
19	Taxi	ABC	1978–83
25	Family Ties	NBC	1982–89
36	Night Court	NBC	1984–92
45	Newhart	CBS	1982–90
46	Kate & Allie	CBS	1984–89
58	Designing Women	CBS	1986–93
64	Who's the Boss?	ABC	1984–92
67	A Different World	NBC	1987–93
79	Benson	ABC	1979–86
82	Growing Pains	ABC	1985–92
89	Diff'rent Strokes	NBC	1978–86
92	The Facts of Life	NBC	1979–88
97	Perfect Strangers	ABC	1986–93
106	Archie Bunker's Place	CBS	1979–83
109	227	NBC	1985–90
125	Too Close for Comfort	ABC	1980–87
130	Gimme a Break	NBC	1981–87
134	Head of the Class	ABC	1986–91
136	The Days & Nights of Molly Dodd	NBC	1987–91
142	ALF	NBC	1986–90
152	The Hogan Family	NBC	1986–91
154	Dear John	NBC	1988–92

Top 25 Situation Comedies of the 1990s

Rank	Program	Network	Aired
3	Frasier	NBC	1993–2004
6	Friends	NBC	1994–2004
10	Seinfeld	NBC	1989–98

Rank	Program	Network	Aired
12	Murphy Brown	CBS	1988–98
20	Roseanne	ABC	1988–97
22	Mad About You	NBC	1992–99
29	Home Improvement	ABC	1991–99
34	The Larry Sanders Show	HBO	1992–98
39	The Wonder Years	ABC	1988–93
48	Coach	ABC	1989–97
52	3rd Rock from the Sun	NBC	1996–2001
71	Evening Shade	CBS	1990–94
73	Empty Nest	NBC	1988–95
78	Dream On	HBO	1990–96
80	Full House	ABC	1987–95
84	Ellen	ABC	1994–98
95	Wings	NBC	1990–97
96	Married ... with Children	FOX	1987–97
100	Family Matters	ABC	1989–98
102	Love & War	CBS	1992–95
105	Spin City	ABC	1996–2002
107	Grace Under Fire	ABC	1993–98
108	The Drew Carey Show	ABC	1995–2004
111	Just Shoot Me	NBC	1997–2003
118	Cybill	CBS	1995–98

Top 25 Situation Comedies of the 2000s

Rank	Program	Network	Aired
7	Everybody Loves Raymond	CBS	1996–2005
16	30 Rock	NBC	2006–13
17	Will & Grace	NBC	1998–2006
27	Two and a Half Men	CBS	2003–15
30	Sex & the City	HBO	1998–2004
37	The Office	NBC	2005–13
44	Curb Your Enthusiasm	HBO	2000–15*
47	Malcolm in the Middle	FOX	2000–06
49	Entourage	HBO	2004–11
81	Weeds	Showtime	2005–12
83	Arrested Development	FOX	2008–13
87	How I Met Your Mother	CBS	2005–14
90	Scrubs	NBC	2001–10
93	Wizards of Waverly Place	Disney	2007–12
94	iCarly	Nickelodeon	2007–12
98	King of Queens	CBS	1998–2007
112	Becker	CBS	1998–2004
115	My Name Is Earl	NBC	2005–09
124	Extras	HBO	2005–07

Rank	Program	Network	Aired
126	Tyler Perry's House of Payne	TBS	2006–12
133	That '70s Show	FOX	1998–2006
135	Hannah Montana	Disney	2006–11
140	The New Adventures of Old Christine	CBS	2006–10
146	Girlfriends	UPN	2000–08
149	It's Always Sunny In Philadelphia	FX	2005–15*

*Still on air as of June 2015

Top 25 Situation Comedies 2010–2015

Rank	Program	Network	Aired
11	Modern Family	ABC	2009–15*
23	The Big Bang Theory	CBS	2007–15*
76	Veep	HBO	2012–15*
77	Nurse Jackie	Showtime	2009–15
104	Louie	FX	2010–15*
128	Mike & Molly	CBS	2010–15*
137	Parks & Recreation	NBC	2009–15
155	Girls	HBO	2012–15*
161	United States of Tara	Showtime	2009–11
180	Hot in Cleveland	TV Land	2010–15
200	Episodes	Showtime	2011–15*
201	The Middle	ABC	2009–15*
215	Good Luck, Charlie	Disney	2010–14
216	House of Lies	Showtime	2012–15*
224	Mom	CBS	2013–15*
232	Victorious	Nickelodeon	2010–13
233	Community	NBC	2009–15*
246	Cougar Town	ABC	2009–15
248	Raising Hope	FOX	2010–14
256	The League	FX	2009–15*
258	Silicon Valley	HBO	2014–15*
261	New Girl	FOX	2011–15*
271	Two Broke Girls	CBS	2011–15*
299	Let's Stay Together	BET	2011–14
300	Anger Management	FX	2012–14

*Still on air as of June 2015

Appendix C:
Top Situation Comedies by Network

Top 25 Situation Comedies Aired on ABC

Rank	Program	Aired
11	Modern Family	2009–15*
19	Taxi	1978–83
20	Roseanne	1988–97
21	Barney Miller	1975–82
26	Bewitched	1964–72
28	Happy Days	1974–84
29	Home Improvement	1991–99
38	Three's Company	1977–84
39	The Wonder Years	1988–93
43	Laverne & Shirley	1976–83
48	Coach	1989–97
56	Soap	1977–81
60	The Odd Couple	1970–75
61	Room 222	1969–74
64	Who's the Boss?	1984–92
66	The Real McCoys	1957–63
79	Benson	1979–86
80	Full House	1987–95
82	Growing Pains	1985–92
84	Ellen	1994–98
85	The Donna Reed Show	1958–66
86	The Adventures of Ozzie & Harriet	1952–66
97	Perfect Strangers	1986–93
99	McHale's Navy	1962–66
100	Family Matters	1989–98

Still on air as of June 2015

Top 25 Situation Comedies Aired on CBS

Rank	Program	Aired
1	All in the Family	1971–79
4	M*A*S*H	1972–83
5	The Mary Tyler Moore Show	1970–77
7	Everybody Loves Raymond	1996–2005
8	I Love Lucy	1951–57
12	Murphy Brown	1988–98
14	The Danny Thomas Show	1953–64
15	The Dick Van Dyke Show	1961–66
18	The Andy Griffith Show	1960–68
23	The Big Bang Theory	2007–15*
24	The Phil Silvers Show	1955–59
27	Two and a Half Men	2003–15
32	The Beverly Hillbillies	1962–71
33	Father Knows Best	1954–60
35	The Lucy Show	1962–68
40	The Jeffersons	1975–85
42	Maude	1972–78
45	Newhart	1982–90
46	Kate & Allie	1984–89
50	Alice	1976–85
51	Hogan's Heroes	1965–71
53	One Day at a Time	1975–84
54	Rhoda	1974–78
55	The George Burns & Gracie Allen Show	1950–58
57	Family Affair	1966–71

*Still on air as of June 2015

Top 25 Situation Comedies Aired on NBC

Rank	Program	Aired
2	Cheers	1982–93
3	Frasier	1993–2004
6	Friends	1994–2004
9	The Cosby Show	1984–2002
10	Seinfeld	1989–98
13	Golden Girls	1985–92
16	30 Rock	2006–13
17	Will & Grace	1998–2006
22	Mad About You	1992–99
25	Family Ties	1982–89
31	Get Smart	1965–70
36	Night Court	1984–92
37	The Office	2005–13
41	Sanford and Son	1972–77

Rank	Program	Aired
52	3rd Rock from the Sun	1996–2001
59	The Bob Cummings Show	1955–59
63	Hazel	1961–66
67	A Different World	1987–93
68	The Life of Riley	1953–58
73	Empty Nest	1988–95
89	Diff'rent Strokes	1978–86
90	Scrubs	2001–10
92	The Facts of Life	1979–88
95	Wings	1990–97
109	227	1985–90

Top 10 Situation Comedies Aired on FOX

Rank	Program	Aired
47	Malcolm in the Middle	2000–06
83	Arrested Development	2008–13
96	Married ... with Children	1987–97
133	That '70s Show	1998–2006
158	The Bernie Mac Show	2001–06
217	Martin	1992–97
225	Living Single	1993–98
248	Raising Hope	2010–14
261	New Girl	2011–15*
305	Til Death	2006–10

*Still on air as of June 2015

Top 10 Situation Comedies Aired on UPN

Rank	Program	Aired
146	Girlfriends	2000–08
183	Moesha	1996–2001
228	One on One	2001–06
241	The Parkers	1999–2004
281	The Hughleys	1998–2002
287	Half & Half	2002–06
291	Malcolm & Eddie	1996–2000
302	Everybody Hates Chris	2005–09
304	All of Us	2003–07
308	In the House	1995–99

Top 10 Situation Comedies Aired on WB

Rank	Program	Aired
204	Reba	2001–07

Rank	Program	Aired
207	Sister, Sister	1994–99
212	The Steve Harvey Show	1996–2002
236	The Wayans Bros.	1995–99
238	The Jamie Foxx Show	1996–2001
239	Unhappily Ever After	1995–99
250	The Parent'hood	1995–99
255	Grounded for Life	2001–05
273	What I Like About You	2002–06
283	For Your Love	1998–2002

Top 10 Situation Comedies Aired on HBO

Rank	Program	Aired
30	Sex & the City	1998–2004
34	The Larry Sanders Show	1992–98
44	Curb Your Enthusiasm	2000–15*
49	Entourage	2004–11
76	Veep	2012–15*
78	Dream On	1990–96
124	Extras	2005–07
141	Arli$$	1996–2002
155	Girls	2012–15*
211	First and Ten	1984–91

*Still on air as of June 2015

Top 10 Situation Comedies Aired on the Disney Channel

Rank	Program	Aired
93	Wizards of Waverly Place	2007–12
135	Hannah Montana	2006–11
165	That's So Raven	2003–07
210	The Suite Life of Zach & Cody	2005–08
215	Good Luck, Charlie	2010–14
240	Lizzie McGuire	2001–04
297	Jonas L.A.	2009–10
331	The Suite Life on Deck	2008–11
339	Even Stevens	2000–03
	Jessie	2011–15

Appendix D:
Top 25 Situation Comedies
That Aired for
One Season or Less

Rank	Program	Network	Aired
122	The Honeymooners	CBS	1955–56
138	My World and Welcome to It	NBC	1969–70
164	Frank's Place	CBS	1987–88
173	He & She	CBS	1967–68
184	The Famous Teddy Z	CBS	1989–90
284	Out of Practice	CBS	2005–06
293	Bridget Loves Bernie	CBS	1972–73
296	The Gertrude Berg Show	CBS	1961–62
315	The Eve Arden Show	CBS	1957–58
316	Sally	NBC	1957–58
319	My Hero	NBC	1952–53
322	Union Square	NBC	1997–98
324	Stark Raving Mad	NBC	1999–2000
326	The Associates	ABC	1979–80
328	The Slap Maxwell Story	ABC	1987–88
330	Life with Luigi	CBS	1952–53
332	Madman of the People	NBC	1994–95
334	Police Squad!	ABC	1982
336	Gloria	CBS	1982–83
337	Leap of Faith	NBC	2002
341	The Jackie Thomas Show	ABC	1992–93
345	Chicken Soup	ABC	1989
346	Me & the Boys	ABC	1994–95
348	Good Heavens	ABC	1976
	Inside Schwartz	NBC	2001–02

Index

The A-Team 35
Aames, Willie 148
Abbot, Jamie 198
Abercrombie, Ian 28, 226
According to Jim 248
Adams, Don 75, 77
Adams, Jane 10
The Addams Family 252
Adiarte, Patrick 13
Adsit, Scott 41
The Adventures of Gracie 134
The Adventures of Ozzie and Harriet 39, 64, 80, 154, 158, 159, 198, 207–210, 247, 254, 259
Aftermash 15, 36, 251
Aikman, Troy 117
Aladjem, Mackenzie 186
Albert, Eddie 221
Alcoa Premiere 240
Alda, Alan 13, 14
The Aldrich Family 249, 254
Alexander, Erika 25
Alexander, Jason 28, 29, 106, 190
Alexander, Reed 228
ALF 248, 256
Alice 120–123, 246, 255, 260
Alice, Mary 163
Alice Doesn't Live Here Anymore 121
All in the Family 5–7, 13, 16, 25, 64, 69, 89, 97, 99, 101, 102, 136, 151, 213, 245, 255, 260
All of Us 252, 261
Alldredge, Michael 121
Allen, Debbie 164
Allen, Gracie 134, 135, 145
Allen, Phillip R. 121
Allen, Raymond 99
Allen, Ricky 158
Allen, Steve 146
Allen, Tim 71, 72

Alley, Kirstie 8, 9, 239
Allman, Elvia 77, 179
Amani, Walid 184
Amen 27, 249
American Gladiators 244
American Graffiti 69, 104
American Idol 89
Amos, John 16, 101
Amos 'n' Andy 80, 134, 249, 254
Amsterdam, Morey 38, 40
Anderson, Harry 87
Anderson, Pamela 71, 72
Anderson, Sam 235
Anderson-Emmons, Aubrey 31
The Andy Griffith Show 38, 45–47, 93, 103, 104, 162, 179, 181, 182, 183, 245, 255, 260
Andy Richter Controls the Universe 253
Angel Heart 164
Angell, David 11, 230
Anger Management 252, 258
Angie 251
Aniston, Jennifer 18, 19
The Ann Sothern Show 250, 254
Annie Oakley 117
Anything But Love 250
Applegate, Christina 232, 233, 234
Archie Bunker's Place 6, 7, 247, 256
Arden, Eve 166, 168
Are We There Yet 252
Arli$$ 248, 262
Arnaz, Desi 23, 24, 85
Arnaz, Desi, Jr. 86, 174, 175
Arnaz, Lucie 86, 174, 175
Arness, James 10
Arnett, Will 200, 201
Arnie 251
Arnold, Tom 50, 51, 242
Arrested Development 185, 200–203, 247, 257, 261
Arthur, Bea 7, 35, 101, 103

Arthur, Rebecca 235, 236
Arthur Godfrey's Talent Scouts 24
Ashley, Elizabet 172, 174
Asner, Ed 16, 17, 132
The Associates 252, 263
Astin, MacKenzie 223
Astor, Shay 126, 128
Auberjonois, Rene 191, 192
Aulisio, Curnal Achilles 156
Austin, Jake T. 226
Austin, Karen 87
Averback, Hy 168
Aykroyd, Dan 112
Azaria, Hank 56
Azzara, Candace 131, 136

Baby Bob 253
Baby Talk 253
Bachelor Father 248, 254
Baddeley, Hermoine 101, 102
Bader, Diedrich 184
Baer, Max, Jr. 77, 78
Baer, Parley 46, 208
Baez, Joan 196
Bailey, G.W. 13
Bailey, Raymond 77, 79
Bain, Conrad 101, 103, 215
Baio, Jimmy 136, 138
Baio, Scott 69, 70
Baker, Leslie David 89, 90
Bakkedahl, Dan 184
Bakula, Scott 32, 143
Balaban, Bob 28
Balding, Rebecca 136, 138
Baldwin, Alec 41, 42
Ball, Lucille 23, 24, 60, 84, 85, 86, 162, 168, 174, 175, 176
Ballantine, Carl 239, 241
Ballard, Michael 121
Banks, Elizabeth 219
Banner, John 123, 124
Baranski, Christine 57
Barbeau, Adrienne 101, 102
Barber, Andrea 193
Barker, Bob 211
Barnes, Priscilla 92, 94
Barney Miller 52–54, 87, 245, 255, 259
Baron, Sandy 28
Barone, Sal 50
Barr, Doug 143
Barr, Roseanne 50, 51, 84
Barrera, Maria Canals 226, 227
Barrie, Barbara 52, 5
Barry, Gene 168, 169
Barry, Rick 117
Bartlett, Diana 77
Bartlett, Robin 54

Baryshnikov, Mikhail 73
Bateman, Jason 200, 201
Bateman, Justine 62
Bates, Jimmy 80
Bates, Kathy 89, 128
Baumgartner, Brian 89
Bavier, Frances 46, 47, 183
Baxendale, Helen 18
Baxter-Birney, Meredith 62
Baywatch 72
Bearse, Amanda 232, 234
The Beatles 64
Beatty, Ned 50
Beavers, Louise 36
Becker 247, 257
Beckman, Henry 239
Bell, Darryl 163, 165
Bell, E.E. 232
Bell, Tina 68
Benaderet, Bea 77, 134, 135, 145, 179, 180
Benben, Brian 188, 189
Bendix, William 165, 166
Benedict, Paul 97, 98
Benjamin, Julia 153, 155
Benny, Jack 86, 176, 189
Benson 139, 190–193, 200, 247, 256, 259
Benson, Dan 226, 227
Berfield, Justin 113, 115
Bergen, Candice 32, 33, 73
Bergen, Edgar 33
Berle, Milton 24, 86, 176
Berman, Shelly 106
Bernard, Crystal 69, 230, 231
Bernhard, Sandra 50
The Bernie Mac Show 248, 261
Berra, Yogi 117
Berry, Ken 46
Bertinelli, Valerie 129
Bessell, Ted 181
Best, Eve 186, 188
Betz, Carl 205, 206
Beulah 251
The Beverly Hillbillies 40, 77–79, 146, 161, 162, 179, 221, 246, 255, 260
Beverly Hills Cop 236
Beverly Hills 90210 74
Bewitched 63–65, 226, 227, 245, 255, 259
Bexley, Don 99
Bialik, Mayim 56, 57
Bichir, Demian 195
Bieber, Justin 227
The Big Bang Theory 56–59, 213, 229, 245, 258, 260
The Big Issue 36
The Bill Cosby Show 250
The Bill Dana Show 251
The Bill Engvall Show 253

Bilson, Rachel 211
Bird, Billie 191
Bishe, Kerry 218, 220
Blair, June 208
Blake, Madge 161, 162
Blake, Whitney 153, 155
Blansky's Beauties 70, 133
Bledsoe, Tempestt 25, 26
Blige, Mary J. 120
Blondell, Gloria 165
Blondell, Joan 161
Bloodworth-Thomason, Linda 142, 143, 172, 174
Blossom 249
Bob 213
The Bob Cummings Show (Love That Bob) 144–146, 246, 254, 261
The Bob Newhart Show 108, 212–214, 247, 256
Bolger, Ray 37
Bon Jovi, Jon 43
Bonar, Ivan 208
Bond, James 75, 79
Bond, Raleigh 121
Bonerz, Peter 213, 214
Bonet, Lisa 25, 26, 163, 164
Bonnie and Clyde 77
Bonsall, Brian 62
Boone 8
Booth, Shirley 153, 154
Borden, Lynn 153, 155
Borgnine, Ernest 239, 240, 242
Bosley, Tom 68, 69
Boston Common 252
Bowden, Katrina 41
Bowen, Julie 30, 31
Bowlby, April 66, 67
Bown, Woody 223
Boxer, Barbara 107
Boxing from St. Nicholas Arena 151
Boy Meets World 248
Boyle, Peter 21, 22
Bradshaw, Sufe 184, 185
Brady, Tom 74, 120
Brady, Wayne 211
The Brady Bunch 6, 145, 248, 256
Braff, Zach 218, 219, 220
Braga, Sonia 73
Bratt, Benjamin 32
Bratton, Creed 89
Breaking Bad 30, 114, 196
Brenna, Bettina 77
Brennan, Walter 161, 162
The Brian Keith Show 252
Brian's Song 117
Bridges, Beau 162
Bridges, Todd 215, 217, 224

Bridget Loves Bernie 251, 263
Bright, Kevin 189
Brinkley, Ritch 32
Brisebois, Danielle 5
Bristow, Patrick 203
Broadside 242
Brooklyn Bridge 250
Brooklyn 99 253
Brooks, Mel 56, 75, 77, 107
Brooks, Peter 158
Brown, Charnele 163, 165
Brown, John 134, 135
Brown, Orlando 242
Brown, Timothy 13
Browne, Roscoe Lee 136
Bryan, Zachary Ty 71, 72
Bryant, Nana 168
Bryce, Scott 223
Buchanan, Edgar 179, 180
Buckley, Andy 184
Buckley, Jackson 32
Buffalo Bill 249
Buffy the Vampire Slayer 212
Buktenica, Ray 131, 133
Bulifant, Joyce 16
Buntrock, Bobby 153, 155
Burghoff, Gary 13, 14, 15
Burke, Delta 142, 143
Burnett, Carol 56, 83, 86
Burnette, Smiley 179, 180
Burns, Catherine Lloyd 113
Burns, George 134, 135, 146
Burns, Jack 46
Burns, Ronnie 134, 135
Burrell, Ty 30, 31
Burstyn, Ellen 162
Burton, Kate 184
Burton, Richard 176
Bush, George W. 43
Bushnell, Candace 74
Butcher, Kasan 113
Butkus, Dick 117
Butler, Dan 10, 12
Buttram, Pat 221
Bye Bye Birdie 39
Byington, Spring 151, 152, 153
Byner, John 136

Caan, Scott 118
Cabot, Sebastian 139, 140, 141
Cady, Frank 179, 208, 221, 222
Caesar, Sid 40
Cagney & Lacey 172
Californication 249
Cameron, Candace 193, 194, 199
Cameron, Kirk 194, 198, 199
Campbell, Duane 121

Campos, Rafael 131
Canfield, Mary Grace 221, 222
Cannevale, Bobby 45
Canova, Diana 136, 138
Can't Hurry Love 253
Cantone, Mario 73
Capps, Lisa 198
Car 54, Where Are You? 248, 255
Card, Kathryn 23
Carell, Steve 77, 89, 90, 91
Carey, Clare 116, 118
Carey, Ron 52, 53, 54
Carlton Your Doorman 133
The Carol Burnett Show 181, 182
Caroline in the City 250
Carroll, Janet 232
Carroll, Pat 36
Carroll, Victoria 121
Carson, Johnny 82, 109
Carter, Dixie 142, 215, 216
Carter, Jimmy 142
Cartwright, Angela 36, 37
Caruso, David 20
Carver, Randall 48
Carvey, Dana 83
Casey, Peter 11, 230
Castillo, Enrique 195
Catlett, Mary Jo 215
Cattrall, Kim 73, 74
Cavanaugh, Tom 219
The Cavanaughs 252
Cera, Michael 200, 202
Chalke, Sarah 50, 211, 218, 219
Chao, Rosalind 13, 215
Chapin, Lauren 80, 81
Chapman, Robert 80
Charles, Ray 157
Charles in Charge 250
Charlie's Angels 142
Chase, Chevy 112
Checking In 7, 98
Cheech & Chong 196
Cheers 7–10, 11, 19, 25, 26, 44, 49, 87, 105, 165, 230, 232, 233, 245, 256, 260
Chicken Soup 253, 263
Chico and the Man 247, 256
Ching, William 168
Chlumsky, Anna 184, 185
Chott, Bill 226
Chriqui, Emmanuelle 118, 119
Christopher, Dyllan 32
Christopher, William 13, 15, 181, 183
Church, Thomas Haden 230, 232
Clark, Fred 134, 135
Clark, Marlene 99
Clark, Oliver 213
Clary, Robert 123, 125

Cleese, John 128
Clennon, David 190
Cleveland, Odessa 13
Clinton, Bill 142, 172
Clinton, Hillary 142, 172
Clooney, George 50, 51, 223, 225
Clyde, Andy 161, 162
Coach 115–118, 246, 257, 259
Coburn, Charles 146
Cochran, Johnnie 217
Cohen, Lynn 73
Cohn, Mindy 223
Coiro, Rhys 118
Colasanto, Nicholas 8, 9
Cole, Gary 118, 184, 185
Cole, Tina 158, 159
Coleman, Gary 215, 216, 217, 224
Colen, Beatrice 68
Coligado, Emy 115
Collins, Mo 201
Colonel Humphrey Flack 36
Come Back Little Sheba 154
The Comeback 251
Community 250, 258
Compton, Forrest 181
Conaway, Jeff 48, 49
Conn, Didi 191, 192
Connick, Harry, Jr. 43, 45
Connolly, Kevin 118, 119
Conreid, Hans 36, 38
Considine, Tim 158, 159
Constantine, Michael 149, 150
Conway, Tim 232, 239, 241, 242
Cooksey, Danny 215, 216
Corbett, John 73
Corley, Pat 32, 34
Corsaut, Aneta 46
Cosby 250
Cosby, Bill 25, 26, 27, 163, 164
The Cosby Show 8, 19, 25–27, 63, 71, 163, 164, 165, 233, 245, 256, 260
Cosell, Howard 148
Cosgrove, Miranda 228
Costa, Peter 25
Costello, Elvis 196
Costello, Lou 189
Cougar Town 250, 258
Coughlin, Kevin 170
Coulier, Dave 193, 194
Coupe, Eliza 218, 220
Couric, Katie 34
The Courtship of Eddie's Father 250
Cover, Franklin 97, 98
Cox, Courtney 18, 19, 30, 62, 63
Crane, Bob 123, 124, 205, 207
Crane, David 19, 189
Cranshaw, Pat 121

Cranston, Bryan 28, 113, 114
Crawford, Edward 99
Crawford, Johnny 209
The Crazy Ones 253
Crenna, Richard 161, 162, 168
Croft, Mary Jane 23, 85, 168, 169, 174, 208
Crombie, Peter 28
Cromwell, James 5
Cronin, Patrick J. 121
Cross, David 200, 202
Cryer, Jon 66
Crystal, Billy 136, 138
Cully, Zara 97
Culp, Robert 25
Cummings, Bob 144, 145
Cuoco, Kaley 56, 57, 58
Curb Your Enthusiasm 105–107, 185, 246, 257, 262
Curran, Kevin 232
Cursed 253
Curtin, Jane 111, 112, 126, 127
Cutter, Lise 235, 236
Cybill 248, 257

d'Abo, Olivia 94, 95
Daily, Bill 213, 214
The Daily Show 90
Dallas 26, 147
Daly, Jonathan 179
Daly, Tim 230, 231
Daly, Tyne 230
Damon, Cathryn 136, 137, 138
Dancing in the Dark 63
D'Andrea, Tom 165, 167
Danner, Blythe 45
The Danny Thomas Show (Make Room for Daddy) 36–38, 46, 153, 245, 254, 260
Danson, Ted 8, 9, 49, 105, 106
Danza, Tony 48, 49, 156
Dave's World 250
David, Larry 29, 106, 107
Davis, Ann B. 144, 145
Davis, Geena 63
Davis, Jennifer 13
Davis, Kristin 30, 73, 74
Davis, Ossie 172, 174
Davis, Rufe 179
Davis, Sammy, Jr. 27
Davis Rules 249
Dawson, Greg 208
Dawson, Richard 123, 125
Day by Day 251
The Days & Nights of Molly Dodd 248, 256
Dayton, Danny 5
Deacon, Richard 38, 40
Dear John 248, 256

DeCamp, Rosemary 144, 145, 146, 180
December Bride 151–153, 246, 254
Dee, Ruby 174
DeFore, Don 153, 154, 208
DeGeneres, Ellen 44, 83, 203, 204
DeGore, Janet 161
Delano, Michael 131, 133
Dell, Charlie 172, 174
DeLuise, David 226
Demarest, William 158, 160
Demetral, Chris 188, 189
Dempsey, Patrick 44
Denman, David 89
Dennis the Menace 248, 255
Derek 253
Dern, Laura 204
de Rossi, Portia 200, 202
Designing Women 141–144, 172, 174, 246, 256
Desperate Housewives 30
Devane, William 9
Devine, Loretta 163
DeVito, Danny 48, 49
DeWitt, Joyce 92
Dharma & Greg 248
Diamond, Selma 87, 88
Diaz, Guillermo 195
DiCaprio, Leonardo 51, 198, 200
The Dick Van Dyke Show 16, 38–40, 245, 255, 260
A Different World 27, 63, 163–165, 246, 256, 261
Diff'rent Strokes 215–217, 223, 224, 247, 256, 261
Diggs, Taye 45
Dillon, Brendon 5
Dillon, Denny 188, 190
Dillon, Kevin 118, 119
Dino, Desi and Billy 175
Ditka, Mike 117
Dixon, Ivan 123, 125
Dodson, Jack 46
Dohring, Kelsey 198
Dohring, Kristen 198
Domino, Fats 209
Donahue, Elinor 46, 80, 81, 146, 148
Donaldson, Colby 107
The Donna Reed Show 117, 159, 198, 205–207, 209, 247, 255, 259
Donovan 196
Donovan, King 144
Donovan, Martin 195
Doogie Howser, M.D. 212, 250
Dooley, Paul 56, 177, 190
The Doors 126
The Doris Day Show 248, 256
Doucett, Linda 82

Douglas, Donna 77, 78
Dourdan, Gary 163
Dragnet 80
Drake and Josh 228, 251
Dratch, Rachel 41
Dream On 19, 83, 188–190, 247, 257, 262
The Drew Carey Show 247, 257
Duchovny, David 83
Duet 253
Duffy, Julia 108, 110, 142, 143
Dulo, Jane 75, 239
Dumbrille, Douglas 166
Dunbar, Olive 158
Dungey, Merrin 237, 239
Dunn, Kevin 184, 185
Dunning, Debbe 71, 72
Durning, Charles 172, 173, 174
Durrell, Michael 121
Dussault, Nancy 56
Dynasty 26

Eastbound & Down 251
Easterbrook, Leslie 103
Ebersol, Dick 111
Ebsen, Buddy 77, 78
Eckholdt, Steven 204
Edelman, Herb 35
Eden, Barbara 227
Edwards, Gail 193
Edwards, Geoff 179
Eigenberg, David 73
8 Simple Rules for Dating My Teenage Daughter 251
Einstein, Bob 106, 201
Ellen (These Friends of Mine) 44, 203–205, 247, 257, 259
Elliott, Abby 211
Elliott, Chris 21
Empty Nest 176–178, 247, 257, 261
Engel, Georgia 16, 17, 22, 116, 132
Enlightened 252
Ennis, Jessie 184
Ennis, John 113
Entertainment Weekly 108
Entourage 118–120, 246, 257, 262
Episodes 249, 258
ER 225
Essman, Susie 106
Evans, Damon 97, 98
Evans, Maurice 64
Evans, Mike 5, 7, 97, 98
Evans, Monica 146, 148
Eve 253
The Eve Arden Show 252, 263
Even Stevens 252, 262
Evening Shade 172–174, 246, 257
Everybody Hates Chris 252, 261

Everybody Loves Raymond 20–23, 25, 71, 238, 245, 257, 260
The Exes 253
Extras 248, 257, 262

F Troop 251
Fabares, Shelley 116, 117, 118, 129, 130, 205, 206, 207, 209
Fabian 225
Fabray, Nanette 117, 129, 130
Facinelli, Peter 186, 188
The Facts of Life 63, 215, 222–225, 247, 256, 261
The Facts of Life Down Under 224
The Facts of Life Goes to Paris 224
The Facts of Life Reunion 224
Fagerbakke, Bill 116, 117
Faison, Donald 218, 219
Falco, Edie 186, 187
Falkner, Anne 50
The Fall Guy 88
Fallon, Jimmy 229
Family Affair 139–141, 246, 255, 260
Family Feud 125
Family Matters 242–244, 247, 257, 259
Family Ties 9, 26, 61–63, 245, 256, 260
The Famous Teddy Z 249, 263
Fancy, Richard 28
Fantasy Island 117
Faris, Anna 120
The Farmer's Daughter 249
Farr, Jamie 13, 15, 151, 183
Farrell, Gwen 13
Farrell, Judy 13
Farrell, Mike 13, 14
Farrell, Will 91
The Father Dowling Mysteries 209
Father Knows Best 79–82, 246, 254, 260
Fatso-Fasano 195
Faustino, David 232
Fax, Jesslyn 168
Fay 253
Faye, Herbie 59, 61, 149
The Feather and Father Gang 133
Fedderson, Don 139
Feldon, Barbara 75, 76, 77
Felker, Brennan 116
Felker, Brian 116
Fell, Norman 92, 93
Felton, Verna 151, 153
Ferdyn, Pamelyn 148
Ferguson, Jay R. 172, 173
Ferguson, Jesse Tyler 30, 31
Fernandez, Evelina 50
Ferrara, Adam 186, 188
Ferrara, Jerry 118, 119
Ferrell, Conchata 66, 67

Ferrigno, Lou 239
Fey, Tina 41, 42
Fiedler, John 213
Fields, Kim 223
Finley, Pat 213, 214
Finn, Pat 32
Fired Up 251
First and Ten 83, 250, 262
Fischer, Jenna 89, 91
Fish 53
Fisher, George Shug 77
Fisher, Joely 203, 205
The Fishing Hole 47
Fishman, Michael 50
Fitzgerald, Paul 184
Flannery, Kate 89
The Flight of the Conchords 250
The Flying Nun 250
Flo 122, 250
Flynn, Joe 208, 239, 240
Flynn, Neil 218, 220
Foley, Ellen 87, 88
Foley, Scott 219
Fonda, Henry 139
For Your Love 251, 262
Ford, Faith 32, 33
Ford, Paul 59, 60
Ford, Tennessee Ernie 86
Forke, Farrah 230, 231
Foster, Donald 153
Foster, Phil 103, 104
Foulger, Byron 179
Foulk, Robert 80
Fox, Bernard 64
Fox, Michael J. 62, 63
Foxworth, Jaimee 242, 243
Foxx, Redd 99, 100, 101
Francis, Anne 158
Franco, Dave 218, 220
Frank, Carl 170
Franklin, Bonnie 129
Franklin, Nelson 184
Frank's Place 249, 263
Frann, Mary 108, 109
Fraser, Elisabeth 59, 61
Frasier 10–12, 25, 30, 83, 245, 256, 260
Frawley, William 23, 24, 85, 158, 160
Freed, Sam 111, 113
Freeman, Kathleen 77, 232
Freeman, Mickey 59
French, Victor 75
Fresh Prince of Bel Air 248
Friebus, Florida 213
Friedlander, Judah 41
Friends 18–20, 25, 30, 31, 36, 56, 157, 189, 200, 210, 245, 256, 260
From Here to Eternity 206

Frome, Milton 77
Frost, Alice 170
Fulger, Holly 203
Full House 71, 193–195, 199, 247, 257, 259
Fuller, Penny 56
Fuller House 195
Fulmer, Ray 153, 155
Fumusa, Dominic 186, 187
Funicello, Annette 36
Funny Face 250
Fury 117

Gable, June 52
Gabor, Eva 221
Gabor, Zsa Zsa 146
Gaffney, Mo 54
Gail, Maxwell 52, 53
Gaines, Boyd 129, 130
The Gale Storm Show 249, 254
Galecki, Johnny 50, 56, 58, 59
Gallagher, Megan 82, 84
The Game 249
Garafolo, Janeane 82, 84, 239
Garde, Betty 161
Gardenia, Vincent 5
Garland, Beverly 158, 160
Garlin, Jeff 54, 106, 226
Garrett, Betty 5, 103, 105
Garrett, Brad 21, 22
Garrett, Jimmy 84, 85
Garrett, Leif 148
Garrison, David 232, 234
The Garry Moore Show 134
Garson, Willie 73
Garver, Kathy 139, 141
Gates, Ruth 170, 171
Gautier, Dick 75, 76
Gaye, Lisa 144
Geeson, Judy 54
Gehring, Ted 121
Gehringer, Linda 172, 174
Gelman, Larry 213
General Hospital 194
George, Sue 80
The George Burns & Gracie Allen Show 133–135, 145, 246, 254, 260
The George Burns Show 135
George Lopez 249
Gerritsen, Lisa 16
The Gertrude Berg Show 251, 263
Gertz, Jami 30
Gervais, Ricky 89, 107
Get Smart 75–77, 246, 255, 260
Getty, Estelle 35, 176, 177
The Ghost and Mrs. Muir 248, 255
Ghostley, Alice 64, 65, 142, 143, 172
Gibbs, Marla 97, 98

Gifford, Frank 117
Gilbert, Sara 50, 56, 58, 59
Gilborn, Steven 203
Gilliam, Burton 172
Gilligan's Island 40, 64, 162, 250
Gilliland, Richard 143
Gillin, Hugh 223
Gilpin, Betty 186
Gilpin, Peri 10, 12
Gimme a Break 248, 256
Girlfriends 248, 258, 261
Girls 248, 258, 262
Glass, Ron 52, 53, 147
Gleason, Jackie 166, 176
Gloria 7, 252, 263
Gold, Missy 191, 192, 200
Gold, Tracey 198, 200
Goldberg, Gary David 62
The Goldbergs 248, 254
The Golden Girls 34–36, 38, 103, 176, 177, 178, 245, 256, 260
The Golden Palace 36, 177
Goldman, Roy 13
Gomer Pyle, U.S.M.C. 47, 181–183, 240, 247, 255
Gomez, Selena 226, 227
Good Heavens 253, 263
Good Luck, Charlie 250, 258, 262
Good Morning, Miami 252
Good Times 7, 102, 215, 247, 256
Good Witch of Laurel Canyon 9
Goodfriend, Lynda 69
Goodman, Dody 215
Goodman, John 50, 51
Goodnight, Beantown 252
Goodwin, Bill 134
Goranson, Lecy 50
Gordon, Gale 84, 85, 162, 168, 174, 175
Gordon, Phil 77
Gordon, Virginia 168
Gordon-Levitt, Joseph 126, 127
Gore, Al 43
Gorme, Eydie 176
Gosfield, Maurice 59, 61
Goude, Ingrid 144
Gould, Alexander 195, 197
Gould, Elliott 18
Gould, Harold 35, 131, 133
Gould, Nolan 30, 31
Goulet, Robert 86
Grace Under Fire 247, 257
Grady 100
Grady, Don 158, 159
Graham, Heather 219
Grammer, Kelsey 8, 9, 10, 11, 230
Grand 252
Grande, Ariana 229

Grandy, Fred 101, 102
Grant, Allie 195, 197
Gray, Billy 80, 81
Grease 49
Green Acres 79, 179, 220–222, 247, 255
Greer, Judy 67, 201, 202
Gregory, James 52, 54
Grenier, Adrian 118, 119
Grey's Anatomy 44
Griese, Bob 117
Griesser, Matt 32
Griffin, Kathy 138
Griffith, Andy 46, 47, 69, 183
Groh, David 131, 132
Gross, Arye 203, 205
Gross, Michael 62
Grosz, Peter 184
Grounded for Life 251, 262
Growing Pains 194, 198–200, 247, 256, 259
Grubbs, Gary 43
Grundy, Reuben 163
Guilbert, Ann Morgan 38
Guillaume, Robert 136, 137, 139, 191, 192
Gunn, Anna 30
Gunsmoke 10
Guy, Jasmine 163, 164

Haddock, Julie Ann 223
Hagen, Earle 47
Hagen, Jean 36, 37
Hahn, Archie 146
Hale, Alan, Jr. 162
Hale, Lucy 226
Hale, Tony 184, 185, 200, 202
Half & Half 251, 261
Hall, Shashawnee 116
Halop, Billy 5
Halop, Florence 87, 88
Halyalkar, Jonathan 156
Hamer, Rusty 36, 37
Hamill, Mark 151
Hamilton, Lynn 99, 100
Hammer, Jay 97
Handler, Evan 73
Hangin' with Mr. Cooper 249
Hanks, Tom 63
Hannah Montana 248, 258, 262
Hannigan, Alyson 210, 212
Hansen, Janis 146, 148
Happy Days 6, 68–71, 103, 104, 139, 246, 255, 259
Happy Endings 252
Harden, Ernest, Jr. 97
Hardin, Melora 89, 91
Hardison, Kadeem 163, 164
Harmon, Kristin 208, 209

Harmon, Mark 209
Harmon, Tom 209
Harney, Michael 195
Harper, Constance 208
Harper, Valerie 16, 17, 131, 132
Harrelson, Woody 8, 9, 12, 44
Harrington, Pat, Jr. 36, 129, 130
Harris, Cynthia 54, 55
Harris, Estelle 28
Harris, Neil Patrick 210, 212
Harris, Susan 177
Harrison, Jennilee 92, 94
Harrison, Shawn 242
Harrold, Kathryn 82, 84
Hart, Ralph 85
Hartley, Mariette 214
Hartman, Paul 46, 179
Harvey, Irene 158
Hastings, Bob 5, 239, 241
Hatcher, Terri 30
Hathaway, Anne 77
Haufrect, Alan 121
Hausner, Jerry 23
Hawking, Stephen 57, 126
Hayes, Sean 43, 44
Haymer, Johnny 13
Haynes, Lloyd 149, 150
Hazel 153–155, 246, 255, 261
He & She 249, 263
Head of the Class 248, 256
Hearts Afire 251
Heaton, Patricia 21, 22
Hecht, Jessica 18
Hecht, Paul 111, 112
Hefner, Hugh 107
Helberg, Simon 56, 58
Heller, Randee 136
Helmond, Katherine 116, 136, 137, 156, 157
Helms, Ed 89, 91
Helton, Percy 77
Hemmings, Sally 97
Hemsley, Sherman 5, 7
Henner, Marilu 48, 172, 173
Hennesey 249
Henning, Carol 144
Henning, Linda Kaye 179, 180
Henning, Paul 180
Henrie, David 226, 227
Henry, Buck 75, 77
Hensley, Sherman 97
Herd, Richard 28
Here Come the Nelsons 208
Here's Lucy 25, 86, 174–176, 246, 256
Hervey, Jason 94, 95, 215
Heshimu 149
Hesseman, Howard 129, 130, 213
Hibbert, Edward 10

Hickman, Dwayne 144, 145, 146
Higgins, David Anthony 203, 204
High on Arrival 129
High School Musical 226
High Society 253
Hill, Anita 164
Hill Street Blues 9
Hiller and Diller 253
Hindman, Earl 71, 72
Hines, Cheryl 106
Hinkle, Marin 66
Hinkley, Tommy 54
Hirsch, Judd 48, 49
Hirson, Alice 203
Hoffman, Dustin 107
The Hogan Family 248, 256
Hogan's Heroes 123–125, 182, 207, 240, 241, 246, 255, 260
Holbrook, Hal 143, 172, 173, 174
Holliday, Polly 121, 122
Holloway, Sterling 166
Hollowell, Todd 223
Holmes, Jennifer 108, 109
Home Improvement 21, 71–73, 246, 257, 259
The Honeymooners 176, 237, 248, 254, 263
Hooks, Jan 126, 128, 142, 143
Hooperman 249
Hope & Gloria 252
Hopkins, Telma 242, 243
Horan, Monica 21, 22
Horne, Lena 165
Hostetter, John 32
Hot in Cleveland 249, 258
Hotchkis, Joan 146
House Calls 249
House of Lies 250, 258
Hovis, Larry 123, 125, 181
How I Met Your Mother 210–212, 219, 247, 257
Howard, John 158
Howard, Ron 46, 47, 68, 69, 70, 139, 183, 201
Howland, Beth 121, 122
Hubbell, Elna 179
Hudson, Haley 197
Hudson, Rock 78, 112
The Hughleys 251, 261
Humperdinck, Engelbert 196
Hunt, Helen 54, 55
Hunter Tab 78
Huskey, Brian 184
Hutson, Candace 172
Hutton, Gunilla 179, 180
Hyland, Sarah 30, 31
Hyman, Earle 25
Hytner, Steve 28

I Dream of Jeannie 226, 248, 255
I Love Lucy 23–25, 85, 132, 134, 151, 153, 160, 176, 245, 254, 260
I Married Joan 250
I Remember Mama 170
I Spy 25–26, 76
I Want to Hold Your Hand 64
iCarly 227–229, 247, 257
Iglesias, Enrique, Jr. 212
I'm Walkin' 209
In the House 252, 261
Incredible Hulk 239
Indigo 195, 196
Inside Schwartz 253, 263
It's a Wonderful Life 206
It's Always Sunny in Philadelphia 248, 258
It's Garry Shandling's Show 249
Ivey, Judith 142, 143
Izay, Connie 13

The Jackie Thomas Show 252, 263
Jackson, Janet 215
Jackson, Jermaine 225
Jackson, Jesse 165
Jackson, Sherry 36, 37
Jackson and Jill 250
Jacobi, Derek 12
Jacobs, Rachel 198
James, Kevin 21, 237, 238
The Jamie Foxx Show 250, 262
Jannis, Vivi 80
Jefferson, Thomas 97
The Jeffersons 7, 96–99, 215, 246, 255, 260
Jenkins, Ken 218, 220
Jenner, Barry 242
Jennifer Slept Here 8
Jergens, Diane 144
Jerins, Ruby 186, 187
Jesse 251
Jessie 252, 262
Jeter, Michael 172, 173
Jewell, Geri 223, 225
Jillian, Ann 153
Joanie Loves Chachi 70
Joey 20
The Joey Bishop Show 249
The John Larroquette Show 248
Johnny Angel 117, 207
Johns Hopkins Science Review 36
Johnson, Ashley 198
Johnson, Cherie 242
Johnson, Jay 136, 138
Johnson, Kristen 126, 127
Johnson, Penny 82, 84
Johnson, Tammy 144
Jolie, Angelina 176
Jolliffe, David 149

Jonas L.A. 252, 262
Jones, Angus T. 66, 68
Jones, Anissa 139, 141
Jones, Gilland 226
Jones, Gordon 208
Jones, Rashida 89
Jones, Wanda 172
Jordan, Jan 13
Jordan, Judy 77
Jordan, S. Marc 87
Joseph, Jeff 188, 190
Josselyn, Randy 242
Juditz, Vicki 116
Julia 248, 255
Jump, Gordon 198
Junior Press Conference 36, 151
Just Shoot Me 247, 257

Kaczmarek, Jane 113, 114
Kaling, Mindy 89, 91
Kamm, Kris 116, 118
Kampmann, Steven 108, 109
Kane, Carol 48, 49
Kaplan, Marvin 121
Karn, Richard 71, 72
Karvelas, Robert 75
Kate & Allie 27, 111–113, 246, 256, 260
Kauffman, Marta 19, 189
Kaufman, Andy 48, 49
Kavner, Julie 131, 132
Kay, Ted 154
Keach, Stacy, Sr. 75
Kearnes, Joseph 168
Keating, Larry 134, 135
Keen, Malcolm 170
Keith, Brian 139, 141
Keith, Richard 23
Kellogg, Ray 77
Kelly, Emmett 189
Kelly, Paula 87, 88
Kemper, Ellie 89
Kenan & Kel 251
Kennedy, John F. 64
Kennedy, John, Jr. 29
Kennedy, Page 195
Kennedy, Robert 64
Kent, Enid 13
Kent, Ethan 195
Kent, Gavin 195
Kenzle, Leila 54, 55
Kerns, Joanna 198
Kerr, Patrick 10
Ketchum, Dave 75
Khali, Simbi 126
Kimbrough, Charles 32, 33
Kimmel, Jimmy 120
Kimmons, Ken 116, 117

Kind, Richard 54
Kindler, Andy 21, 226
King, B.B. 27
King, Martin Luther, Jr. 64
King, Rodney 165
The King of Queens 237–239, 247, 257
Kinney, Kathy 110
Kinsey, Angela 89, 90, 91
Kirchenbauer, Bill 198
Kirk, Justin 195, 196
Klemperer, Werner 123, 124
Kline, Richard 92, 93
Klugman, Jack 146, 147, 148
Knight, Gladys 165
Knight, Ted 16
Knight, Wayne 28, 29, 126, 128
Knotts, Don 46, 47, 92, 93
Koehler, Frederick 111, 112
Koenig, Josh Andrew 198
Koosman, Jerry 199
Kopell, Bernie 75, 76
Korologos, Paula 32
Krakowski, Jane 41, 42
Kramer, Kenny 29
Krasinski, John 89, 91
Kravitz, Lenny 164
Krenn, Sherrie 223
Kress, Nathan 228
Kudrow, Lisa 18, 19, 20, 56
Kulky, Henry 166
Kulp, Nancy 77, 79, 144, 145, 146, 162
Kutcher, Ashton 66, 67
Kuter, Kay E. 179, 221

LaBrie, Donna 191
Ladd, Alan 146
Ladd, Diane 121, 122, 123
Laire, Judson 170, 171
Lander, David L. 103, 104
Landesberg, Steve 52, 53, 54
Lane, Charles 84, 85, 179, 180
Lane, Nancy 131
Lane, Nathan 32
Laneauville, Eric 149
Langard, Janet 205
Langham, Wallace 82, 84
Lansing, Joi 144
Lanteau, William 110
LaPaglia, Anthony 12
Larroquette, John 87, 88
The Larry Sanders Show 82–84, 246, 257, 262
Lassie 205
Last Man Standing 72
Late Night with David Letterman 21
The Late Show with David Letterman 190
Lauper, Cyndi 56
Lauria, Dan 94, 95

Laurie, Hugh 184
Laverne & Shirley 6, 70, 103–105, 148, 151, 246, 255, 259
Lavin, Linda 52, 121, 122
Lawford, Peter 145
Lawlor, John 223
Lawrence, Bill 220
Lawrence, Mary 144
Lawrence, Steve 176
Leachman, Cloris 16, 17, 113, 114, 132, 223, 225
The League 251, 258
Leap of Faith 252, 263
Lear, Norman 5–6, 99, 101, 102
Leave It to Beaver 207, 247, 254
Le Beauf, Sabrina 25, 26
LeBlanc, Matt 18, 19
Lee, David 11, 230
Lee, Justin 201
Lee, Rex 120
Leeves, Jane 10, 11, 12, 30
Leigh, Jennifer Jason 195
Leisure, David 176, 178
Lembeck, Harvey 59, 61
Lembeck, Michael 129, 130
Lemmon, Jack 147
Leno, Jay 82, 120
LeNoire, Rosetta 242, 243
Leonard, Sheldon 36, 37, 57
Leonetti, Tommy 181
Less Than Perfect 251
Lesser, Len 28
Lessy, Ben 36
Lester, Tom 179, 221, 222
Let's Make a Deal 148
Let's Stay Together 252, 258
Letterman, David 83
Levin, Charles 121, 123
Lewis, Cathy 153
Lewis, Clea 203, 205
Lewis, Dawnn 163, 165
Lewis, Huey 239
Lewis, Jason 73
Lewis, Richard 106
Libertini, Richard 136
Lieb, Robert P. 153, 158
Lieberstein, Paul 89
The Life of Riley 50, 165–167, 246, 254, 261
Life with Bonnie 251
Life with Lucy 175
Life with Luigi 252, 263
Light, Judith 156
Lime, Yvonne 80
Linden, Hal 52
Lindley, Audra 92, 93
Lindsey, George 46, 47, 183
Linkletter, Art 86

Linn-Baker, Mark 235, 236
Linney, Laura 12
Linville, Larry 13, 14, 15, 151
Lippin, Renee 213
Lithgow, John 126, 212
Little, Jimmy 59
Little Boxes 196
Little Shop of Horrors 114
Living Single 250, 261
Livingston, Barry 158, 160
Livingston, Ron 73
Livingston, Stanley 158, 159, 160
Lizzie McGuire 250, 262
Lloyd, Christopher 48, 49
Lloyd, Sam 218
Lockhart, June 179, 180
The Lone Ranger 80
Long, Shelley 8, 9, 12, 32
Longet, Claudine 240
Longo, Tony 121
Lord, Marjorie 36, 37
Lorne, Marion 64, 65
Lorre, Chuck 59, 67
Lost 210
The Lot 252
Loughlin, Lori 193, 194
Louie 247, 258
Louis-Dreyfus, Julia 28, 29, 184, 185, 202
Louise, Tina 162
Love American Style 69, 117
Love & War 247, 257
The Love Boat 241
Love, Sidney 250
Lucky 253
The Lucy-Desi Comedy Hour 25
The Lucy Show 25, 84–86, 175, 246, 255, 260
Lunden, Joan 34
Lutter, Alfred 122
Lutz, Joleen 87
Lyn, Dawn 158, 160
Lynch, Jane 202
Lynde, Paul 64, 65
Lynn, Betty 46
Lynn, Cynthia 123, 124
Lynskey, Melanie 66, 67

MacGibbon, Harriet 77, 79
Mackenzie, Will 213, 214
MacLachlan, Kyle 73
MacLeod, Gavin 16, 17, 239, 241
MacMichael, Florence 158
MacMurray, Fred 158, 159, 160
MacRae, Elizabeth 181
MacRae, Meredith 158, 159, 179, 180
Macy, Bill 101, 102
Mad About You 54–56, 245, 257, 260
Madden, Dave 121

Madera, Hemky 195
Madison, Bailee 226
Madman of the People 252, 263
Magnum, P.I. 26
Maguire, Mady 77
Maguire, Tobey 51
Mahoney, John 10, 11, 12
Major Dad 249
Make Room for Granddaddy 38
Malco, Romany 195, 196
Malcolm & Eddie 251, 261
Malcolm in the Middle 113–115, 246, 257, 261
Malick, Wendie 10, 112, 188, 189
Maloney, Lauren 129, 130
Maloney, Paige 129, 130
Mama 170–172, 246, 254
The Mamas and Papas 129
Mama's Bank Account 170
Man About the House 92
The Man from U.N.C.L.E. 75
Mandan, Robert 136, 137
Mandrell, Barbara 178
Manfrellotti, Joe 21
Manimal 8
Mann, Aaarti 58
Mann, Iris 170
Manoff, Dinah 136, 138, 176, 177
The Many Loves of Dobie Gillis 146, 249, 255
March, Hal 134, 135
Marcus Welby, M.D. 80
Mardi, Danielle 77
Marie, Rose 38, 40
Marinaro, Ed 103
Marky Mark and the Funky Bunch 119
Married ... with Children 232–234, 247, 257, 261
Mars, Kenneth 113
Marshall, Garry 32, 148
Marshall, Gloria 144
Marshall, Gregory 165, 166
Marshall, Penny 103, 104, 146, 148, 213
Martel, K.C. 198
Martin 250, 261
Martin, Barney 28
Martin, Dean 86
Martin, Dick 84
Martin, Melissa 172
Martin, Millicent 10
Martin, Steve 60
The Martin Short Show 253
Martinez, Tony 161, 162
Marx, Groucho 189
Mary Poppins 39
The Mary Tyler Moore Show 12, 15–18, 25, 33, 131, 132, 133, 213, 241, 245, 255, 260
Maschio, Robert 218

*M*A*S*H* 11, 12–15, 19, 25, 151, 183, 213, 240, 245, 255, 260
Masterson, Christopher Kennedy 113, 114
Masur, Richard 129, 130, 131, 133
Mathews, Larry 38, 39
Matthau, Walter 147
Maude 7, 69, 101–103, 246, 255, 260
Maxwell, Jeff 13
May, Deborah 82
Mayberry, RFD 47, 249
Mayo, Whitman 99, 100
Mazar, Debi 118
McBrayer, Jack 41, 42
McClanahan, Rue 35, 101, 103
McCleister, Tom 232
McClure, Bryton 242
McClurg, Bob 121
McConnell, Judy 77, 221
McCormack, Eric 43, 44
McCormack, Patty 170
McCrary, Darius 242
McCrea, Ann 205, 207
McCullough, Julie 198, 199
McCurdy, Jennette 228, 229
McDevitt, Ruth 5
McDonald, Ryan 146
McGinley, John C. 218, 219
McGinley, Ted 69, 232, 234
McGovern, George 110
McGowan, Tom 10
McGuire, Betty 198
McHale's Navy 64, 239–242, 247, 255, 259
McKean, Michael 103, 104, 188, 190
McKellar, Crystal 96
McKellar, Danica 94, 96
McKenna, Travis 116
McKeon, Nancy 223, 224
McKeon, Philip 121, 122
McLachlin, Kyle 211
McLeod, Gavin 132
McMahon, Ed 83
McMahon, Horace 36
McMillan, Gloria 168, 169
McMillan, Ken 131
McMillan and Wife 112
McNear, Howard 46, 47, 181
McNichol, Kristy 176, 177, 178
McWilliams, Caroline 136, 191, 192
Me & the Boys 253, 263
Meara, Anne 131, 133, 238
Mechoso, Julio Oscar 116
Meet Millie 249, 254
Meet the Browns 249
Meiklejohn, Linda 13
Mekka, Eddie 103, 10
Melissa & Joey 252
Meloni, Christopher 184, 185

Melrose Place 74
Melton, Sid 36, 221, 222
Melvin, Allan 5, 59, 61, 181
Mendler, Bridget 226
Meredith, Judi 134
Merman, Ethel 86
The Merv Griffin Show 29
Messing, Debra 30, 43, 44
Metcalf, Laurie 50, 57, 59, 128
Mettey, Lynette 13
Metzinger, Kraig 101
Meyers, Ari 111, 112, 172
Miami Vice 35, 147, 177
Michaels, Al 117
The Middle 249, 258
Midler, Bette 33
Mike & Molly 248, 258
Milano, Alyssa 156
Milder, Andy 195
Milioti, Cristin 210, 211
Miller, Alan 136
Miller, Christa 218, 219, 220
Miller, Dean 151, 152
Miller, Jeremy 198
Miller, McKaley 226
The Millers 253
Millicano, Pat 232
Mills, Alley 94, 96
Milner, Martin 166
Minnelli, Liza 200, 202
Minnow, Newton 79
Minor, Mike 179, 180
Mr. Adams & Eve 250
Mr. Belvedere 249
Mister Ed 40, 248, 255
Mr. Peepers 247, 254
Mr. Smith 8
Mitchell, Bobbie 13
Mitchell, Scoey 131
Mobley, Mary Ann 215, 216
Modern Family 30–32, 245, 258, 259
Modine, Matthew 195
Moesha 249, 261
Molinaro, Al 69, 146, 148
Moll, Richard 87, 88
Mom 250, 258
Mond, Steven 215
Monday Night Football 117
Mondo, Peggy 240
Money, Eddie 239
The Monkees 248, 255
Montagne, Edward J. 240
Montgomery, Elizabeth 64, 65, 227
Moody, King 75, 76
Moody, Lynne 136
Moonlighting 235
Moore, Alvy 221

Moore, Candy 84, 85
Moore, Mary Tyler 16, 33, 38, 39
Moorehead, Agnes 64, 65
Moran, Erin 68, 69
Moreno, Belita 235, 236
Moreno, Rita 177
Morgan, Harry 11, 13, 14, 15, 151, 152, 153
Morgan, Jane 168, 169
Morgan, Robin 170, 171
Morgan, Sean 208
Morgan, Tracy 41, 42
Morgan, Wesley 165, 166
Morin, D. David 177
Morita, Pat 69, 70, 99
Mork & Mindy 70, 126, 235, 248, 256
Morrill, Priscilla 16
Morris, Phil 28
Morrison, Brian 101, 102
Morrison, Jennifer 211
Morrison, Shelley 43
Morton, Joe 163
Mosley, Michael 218, 220
Most, Donny 68, 69
Moynahan, Bridget 73, 74
Mull, Martin 50
Mullally, Megan 43, 44, 45
Mulligan, Richard 136, 137, 138, 176, 177
Munck, Noah 228, 229
Muniz, Frankie 113, 114
The Munsters 251
Muppet Babies 194
Murdock, George 52
Murphy, Diane 64
Murphy, Erin 64
Murphy Brown 32–34, 144, 245, 257, 260
Music, Lorenzo 131, 133
Mustin, Burt 5, 46
My Big Fat Greek Life 253
My Boys 252
My Cousin Vinny 164
My Dad 207
My Favorite Husband 24
My Favorite Martian 64, 250
My Hero 252, 263
My Little Margie 249, 254
My Name Is Earl 247, 257
My Sister Sam 253
My Three Sons 6, 64, 139, 158–160, 246, 255
My Two Dads 251
My Wife and Kids 249
My World and Welcome to It 248, 255, 263
Myeres, Lou 163

Nabors, Jim 46, 47, 181, 182, 183
Najimy, Kathy 184
Nakahara, Kellye 13
The Naked Truth 251

Namath, Joe 116, 175
The Nancy Walker Show 133
The Nanny 248
Nayyar, Kunal 56, 58
Nealon, Kevin 195, 196
Nelson, Craig T. 116, 117, 118
Nelson, David 208, 209
Nelson, Frank 23
Nelson, Gunnar 209
Nelson, Harriet 208, 209
Nelson, Matthew 209
Nelson, Ozzie 189, 208, 209
Nelson, Ricky 207, 208, 209
Nelson, Tracy 209
Nemes, Scott 94
Nenninger, Eric 113
Netherly, Pendrant 149
Neuwirth, Bebe 8, 9, 12
The New Adventures of Old Christine 184, 185, 248, 258
The New Bob Cummings Show 145
The New Dick Van Dyke Show 251
New Family in Town 69
New Girl 251, 258, 261
New Kids on the Block 119
The New Mickey Mouse Club 194
The New Odd Couple 146
New York Post 41
New York Times 18, 106
Newhart 108–110, 143, 213, 246, 256, 260
Newhart, Bob 108, 213, 214
Newman, Edwin 110
Newsradio 250
Newsweek 137
Newton, Wayne 175
Nicholas, Denise 149, 150
Nielsen, Leslie 35, 157
Night Court 9, 86–88, 246, 256, 260
9 to 5 250
Nixon, Cynthia 73, 74
Nixon, Richard 6
Noble, Chelsea 198, 199
Noble, James 191
Nolan, Kathy 161, 162
Norris, Chuck 151
Noth, Chris 73, 74
Novak, B.J. 89, 91
Novello, Jay 240, 241
Nozick, Bruce 195
Nunez, Oscar 89, 90
Nurse Jackie 186–188, 247, 258
Nurses 177
Nye, Louis 77
NYPD Blue 20

Oatman, Doney 148
Obama, Michelle 229

O'Connor, Carroll 5, 6, 56
The Odd Couple (1970) 146–149, 235, 246, 255, 259
The Odd Couple (2015) 147
Odenkirk, Bob 82, 84
O'Donnell, Rosie 44, 83
The Office 89–91, 246, 257, 260
O'Hanlon, George 166
O'Hara, Jenny 223
O'Herlihy, Gavan 68, 69
O'Hurley, John 28, 29
O'Keefe, Michael 50
Oleynik, Larisa 126, 128
Olin, Ken 24
Olsen, Ashley 193, 195
Olsen, Mary Kate 193, 195
Olyphant, Timothy 89
On Our Own 253
One Day at a Time 117, 128–130, 246, 255, 260
One Life to Live 156
One on One 250, 261
O'Neill, Dick 242
O'Neill, Ed 30, 232, 233, 234
O'Neill, F.J. 235
O'Neill, Shaquille 107
Onorati, Peter 111
Oppenheimer, Alan 32
Orchard, John 13
O'Rourke, Heather 69
Osment, Haley Joel 32
Oswalt, Patton 184, 237, 239
Our Miss Brooks 154, 161, 166, 167–170, 246, 254
Out of Practice 251, 263
Overall, Park 176, 178
Owens, Geoffrey 25

Pace, Amanda 195
Pacheco, Frank 226
Page, LaWanda 99, 100
Palin, Sarah 42
Palmer, Sean 73
Pancholy, Maulik 41, 195
Pankow, John 54, 55
Pantomime Quiz 36
Papenfuss, Tony 108, 109
The Parent'hood 250, 262
Paris, Jerry 38
Park, Randall 184
Parker, Jacob 172
Parker, Mary-Louise 195, 196, 197
Parker, Penney 36, 37
Parker, Sarah Jessica 73, 74
Parker Lewis Can't Lose 252
The Parkers 250, 261
Parks & Recreation 248, 258

Parnell, Emory 166
Parrish, Hunter 195, 197
Parry, Matthew 200
Parsons, Estelle 50
Parsons, Jim 56, 57, 229
The Partridge Family 6, 146, 249
Pasquesit, David 184
Password 148
Pastorelli, Robert 32, 34
Patano, Tonye 195, 196
Patrick, Butch 161
Patterson, Elizabeth 23
Patterson, Hank 221, 222
The Patty Duke Show 249
Paul Sand in Friends and Lovers 253
Payne, Carl Anthony, II 25
Payton-France, Jo Marie 235, 236, 242
Pearce, Alice 64, 65
Pearlman, Rhea 48
Penn, Kal 212
Pennell, Larry 77
Pennington, Marla 136
Pentland, Bill 51
The People's Choice 251
Pepper, Barbara 221, 222
Pepper, Cynthia 158
Perfect Strangers 193, 234–237, 242, 247, 256, 259
Perkins, Elizabeth 195, 197
Perkins, Ron 50
Perlman, Philip 8
Perlman, Rhea 8, 9
Perry, Matthew 18, 19, 157
Perry, Roger 223
Pete and Gladys 153, 251
Peters, Kelly Jean 13
Petersen, Patty 205, 207
Petersen, Paul 205, 206, 207, 209
Peterson, Arthur 136, 138
Petticoat Junction 79, 145, 178–181, 221, 247, 255
Phantom of the Opera 87
Phenom 253
The Phil Silvers Show 39, 59–61, 124, 240, 245, 254, 260
Philbin, Regis 90
Philipp, Karen 13
Phillips, Ethan 191, 192
Phillips, John 129
Phillips, Joseph C. 25
Phillips, Mackenzie 129, 130
Phillips, Sally 184
Phyllis 17, 250
Pickles, Christina 18
Piekarski, Julie 223
Pierce, David Hyde 10, 11
Pinchot, Bronson 235, 236

Pinkett, Jada 163
Pintauro, Danny 156
Pitlik, Noam 99, 213
Pitt, Brad 19, 176, 200
Piven, Jeremy 82, 84, 118, 120, 203, 205
Plakson, Suzie 54
Plato, Dana 215, 217, 223
Platt, Edward 75, 76, 99
Playboy 199
Pleshette, Suzanne 108, 213, 214
Plotnick, Jack 203
Poehler, Amy 201, 202
Police Squad! 252, 263
Pollack, Sydney 45
Pollan, Tracy 62, 63
Pope, Peggy 136
Porky's 74
Porter, Alisan 235
Porter, Arthur Gould 77
Post, Markie 87, 88
Poston, Tom 108, 109
Potter, Jerry 121
Potts, Annie 142
Powell, Jane 198
Powell, Keith 41
Powers, Mala 153
The Practice 117
Price, Mark 62
Price, Shannon 217
The Price Is Right 211
Prickett, Maudie 153
Prince, Jonathan 121
Prince, Karim 113
Private Benjamin 249
Private Secretary 247, 254
The Producers 107
Provenza, Paul 176, 223
Pulliam, Keshia Knight 25, 26
Purl, Linda 68, 70

Quayle, Dan 34
Quinn, Bill 5
Quinn, Glenn 50

Radnor, Josh 210
Rae, Charlotte 215, 223, 225
Rafferty, Frances 151, 152
Raising Hope 250, 258, 261
Rajskub, Mary Lynn 82, 84
Ralph, Michael 163
Ralph, Sheryl Lee 142, 143
Ramsey, Anne Elizabeth 54, 55
Randall, Tony 146, 147
Randolph, Isabel 168
Rasche, David 184
Rashad, Phylicia 25, 26, 164
Ratzenberger, John 8

Rauch, Melissa 56, 58
Raven-Symone 25
Raye, Martha 121
Reagan, Nancy 216
Reagan, Ronald 189
The Real McCoys 160–163, 246, 254, 259
Reba 249, 261
Recanser, Marie-Alise 163
Reed, Donna 205, 206, 207
Reed, Lydia 161, 162
Rees, Roger 8
Reeves, Perrey 118
Reeves, Phil 184
Regalbuto, Joe 32, 33
Reid, Tara 219
Reiner, Carl 38, 40
Reiner, Rob 5, 7, 148, 151
Reiser, Paul 54, 55
Remar, James 73
Remini, Leah 172, 237
Reubens, Paul 32, 33
Reyes, Judy 218, 219
Reynolds, Burt 172, 173, 174, 239
Reynolds, Debbie 45
Reynolds, Kathryn 136
Reynolds, Malvina 196
Reynolds, Marjorie 165, 166
Rhoades, Barbara 136
Rhoda 17, 131–133, 246, 255, 260
Rhodes, Donnelly 136, 138
Ribisi, Giovanni 94
Rice, Condoleezza 43
Rice, Howard 149
Rice, Rosemary 170
Rich, Buddy 175
Rich, Christopher 32
Richard, Darryl 205, 207
Richard Diamond, Private Detective 39
Richards, Beah 99
Richards, Michael 28, 29
Richardson, Patricia 71, 72
Richardson, Sam 184
Richmond, Deon 25
Rickles, Don 138
Rieffel, Lisa 176, 178, 237
Rifkin, Ron 129, 130
The Rifleman 209
Riley, Jack 213, 214
Riley, Jeannine 179, 180
Ringwald, Molly 223, 224
Rist, Robbie 16
Ritter, John 92, 93, 94, 231
Rivers, Joan 82, 176
Rivers, Johnny 75
Roberts, Doris 21, 22, 236
Roberts, Randolph 68, 69
Roberts, Roy 77, 85, 179

Robinson, Charlie 87, 88
Robinson, Doug 121
Rob 253
Roc 252
Roche, Eugene 136, 235
Rock Around the Clock 69
Rockwell, Robert 168, 169, 198
Roddy, Rod 139
Rodriguez, James 113
Rodriguez, Lukas 113
Rodriguez, Rico 30
Rogers, Kasey 64
Rogers, Wayne 13, 14, 183
Roker, Roxie 97, 98
Rolle, Esther 101, 102
Romano, Larry 237
Romano, Ray 21, 22, 238
Romanus, Robert 223
Romeo! 252
Room for Two 252
Room 222 149–151, 246, 256, 259
Rooney, Mickey 86
The Ropers 252
Roseanne 21, 49–51, 59, 71, 245, 257, 259
Rosenthal, Philip 22
Ross, Joe E. 59, 61
Ross, Lonny 41
Ross, Marion 68, 69
Ross, Shavar 215, 242
Rowe, Misty 68
The Royal Family 100
Rubinek, Saul 10
Rubinstein, John 226
Rudd, Paul 18, 20
Rudolph, Amanda 36
The Ruggles 251
Rules of Engagement 249
Ryan, Amy 89, 91
Ryan, Frank 221
Ryan, Irene 77, 78, 162, 179
Rydell, Bobby 225

Sabella, Ernie 235, 236
Sabo, Shari 13
Sabrina, the Teenage Witch 249
Sagal, Katey 232, 233, 234
Saget, Bob 120, 193, 194, 210, 211
St. Clair, Jessica 184
Saint James, Susan 111, 112
Salata, Gregory 111
Sale, Virginia 179
Salerno, Charlene 208
Sally 252, 263
Salt, Jennifer 136, 138
Sam & Cat 229
Samantha Who? 249
Sanders, Ajai 163

Sanders, Lugene 165, 166
Sanderson, William 108, 109
Sandler, Adam 239
Sands, Billy 59, 61, 239, 241
Sanford, Isabel 5, 97, 98
Sanford and Son 99–101, 246, 255, 260
Sansberry, Hope 59, 60
The Sarah Silverman Program 251
Sarandon, Susan 19
Sargent, Dick 64, 65
Saturday Night Live 41, 42, 112, 143, 184
Saunders, Lori 179, 180
Savage, Fred 94, 95
Saved by the Bell 251
Saviano, Josh 94, 96
Scarpelli, Glenn 129, 130
Schacter, Felice 223
Schell, Ronnie 181, 182
Schramm, David 230, 232
Schroder, Rick 219
Schuldt, Travis 218, 219
Schull, Rebecca 230, 232
Schulze, Paul 186, 187
Schur, Michael 90
Schwartz, Neil J. 68
Schwimmer, David 18, 20, 94, 95
Scolari, Peter 108, 110
Scooby-Doo and Scrappy-Doo 194
Scorsese, Martin 107, 121
Scott, Lucien 213
Scott, Reid 184, 185
Scott, Simon 239, 240
Scrubs 211, 217–220, 247, 257, 261
Seagram, Lisa 77
Seagren, Bob 136
Seaver, Tom 199
Secret Agent Man 75
The Secret World of Alex Mack 251
Sedaka, Neil 239
Sedan, Rolfe 134
Segall, Pamela 223
Segel, Jason 210
Seinfeld 19, 21, 27–30, 55, 71, 106, 107, 184, 204, 210, 238, 245, 256, 260
Seinfeld, Jerry 28, 29, 42, 84, 106, 191, 192
Selby, Sarah 80
Selleck, Tom 18, 20, 26
Sgt. Bilko (Movie) 60
77 Sunset Strip 39
Sex and the City 30, 73–75, 83, 246, 257, 262
The Shaggy Dog 159
Shakur, Tupac 165
Shalhoub, Tony 230, 231
Shandling, Garry 82, 83
Sharma, Barbara 131, 132
Shatner, William 128
Shaud, Grant 32, 33

Shawkat, Alia 200, 202
She Can't Find Her Keys 207
Sheen, Charlie 66, 67, 144, 145
Sheldon, Cali 18
Shelly, Carole 146, 148
Shelson, Noelle 18
Sheridan, Bonnie 50
Sheridan, Liz 28
Shore, Roberta 80
Short, Martin 107
Sibbett, Jane 18
Sideways 232
Siebert, Charles 129
Sierra, Gregory 52, 53, 99, 100, 136, 137
Sigler, Jamie Lynn 119
Silicon Valley 251, 258
Silver, Ron 131, 133
Silver Spoons 249
Silverman, Fred 137
Silverman, Sarah 84
Silvers, Cathy 69
Silvers, Phil 59, 60, 77
Simon, Neil 146
Simon, Robert 13
Simons, Timothy 184, 185
Simpson, O.J. 217
Sinatra, Frank 21, 157
Sinbad 163
The Single Guy 251
Singleton, Doris 23
Sister, Sister 249, 262
60 Minutes 33
$64, 000 Question 24, 135
Skeritt, Tom 8
The Slap Maxwell Story 252, 263
Sledge, Percy 94
Sleiman, Haaz 186
Slimer and the Real Ghostbusters 194
Smart, Amy 219
Smart, Jean 12, 142, 143
Smith, Allison 111, 112
Smith, Anna Deavere 186, 188
Smith, Bee-be 163
Smith, Ebonie 97
Smith, Hal 46
Smith, Howard 153
Smith, Leonard 168, 169
Smith, Patricia 213
Smith, Phyllis 89
Smith, Roger 80
Smith, Taran Noah 71, 72
The Smith Family 139
Smollett, Jurnee 193
The Smothers Brothers 21
Smulders, Colbie 210, 211
Snoopy and the Red Baron 77
Soap 136–139, 177, 191, 192, 246, 255, 259

Sokoloff, Marla 193
Somers, Brett 146, 148
Somers, Suzanne 92, 93
Sonny with a Chance 253
Soo, Jack 52, 53
The Sopranos 119, 186, 210
Sorkin, Aaron 116, 184
Sothern, Ann 85
The Soul Man 253
Soule, Olan 158
Spader, James 89, 91
Speedway Junkie 72
Spelling, Aaron 175
Spin City 247, 257
Sports Night 116, 249
Springsteen, Bruce 19, 63
Stacy, James 208
Stadlen, Lewis J. 191, 192
Stahl, Richard 148, 149
Stalag 17 124
Stamos, John 193, 194
Stanley, Florence 52, 53
Stapleton, Jean 5, 6, 7
Star Wars 151
Stark Raving Mad 252, 263
Starr, Darren 74
Steenburgen, Mary 106
Steffan, Sirry 77
Stehlin, Jack 195
Stein, Ben 94
Steinbrenner, George 29
Step by Step 248
Steptoe and Son 99
Stern, Daniel 94, 95, 96
Stern, Howard 48
Stern, Shoshannah 195
Sternhagen, Frances 73
The Steve Harvey Show 250, 262
Stevens, Patricia 13
Stevenson, McLean 13, 14
Stewart, French 126, 127
Stewart, Jon 83, 90
Stewart, Mel 5, 7
Stiers, David Ogden 13, 15
Stiles, Ryan 66
Still Standing 30, 250
Stiller, Ben 202
Stiller, Jerry 28, 237, 238
Stockard Channing in Just Friends 253
Stoller, Fred 226
Stone, Jennifer 226, 227
Stone, Pam 116, 117
Stonestreet, Eric 30, 31
Strangis, Judy 149
Strassman, Marcia 13
Stroll, Edson 239
Struthers, Sally 5, 7

The Stu Erwin Show 249, 254
Stuart, Barbara 181
Stuart, Roy 181
Suburgatory 253
Suddenly Susan 250
The Suite Life of Zach & Cody 250, 262
The Suite Life on Deck 252, 262
Sulkin, Gregg 226
Sullivan, Erik Per 113, 115
Sullivan, Nicole 237, 238
Summer, Cree 163
Summers, Hope 46
Sundstrom, Florence 166
Superman 64
Survivor 107
Susi, Carol Ann 58
Sussman, Josh 226
Sussman, Kevin 56, 59
Sussman, Todd 108, 110
Sutherland, Sarah 184
Sutton, Frank 181, 182
Swank, Hilary 172
Swanson, Jackie 8
Swasey, Nikki 215
Swedberg, Heidi 28, 226
Sweeney, Robert 166, 168
Sweet, Shane 232
Sweeten, Madylin 21
Sweeten, Sawyer 21
Sweeten, Sullivan 21
Sweetin, Jodie 193, 195
Swenson, Inga 191, 192
Swit, Loretta 13, 14
Sylvester, Harold 232

Ta-Tanisha 149
The Tab Hunter Show 39
Tabitha 65
Taggart, Rita 116
Talbot, Lyle 144, 208
Tamblyn, Amber 66, 68
Tambor, Jeffrey 82, 83, 200, 201, 202
Tape, Amanda 226
Tari, Le 215
Tartikoff, Brandon 8
Tate, Sharon 77
Taxi 47–49, 156, 245, 256, 259
Tayback, Vic 121, 122
Taylor, Clarice 25
Taylor, Elizabeth 176
Taylor, Holland 66, 67
Taylor, Jennifer Bini 66, 67
Taylor, Meshach 142
Taylor, Nathaniel 99
Taylor, Renee 188
Tessier, Michael 52
Texaco Star Theatre 24

That Girl 38, 145, 247, 255
That '70s Show 248, 258, 261
That's So Raven 249, 262
Theismann, Joe 117
Theron, Charlize 201, 202
They Might Be Giants 115
Thicke, Alan 198
3rd Rock from the Sun 125–128, 246, 257, 261
30 Rock 40–43, 245, 257, 260
thirtysomething 24
Thomas, Clarence 164
Thomas, Danny 36, 37, 38, 46
Thomas, Jay 8
Thomas, Jonathan Taylor 71, 72
Thomas, Marlo 38
Thomas, Michelle 242
Thomas, Tony 38
Thomas, William L. 184
Thomas, William, Jr. 25
Thomason, Harry 142, 143, 172, 174
Thompson, Scott 82
Thorne-Smith, Courtney 66, 68
Thornton, Billy Bob 196
3 Men and a Baby 193
Three's a Crowd 94
Three's Company 70, 92–94, 246, 255, 259
Thunder Alley 252
Thyre, Becky 195
Til Death 252, 261
Tinker, Grant 8
Tobias, George 64
Todd, Daniel 158
Todd, Joseph 158
Todd, Michael 158
Tolbert, Berlinda 97, 98
Tomei, Marisa 29, 163, 164
Tomlin, Lily 32
The Tonight Show 82, 83, 182, 229
The Tony Randall Show 252
Too Close for Comfort 248, 256
Toomey, Regis 179
Top of the Heap 253
Topper 250
Torn, Rip 82, 83
Torres, Liz 5
Torrey, Roger 77
Townsend, Tammy 242
Trainor, Jerry 228
Traylor, Craig Lamar 113
Troup, Ronnie 158, 160
True Jackson, VP 253
Tucker's Witch 9
Tullis, Dan, Jr. 232
Tuomy-Wilhoit, Blake 193, 194
Tuomy-Wilhoit, Dylan 193, 194
Turman, Glynn 163

Turquand, Todd 131
TV Guide 175
Two and a Half Men 65–68, 235, 245, 257, 260
Two Broke Girls 251, 258
Two Guys, a Girl and a Pizza Place 251
227 27, 98, 247, 256, 261
Tyler, Aisha 18
Tyler, James Michael 18, 20
Tyler Perry's House of Payne 248, 258
Tyson, Mike 157

Ulrich, Kim Johnson 231
Underwood, Blair 73
Unfabulous 253
Unforgettable 48
Unhappily Ever After 250, 262
Union Square 252, 263
United States of Tara 248, 258
The Untouchables 23
Urich, Robert 136, 137

Valdetero, John 116
Valdis, Sigrid 123, 124
Valentine, Karen 149, 150
Valentine, Scott 62
Vance, Vivian 23, 24, 84, 85, 175
Van Dyke, Dick 38, 39, 118
Van Dyke, Jerry 116, 117
Van Patten, Dick 170, 17
Varden, Norma 153
Vaugier, Emmanuelle 66
Veep 183–186, 247, 258, 262
Vega, Alexa 172
VelJohnson, Reginald 236, 242
Vera, Ricky 168
Verdon, Gwen 190
Vergara, Sofia 30, 120
Vernon, Irene 64
Veronica's Closet 249
Victor, Renee 195
Victorious 229, 250, 258
Vigoda, Abe 52, 53
Vinson, Gary 239, 240
Viscuso, Sal 136, 138
Voland, Herb 13
Volstad, John 108, 109
Volz, Nedra 215
von Bargen, Daniel 113
Von Zell, Harry 134, 135

Wade, Justin Grant 201
Wagner, Jack 208
Wahlberg, Mark 119
Wahlgren, Kari 226
Walberg, Garry 146
Walker, Nancy 131, 133, 139

Walking Across Egypt 72
Wallace, Marcia 213, 214
Wallace, Paul 80
Wallem, Stephen 186
Walsh, Matt 184, 185
Walter, Jessica 200, 201
Walters, Barbara 143
Walther, Susan 179
The Waltons 100
Warburton, Patrick 28, 29
Ward, Sandy 113
Warfield, Marlene 101, 102
Warfield, Marsha 87, 88, 176, 177
Warlock, Billy 69
Warner, Malcolm-Jamal 25, 26
Warren, Lesley Ann 45
Washington, Kenneth 123
Wass, Ted 136, 138
The Waverly Wonders 116
Wayans, Kim 163
The Wayans Bros. 250, 262
Wayne, John 86
We Got It Made 8
Weber, Ben 73
Weber, Steven 230, 231
Webster 249
Wedgeworth, Ann 92, 172
Weeds 195–197, 247, 257
Weege, Reinhold 87
Weinger, Scott 193
Welcome Back, Kotter 21, 248, 256
Welles, Jesse 136
Wells, Danny 97
Wendel, Elmarie 126, 128
Wendt, George 8, 49
Wertimer, Ned 97
West, Adam 162
West, Kanye 120
West, Natalie 50
West, Ron 126, 128
The West Wing 184
Weston, Celia 121, 123
Wettig, Patricia 24
Wever, Merritt 186, 187
What I Like About You 251, 262
What's Happening!! 251
Wheeler, Maggie 203
Whelchel, Lisa 223, 224
When a Man Loves a Woman 94
Where's Raymond? 37
Whitaker, Johnny 139, 140
White, Betty 16, 17, 35, 157
White, Carole Ita 103
White, David 64
White, Jaleel 242, 243
White, Jesse 36
White, Karen Malina 163

White, Slappy 99
Whitehead, Paxton 54
Whitlock, Isiah, Jr. 184
Whitman, Mae 201, 202
Who's the Boss? 155–157, 235, 246, 256, 259
Wickes, Mary 36
Wilcox, Frank 77
Wilfred 252
Wilkof, Lee 108
Will & Grace 30, 43–45, 245, 257, 260
Willard, Fred 21, 22
Williams, Amir 163
Williams, Anson 68, 69
Williams, Ashley 211
Williams, Cara 131, 153
Williams, Cindy 103, 104, 105, 151
Williams, Hal 99
Williams, Kellie Shanygne 242, 243
Williams, Robin 70, 126
Williams, Victor 237, 239
Willis, Bruce 19
Wilson, Demond 99, 100, 101, 147
Wilson, Dick 240
Wilson, Dorien 188, 190
Wilson, Mary Louise 129
Wilson, Melanie 235, 236
Wilson, Paul 8
Wilson, Rainn 89, 90
Winbush, Troy 25
Window on Main Street 80
Winfrey, Oprah 43, 129, 204
Wingreen, Jason 5
Wings 10, 230–232, 247, 257, 261
Winkelman, Michael 161
Winkler, Henry 68, 69, 70, 201, 202
Winslowe, Paula 168
Winter, Ariel 30, 31
Winter, Lynette 179

Winters, Roland 170
The Wizards of Waverly Place 225–227, 247, 257, 262
Wizards Return: Alex vs. Alex 226
WKRP in Cincinnati 247, 256
Woman of the House 143
Wonder, Stevie 27
The Wonder Years 94–96, 246, 257, 259
Wood, Peggy 170, 171
Woodburn, Danny 28
Woodell, Pat 179, 180
Woods, Zach 89, 184
Wrage, Glenn 184
Wright, Aloma 218
Wright, John 239, 241
Wright, Joseph 242
Wright, Julius 242
Wyatt, Jane 80, 82
Wyndham, Anne 52

Yasbeck, Amy 230, 231
Yes, Dear 248
Yoda, Yoshio 239, 241
York, Dick 64, 65
York, Rebecca 108
Yothers, Tina 62
You Again? 252
You Came Along 144
Young, Robert 80, 82
Young, Skip 208
Your Show of Shows 40
You're Not the Boss of Me 115

Zahn, Paula 34
Zoey 101 250
Zorich, Louis 54, 55
Zucker, Jeff 19